*Oracle Press*™

Oracle Application Express (APEX)

Build Powerful Data-Centric Web Apps with APEX

About the Authors

Arie Geller is an independent IT consultant and software developer with more than 35 years of experience in IT work, including software development, systems analysis, and IT infrastructure. He has been using APEX since its first public version (HTML DB back then), and over the years, he has accumulated vast experience with globalization, localization, and translation aspects of APEX applications, especially with right-to-left support.

Brian Spendolini is currently the product manager of Oracle's Exadata Cloud Service and previously served as a product manager for the Oracle Enterprise Database Cloud Service (DBCS). Prior to his product management roles, Brian had been developing APEX applications, used by thousands of people to this day, in many various industries as well as internal to Oracle. He started using APEX back in 2000, when it was an internal project at Oracle, being passed around the office in an 80MB zip file. APEX runs in his blood; his brother, Scott Spendolini, has authored several APEX books as well.

About the Technical Editor

John Snyders is a consulting member of technical staff at Oracle. He has been a software engineer for more than 30 years and a member of the Oracle Application Express development team for 4 years. Prior to joining the APEX team, he worked on the WebLogic Server Administration Console. Being a longtime advocate for declarative software development and its productivity benefits, he was a natural for joining the APEX team. He has 9 years of experience in JavaScript programming and has been a key designer and developer of the Page Designer and Interactive Grid APEX features. He also created the Survey Builder APEX packaged application.

ORACLE®   *Oracle Press*™

Oracle Application Express (APEX)

Build Powerful Data-Centric Web Apps with APEX

Arie Geller
Brian Spendolini

Mc
Graw
Hill
Education

New York   Chicago   San Francisco
Athens   London   Madrid   Mexico City
Milan   New Delhi   Singapore   Sydney   Toronto

Cataloging-in-Publication Data is on file with the Library of Congress

McGraw-Hill Education books are available at special quantity discounts to use as premiums and sales promotions, or for use in corporate training programs. To contact a representative, please visit the Contact Us pages at www.mhprofessional.com.

Oracle Application Express (APEX): Build Powerful Data-Centric Web Apps with APEX

1 2 3 4 5 6 7 8 9 LCR 21 20 19 18 17

ISBN   978-0-07-184304-1
MHID   0-07-184304-3

Sponsoring Editor	**Technical Editor**	**Production Supervisor**
Wendy Rinaldi	John Snyders	Pamela Pelton
Editorial Supervisor	**Copy Editor**	**Composition**
Jody McKenzie	Lisa Theobald	Cenveo® Publisher Services
Project Editor	**Proofreader**	**Illustration**
Rachel Gunn	Paul Tyler	Cenveo Publisher Services
Acquisitions Coordinator	**Indexer**	**Art Director, Cover**
Claire Yee	Jack Lewis	Jeff Weeks

Brian dedicates this book to his parents, who didn't have him committed when he grew his hair long and all he wanted to do was rock. And to his brother, who always helped him find the perfect piece of cardboard for his break dancing lessons.

Arie dedicates this book to his dear departed father, Asher Geller. At the age of 91, he was a big fan of APEX in general and this book project in particular. It saddens Arie deeply that he didn't get to see it through to completion.

Contents at a Glance

Contents

Acknowledgments

I'd like to thank my partner in life, Hana, and all the other great members of my family. Writing a professional and technical book is a very time- and energy-consuming task. Without their understanding, patience, and support, I would not have been able to complete this project. They mean the world to me.

—Arie

Behind this type of book is a well-oiled mechanism composed of highly trained and experienced McGraw-Hill teams that initiated this project and then helped and pushed it all the way to completion. Many of them are the behind-the-scenes, hard-working staff, and without them, the book wouldn't be published. Our sincere gratitude to all of them.

Special thanks to John Snyders, our technical editor. His vast experience, intimate knowledge of APEX, and wise comments on the raw manuscripts raised the bar for the final outcome and made this book better for the readers.

Last, but not least, special thanks to Joel Kallman, the leader of the APEX development team. Joel gave us much more than just friendly moral support throughout this project. His valuable professional advice and profound insights on APEX were priceless.

—Arie and Brian

Introduction

This book is about Oracle Application Express (APEX)—its development and running environments. APEX is a rapid application development (RAD) tool, and its integrated development environment (IDE) is web-based, which means you are using your local browser during development. APEX lives in the Oracle Database and was natively designed to develop data-centric web applications that can use cutting-edge technologies in the current web environment, such as HTML5, CSS3, JavaScript (including built-in and external JavaScript libraries), and such. All these enable you to develop robust, efficient, and secure web applications that can run on both stationary (desktop) or mobile devices, while featuring modern, rich user interfaces to enhance the user experience provided by your developed application.

Throughout this book, we explain all the important terms you need to know and review the APEX architecture, concepts, and what is under its hood. The book leads you through the development cycle: right from the start, when you should plan and design your application; through functionality, the data model, appearance, and such; up to the end, when you deploy your application for the end users. In between, we discuss the concepts you need to know and understand to use the APEX IDE optimally, plus the elements and building blocks APEX provides for your application. In this book, we use real working code and hands-on examples, and we concentrate on covering the new and updated features that APEX 5.0, and especially version 5.1, introduced.

Writing this book was our humble attempt to increase even further the (thriving) APEX community, by helping novice developers join and fit in more easily. We like to share our many years' experience with APEX and hope to help even veteran developers enrich their knowledge and ease their way into using the new APEX 5.0/5.1, which introduced many exciting and productivity enhancing features, wizards, and tools.

The main target audience for this book is novice developers who want to become familiar with Oracle APEX and to learn how this web-based RAD tool can help them develop data-centric web applications in the Oracle Database environment. Moreover, experienced APEX developers can also find much of interest in this book, as it thoroughly covers the notable new and updated features that APEX 5.0/5.1 introduces.

This book covers the theoretical and practical aspects of APEX—planning and designing a new application, concepts behind the APEX development cycle, APEX building blocks and their characteristics, and more. Alongside the theoretical discussion, we cover practical aspects of APEX by reviewing how to operate the APEX IDE and how to build a real application, by using examples with working code and many hands-on examples.

To make the most of this book, you should have access to an APEX instance. If you don't have access to your own local APEX instance, you can go to apex.oracle. com and request an APEX Workspace (as we explain in the book). Oracle provides this service for free; use it to practice working through the examples in this book and gain valuable experience.

The book is organized in a logical order that corresponds to the real-life development cycle. We start with general discussions about the APEX environment and architecture, reviewing the concepts behind the APEX applications and their building blocks. Each chapter deals with specific APEX features, tasks, and functionalities, and lays out the fundamentals for these and others that follow in the next chapters. Hence, we recommend that you read the book chapter-by-chapter, in sequential order.

Chapter 1: Introduction to Oracle Application Express

This chapter introduces APEX as a native web-based RAD tool for data-centric web applications and explains what it all means. The APEX architecture is explored in detail, followed by discussions about installation and configuration of a new APEX instance and upgrade aspects for an existing environment.

Chapter 2: Getting Ready

This chapter covers the homework you'll need to do before you start using APEX, including the prerequisite knowledge we recommend that you have (and preferably have mastered) in order to use APEX optimally and make the most of its IDE.

The chapter includes a list of books you can consult if you need to complement your knowledge. Next, we discuss High Level Design (HLD) actions you should take, as the first stage of your development cycle, to ensure a good and smooth process. We apply this strategy on the demo application that will accompany us throughout the book, and provide examples of some HLD actions, such as planning and implementing the application data model, QA scenarios, and more.

Chapter 3: APEX IDE: Quick Tour and Basic Concepts

You will take a quick but thorough tour around the APEX IDE and its five major modules—App Builder, SQL Workshop, Team Development, Packaged Apps, and Instance Administration. We discuss the operational aspects of these modules, alongside their functionalities, and how they can help you in your development efforts.

Chapter 4: APEX Applications: Concepts and Building Blocks

This chapter covers the fundamental APEX building blocks and the concepts behind them by reviewing the hierarchical structure of the APEX environment. We start from the top—the APEX instance—and work our way through Workspaces, applications, themes, templates, application pages, regions, page items, buttons, and more.

Chapter 5: The Page Designer

Here you learn about the Page Designer, which was introduced in APEX 5.0 and enhanced in APEX 5.1. The operational aspects of the Page Designer are reviewed; you'll learn how to work with it, how to use it to create and define various APEX elements, and how to position APEX items on your application pages.

Chapter 6: APEX Wizards

Create APEX components in minutes with the multitude of wizards and guides provided. We start with the Create an Application wizard, where with a few clicks of the mouse, you can create your very first application. Then you'll create forms and reports with minimal to no code, adding, modifying, deleting, and displaying data in a simple and quick manner.

Chapter 7: Computations, Validations, and Processes

Oracle Application Express provides a complete framework for working with data, ensuring consistency and business rules. In this chapter, you will learn how to display and alter data on both the page Rendering (page load) and Processing (after page submit) phases, using computations; how to ensure data consistency and accuracy with validations; and how to implement the application logic by using built-in or custom DML processes, with APEX processes.

Chapter 8: Crafting a Powerful UI

APEX 5.0 and 5.1 provide a complete set of tools behind all UI aspects, enabling developers to tailor UI components like never before. Learn how to alter the colors of your pages and application components without writing a single line of code. Also covered is the Universal Theme, the most flexible UI found in any development environment, that gives you complete control of layout, formatting, and style.

Chapter 9: Dynamic Actions

JavaScript doesn't have to be difficult. Using Dynamic Actions, you can create common and custom UI elements programmatically, with little or no code at all. This chapter will guide you through creating dynamic actions that once would have taken hundreds of lines of code.

Chapter 10: APEX Security

Security of our applications and data is paramount. With the daily data breaches we hear about in the news, security has come to the forefront of application development. This chapter covers the security aspects of APEX and how the tool helps developers secure data and forms by default, and not after the fact.

Chapter 11: Packaging and Deployment

One of the great aspects of APEX is that it can run anywhere—on premises, in the cloud, or on a laptop. Strengthening this portability is the packaging and deployment framework built right into the tool. The chapter will guide you through creating an application bundle that contains not only the application, but the database objects as well.

CHAPTER
1

Introduction to Oracle
Application Express

This book is all about Oracle Application Express, also known as APEX (pronounced ā'-pĕks, with a long "a" as in "angle" or "acorn").

You are likely reading this book because you are curious about developing web applications, possibly in a database environment, and you want to learn more about it. Oracle Application Express (APEX) is a native web integrated development environment (IDE) for creating web applications that is implemented as a rapid application development (RAD) tool with strong declarative features. With APEX running in an Oracle database, you can develop data-centric native web applications.

This description of APEX includes many technical terms, some of which may be new to you, and it might sound a bit intimidating. But what we will show you is a friendly, browser-based environment to use for making powerful web applications, with a beautifully modern look and feel, that is driven from your database and by your data.

In this chapter, we'll dig into the core definition of APEX. We will review the architecture, major features, and main concepts behind APEX and give you the necessary tools and information to decide whether this development environment is right for you. We'll review what it takes to work with APEX and what you should consider to install, upgrade, and configure it correctly.

NOTE
Experienced APEX developers may find some new perspectives on APEX in this chapter, or you can skip to the chapters on APEX 5.1 (Chapters 3 onward). Rest assured that they are filled with APEX 5.x–specific information that we are sure you'll find useful.

Let's take apart our definition of APEX and learn what each component means.

A Native Web Tool for Developing Web Applications

APEX is a native web development tool that is (most likely) already installed on your Oracle Database (more about this in a bit). The only thing you need to start working with it on the client side is a modern browser.

As you'll see throughout this book, the APEX IDE leverages some of the latest, most cutting-edge technologies in the web world. Only by using a modern browser will you enjoy and benefit from these technologies that are embedded in the APEX IDE. A modern browser supports Hypertext Markup Language version 5 (HTML5) and Cascading Style Sheets version 3 (CSS3), and it can handle JavaScript.

NOTE
A list of tested and approved browsers and versions can be found in the Release Notes *or the* Installation Guide *for the latest APEX version. These documents are also available in the APEX home page of the Oracle Technology Network (OTN) web site under the "Learn More/Getting Started Guide" section. As of APEX 5.1, the official policy is to support only the last two major versions of the various major browser brands. For example, where Microsoft is concerned, only Internet Explorer 11 and Microsoft Edge are fully supported.*

The final product of the APEX IDE, the developed APEX application, is a native, cross-browser web application. It means that we are dealing with a collection of HTML, CSS, and JavaScript code that can run directly on a variety of web browsers. This code is generated at runtime by the APEX engine, making it dynamic and source-file free. We'll elaborate more in the APEX engine discussion. All the end user needs to run the developed APEX application is its URL. No other deployment actions are needed, and that makes an APEX application very simple and very easy to use.

NOTE
Although we are talking about a web application, the APEX application does not comprise prebuilt HTML files that are stored somewhere on a (web) server. Each application page is generated by the APEX engine per a specific request from the client browser. We'll elaborate on this later in the chapter in the section "APEX Architecture."

Native to the Web World

We have used the term "native" in respect to both the APEX IDE and its final product, the developed APEX application. *Native* means that the Oracle development team designed APEX from the outset to operate in the web environment. This path enables the APEX engine to take optimal advantage of the perks of the Web, such as the advanced HTML5 and CSS3 technologies, alongside seasoned JavaScript and Ajax (asynchronous JavaScript and XML). Moreover, the native web design gives the APEX engine an opportunity to overcome some of the challenges the web environment poses, such as stateless HTTP and cross-browser compatibility issues. All this is packed into a modern, dynamic, and flexible web-browser UI. Of course, all these web-oriented features are fully available to us, as developers, to be used in our developed applications. It directly leads to high-level web-oriented APEX applications for the end users.

It's important that we distinguish between the modern browsers you should use while developing with APEX and the target browsers for which you can develop. As you will see later, APEX includes some legacy resources that enable you to develop to some older versions of browsers (which don't necessarily support HTML5, CSS3, and so on). Although you hope all clients and end users use the latest version of a browser, in reality, this is often not the case. The native web abilities of APEX help widen the target audience for the developed APEX application.

Cross-Browser Code

Cross-browser application means that the application runs not only on various available browsers (including the multiple versions of each maker), but that the application displays a similar behavior with each of these different browsers. This is one of the biggest challenges Web developers face, and APEX is doing a very good job in meeting this challenge.

To achieve this, the APEX engine generates *cross-browser code*. The use of cross-browser JavaScript libraries, such as jQuery and jQuery Mobile, make it even simpler to develop cross-browser web applications quickly and efficiently.

Client-Side Platform Independent

Working in and developing for the Web gives APEX one of its most significant advantages: a high degree of client-side platform independence. As earlier stated, all you need to develop or run an APEX application is a web browser. You are not restricted to any specific combination of hardware and local operating system (OS). Any hardware that runs an OS supporting a (modern) browser can be used to develop, and more so to run, APEX applications. You are not limited to the "Wintel coalition" or Apple iOS hardware/software combinations; you can use a variety of alliances that support UNIX/Linux systems and countless Android devices. This opens the huge world of mobile media in addition to non-Windows workstations.

TIP
Although technically possible, using a handheld device to develop with APEX, especially with APEX 5.x, is not advised. As you'll see later in the book, the new development practices introduced in APEX 5.x need more screen real estate, making handheld development a challenge. However, developed applications can be easily fitted to a large assortment of mobile devices.

Using the APEX technology enables you, in many cases, to develop and maintain only a single APEX application for both the stationary workstation sector and the mobile one, yielding significant savings in development resources and efforts.

Effortless Deployment to Clients

It is highly probable that any combination of hardware and OS you choose already includes a preinstalled web browser. This means that an APEX application can be available to the client right from the start, without the need to take any extra client-side installation actions. As mentioned, a specific APEX application URL is the only resource the client needs to gain access and run the application. The ease of client-side deployment is a major advantage.

A Declarative RAD IDE

APEX is a *declarative rapid application development tool* that includes an *integrated development environment*. Let's look at what that means.

Declarative technologies deal with what we want to do and not how we want to do it. You are likely familiar with a good example—SQL. SQL is a declarative language. When you are running a **SELECT** statement, for example, you are telling the SQL engine the characteristics of the data set you want to fetch from the database, such as table and column names, filters, sort order, and so on. You say nothing about how it should build this data set, such as which indexes to use, the algorithm for sorting the retrieved records, and so on. In the context of APEX, we are implementing the declarative feature through a collection of wizards that enable us to declare our wishes to the *APEX engine*, which in turn, fulfills them for us.

The new *Page Designer*, introduced in APEX 5.0, is a great example of the declarative feature of APEX. This principal wizard includes some subwizards that help us use a drag-and-drop technology to position items on the application page (the *Layout grid*) and define their necessary properties (the *Property Editor*). We are not telling the APEX engine what HTML code to use to generate the type of item we want, what CSS code to match it with the general look and feel of the application (which, as you'll see later in the book, is also being determined in a declarative manner), and what combination of HTML and CSS code to position the item in place. It is all being done by the APEX engine, and that is why we call APEX a *declarative RAD tool*.

TIP
The declarative nature of APEX doesn't limit your development options. It is impossible to foresee all the possible needs and requirements developers may encounter and cover them all in a declarative manner. If APEX doesn't have a suitable declarative solution, it lets you manually feed the appropriate code needed to achieve your development goals. APEX is not a black box, limited only to out-of-the-box features. You can almost always manually intervene, adding your own code (or changing the APEX engine's initially generated code), and you'll review these options throughout the book. This is one more of APEX's strengths.

The APEX 5.*x* Page Designer is also a classic implementation of the RAD philosophy, and we dedicate the entire Chapter 5 to this APEX wizard. It enables you to design the look and feel of an APEX application page by using, among others, a drag-and-drop technology to position various page elements, without the need to write a single HTML tag or CSS selector code.

But what is a RAD tool, exactly? There is more than one concept or explanation behind this term, which mainly aim to interpret what "rapid" actually means. One concept claims that rapid development puts more emphasis on the code development phase itself and allocates less attention to the plan and design phase. Although APEX can be used this way, this is *not* our recommended approach, as Chapter 2 will clearly show. We are more inclined to adopt the graphical user interface (GUI) builder approach, in which we are using an assortment of wizards to generate portions of the application code, instead of manually writing it. It is most notable in developing the UI segment of the application, using, for example, a drag-and-drop and/or WYSIWYG technology, but it also can be applied to the development of the business logic code.

As an IDE tool, APEX includes a variety of modules (tools and utilities) that support the entire development cycle. All these modules (which we will review in Chapter 3), with all their different and sometimes complementary functionalities, are integrated into the same look, feel, and operational environment that is available after a single authentication process (login) into the APEX IDE. Under the same roof, we can develop the application and test it as both developers (privileged users) and as regular end users; we can manage and track the development process, especially if we are part of a development team. We can perform various data model–related actions on the database (which we'll discuss in Chapter 2) and can also manage the APEX environment itself— the developers, users, database resources, APEX resources, and more.

The new APEX 5.*x* IDE includes many new features that improve the ease and comfortable use of the IDE and increase the productivity of developers. We'll review these features in the chapters ahead.

Oracle Database Data-Centric Applications Tool

APEX is an Oracle tool that runs in the Oracle Database. On the downside, if your IT infrastructure doesn't include Oracle Database(s), APEX is not for you. On the other hand, if you are operating in an Oracle workshop, APEX is likely already included (and even installed) as a free-of-charge feature of your database. Let's break apart this tool a bit further as an Oracle Database tool and a data-centric application.

Oracle Database Tool

Starting with Oracle Database 11g and continuing with Oracle Database 12cR1, all Oracle Database editions (including the free XE version) have APEX preinstalled as part of the default installation script. With the upcoming (at the time of writing) 12cR2 Database version, APEX will continue to be included in the distribution files, but it will not be installed by default. APEX is also an integrated module in the Oracle Cloud.

TIP
The pace of releasing new APEX versions is much higher than the pace of releasing new database versions. As such, the APEX version shipped or installed by default is almost always not the latest one available. We'll discuss this in more detail later in the chapter, but for now, you should remember that the latest version of APEX is always available for downloading, at no cost, from OTN, and it can easily be installed on the database as a fresh installation (12cR2 and later) or as an upgrade process on databases that include default installation.

APEX gains some high-quality features from running in the Oracle database. First, APEX is available on the main platforms that support Oracle databases. The APEX downloads page on OTN includes a list of the hardware/software platforms that support the installation of APEX, and currently the most noteworthy are Microsoft Windows (32- and 64-bit), Linux x86 and x86-64, Oracle Solaris systems, HP-UX Itanium systems, and some specific IBM platforms. Although there is not the high degree of platform independence that APEX enjoys on the client side, APEX still provides an impressive range of hardware/software server options.

APEX was designed to take full and optimal advantage of all the benefits that various Oracle Database technologies have to offer. First and foremost, the APEX engine uses SQL and PL/SQL, which are the fastest and most efficient resources to store, query, and manipulate data in the database. Moreover, APEX can use several more notable database technologies such as Oracle XML DB, Oracle Text, and so on. On top of that, APEX enjoys the very high degree of scalability, advanced security features, globalization, and localization characteristics available with the Oracle Database—and much more.

NOTE
The Oracle XML DB is a high-performance technology that natively deals with XML-related data, using common XML standards. The embedded PL/SQL gateway (EPG), which we'll discuss in the "APEX Architecture" section, is part of Oracle XML DB.

APEX also inherits all the database infrastructure enhancements made by its owner, such as advanced storage units and smart backup/restore systems. If, for example, your environment includes investments in load-balancing and fault-tolerance systems such as Real Application Clusters (RAC), Data Guard/standby database, or any other data disaster recovery planning, APEX will benefit from them as well. Thus, although APEX is limited to the Oracle Database environment, it makes the most out of it.

Data-Centric Applications

Oracle databases handle data. When you are on the Web, APEX is the best way to generate and store new data or access and manipulate data already stored. Hence, if your application revolves around the data and is driven by it, APEX is the best tool for you. Every application that deals with gathering data and information; processing and storing it; or retrieving, analyzing, and reporting about it is a perfect candidate to be developed as an APEX application. APEX also includes a special module, the Websheet, that allows power users (not necessarily IT specialists) to develop spreadsheet-like applications by extensively using the very friendly declarative RAD features of APEX.

NOTE
The Websheet module is not supported in the APEX runtime-only environment.

APEX Architecture

Now that we have covered the definitions around APEX, you have likely started thinking about what it can do for you. Let's take a deeper view at the APEX architecture, peek under the hood of its environment, and see how it actually works.

The basic APEX architecture is a simple (physical) two-tier model with a client side (essentially a web browser), a server side (here, an Oracle database with APEX installation that we'll refer to as the *APEX engine*), and something in between (a communication broker that will act as a bidirectional channel between the web browser and the APEX engine).

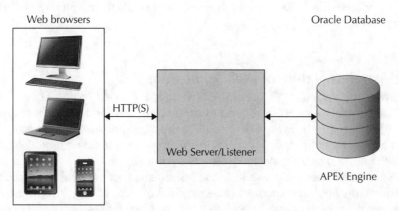

In the APEX architecture, the communication broker is a web server (or emulation of it) that provides HTTP(S) listener services, and we'll reference this functionality as the *web listener*.

NOTE
In the basic APEX infrastructure configuration, the web server/listener is installed on the same hardware server as the database and has no extra costs (such as licensing and hardware). There are options to expand the architecture into a (physical) three-tier model, in which the web server/listener is installed on its own machine. In these cases, on top of the additional hardware, extra licensing fees may apply, depending on the specific web server/listener you choose to use. We will review the available options later in the chapter.

The web listener receives the HTTP request from the browser—a specifically formatted URL, which we'll discuss later—and maps it to a database PL/SQL stored procedure. The web listener communicates with the database by opening a new database session, and in the APEX context, its main entry point to the APEX engine is a procedure called "F" (we'll remind you of the F procedure when we discuss the APEX URL notation). During your browser work with APEX, you'll likely encounter two more very important procedures: the **WWV_FLOW.SHOW** procedure, which is responsible for generating the rendering code for the application page, and the **WWV_FLOW.ACCEPT** procedure, which is responsible for the after submit activities of the page.

When the APEX engine has done its job with regard to the specific request it received from the web listener, another new database session is opened, and the web listener takes the APEX engine job results and sends them to the client browser to be rendered.

The Stateless Nature of Web Applications

As a web application, APEX uses HTTP, which is a *stateless protocol* by nature. This means that every HTTP request must stand by itself, independent of any other HTTP requests. Every HTTP request must include all the necessary information for the receiving party to be able to process it. Some protocols (such as FTP) maintain persistence and interactive communication channels between the client and server, make available the results/effects of previous interactions, and allow previous interactions to affect current ones. With stateless protocols, however, there is no persistent channel, and past interactions cannot influence the present ones, which can rely only on themselves.

In a security context, for example, it means that the current HTTP request cannot rely on any past authentication (login) process performed by the user by using a previous HTTP request, and every new request must include some sort of information that will enable the server to identify the origin of the HTTP request and validate it. In the APEX environment, you'll see that each HTTP request indeed includes such information, called a *session ID*. This parameter, in conjunction with two nonpersistent browser cookies (known as *session cookies*) that are generated and sent to the local browser during a successful login/authentication process, allows the APEX engine to associate the request with a specific APEX logic session and revalidate its authentication. The APEX engine operates a special mechanism called *Session State*, and this mechanism helps overcome the stateless nature of HTTP and effectively turns the APEX applications to be conducted in a *stateful* manner.

Another important thing you should learn from the HTTP stateless nature is that a new database session is opened each time the web server/listener needs to communicate with the database, and it has a very short life span—the time it takes the HTTP request to reach the server, or back to the client browser. When we cover the concept of an *application page* in Chapter 4, you'll see that every APEX application page actually uses at least two database sessions: one at the rendering phase, when information flows from the APEX engine to the client browser, and another one in the page submit phase, in which information flows from the browser to the APEX engine. We'll remind you of that when we discuss the nature and responsibilities of the APEX engine (hint: PL/SQL packages that are influenced by database sessions).

The APEX Engine

The APEX engine is a collection of Oracle Database objects, and as such it actually lives in the database. Its main components include around 445 metadata tables that are being populated, queried, and manipulated by approximately 281 PL/SQL packages.

The APEX tables include all the metadata needed by the APEX engine to do its job. This includes all the information needed to render a specific APEX application page, which means all the HTML attributes for generating the appropriate HTML tags; all the CSS information needed to produce the corresponding CSS selectors that will shape the page; information about external files that we need to link to the page; and all the instructions on how to populate the page items with their initial values and how to compute them (for example, fetch them from the database, rely on values previously computed, static values, and so on). The APEX metadata tables also include all the information the APEX engine needs to implement the business logic when a page application is being submitted to the server, and where to go after it has done its job (usually, the next application page that we need to process).

NOTE
As you'll later see, the APEX IDE itself is actually an assortment of APEX applications. Hence, as part of the APEX installation process, the APEX tables are populated with all the necessary metadata needed to run the APEX IDE.

The APEX database objects are stored in two major schemas. The primary schema is version dependent, and its name is derived from the APEX version: APEX_*nnnnnn*. The first *nn* digits stand for the major APEX version, so for APEX 5.x they are set to 05. The next *nn* digits stand for the (major) sub-version. For APEX 5.0 they are set to 00, and for APEX 5.1 they will be set to 01, and so forth. The last *nn* digits were not in use so far, and they are set to 00. Ergo, the primary schema of APEX 5.1 is called APEX_050100, and the one for a major previous version is APEX_040200.

NOTE
The fact that the last two digits of the schema name remain 00 means that minor version upgrades and patch sets are being installed into the same current APEX schema. For example, the last version of APEX 4.x, 4.2.6, is still installed into the APEX_040200 schema.

The second schema that serves APEX is FLOWS_FILES, and this name remains the same for all the APEX versions. APEX uses this schema to manage and store its uploaded files (a feature that both the APEX IDE and developed applications support).

A third schema, APEX_INSTANCE_ADMIN_USER, was introduced in APEX 5.1. This schema serves a new feature, the REST Administration Interface. This interface enables an APEX instance administrator, using the REST Administration API, to run administrative functions on its APEX instance(s), only over REST and HTTP. This may come in handy, for example, in a cloud environment, where SQL*Net is not possible. Moreover, by using a REST client with an access token that follows the OAuth Client Credentials authentication flow, which can be created as part of enabling the REST Administration Interface, administrators can gain easy access to statistics information about the APEX instance(s) usage. A packaged application that permits easy collection and analysis of these statistics is anticipated in a future release. More details about these new features and options can be found in the Application Express Administration Guide and Application Express API Reference documentation.

TIP
The REST Administration Interface is disabled by default. To enable it and take advantage of these new features, the APEX architecture should include Oracle REST Data Services (ORDS) 3.0.5 and later. We'll discuss ORDS later in this chapter.

The APEX installation script also creates a few objects in the SYS schema. Although it might be considered an unorthodox behavior, this is done for security reasons. In the context of this chapter, we'll only say that ultimately it allows APEX to use a low privileged user, APEX_PUBLIC_USER, to establish a database connection with the web server/listener, and at the same time the APEX engine uses a very powerful (undocumented) SYS package called SYS.DBMS_SQL_SYS. This package allows the APEX engine to parse the PL/SQL code that is part of the application (for example, the implementation of the application business logic) under the security privileges of the schema that we associated with our application. These privileges, which are determined according to the specific needs of the application, are usually much higher than those granted to the public user. We'll remind you of that in Chapter 4 when we discuss the concept of APEX Workspace.

APEX Engine Responsibilities

In the following sections, we'll review some of the major tasks for which the APEX *engine* is responsible (not necessarily in any order of importance):

- Generating the rendering code for each APEX application page
- Running the application business logic and controlling its flow
- Security (authentication and authorization)
- Session State

The Rendering Engine   The APEX engine is responsible for generating the rendering process of each APEX application page. (Don't get confused: the actual rendering process—running the HTML code that was generated by the APEX engine and translating it into visual elements on the browser screen—runs only on the client-side browser.) As we already discussed, each APEX HTTP request includes specific page information that allows the APEX engine to query its metadata tables and fetch all the information necessary to generate the page HTML, CSS, and JavaScript code. Because APEX doesn't adhere to the classic web application three-tier model, and the logic module is not separated from the data module (they actually share the same hardware and database), the metadata is being fetched and processed in lightning speed as no network communication is involved.

NOTE
Although scalability is not just about enhancing your hardware, and it has a lot to do with the way you write your code, hardware enhancements are a popular action to take when you want to increase and improve your scalability. In the APEX architecture, it means that the APEX engine enjoys these measures immediately and directly.

After fetching all the necessary metadata, it is time to produce the application page code, and for that the APEX engine extensively uses the PL/SQL Web Toolkit. This toolkit is a set of PL/SQL packages that enable developers to exploit the PL/SQL strength fully in the Oracle Database (for example, query and data manipulations using DML, use dynamic SQL to generate dynamic on-the-fly data sets, and so on) to translate the metadata into HTML code that can be run directly on a web browser. In comparison with the alternative of writing the entire page code manually, using the full range of the HTML syntax, the PL/SQL Web Toolkit does it in a simpler and relatively hassle-free manner.

NOTE
More experienced APEX developers are likely familiar with the HTP and OWA_UTIL packages, which are included in the PL/SQL Web Toolkit. As APEX developers, we sometimes directly use some procedures from these packages (such as HTP.PRN, OWA_UTIL.HTTP_HEADER_CLOSE, and so on), especially in the Ajax-related PL/SQL anonymous blocks.

The PL/SQL Web Toolkit stores its work products in a dedicated PL/SQL array. After the APEX engine completes the page rendering task, the web server/listener invokes a procedure that takes the content of the PL/SQL array—the page rendering code—and sends it to the client browser to be actually rendered.

TIP
Now you can better understand why APEX applications do not store any persistent page application code files on the web server. They simply don't have any to store. Each application page is dynamically generated at runtime, according to the current metadata. However, it doesn't mean that APEX cannot use the web server to cache static files that were linked to the application page. These files—external JavaScript files (libraries), external CSS files, images, and so on—are being cached. APEX is optimally taking care of both its dynamic and static aspects.

The Business Logic Engine   The APEX engine is responsible for running the application business logic, which is implemented through several declarative and manual mechanisms. These mechanisms implement some of the fundamental building blocks of APEX, and we'll cover them all in Chapter 7. The mechanisms enable us to query the database and manipulate the data stored in it; condition parts of the code according to the business logic terms; validate the data fed by the end user, before processing it and/or saving it in the database; and control the general application flow (the order in which tasks are performed, application pages branched to, and so on).

For each application page, the APEX engine considers the business logic at least twice: The first time, as part of producing the rendering code, it determines how to populate/initialize the page items and how to treat validation (or other logic) errors the APEX engine encounters. The second time occurs when it needs to implement the application business logic, after the end user has submitted the application page.

The APEX Engine and Ajax

Between the page rendering and page submit phases, the APEX engine is also responsible to run the server-side, Ajax-related PL/SQL anonymous blocks. This activity can be characterized as either rendering related (such as dynamically generating a page item with values that are dependent on user input at runtime) or as business logic related (such as updating a database table[s] even before or in place of submitting the page).

The business logic engine is also not separated from the data module, and they share the same hardware and database, similar to the rendering engine. The result is very high application performance, with very low overhead of the APEX engine.

APEX Security   The APEX engine is responsible for the APEX security in both the development environment (we already mentioned that the APEX IDE itself is an assortment of APEX applications) and our APEX-developed application.

The APEX IDE always operates in a *protected environment*, which means that we need to authenticate ourselves (log in) before we are allowed in. The developed applications can be public—that is, they don't require any authentication process— or they can be protected.

APEX implements security in two phases: The first phase is *Authentication*, in which we start from outside the APEX environment and need to identify ourselves to gain access. APEX provides us with several out-of-the-box authentication schemes, which are based on internal managed APEX users, database users, the LDAP directory, and Single-Sign-On (SSO). Once we pass the authentication process, the APEX engine enables us to implement an *Authorization* scheme that can determine which APEX resources will be available to us, what business logic we'll be allowed to use, and what data we can be exposed to. The authorization scheme allows us to define several levels of users in the same application with different access/usage privileges.

In the context of security, you should remember that the stateless nature of HTTP compels the APEX engine to identify each APEX HTTP(S) request, classify it to an APEX session (which we'll discuss next), and treat it according to the APEX session authentication and authorization schemes.

APEX Session State   *Session State* is an essential concept and mechanism in APEX, and we'll cover it thoroughly in Chapter 4. In the context of the APEX engine, Session State helps overcome the stateless nature of HTTP and effectively causes APEX applications to behave in a stateful manner.

Every dialog between the client-side browser (including public applications, which don't force the users to be identified) and the server-side APEX engine must take place within an active logic APEX session. The APEX session must be active; should conditions exist where it becomes inactive, it also becomes unusable. This stands logically, as there is no persistent physical connection between the two sides. The APEX engine attaches a unique session ID to every APEX session and manages the entire operation in a special table that includes all the active session IDs.

On the client-side, we are using a browser cookie (which expires when the APEX session is no longer active, including when we close the browser) to hold a hashed version of the session ID. The session ID itself is included in every HTTP request that goes to the APEX engine. The APEX engine verifies that the session ID belongs to an active APEX session. If it belongs, the engine will continue handling it. If it does not, or the session ID is not included in the HTTP request (which can occur if the APEX

Active and Inactive APEX Sessions

An *active* APEX session can become *inactive* (expired) in three major cases:

- The end user signs out from the application.
- The life span of the APEX session exceeds the session maximum lifetime parameter, which is set by default to 28,800 seconds (8 hours).
- The APEX session is idle longer than the idle time parameter, which is set by default to 3600 seconds (1 hour).

These parameters can be changed by the APEX instance administrator. Every hour, the APEX engine runs a background database "garbage collection" job, which scans the APEX sessions table and purges all the expired sessions.

URL were manually constructed by the end user), the APEX engine initializes a new authentication process. If we are dealing with a public application, a new APEX session with a new session ID will be created instantly, and we'll be granted access to the application. If the application is protected, a full authentication process will be launched and a new APEX session will be created upon its success.

The APEX Runtime Environment

APEX includes a runtime-only environment in which the APEX IDE is not exposed (including the Administration module and its web interface, as we'll describe in Chapter 3). With this configuration, the APEX engine solely deals with running existing APEX applications, which means that this configuration is suitable for production instances. Security wise, this configuration is a big advantage as the running applications cannot be changed or harmed while in the runtime production environment.

TIP

An APEX runtime instance can be upgraded to a full development environment, and vice versa. This gives you the flexibility to start with one and later move to the other. You can experience both environments and ultimately decide which one is best for your specific needs.

Everything in Between

In our APEX architecture discussion so far, we've covered the client side (a common, and preferably modern, web browser) and the server side (the APEX engine). Now it's time to see what the APEX architecture has to offer us for the "in between"—the web servers/listeners.

APEX supports three options for the communication broker between the web browser and the APEX engine:

- **Oracle HTTP Server (OHS)**   Based on an Apache server with an Oracle extension called mod_plsql.

- **Embedded PL/SQL Gateway (EPG)**   This embedded HTTP server runs in the database as part of the Oracle XML DB database features. It provides similar functionality to the mod_plsql extension in OHS.

- **Oracle REST Data Services (ORDS)**   This Java application, formerly known as APEX Listener, runs in a J2EE container (application/web server).

NOTE
As you'll see in a moment, some options can be installed on the same server as the database, while others can be installed on a different machine. Using a separate machine for the application/web server doesn't turn the APEX architecture to a (classic) web application three-tier model. In any infrastructure used for the APEX environment, the data model (APEX metadata and application data) and the logic model (the APEX engine) will always share the same database server.

Oracle HTTP Server

The OHS was the first option available to APEX, which was known at that time as HTML DB. It is still available for the latest APEX version.

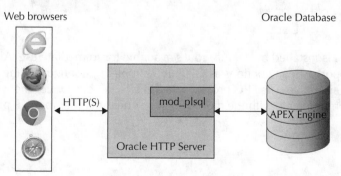

The OHS is actually an Oracle adaptation of the seasoned Apache server, with some plug-in extensions that optimized it for the Oracle environment. In our context, we are using the mod_plsql plug-in. This extension is responsible for mapping HTTP requests to database stored procedures, and then taking the results from the database and sending them back to the client web browser.

OHS being the first, there is a lot of good experience with it, and its installation and configuration are fairly simple. On the other hand, mod_plsql poses some limitations, and the most notable in the APEX context is the 32K size limit of a single parameter that can be passed to a procedure. This means that we cannot simply submit text items that are longer than 32K.

NOTE
The APEX licensing agreement allows us to install the OHS on the same server as the database, without any additional costs. Although it is possible to install OHS on its own machine, extra licensing fees may apply.

Embedded PL/SQL Gateway

The EPG was introduced to APEX users with the first version of Oracle Database Express (10g), and then as part of Oracle 11g and later. The EPG is part of the XML DB HTTP server, which is a feature of the database. Similarly to APEX, it is implemented as a collection of built-in database packages, and, therefore, it also lives in the database.

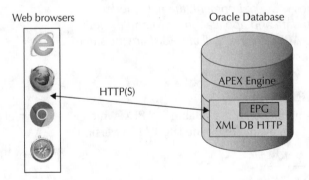

The EPG is installed by default, so it's available for immediate use. Although it doesn't support as many options as OHS, it is simpler to configure using the built-in DBMS_EPG package. The EPG provides the HTTP listener services the web browser needs to communicate with the database, in a similar manner to mod_plsql in OHS.

Running in the database, the EPG doesn't support the use of a firewall to buffer between the client side and the server. In some environments, this could be a serious limitation. Moreover, the static files that accompany APEX (the images directory), such as external JavaScript, CSS, or graphical (image) files, should be uploaded into the database (as opposed to being part of the OS file system). This might degrade performance.

TIP
The EPG is not intended to serve in a high-workload production environment. It will best serve a development environment.

Oracle REST Data Services

ORDS 3.0.*x* is the third major version of the product formerly known as APEX Listener. With previous versions, the product was tightly tied with APEX as it was using the APEX repository to save data. Version 3.0 was extended to provide services beyond those that are APEX-related only, and ORDS can now be installed without APEX.

ORDS is basically a Java application that can be run under any J2EE container, but it is fully supported against Oracle WebLogic Server, Oracle GlassFish Server, and Apache Tomcat. The previous version, APEX Listener 2.0, is also supported under Oracle Application Server Containers for J2EE (OC4J). ORDS also has a standalone version, which doesn't require a full-scale application server, can be easily installed from a command line, and can be a good choice for a development environment.

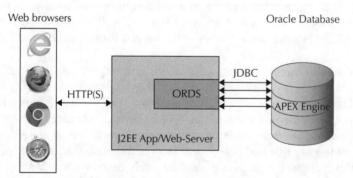

ORDS is the latest and most advanced web listener technology that APEX can offer. It was designed to overcome some of the limitations that were posed by the OHS and mod_plsql (such as the 32K limit) and add some long-demanded features such as PDF report printing support and better caching services to APEX static files. As of writing this book, ORDS is Oracle's recommended option for using with APEX.

The Preferred Option, and How to Choose It

Choosing the preferred web listener option should be based on the specific characteristics of the current APEX installation. Consider the following when deciding which web listener option is right for your installation. Make sure that any decision you make coincides with your future needs, those of your development environment, and of your developed APEX application.

NOTE
This list is intended to make you think. In the next chapter, we'll discuss the importance of good planning and design. Do your homework, learn as much as you can about the options you are facing, and make an informed decision.

Oracle Recommendation   Listen to Oracle's advice and recommendations. By choosing APEX, you trusted Oracle with your most valuable asset: your data. Rely on Oracle's expertise for these more technical parts. Currently, Oracle recommends the use of ORDS 3.0.x, as the latest, most advanced, and most feature-rich technology offered for the APEX environment (and as we discussed earlier, some of the new APEX 5.1 features are dependent on it). In past years, one of the common reasons for not using the ORDS/APEX listener was that the technology was relatively young with limited experience. We have now seen this technology mature and gain a lot of good experience. Oracle recommends it and follows its own advice. The ORDS technology is being used with very important and high-profile services, including the Oracle Public Cloud. It's also being used as the web listener of the free hosting site for APEX developers: apex.oracle.com. This is a strong positive indication.

Needs and Requirements   Check your needs and requirements, and the environment in which you are going to fulfill them, both as a developer and an end user. Development, testing, and QA are often scaled quite differently than the production environment, and each can have its own best choice. Remember that APEX applications are independent of the database version they were developed on and the web listener that had been used. Even if you have started an application and now want to change your decision, you can safely do so without losing any APEX code. If you are unsure of where to begin, start small and grow as needed.

Existing Infrastructure   If your currently installed infrastructure serves you well, you may want to consider not replacing it, even for a newer and better featured product. Check whether you really need to use all the new features that are available in the newer technologies, mainly if you are currently using OHS and consider upgrading to ORDS. On the other hand, if your current infrastructure already includes a suitable J2EE container, choosing ORDS seems logical.

Known Advantages and Added Values   ORDS exposes you to RESTful web services and allows you to use them. It also supports simple PDF printing. These specific features are not supported with the other options, so if they are needed, it makes your selection decision easier.

Known Limitations   Review the known limitations of the options you are considering, and see how they might affect you. For example, the EPG or the standalone version of ORDS are not intended to be used in a production environment with a high workload. The EPG architecture doesn't support a firewall, and the standalone version of ORDS doesn't support HTTPS. The OHS with mod_plsql has a limit of 32K on the size of a single item. If any of these limitations is in conflict with your environment or application requirement—production versus development, high workload versus low, large development team versus small one, external (out on the Internet) application versus an internal one, with or without a firewall, HTTP versus HTTPS, larger than 32K text fields, and so on—it should steer you to the right direction. Furthermore, one of the popular uses of APEX is simply and quickly enhancing the capabilities of the Oracle E-Business Suite (EBS). The latest version, EBS R12, no longer supports OHS. If integration with this suite is one of your APEX working goals, ORDS is the right choice for you.

Cost   The costs of various options vary considerably, starting with completely free (OHS on the database server, Apache Tomcat, the Oracle GlassFish Community Edition) and going to thousands of dollars for high-end application servers. Check your budget, check your financial possibilities, and check your existing inventory for installed and licensed products and infrastructure. Make your decision accordingly.

Support, Standards, and Regulations   If you operate under a support agreement with Oracle, make sure that the solution you choose is fully supported. For example, ORDS is no longer supported under OC4J. Your environment may also include fully compatible J2EE application servers that service other installed software, such as IBM WebSphere, SAP NetWeaver, JBoss Application Server, and others, but these are not supported by My Oracle Support. If your organization is bound by (internal or external) rules and regulations, make sure the chosen solution meets them all. For example, your organization may prohibit the use of open source products like Apache Tomcat (even though it is a supported platform).

Look to the Future   Look at the direction Oracle is taking. The mod_plsql plug-in extension is deprecated as of Oracle HTTP Server 12c (12.1.3), so OHS will not continue evolving in a manner that APEX supports, and the integration with current (EBS R12) and future products will not be supported. On the other hand, ORDS is definitely the current trend, and as we mentioned, Oracle is using it in some major strategic projects of its own. The company's March 2014 statement of direction includes the following: "As a key component of the Oracle Database, Oracle intends to continue enhancing Oracle REST Data Services. Oracle REST Data Services will be included with the next each new version of the Oracle Database as a standard database component."

Installation, Configuration, and Upgrade

Many users have the tendency to skip new software installation guides and dive right in. In many cases, and APEX is definitely included, this might turn out to be a gross mistake, and the short way becomes a very long one. However, if you can't wait and simply want to try it out first, or if you don't have the hardware or software means to install your own local APEX instance, you can visit the APEX hosting site at apex.oracle.com and apply for a free-of-charge APEX workspace. This personal APEX sandbox will enable you to practice everything covered in this book.

The APEX installation is a technical, platform-dependent procedure, and it should be a very precise one. You should understand what you are going to do, make the necessary pre-installation decisions, and only then start the actual installation work.

CAUTION
Both the APEX installation and APEX upgrade procedures, which we'll discuss next, are fairly safe, but something can always go wrong with a new installation. Before you start, always back up your database, in general, and your APEX work (workspaces, users, and applications) in particular. Better safe than sorry—a very old, but true, cliché.

The Installation Process

The APEX installation process has three major stages—pre-installation, installation, and post-installation tasks—and you must not skip any of them. It is highly important that you read and carefully follow all the instructions in the installation guide, as some of them pertain to a specific platform, mainly database versions (pre-11*g* if you are installing a pre-APEX 5.*x* version, 11*g* and 12*c* for APEX 5.*x*), and there are particular actions to take for each version. Platform-dependent instructions are also included for the various web listener options, and in the case of ORDS, installation and configuration instructions are included for each of the fully supported application/ web servers. Moreover, some of the tasks pertain to significant database and APEX initialization parameters that have a considerable impact on the availability of some services and the performance of others. Another important aspect that needs your attention is security, and security considerations and tasks are also included in the installation process.

The Installation Guide

The *Oracle Application Express Installation Guide* is available online at the APEX home page on OTN and can currently be downloaded in three different formats: PDF, ePub, and Mobi. This is a very detailed guide that explores most all of the essentials you need to know to install, upgrade, and configure APEX properly according to the infrastructure architecture you chose and its specific components. Please refer to this for detailed technical instructions, and use the following notes to further guide your installation, upgrade, or configuration.

Single APEX Version Installation per Database

A single Oracle database can hold a single APEX instance. This emanates mainly from security reasons: the way APEX objects are dispersed and stored in the database (including in the SYS schema) and the way APEX uses public synonyms with non-APEX version–dependent names (such as public API packages). Therefore, two APEX versions cannot be installed on the same database.

Oracle Database 12*c* introduced a new multitenant architecture for the database, which provides a multitenant database container (CDB) that may include more than one pluggable database (PDB)—a user configured database that can be treated as a separate (standalone) database.

NOTE
*In the jargon of 12*c*, a PDB is treated as a non-CDB, a definition that fits all the pre–Oracle Database 12*c* versions.*

The APEX engine, and the APEX installation script, were adapted to the multitenant 12*c* architecture, and the default 12*c*R1 installation includes an APEX instance in the root container. In our context, one of the available configurations for 12*c*R1 is to remove APEX from the root container and install a complete (local) APEX version in a PDB. Each PDB, being treated as a separate database, can hold a different version of an APEX instance. Generally speaking, it is still a situation of one APEX version per one database, even though this database (a PDB) is included in a larger entity. The same concept will apply to 12*c*R2, but in this case, no removing of installed-by-default APEX instance will be needed.

The APEX installation guide includes a detailed discussion about installing APEX in a 12*c* database: "Utilizing the Multitenant Architecture in Oracle Database 12*c*." If this is your database version, please read it carefully.

APEX Upgrade

The APEX upgrade procedure is quite simple and straightforward. It is fully automated for the APEX engine and almost fully automated where developed applications are concerned. If the new version installation script identifies an older APEX version instance on the database, it will automatically invoke the upgrade procedure, which will migrate all the existing applications into the new APEX instance.

The upgrade process for APEX 5.1 was considerably improved, especially with regard to downtime, which was optimized and reduced to a minimum. For example, the total outage time while upgrading the apex.oracle.com instance was about 45 minutes, and this is an instance that held 31,600 distinct Workspaces, which is very impressive. This should make the decision to upgrade production sites a bit simpler, and the upgrade process itself less painful.

NOTE
The upgrade procedure will not delete the previous APEX instance; it will just disable it. It allows you to go back to the original APEX instance in case of a serious problem. You can find further detail in the installation guide.

The upgrade procedure migrates the current applications into the new APEX instance, but it doesn't change the application's basic look and feel. It actually retains the application's original theme and templates—hence, the "almost fully automated" with regard to upgrading the APEX application. Each new APEX release introduces new features to existing elements and new themes you can use. If you want to use these new features (and APEX 5.x includes some major ones), you need to complete the upgrade process manually—although, as usual, APEX is there to help.

The Upgrade Application Utility

The Upgrade Application wizard is a lesser known but very powerful utility that can save you a lot of hard and tedious work, while marching your application to a new and upgraded environment. It scans your recently upgraded application and finds all the APEX components that could potentially be elevated to a newer level, thus taking advantage of the new release features.

The following are just a few examples from the wizard:

- Upgrade tabular forms to the new APEX 5.1 interactive grid.
- Migrate AnyChart charts to the Oracle JET charts (HTML5 based).
- Update text field items to number field items, where appropriate.

- Upgrade date picker (classic) to the new date picker.

- Convert a theme-based calendar to a CSS calendar.

- Enable fixed report headers to the top of the page, for interactive reports.

This is a partial list. Look for this utility in the *APEX App Builder User's Guide* and see how you can exploit it to the fullest.

Switching to the Universal Theme

We will continue discussing the concept of APEX Theme and devote an entire chapter to it, particularly the Universal Theme, which is considered one of the major new features of APEX 5.x. For now, let's just say that APEX includes a Switching Theme wizard that enables you to switch the current active theme with a new one. With the Universal Theme, it's a bit more complicated than usual, and we encourage you to look for the *Universal Theme Migration Guide* at apex.oracle.com/ut.

TIP
If you are already using the Universal Theme, have upgraded from APEX 5.0 to 5.1, and want to use the new features that were added in APEX 5.1 (such as out-of-the-box RTL support), you should refresh the theme. Go to Shared Component | User Interface | Theme, and double-click the theme name – Universal Theme – 42. In the Theme Subscription section, click the Refresh Theme button. You should see the following success message: "Templates and templates options refreshed from master theme." The new theme features are available to you now.

Summary

APEX is a native web declarative rapid application development (RAD) integrated development environment (IDE) for developing Oracle Database data-centric web applications. In this chapter, we explained what that actually means and reviewed the architecture behind it. You should now be able to determine whether APEX is the right tool for you and should have a basic understanding of the APEX installation, upgrade, and configuration processes. In the next chapter, we'll review what you need to know to use APEX fully and optimally exploit its development cycle.

CHAPTER
2

Getting Ready

I n this chapter, we'll review some of the processes and planning actions you should take as part of what we consider to be a best-practice path to a smooth and efficient application development cycle.

We'll start with the prerequisite knowledge we believe you should master (or at least be familiar with and basically understand) in order to use the Oracle Application Express development environment in the best and optimal ways. We'll review some of the basic application development planning we recommend you should take as the first stage in your application development process. We'll end up applying our own advice to the demo application that we will develop throughout this book.

Recommended Prerequisite Knowledge

As you learned in the first chapter, APEX is a declarative rapid application development (RAD) tool, which means that we can often use its built-in wizards to define and develop the application components that we need, without writing any code. However, the APEX engine itself does use various technologies and programming languages to generate each page of our developed application. Being familiar with and having an understanding of these technologies and programming languages should give you an edge in using advanced technologies (such as Ajax) and gaining full control over all aspects of the application, including the option to add, enhance, or overwrite the standard (default) output of the APEX engine, and thus customize it to your exact requirements. Furthermore, when reviewing the APEX development capabilities, you'll see that you can implement many scenarios that are not directly supported by the APEX wizards. To do that and reach the full potential of APEX, you must manually code the elements you need using the technologies and programming languages we'll review in this chapter.

SQL and PL/SQL

We categorized the applications developed with APEX as data-centric. To be more precise, these applications are Oracle Database data-centric. As such, the best way to deal with this type of data is by using SQL and PL/SQL. These are the fastest and most efficient languages to query and manipulate Oracle Database data.

Mastering SQL, mainly the **SELECT** statement and the **INSERT**, **UPDATE**, and **DELETE** DML statements, will enable you to generate APEX reports and easily manipulate data in scenarios that are not supported directly by the APEX wizards (such as simultaneously manipulating data in more than one table).

Mastering PL/SQL will enable you to implement your application logic easily, especially in more complex scenarios, and use advanced technologies such as Ajax to invoke PL/SQL code on the server, without submitting the application page.

HTML/HTML5, CSS, and JavaScript

The final product of the APEX engine is an HTML/HTML5 code page, which includes some links to built-in Cascading Style Sheets (CSS), JavaScript, and jQuery external files/libraries. However, APEX enables us also to include our own external CSS and JavaScript files, alongside inline code that can be embedded in each application page (using the APEX Page Designer, which will be discussed in great detail in later chapters).

By understanding and mastering these technologies, you will have full control over the final look and feel of your application to manipulate the page HTML code (the DOM, or Document Object Model interface), either by using the APEX wizards (such as Dynamic Actions) or by writing your own code.

jQuery

The APEX 5.1 environment includes the JavaScript libraries jQuery 1.11.3 and 2.2.3, jQuery UI 1.10.4, and jQuery Mobile 1.4.5. The APEX IDE uses jQuery features extensively in its various modules, and the APEX engine embeds the appropriate and relevant links in each of the developed application pages. Hence, these libraries are also available to us, as developers, to use in our own applications.

By having a working knowledge of jQuery, you can harness the power of these libraries to use in your applications. It will also increase your productivity by enabling you to write less or smaller code and use the built-in cross browser features.

Ajax

Ajax is an advanced technology that enables you to invoke server-side (database) actions without submitting your current web page. Ajax is fully supported by APEX, either via APEX wizards (Dynamic Actions) or manually using the APEX Ajax framework.

Having an understanding of the principles of Ajax will enable you to exploit this advanced technology efficiently using the tools APEX makes available to you, to enhance the look and feel of the UI by making it more responsive and dynamic. It will also increase the efficiency of your developed applications, by enabling you to invoke database resources without submitting the page.

Need to Complement Your Knowledge?

If you need to complement your knowledge in any of the recommended subjects, the following list of books may be good places to start:

- **Oracle Database 12c SQL** by Jason Price (Oracle Press, 2013)
- **Oracle Database 12c PL/SQL Programming** by Michael McLaughlin (Oracle Press, 2014)

(continued)

- *HTML & CSS: The Complete Reference,* **5th Edition (Complete Reference Series)** by Thomas A. Powell (McGraw-Hill, 2010)

- *JavaScript: The Complete Reference,* **3rd Edition** by Thomas Powell and Fritz Schneider (McGraw-Hill, 2012)

- *jQuery: A Beginner's Guide* by John Pollock (McGraw-Hill, 2014)

- *Ajax: The Complete Reference* by Thomas A. Powell (McGraw-Hill, 2008)

This list is a personal one. The amount of books that cover the issues we are dealing with is staggering. You are encouraged to explore the major book sites and compile your own list. But this list is a good place to start.

The Internet can also be a great (and free) source of knowledge in the subjects we are dealing with. The following sites are merely the tip of the iceberg:

- **Oracle Learning Library: apexapps.oracle.com/pls/apex/ f?p=44785:1**   Where Oracle technologies are concerned, this is a good place to start. The Oracle Learning Library, by the way, is a great example of a public APEX application.

- **The APEX home page: apex.oracle.com**   This site includes many resources that can help you learn and better understand the APEX concepts. It includes an option to request a free APEX Workspace, hosted by Oracle. The hosting site always runs the latest (production) APEX version, and you can use it as your sandbox.

- **Web-related development technologies: www.w3schools.com/ default.asp**   This site is a very useful resource for learning about web development. Along with its simple and coherent tutorials, this is a great reference site.

Application Planning

Single developers, or members of small development teams (in which you are expected to be involved in all aspects of the application development, and not just writing code), often tend to dive directly into the code development stage, and skip the application planning stage, which should include several processes and actions that we'll review next. Some of these processes, such as data modeling or defining and creating the application data tables, include actions that can't be avoided, even if you are working alone.

If you don't have a methodical application planning stage, it usually means that you'll create each data table when you first need it. Reality shows, however, that often enough, this translates into tables that are not structured optimally, that are not always normalized, and that don't include all the necessary indexes, not to mention missing foreign keys and other elements. These potential problems, which can easily impair the final quality and performance of a developed application, can simply be solved by implementing a proper application planning stage.

In the next sections, we'll describe some of the processes and actions we believe should be included in a basic application planning stage, regardless of the nature and size of the developed application and the number of people developing it. The volume of this stage should be scaled to the nature and size of the developed application and its development environment. As long as you are working in a procedural manner, you should choose the planning processes and actions that will best serve your needs and objectives.

High Level Design

The main objective of the High Level Design (HLD) process is to construct the big picture of the newly developed application and its operational environment. It should include an abstract overview of the application functionality and business logic, the elements needed to achieve these objectives, and all the external (to the application) systems that the application is depending on or going to invoke, if any. In this context, *abstract overview* means verbal descriptions with a minimal use of specific technical terms and references, or implementation strategies.

 NOTE
We are not going to teach you how to construct and write an HLD document, as this is beyond the scope of this book. Searching the Internet for "high level design examples" will yield many examples of HLD documents, recommended templates for such documents, and examples of diverse types of diagrams for illustrating various aspects of the HLD. Those will give you a clear view of what you should do, and how.

We will discuss some design elements that we find important to be included in your HLD process and document. Their scope, volume, and level of detail should be determined by you and be scaled according to the nature, size, and complexity of the developed application and its running environment.

Visual Aids

Depending on the complexity of the application and the environment in which it will run, visualization aids such as simple diagrams can be very helpful in clarifying the verbal descriptions used in the HLD document. A *diagram* is a (relatively) uncomplicated technique used to abstract complex structures and systems and display the essential information we are interested in. The diagram may include the various elements we are going to deal with and the relationships among them. In our context, this would include the connections between the application and its surroundings. It may also include graphical representations of the application workflow according to the business logic, the dataflow based on both the business logic and the data model, and other information.

Following is an example of a very simple diagram that can be used to represent the application environment, participating elements, dataflow directions, and other information:

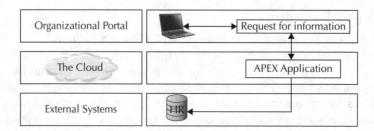

From this diagram, we can easily learn that the APEX application is going to reside in the cloud. It can be called from the organizational portal, and it queries an external Human Resources (HR) system.

Business Logic

If your development team includes system analysts, it will be their responsibility to formalize the developed application *business logic* and functionalities, and to make sure that you, as the code developer, fully understand what the application is expected to do. However, if system analysts are not included in the development team, and you're on your own, it will be your job, and your responsibility, to describe and formalize the business logic, and you should do this prior to writing any piece of code.

It is always a good thing to understand fully what is required of you as the application developer, and formalizing the business logic is a very productive way of learning what needs to be implemented in order to achieve the application goal(s). Productive, and important, because the business logic has a major bearing on many aspects of the development process, including constructing the data model, the QA (Quality Assurance) process, and, finally, writing the application code itself. We'll take a closer look at these processes in a moment, but let's start by looking at the business logic impact on them.

The Data Model   The business logic determines the volume and type of data we are going to use in the application, how it should be stored (various tables according to the nature and functionality of the data in the application), how it should be queried (according to the business logic reporting requirements), and how it should be manipulated (all the data manipulating actions required to achieve the application goals). These have direct bearing on the construction of the database tables, their primary key, and possible internal connections through foreign keys. Moreover, the business logic should influence the setting of extra indexes to the application tables, which will optimize and enhance the performance of certain application tasks.

Validations and QA   The business logic determines many of the data validations and conditioned actions we'll need to implement during the application development, such as required input fields, workflow conditions, and much more. Formalizing the business logic makes it simpler to detect and implement all these constraints.

The business logic is also responsible to some of the QA scenarios we need to compile in order to verify that the application is indeed doing what is expected of it and to uphold all the business logic constraints. As with validations, formalized business logic makes it easier to detect and compose the necessary QA scenarios.

Code Development   The sole purpose of the application code is to implement the application business logic, which defines its goal(s). If the business logic is made coherent and understandable to the developer(s), using a systematic procedure, the code development becomes much simpler and quicker. If we are developing according to a methodical plan, we are less prone to make mistakes and miss our goals.

Data Modeling

APEX applications are data-centric, and the data needs to be organized within the database. "Organized" is the key word here, because the structures (database elements) that hold the data can have a profound influence on how good, or bad, our application will perform, and how reliable and consistent are the results it produces.

We already established that the application business logic is the ultimate source for identifying the data our developed application is going to use. We should categorize and differentiate this data according to its nature and functionality within the application, and associate the formed data groups to database tables. Based on the data access needs posed by the application, while taking into account database design good practice rules, we should set a primary key (PK) for each table and decide how we are going to populate it (sequence, trigger, function, and so on). If required, extra indexes (and index types) that will optimize the data access should also be defined.

We should normalize the tables as much as possible to avoid, among other things, storing the same information in more than one place (table). While doing so, the FKs become obvious, and we should set them as well. Normalized tables, and internal table connections based on FKs, ensure a higher data consistency level in our data model.

As you'll see in the next chapter, the APEX IDE includes a module, SQL Workshop, that enables us to define and generate all the database objects we'll need during the development process (and which are included in our data model). Other tools are available in the market that can give us the same functionality, including a free tool by Oracle, SQL Developer, which can be downloaded from the Oracle Technology Network (OTN) site.

On top of enabling us independently to create all the database objects we'll need, the SQL Developer includes an extension (which can also be downloaded as a standalone utility), the Data Modeler. This very powerful extension/utility enables us to perform forward and backward engineering on the data model we are constructing, against the corresponded database schema that stores our data.

One of the possible results the Data Modeler can provide us is a graphical diagram of our data model, a simple representation of all the tables we created or that are going to be used with the application, their PK, FK, and internal table connections. An example of such a diagram is shown in Figure 2-1, later in the chapter, as part of a discussion about the demo application that will accompany us throughout the book.

TIP
Bear in mind that the data model logical design you have constructed is being translated into database objects, and these might be considerably influenced by the database configuration and the hardware running it. Also remember that what seems to be highly reasonable on paper (or on screen) does not always turn out to be the same in the real world. In our context, a full table scan, for example, is not necessarily slower than using an index, and too many indexes on a table might slow down a bulk load of data into it. So, should these objects and others be included in the data model? Should they be left out? The best authority on these issues, and the one who can highlight such potential pitfalls in the data model and who can make it more optimized, is the system DBA. Thus, it is highly advisable that you consult a DBA while constructing your data model.

Logical Constraints

We already established that the business logic has a significant impact on the code we are going to develop. The business logic may impose many constraints that we need to address in our code, and these should be mapped in advance, as they may influence the code control flow and the conditions it needs to meet in order to run.

Following are a few examples of simple/common constraints we should identify and address:

- Access to the application is for registered and authenticated users only.

- Certain operations are available to specific (privileged) users only.

- Certain information (such as reports) is exposed to specific (privileged) users only.

- Regulations or rules (such as banking, credit card, or insurance regulations) must be enforced.

- Organizational workflow rules (such as order of approval) must be enforced.

- Certain fields are required (not NULL).

- Fields should be classified as unique/non-unique.

- Fields can hold only specific types of data (such as numbers/digits only).

- Geographical boundaries (such as only US-associated IP addresses are allowed to connect to the application; using the correct date, currency, and decimal point formats) must be enforced.

If we identify all these logical constrains in advance, prior to writing any code, our development efforts will be much more comprehensive and more targeted in achieving the application goal(s).

Validations

On top of the logical constraints we should identify are *data validation* actions we should take to ensure the validity of the data entered by the application users. Often, these validations emanate from the nature of the data, or its data type. Following are a few simple common examples of validations we can use in applications:

- **Date validation** After validating that we are using the correct date format (for example, an American format versus a European one), we should make sure that the input date is valid. For example, February 29 is a valid date only in a leap year (and you may want to implement an algorithm to establish that), and June 31 is not a valid date any time.

- **Check/control digit verification** This helps us verify that the data was keyed correctly (for example, the ninth digit in SSN).

- **Enforcing field format** The entered data should follow certain rules. For example, an e-mail address must include the @ character, an international phone number must include a country prefix, a specific field length is required, and so on.

NOTE
As you'll see later in the book, the APEX IDE includes some prebuilt validations. Some of these are being used by the APEX wizards and are added automatically to the wizard-generated code; others can be implemented or set manually.

Don't Trust Client-Side Validations   One of the major challenges every web application developer faces is implementing an interactive and responsive user interface (UI) that gives the end user immediate feedback on his actions on screen. And, of course, the guiding rule is always "the quicker the better." That usually leads to client-side validations, usually based on JavaScript, which can immediately—without the need to submit the entire web page—alert the user to faulty input actions such as empty required fields, illegal dates, and other field format violations. Using Ajax, client-side validations can also rely on database queries to alert against database-level violations (such as non-unique values, illegal values, and so on).

Client-side actions should be considered easy to hack, however, and as a result, the information sent to the server can be manipulated and changed, so *client-side validations should not be trusted* and should be repeated on the server (database) side.

NOTE
The fact that client-side validations should not be trusted as final data validations doesn't mean we should not use and implement them. These validations can have a major role in increasing the dynamic and responsiveness of our UI, and this is a worthy cause by itself.

Design Points on Validations
The following are a few considerations regarding validations:

- *General types of data validations can be reused between applications,* such as date validation, regular expressions for e-mail/phone format validation, and so on. Other validations are specifically dependent on the business logic of the application and should be formalized for the specific application.

- *APEX supports various page item types that can help the user avoid unintentional input errors.* Item types such as select lists, checkbox/radio groups, date pickers, and others restrict the end user selection to legitimate and well-formatted options. However, even with these items, we are required to use server-side validations on the submitted data.

- *Client-side validations should not be trusted for data validation and business logic verification.* These validations provide an important service to the enduser—quick and immediate feedback—and should

(continued)

be implemented. However, the business logic verifications and data validations should be performed only on the server side, using the data that was submitted to the server (database).

■ *Best practice for validations is not to rely on database constraints.* Those are very important on the database level, and this helps us to maintain data integrity and consistency. However, in the developed application, our validation strategy should include performing all the necessary validations as part of the application, prior to any data save in the database. Performing the validations within the application enables us to alert users about validation problems and give them proper options for fixing them. Capturing database error messages, as a result of database constraint violations, and relaying them to the end user might be much more complicated and much less user friendly.

Quality Assurance Scenarios

Many developers believe (and act accordingly) that QA comes only after the code development process has ended. This might very well be proven as a misguided concept.

We already discussed how the business logic can affect QA, but sometimes the QA scenarios can take us further ahead than the pure business logic can—right into the real world. For example, business logic requires the application to communicate with an external system, but what should happen if this external system is not available for us online at runtime? The answer should be implemented in the application code.

If these real-world scenarios are detected and drafted as part of the application planning stage, the developed code would be able to address them properly, and as such, it would be more robust in its running environment.

Some More Added Values to HLD

For either a single developer or a (much) larger development team, the HLD process can be an efficient tool for estimating the resources it will take to implement the project—the application development. These resources may include IT facilities (servers, workstations, database resources, communication resources, and so on), human resources (developers, system analysts, DBAs, QA experts, and so on), the time frame for the development process (allocating and scheduling the variety of development tasks), and, finally, the budget calculations to complete the project.

If the application is ordered and financed by a client (a commercial project), the HLD process can also serve you in a very important task: it can reconcile the expectations between the wishes of the client side and the deliveries of the development side. Many software projects fail because the client side has very high expectations regarding the features and functionality of the application to be created which the development side cannot always meet, be that for technical or technology reasons or for some other reasons, such as delivery time constraints, budget deficits, and so on. It is vital to the general success of the development project that you, as the developer, fully understand what the other side is expecting to gain from using the application; and, just as important, the client side must be aware of the true capabilities of the application at the end of the development process. The HLD document can be a very good platform to synchronize the two sides and reconcile the client expectations with the development abilities and deliveries.

Best Practice: Document Your Work

We all know that many developers out there cannot stand the verb "document." Documentation is perceived as an extra burden on the developer, a tedious task that we can do without. However, one of the best practice rules that is always proven correct is "document your work."

Documentation is important to you as a single developer, but it's much more important if you are part of a team. In both cases, after a while, nobody can really remember all the intricacies of their work—the reasons for a specific decision they made, specific details about code they developed, (smart) shortcuts they took, and so on—especially if you are working on a large or complex application. Furthermore, if you are part of a team, documentation is the best way to share your work, and the accumulated knowledge that follows it, with other members of the team.

And we haven't mentioned important issues such as maintenance, which is usually the next step in the application life cycle, after the development stage has ended. Fixing bugs, enhancing current features, and other tasks that may be required to maintain the viability of the application might turn out to be real nightmares without proper documentation, especially when there is no guarantee that the original developers are still available to do the job.

TIP
A good "getting ready" move will be to decide that your project will be documented properly, right from the start.

Documenting APEX-Developed Applications

As you'll see throughout this book, the APEX IDE gives us ample options to document our work (including our work as part of a team) and the various APEX elements we are using in the course of our development. **Use them**!

In some cases, where the components of an element are not stored together and not necessarily in direct correlation to the invoking element (usually to allow reuse options), proper documentation may be proven as a must. Notable examples are the application-level on-demand PL/SQL processes, which serve as the server-side actions in Ajax calls; LOV (List of Values) objects that can be shared among the various application pages; and basically all the other APEX Shared Components that we'll discuss in the relevant chapters of the book.

The Book Demo Application: Contacts in the Cloud

To help solidify the concepts and chapters in this book, we need to center it on a project or application as a common thread to tie it all together. The demo application we will gradually build and then use is a contacts, or people information, application. In the following sections, we'll describe this application while using some of the HLD concepts we reviewed so far in this chapter.

Whether you use the contacts application on your phone, your e-mail client, or a physical rolodex, the concept of a contacts manager is a familiar one. Through this simple app, the chapters in this book can present very simple as well as complex concepts of APEX.

But before we get started, let's list out some basic requirements for this application. To make this a complete contacts application, it needs to perform the following tasks:

- Ability to collect people's names, addresses, and contact info

- Ability to store multiple addresses and multiple contact types (phone, e-mail, and so on)

- Ability to store a photo of the contact

- Ability to add notes about that contact

- Ability to search the contact database easily

- Ability to classify the contact

Basic? Yes, but the final result will be a very feature-rich web application. Just thought of an additional requirement? Write it down quickly, and after you have finished this book, use that idea to extend the app in any direction you want.

Application Business Logic and QA Scenarios

The next pieces of our application foundation are the business logic, or rules of the application, and our QA scenarios, or what we want to capture. The business logic will bind the foundation together with how we want the application to function. It will also help to craft in our minds what the application will look like. QA scenarios will be the blocks in our application foundation. These will define data that we want to capture and how we want to capture it. This will further help us craft our application.

Application Business Logic

To better understand our application and the data model, it is always good to discuss how the application will be used, or the business logic. What scenarios will we be performing with our application?

Let's start by discussing how the requirements translate into business logic. We need to store names of contacts, and with a particular name, we need the ability to store multiple addresses and contact methods. Here's the first scenario: A user needs to enter the name of a recent acquaintance. At a minimum, the application should require a contact type and a part of the name. The user should be able to select from a set of contact types such as business, personal, or family. We also need to capture as much of each contact's name as possible. Minimum acceptable combinations can be a formal prefix and last name or a first name and last name. All other combinations would be fine. The application cannot allow the user to add the same contact twice; it needs checks in place to prevent duplicate names. No two contacts can share the same first, middle, and last names.

Next, the user is going to need to add a contact method, an address, or both. As with a person contact type, the user needs to select either a postal address or another contact method. If adding a postal address, the minimum amount of information should be an address type (home, business, or other), one address line, city, and state. If adding a contact method, the type of method (e-mail, business phone, home phone, or mobile phone) and the method value should be required. The application has to store the addresses and contact methods in context of that particular user. The user has to be tied to those pieces of information; otherwise, we would not be able to recall the correct information. As with the duplicate checking with names, we should not allow duplicate address or contact methods for the same user. Different contacts can share addresses or phone numbers, but the same contact cannot have duplicate information.

Once a contact is in, the application needs to allow updates to the person and contact information, but also provide the ability to add a picture and notes about that person. One picture per contact and a limit on the amount of text a contact note can have should be enforced.

These scenarios, or business logic, can now help us define not only how the application will flow, but can aid in the creation of our backend tables and the data integrity we must keep.

QA Scenarios

The business logic of the application enforces several constraints we need to verify. Let's describe some of them and compile some test cases to check on them.

- Every record must include a person type. It means that the PERSON_TYPE field is required and cannot be NULL.

    - QA1 – submit a contact record without a PERSON_TYPE.

- Each contact name must include at least a prefix and last name. Another valid combination is first and last name. It means that the PERSON_LAST_NAME field is required and cannot be NULL.

    - QA2 – submit a contact record without a PERSON_LAST_NAME.

    - QA3 – submit a contact with PERSON_LAST_NAME but without PERSON_FIRST_NAME.

    - QA4 – submit a contact with PERSON_LAST_NAME but without PERSON_PREFIX.

- Duplicate records for the same person are not allowed.

    - QA5 – create a contact for John A. Doe. Submit another contact with the same name.

    - QA6 – create a contact for John B. Doe. This record should be saved (what the QA people call a *happy path*).

There are many more QA scenarios we can compile, just from the business logic, but we are sure you get the point by now, so we'll stop here.

TIP
Every QA scenario with an unhappy path should raise an appropriate error message. The validity of the error message should also be tested.

APEX Code Development

As we mentioned earlier in the chapter, the business logic and QA scenarios have direct influence on the application code we are going to develop. For example, we need to develop the appropriate validations for the NOT NULL fields (or make sure that the appropriate APEX wizard created them for us). The unique combination of several fields should also be developed, and because we don't want to rely on the database constraints to be the first to detect possible violations, we need to develop an error detection mechanism, which will properly alert the end user and enable her to fix the problem.

We mentioned real-world QA scenarios that our application code should address. If we look at the uniqueness constraints, it should be clear to us that this kind of validation involves database query. In our case, the database is in the cloud. This means that there are some availability and response time issues that we'll need to address in our code. As we are dealing with the HLD process now, everything is simple and abstract, but when code development starts, we'll need to be more specific and technical. A good (best practice) move can be to thicken the HLD document into a *detailed design (DD) document*, which includes the technical aspects of our development. In our example, we can say that the uniqueness validation will include an asynchronous Ajax call to the database. Why an asynchronous call? Because in the cloud, the response time can be longer, and we don't want the client browser to freeze for too long. And what does "too long" mean? Well, we are in the design phase, and it is up to you to determine that and act (develop) accordingly.

Designing the Data Structures

We know what the application is going to do, so let's go into how we are going to store all the data we are going to capture. First, we need a table to store the basic contact information such as name, type, and a picture. This table will be called the PERSONS_TABLE (see Table 2-1).

NOTE
We will capture and use three types of data: numbers, text, and dates. In our tables, we will use these terms for the data types, and in the next section, we'll use the corresponding database terms.

Here's how the table can be laid out:

Column Name	Column Data Type	Can Be NULL?	Primary/ Foreign Key	Column Description
Person ID	Number	No	Primary	Acts as the primary identification for the contact in the database (such as SSN or passport ID)
Person Type	Text	No		Type of contact (Business, Personal, Family)
Person Prefix	Text	Yes		Formal prefix (Ms., Mrs., Mr.)
Person First Name	Text	Yes		First name of the person
Person Middle Name	Text	Yes		Middle name of the person
Person Last Name	Text	No		Last name of the person
Person Birthday	Date	Yes		Person's birthday (reminder so you can get them a present)
Person Picture	Image	Yes		Picture of the person
Person Notes	Text	Yes		Notes and reminders for the person

TABLE 2-1. *The PERSONS_TABLE*

Next, we need to define the address table for the contact, called the ADDRESS_TABLE (Table 2-2).

Column Name	Column Data Type	Can Be NULL?	Primary/ Foreign Key	Column Description
Address ID	Number	No	Primary	Acts as the primary identification for the address in the database
Person ID	Number	No	Foreign	Corresponds to the person ID in the PERSONS_TABLE; use this to link the pieces of data together
Address Type	Text	No		What kind of address (Personal, Business, Other)
Address Line 1	Text	No		First line of the address
Address Line 2	Text	Yes		Second line of the address
Address Line 3	Text	Yes		Third line of the address
Address City	Text	No		City
Address State	Text	No		State
Address Postal Code	Text	Yes		Postal code (not a number because some countries use alphanumeric postal codes)
Address Country	Text	Yes		Country in which the address is located

TABLE 2-2. *The ADDRESS_TABLE*

The last table is for other methods of contact such as phone numbers and email addresses, called the CONTACTS_TABLE (Table 2-3).

Column Name	Column Data Type	Can Be NULL?	Primary/ Foreign Key	Column Description
Contact ID	Number	No	Primary	Acts as the primary identification for the contact in the database
Person ID	Number	No	Foreign	Corresponds to the person ID in the PERSONS_TABLE; use this to link the pieces of data together
Contact Type	Text	No		What kind of contact (Phone, Email, Mobile, Other)
Contact Line 1	Text	Yes		First line for storing text contact information
Contact Line 2	Text	Yes		Second line for storing text contact information
Contact Number 1	Text	Yes		First line for storing numeric contact information
Contact Number 2	Text	Yes		Second line for storing numeric contact information

TABLE 2-3. *The CONTACTS_TABLE*

These three simple tables will be the foundation of our application. As you noticed, person ID is in all three of our tables. In our requirements, we needed to store multiple addresses and multiple contact types for a single person. With the person ID being stored in all three tables, we form a relationship in which we can relate this information back to the main person table.

Data Modeling

Now let's put our application concept into action. Before we do this, though, we must move the table structures that we previously defined into the database. We can accomplish this in many ways. One method is to use Oracle's own SQL Developer Data Modeler tool. This free tool can be downloaded from the OTN at oracle.com/technetwork/developer-tools/datamodeler/overview/index.html. With this tool, we can design the database tables, their relationships, and DDL scripts to run in the database to create the tables.

Not comfortable with the SQL Developer Data Modeler? No worries! We will go over creating tables, indexes, and other database objects, with the **SQL Workshop** module of APEX in the next chapter. For now, let's look at what the table design looks like in Data Modeler (Figure 2-1).

A few important elements to the table diagram in Figure 2-1 need to be pointed out. First you will notice a "P" next to the top column in each table. This signifies the primary key (PK) of that table. This number will uniquely identify each person we enter into our contacts application. Next is the "F" on the ADDRESS_TABLE and CONTACTS_TABLE tables. This designates a foreign key (FK) relationship. A foreign key relationship enforces referential integrity between tables, with the table containing the FK being the child table and the referenced table being the parent. This helps with the one-to-many requirement we have for our application.

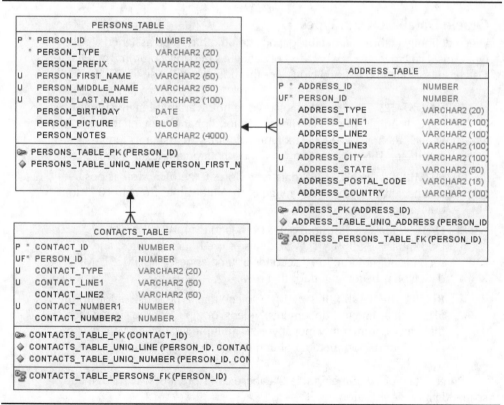

FIGURE 2-1. *The Contacts in the Cloud data model*

Referential Integrity

Referential integrity in a database ensures that relationships between two or more tables remain constant. This is done with foreign keys, setting up a parent–child relationship. The child table cannot contain data that is not in the parent table on the column that is linked with the FK. For example, in our ADDRESS_TABLE table, we cannot have a person ID value that is not in the PERSONS_TABLE table. This relationship also prevents the deletion of the person ID in the PERSONS_TABLE table if there are linked records in the ADDRESS_TABLE table.

The data types have also been replaced with database-level terms. Text fields are now VARCHAR2 types of various lengths. Number types are still NUMBERS types in the database as well as DATE types.

Oracle Database Data Types

When defining a table in a database, each column has to be assigned a data type. This data type tells us what kind of data goes into this column. The Oracle Database has many predefined types. For this book we will use the following:

- **VARCHAR2** This data type is used to hold variable-length strings—or, to put it simply, this data type is used for alphanumeric characters. When creating a VARCHAR2 type column, you assign its length as a parameter. This is for the app columns that contain text.

- **NUMBER** The NUMBER data type stores 0 (zero) as well as positive and negative numbers. The range is absolute values from 1×10^{-130} to but not including 1×10^{126}.

- **DATE** Here we can store dates from January 1, 4712 BC, to December 31, 9999 AD. We can also store hours, minutes, and seconds but not fractional seconds or time zones. The TIMESTAMP data type is better suited for that data.

- **BLOB** The BLOB (Binary Large Object) data type is useful for storing files such as images, documents, videos, or zip files. The size of these files can be from a few megabytes to multiple terabytes. We will use this for our person picture column to store a person's image.

Other data types that the Oracle Database can store are XML, JSON, and spatial data for geolocation.

Lastly, we have constraints on all the tables. A constraint enforces data integrity on the table. We have used a *unique constraint* across the first, middle, and last name columns in the PERSONS_TABLE table. This will ensure that we cannot enter multiple contacts with the exact same first, middle, and last name. We also have a unique constraint on the ADDRESS_TABLE table. We restrict the ability to store the same PERSON_ID, ADDRESS_LINE1, ADDRESS_CITY, and ADDRESS_STATE. This combination of data must be unique. We have a similar constraint on the CONTACTS_TABLE table. The first constraint restricts duplicate data for person_id, contact_type, and contact_line1. A similar constraint is used on PERSON_ID, CONTACT_TYPE, and CONTACT_NUMBER1. This is signified in the data model in Figure 2-1 by the letter "U" in front of the column names.

From now on, in every relevant chapter in which we will learn how to implement and developed APEX elements, we will use the Contacts application to get hands-on practice and experience. By the end of the book, we are going to have a fully working APEX application.

Summary

We started this chapter with the prerequisite knowledge we believe you should possess in order to get the best out of APEX. That includes SQL and PL/SQL, HTML/HTML5, JavaScript, and CSS. If you think that your knowledge needs to be complemented in some areas, we compiled a list of recommended books that can help you with that. Once the knowledge issues are behind you (or at least you are aware of them and know what needs to be done), you are ready to start.

We showed you that a good (best practice) development cycle should start with an appropriate application planning process, which should include various stages of High Level Design (HLD). These stages may include processes and activities to formalize the application business logic, constructing a data model, compiling lists for business logic constraints and data validation, and composing some real-world QA scenarios, on top of all those that emanate from the application business logic and the data it uses.

We emphasized the importance of a full documentation process, starting right from the get-go of the development process. We ended the chapter with a description of the demo application we are going to use and gradually develop throughout the book—Contacts in the Cloud—while applying some of the HLD concepts we reviewed in this chapter.

CHAPTER
3

APEX IDE: Quick Tour and Basic Concepts

APEX is an *integrated development environment* (IDE). That means it includes an assortment of modules that were designed to assist you and facilitate the development cycle. In this chapter, we'll take a quick tour of the major modules of the APEX IDE to help you get familiar with the development environment, to learn how it can help with your development efforts, and to discover where to look for help when you need it.

Working with the APEX IDE

The APEX IDE is a *secured environment*, which means you need to log into it using a username and password. During the APEX installation process, a super user—*instance administrator*—is created; this user can define more APEX users, with three levels of privileges that translate to three levels of development and management functionalities within the IDE.

Figure 3-1 shows the login page of the apex.oracle.com hosting site. The first field you should provide is a Workspace name. We'll discuss APEX Workspaces in the next chapter, but for now, know that a Workspace is the private logical framework that is allocated for you to work in.

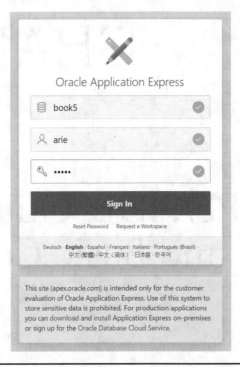

FIGURE 3-1. *The APEX IDE login page*

Requesting an APEX Workspace

If you already have access to your own local APEX instance, you're ready to go. If not, the simplest and quickest way to track the content of this book easily, while gaining valuable hands-on experience, is to request your own Workspace at the apex.oracle.com hosting site. The Workspace is free, and you can ask for it by clicking the Request A Workspace link on the login page. Bear in mind that this link is available according to the APEX instance configurations, so it's not always visible.

Requesting a Workspace is a very good start to our APEX IDE tour. It will redirect you to an APEX implementation of Workspace provisioning, where you can see some APEX features in action, including a wizard for the application end user that includes several tied-up application pages, various page item types, and built-in security measures like a CAPTCHA (Completely Automated Public Turing Test To Tell Computers and Humans Apart) mechanism. As we are dealing with an APEX implementation, every feature that you see during this process can be fully implemented in your own application.

In addition to the other elements, the login page shows a list of the ten languages supported by the APEX IDE. The visibility of this list depends on whether other (than English) languages are installed on the APEX instance. If so, the list will include only the installed language(s).

A successful login leads to the home page, or Workspace home page, of the APEX IDE, as shown in Figure 3-2.

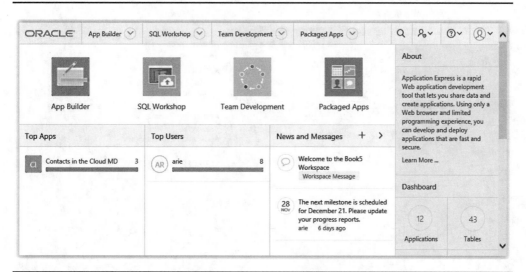

FIGURE 3-2.   *The APEX IDE home page*

This home page includes four large clickable icons that represent and lead to four major modules of the APEX IDE: App Builder, SQL Workshop, Team Development, and Packaged Apps. But before we tour these modules, we'll take a look at several informative and navigational elements on this page that will be present on most pages of the APEX IDE.

Main Menu

The main (responsive) pull-down menu for the APEX IDE is located at the upper-left corner of the page, and it includes five options. Starting on the left side, the first menu option leads to the Workspace home page (its tooltip says Application Express Home). The other four options across the menu correspond with the four large icons on the Workspace home page, and lead to the home page of four major modules of the IDE: App Builder, SQL Workshop, Team Development, and Packaged Apps.

To access the menu options, click the down arrow next to the menu name; each menu includes specific options or tasks available within the module, such as the App Builder menu, shown next, which also includes a submenu of Workspace Utilities options.

NOTE
The APEX IDE uses a responsive theme, which means that the layout grid of the screen is flexible and adaptable, to some extent, and not fixed. It allows the system (both the APEX engine and the client browser) to adapt the layout of the page components automatically to the actual size of the screen you are currently using. This is very useful with mobile devices with much smaller screens, so that the application pages can be displayed accordingly. Depending on the size of the screen and the available screen real estate, the first menu will be labeled either "Oracle" or "ORACLE Application Express," both of which are shown in the preceding images. Figure 3-2, for example, shows the menu selections on a narrower screen, and you can see that the menu label was shrunk to include the ORACLE logo only, and the large graphical icons of the major IDE modules are smaller in size. If the screen is even narrower, the main menu will span two rows, so the first menu, which still includes only the Oracle logo, is positioned on the first row, and the rest of the menus are on the second row. If the second row is not wide enough, an overflow behavior will be applied (so no third row for the main menu).

Developer Navigation Tools

The Developer navigation tools are located in the upper-right corner of the page. A responsive smaller version of the tools menu is shown next, while the full version, which is also context-sensitive, is shown in Figure 3-3. This menu/toolbar offers quick and direct access to various tasks, locations, and resources within the APEX IDE and on the Internet.

Search Tool

From the left, the first tool is a context-sensitive Search mechanism. The context—the location within the APEX IDE—determines the availability of the mechanism (it will not appear in the SQL Workshop and the Packaged Apps modules) and the target and scope of the search.

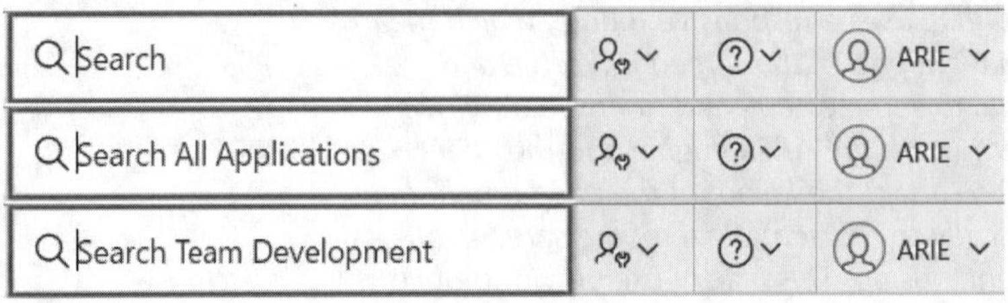

Q Search	♨ ∨	⑦ ∨	⑧ ARIE ∨
Q Search All Applications	♨ ∨	⑦ ∨	⑧ ARIE ∨
Q Search Team Development	♨ ∨	⑦ ∨	⑧ ARIE ∨

FIGURE 3-3. *Various contexts of the Search field*

The expanded search field includes a prompt text (called a *value placeholder* in APEX terminology) that hints about the target and scope of the search, as the three examples from three different contexts show in Figure 3-3.

TIP
If you are working with a narrow screen/window that displays the responsive shrunken version of the toolbar, hovering over the magnifying glass icon will expand it to a search field, with the appropriate context-sensitive hint.

The context of the first example (at the top of Figure 3-3) is the Workspace home page. The prompt text in this case—Search—is very general and doesn't specify the target of the search. This might be a bit baffling, because the target in this case is an Interactive Report (Chapter 6) that doesn't display on this page permanently and is opened only as the search results. This report lists information about all the applications in your Workspace, and it includes searchable columns for the application full name, owner (schema), and last developer who updated the application and when.

TIP
A similar functionality can be achieved on the App Builder home page by filtering the applications list that the Interactive Report displayed on this page.

The context of the second example (in the middle of Figure 3-3) is the App Builder home page. The search target of this context—Search All Applications—is the metadata of all the applications in our Workspace. If, however, the invoking context is within a specific application, the prompt text would say Search Application, and the scope of the search would be limited to the metadata of this particular application.

The context of the bottom-most example in Figure 3-3 is the Team Development module, and the target search in this case is the metadata for the Team Development objects, which we'll review as part of our tour in the module, a little later in this chapter.

TIP
If you have Workspace administrator privilege (discussed in the next chapter), you may encounter another context—Administration. The prompt text in this context is Search Users, and the target is an Interactive Report that lists identified details of all the users defined in the current workspace.

Search Criteria   The Search mechanism is case-insensitive by default and acts as if a wildcard is attached to the search string, both as prefix and suffix. This means that the result set of a search action will include every appearance of the search string in the target search scope, regardless of its location in the searched strings—beginning, middle, or end—as demonstrated in Figure 3-4.

In the context of the search shown in Figure 3-4, the target search is the metadata of the Workspace applications, and it includes various objects that contain the search string (which, on-screen, is highlighted in red). You can see the case-insensitive feature, because the result set includes an appearance of "EMPNO"; and you can also see the wildcard effect, because the result set also includes an appearance of "P26_EMPNO."

Figure 3-4 also includes two options to refine your search. The first option, Case Sensitive, enables you to run a case-sensitive search. The other, Current Page Only, is applicable only if you invoked the search from an application page. In this case, the search scope will be limited to the metadata of this specific page.

Searching the Metadata

The APEX IDE, even in versions prior to APEX 5, includes a (query-builder like) wizard to help you explore the metadata of the developed applications. However, using this declarative wizard limits you to a single APEX view at a time, and its result set is purely informative. By using the Search mechanism of the Developer navigation tools, you can explore the full scope of the application(s) metadata, and more so, the search's result set has a navigational functionality. Clicking the View button of a result record will redirect you to the appropriate location within the App Builder (editor/wizard) so that you can review the object in more detail and edit it, if necessary.

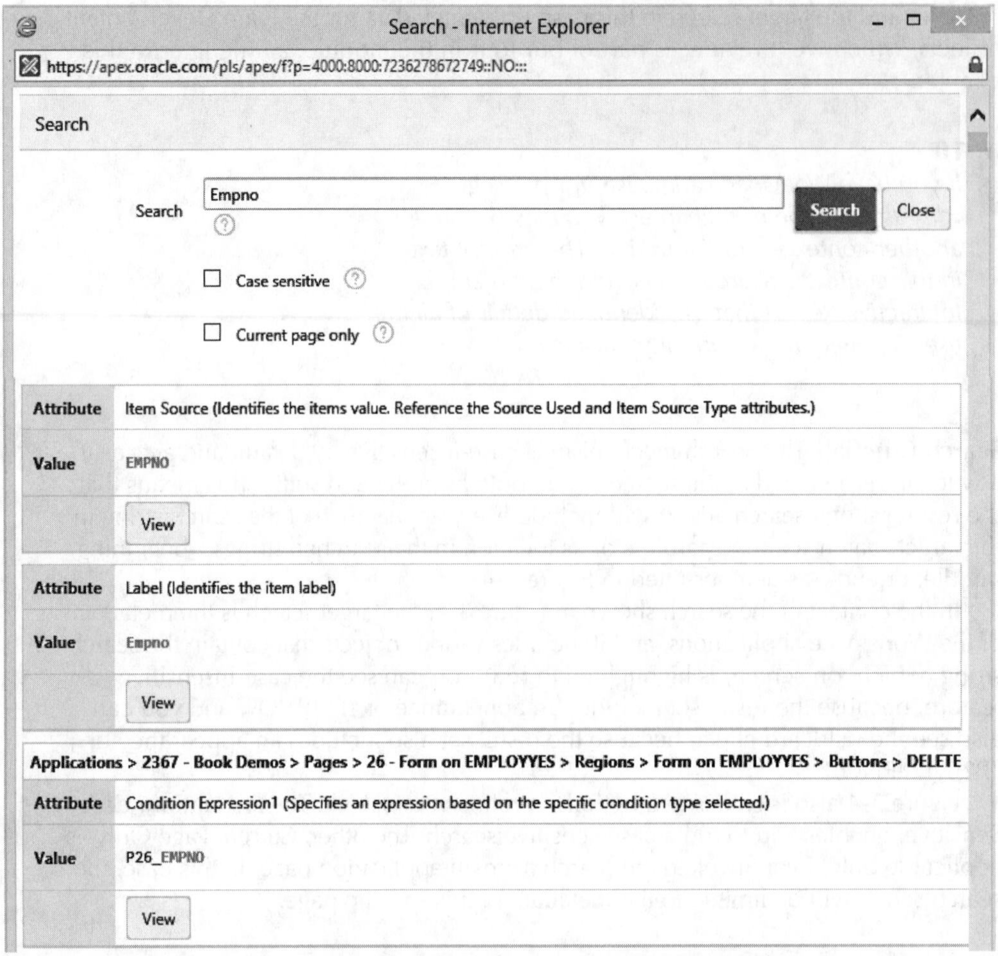

FIGURE 3-4. *A snippet of the result set for a search in the App Builder home page context, using the search string "Empno"*

Using a wildcard base and case-insensitive search might yield a large result set, especially when metadata is involved. In some cases, you'll be interested in a more precise and targeted result set, and regular expressions may come in very handy. You can use them if the context of the search is the App Builder home page or is within a specific application.

To define a search based on regular expression, you use the literal text **regexp:**, followed by a regular expression. Figure 3-5 shows an example that uses a case-sensitive search, based on the regular expression **^EMPNO$**. The result set of this

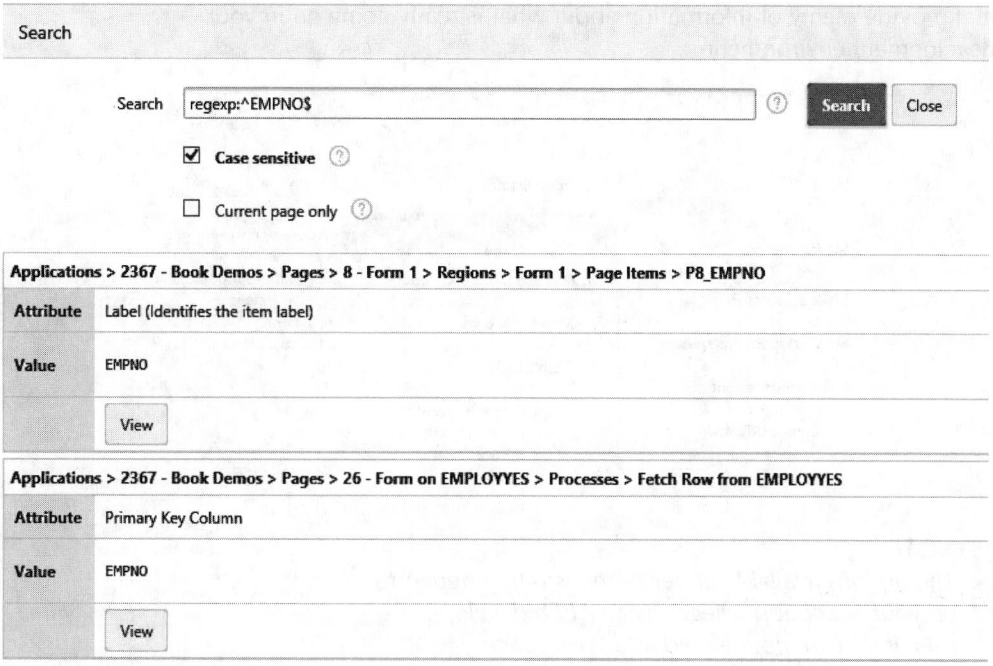

Search			
Search	regexp:^EMPNO$ ⑦	**Search**	Close
	☑ **Case sensitive** ⑦		
	☐ Current page only ⑦		

Applications > 2367 - Book Demos > Pages > 8 - Form 1 > Regions > Form 1 > Page Items > P8_EMPNO	
Attribute	Label (Identifies the item label)
Value	EMPNO
	View

Applications > 2367 - Book Demos > Pages > 26 - Form on EMPLOYYES > Processes > Fetch Row from EMPLOYYES	
Attribute	Primary Key Column
Value	EMPNO
	View

FIGURE 3-5. *A case-sensitive search*

search will include all the metadata appearances of the whole word EMPNO, in all capital letters (for example, all the places in which the column EMPNO is used as a primary key).

TIP
Regular expressions are outside the scope of this book. However, they are very powerful tools, and APEX supports them in several functionalities. You are encouraged to explore and learn about them. It will be worth your while.

Administration Tool

The next (from the left) set of options and tools on the Developer navigation tools menu/toolbar is the Administration tool set, which includes various navigational options to Workspace-related administrative tasks, such as Set Workspace Preferences, Manage Users and Groups, or simply Change My Password. It also enables you to monitor real-time activity and navigate to some Dashboard reports that provide plenty of information about what is really going on in your development environment.

NOTE
The options available under Administration depend on your account privileges as an APEX developer user. If you are not defined as a Workspace administrator, only the Change My Password and the informative options (monitoring and Dashboard reports) will be visible.

Help Tool

The Help tool contains navigational options to some very useful resources on the Internet, including the full APEX Documentation library, the APEX Discussion Forum, and the Oracle Technology Network (OTN). It also includes an About section with useful information about your specific APEX instance and its running environment.

Account Menu

The last section on the Developer navigation tools is the Account menu. Its header includes the developer username (if the screen/window is wide enough; otherwise, the responsive theme will not display it), and its options include general information about the user, with options to Edit Profile, Preferences, and Sign Out of the APEX IDE.

Other Elements on the Workspace Home Page

Looking back at the APEX Workspace home page in Figure 3-2, you can see some elements that are positioned only on this page. The most notable are the four large graphical icons, each of which leads to the home page of one of the major modules of the APEX IDE, which we will explore shortly. Some of the other elements act as real-time informative dashboards, and some of them have navigational options, as shown in Figure 3-6.

Starting on the left is Top Applications, which lists the applications with the most page events in a timeframe that you can set through a link at the bottom-left of the page. Clicking the application name will redirect you to the development home page of the application. Next is Top Users, which lists the users with the most page events in the same timeframe. If you want more information about a specific user,

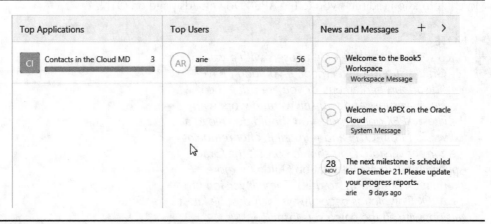

FIGURE 3-6. *Informative elements on the home page*

you can click the username and be redirected to an Interactive Report about Page Views by User.

Next is the News And Messages billboard, which includes a System Message that will be displayed to all the users of the APEX instance. (If the APEX instance includes more than one Workspace, all the users in all the Workspaces will see this message.) Another type of message, a Workspace message, will be displayed to all the users of this Workspace. Lastly, users can share their own news with their colleagues by creating new messages or editing existing ones by clicking the plus or the right-arrow icons.

On the right side of the Workspace home page, you also can see the Dashboard section, shown here. It displays statistics about the number of Applications included in the Workspace, the number of Tables in the schema(s) associated with the Workspace, the number of Features defined in the Team Development module, and the number of Packaged Apps installed.

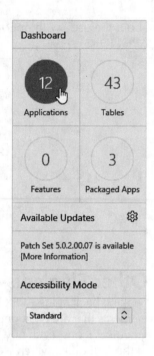

TIP
Each of these stats is related to one of the major APEX IDE modules. Clicking them will redirect you to the home page of the related module, similar to clicking one of the large graphical icons.

Below the Dashboard is the Available Updates section. If you have an Internet connection, this section will display available updates, if any, to your APEX version. If you are using ORDS, available ORDS updates will also be displayed. Clicking More Information redirects you to the APEX Downloads page on OTN.

NOTE
Patch sets are available only to users with a valid My Oracle Support agreement. If you don't have a valid support agreement, or you are using the Oracle XE version, and you still want to work with the latest APEX dot version, you should download a full version from OTN and reinstall it, after removing the current version. (You should consult the Oracle Application Express Installation Guide for more information on how to do that). The full version on the APEX Downloads page always includes the latest version, with all the patch sets installed.

Major Modules of the APEX IDE

The APEX IDE includes five major modules, the first four of which have corresponding graphical icons on the Workspace home page and are intended for the APEX IDE developers. The fifth module, Instance Administration, is intended for the APEX instance administrator only. Let's take a quick tour of these modules.

App Builder Module

The App Builder (prior to APEX 5.1, this was called Application Builder) is the core of the APEX IDE and the module you will use the most as a developer. This module includes all the wizards you need to develop an APEX application (unlike the other modules that mostly help you manage the development cycle, making it easier and efficient, alongside managing the related database resources). As mentioned, most of the App Builder wizards are declarative by nature, but they also include options for manual coding for all the cases and features that can't be set declaratively. In the following chapters, we will review most of the App Builder wizards, and you will learn how best to use them in your development efforts.

The App Builder home page, part of which is shown in Figure 3-7, includes four big graphical icons—similar to the home page's design motif:

- **Create**   Click to launch a wizard that helps you create new APEX Desktop, Mobile, or Websheet applications, or install one of the Packaged Apps included with the APEX IDE.

- **Import**   Click to launch a wizard that enables you to import a full APEX application or some individual major components of an APEX application, such as a single application page or even a specific object on the page.

- **Dashboard**   Click to launch various informative and statistic reports and gauges about the existing applications in the App Builder and their development-related activities and events.

- **Workspace Utilities**   Click to access utilities that help you define, manage, or query App Builder resources such as preferences and default values, themes, or APEX (metadata) views.

Below these icons is an Interactive Report of all the applications in the Workspace to which you are connected. This IR can be viewed in two ways: via the View Icons (shown in Figure 3-7) or the View Report.

View Icons displays a compound icon for each application. The center of the icon includes the application full name and ID number. A colored square with two capital letters, derived from the application name, is located on the left side, and two mini-action icons are on the right side. The upper icon, in the shape of a pencil, leads to the Application home page, and has the same effect as clicking anywhere

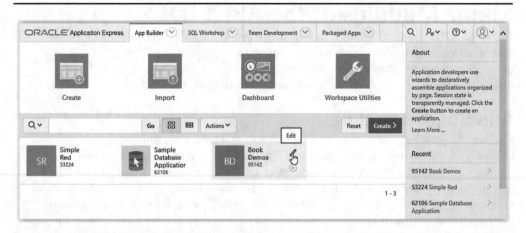

FIGURE 3-7. *Part of the App Builder home page*

else on the compound icon (except clicking the bottom mini-action icon will directly run the application within the App Builder).

View Report is displayed as a conventional row-based report, with a row to every application, which includes columns for the application full name and ID, the application type, the last developer who updated the application and when. It also includes a column with an action icon to run the application directly from the home page.

NOTE
Because we are dealing with an IR, it includes a toolbar that enables you to search it or customize it by choosing the participant columns, or to apply other IR filters. In crowded Workspaces, it can be helpful to be able to locate the application you need quickly. You can also use the Recent list on the right sidebar of the home page, which includes the most recent applications the developer visited.

Application Home Page
From the App Builder home page, you can choose the application you want to work with, and your choice will lead to the Application home page. Shown in Figure 3-8, the Application home page includes various tools and navigational aids to facilitate the application development process.

Globalization, Localization, and Translated Applications

As shown in the APEX IDE login page in Figure 3-1, the APEX IDE natively supports nine languages in addition to English. This means that you can run and use the App Builder in any of these languages. Moreover, with the App Builder, you can develop applications in any language supported by the Oracle Database, and you can set localization preferences for these applications, including date format, currency, decimal character, and more. The App Builder includes a translation mechanism that enables you to translate the UI strings to any language you need, while maintaining a single business logic code. You can read more about it in Chapter 20, "Managing Application Globalization," in the *App Builder User's Guide*.

In our context, it's important that you remember that the IR on the App Builder home page lists only the primary language applications. The translated version(s) of the applications are managed and edited through the APEX translation mechanism.

As you have seen in previous APEX home pages, the Application home page also includes five large icons, which represent important repetitive (on the application level) tasks or lead to submodules that help you handle various stages of the development cycle. We'll review them from left to right.

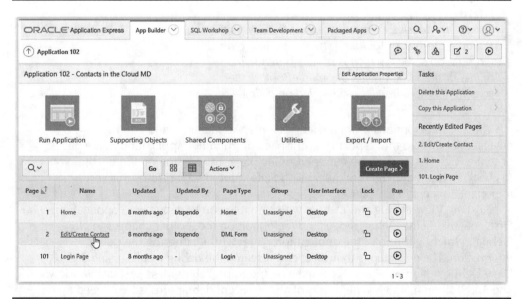

FIGURE 3-8. *The Application home page*

Run Application Because you are working with an IDE, you don't have to leave the development environment to run and test your application. Clicking this icon will run the application (the default preference is to run it on a new browser tab) in the same way that an end user would do it. This means that if you are developing a secured application, you'll need to perform a successful login to the application, even though you already authenticated in the APEX IDE.

TIP
You can authenticate to (log into) the running application using a different user than the developer user you used to log into the APEX IDE. This makes sense when you want to test different users with different levels of security to make sure the application is performing correctly.

The App Builder embeds the Runtime Developer toolbar, shown next, on every application page that was invoked from the APEX IDE, which is displayed on the page at a location of your choice (top, left, bottom, or right side of the application page).

NOTE
Using a responsive theme, our example displays the Runtime Developer toolbar in two rows. In a typical workstation screen, which is usually much wider than a printed book page, or on an eBook reader screen, the toolbar will be displayed on a single row.

The first three options (from the left)—Home, Application, and Edit Page—are navigational links to the respective Workspace or (running) Application home pages, or to the Page Designer of the current running page. The Session option enables you to check, in real-time, the runtime Session State values (we'll discuss this very important concept in Chapter 4).

Next are View Debug and Debug, which enable you to debug your application. First, you enable the Debug mode (and the option on the toolbar changes to No Debug), which will reload the application page, while gathering the debug information. The next step is to inspect and research the debug results, using the View Debug option, which will open a new (pop-up) Debug Message Data window. The App Builder maintains the results of all the recent debug runs, so you need to select the relevant one.

While running in a debug mode, each program statement or activity (that is, page request) is timed by two factors: the elapsed time from the beginning of the page run, and its execution time. The gathered data is presented in two ways. The first is a bar chart based on the execution times, with one bar per statement. Hovering over a bar will display a tooltip with debug details pertaining to the bar, which helps you identify and locate it in the IR that follows.

TIP
The bar chart can help you understand how the running resources are distributed across the page rendering, what actions take the most time, and where potential bottlenecks are located. The fact that you have a history of debug runs enables you to compare different runs and see if the changes you made (such as code optimization) were effective.

Just below the chart is an IR. In addition to the Elapsed and Execution columns, it includes a Message column that holds the detailed debug messages, which help you identify the related activity. Because this is an IR, you can search and filter it to target the activities you want to debug.

If your application page raises a runtime error, the IR will include detailed debug messages up to the point the error occurred. This helps you pinpoint the exact activity that raised the error, and if it's database related, you'll see the original ORA error message. It makes fixing the bug much easier.

Figure 3-9 shows a customized version of the IR rather than the default, with an added first column for the row number (which you'll learn how to do in Chapter 6). The Row column makes it much easier to match bars from the chart with rows on the report; the row number matches the group number in the tooltip of the bar. Clicking the bar will scroll the IR toward the matching record.

As the upper row of tabs in Figure 3-9 may hint, the View Debug is part of a wider tool: Find. The Debug mechanism is accessible not only from a running application, but also from the App Builder itself. You can access and research previous debug runs, regardless of the running application in the background.

NOTE
The View Debug is a declarative tool that is quite easy to use. The APEX API includes the APEX_ DEBUG package that lets you manually control the level of details the debug run collects and embed your own debug messages in your manually coded PL/SQL. For more details, see the APEX API Reference.

FIGURE 3-9. *A customized version of the IR for debug activity*

The Application Tool Icons

At the upper-right corner of the Application home page shown in Figure 3-8, just below the Developer navigation tools, is a set of icons that represents various actions and tools related to the application development process. This set of icons, shown in the following illustration, extends or shrinks according to its display context (such as the Application home page, the Page Designer, or the Component View). It gives you quick and direct access to common tasks, from various locations under the Application home page, without the need to pass through the home page itself. We'll review these icons throughout the book, according to context and relevance.

The Show Layout Columns option (in APEX 5.0 it was called Show Grid) is next on the Runtime Developer toolbar. It highlights the layout grid on the application page. Earlier (non-responsive) APEX Themes place elements on the page according to table-based grids. This option highlights all the table cells' borders and makes it easier for the developer to understand the layout context of each element on page. The modern (responsive) themes, mainly the Universal Theme, are based on the Bootstrap framework. For these, the basic (12-column) Bootstrap layout grid is also highlighted.

NOTE
*Not all the legacy themes support the Show Layout
Columns functionality.*

Next is the Quick Edit option, which enables you to point at an object, or APEX component, on the page. Clicking it will populate the matching Property Editor attributes into the Page Designer. This is a quick-and-easy way to pinpoint the exact component on a page that you want to change or edit, providing immediate and direct access to it in the Page Designer.

APEX 5.1 debuted a productivity enhancer feature for those using the Universal Theme, called Live Template Options. When pointing to the APEX component you want to edit, a small wrench icon appears at the upper-right corner of the component borders, as shown in the next illustration. Clicking it opens the Live Template Options pop-up dialog, where you can change, in real time, some common display-related properties of the component and save them directly, without passing through the Property Editor (more details in Chapter 8, which is dedicated to the Universal Theme).

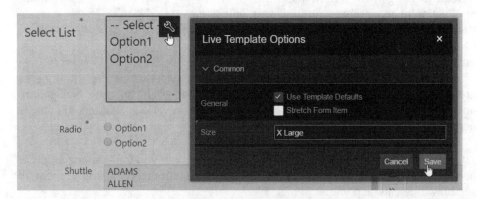

The Theme Roller option is a conditioned option that is visible only if the running application implements the Universal Theme. If it is visible, this option enables you to change or tweak the color palette associated with the application theme. (More on that in Chapter 8.)

The last option on the Runtime Developer toolbar is its setting menu, where you can customize the appearance of the toolbar and its location on page.

Now that you know how to handle running applications within the App Builder, let's continue reviewing the other modules behind the icons on the Application home page.

Supporting Objects   You already know that APEX applications are database-centric, which means they are relying on database objects (database tables, views, indexes, packages, and more) that need to be distributed with the APEX application itself. The Supporting Objects module lets you easily identify the relevant database objects that support the application and packages them in a script that is included in an APEX application Export script (discussed later in the chapter). This enables you to distribute the application with all the database objects the application needs to perform correctly. It makes the application installation much simpler and error-free.

Shared Components   Shared Components are APEX elements that you define once, on the application level, and then reuse on multiple application pages. Look at the APEX main menu or the Developer navigation tools, which are repetitive elements on all the pages of the App Builder—which, by the way, is itself an APEX application. There is no logic in redefining these elements over and over again on each page. Using Shared Components, you can define them only once and reuse them wherever you need, saving you time and effort and ensuring consistency among identical elements used throughout the application.

Shared Components are also available from the Application tool icon set, shown here, making this option available for use in a variety of cases. It's very useful to have direct access to this module without needing to go through the home page.

Moreover, when the Shared Components module is being invoked from a specific application page, another icon in the set, Edit Page, enables you to be redirected back to the calling page. This is a useful productivity-enhancement feature.

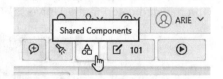

Figure 3-10 shows the Shared Components home page, where the components are categorized according to functionality: Application Logic, Security, Navigation, and more. We'll discuss specific shared components in various chapters to come, according to their specific role.

Utilities   The Utilities module includes utilities that help you track, manage, debug, and optimize your developed applications. You are encouraged to explore them and see how they can help you.

Export / Import   This module includes some wizards that help you generate various APEX export scripts, and some that help you use these scripts for import actions.

Using the main Export wizard, you can export a full APEX application, including determining which special features should be included in the export script (Export Preferences). Using other wizards, you can export a single page or individual APEX components.

Using the Import wizard, you can import an entire APEX application, a single application page, or individual APEX components, using export scripts that were generated by the Export wizards.

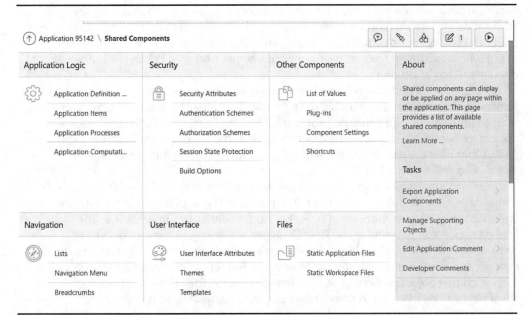

FIGURE 3-10. *Shared Components home page*

NOTE
A full APEX application can be imported to any APEX Workspace. Single pages and individual components can be imported only to an identical Workspace. That may be the same Workspace from which you exported the page or components or a Workspace on a different APEX instance with the same Workspace ID. We'll elaborate more on this when we discuss Workspaces in the next chapter.

Edit Application and the Page Designer

Looking back at the Application home page (Figure 3-8), just under the graphical icons, an IR is displayed, listing all the application pages. You can use the IR to search, sort, or filter information according to your needs and to quickly find the application page you want to work on. Another quick loading option is Recently Edited Pages, on the right sidebar of the home page, which is similar to sorting the IR by the Updated column (descending order).

The IR includes two action icon columns. By clicking the Lock icon, you can lock the page you want to work on to prevent others from changing it while you are working on it. If you are part of a development team, for example, the locked page will be available to all the other developers in read-only mode. Using the corresponding wizard, you can enter informative comments that are displayed on the Lock History report, which is viewable by other developers, who are also able to see who holds the page and his or her comments. Adding a comment is a documentation good practice.

Clicking the second action icon, Run, enables you to run a specific page. The App Builder doesn't support uncontrolled deep linking. That means if you are working on a secured application, and you didn't authenticate to the developed application itself—not just to the APEX IDE—you'll be redirected first to the developed application login page. Only after a successful login will you be allowed to run individual pages—exactly like in the real world.

The most important column in the IR is the Name column. Clicking the page name loads it (by default) into the Page Designer. This is one of the more notable and important new features introduced by APEX 5.0 and enhanced in APEX 5.1. The leading concept in developing the Page Designer is to increase the productivity of APEX developers by making things simpler, clearer, and more quickly accessible. The enhanced version implements the most common and repetitive development actions, such as editing object properties, in addition to requiring fewer mouse clicks and fewer pages to be loaded and saved; more use of the drag-and-drop technique; real-time interactive alerts on the client-side, which immediately enable errors to be fixed; important declarative tasks, such as Dynamic Actions, concentrated under a single tab; and much more. Chapter 5 is dedicated entirely to the new Page Designer.

NOTE
By default, the Page Designer displays the APEX components (which we'll discuss in the next chapter) by the page Layout. However, the Page Designer still supports the page component view concept, which should be familiar to veteran developers. Ergo, it includes a Component View tab, where you can access the page components, based on page life-cycle grouping (Page Rendering, Page Processing, and Shared Components), and not by the page layout. While using the Component View tab, you can still enjoy the new Property Editor, so you can work with the page view that is most comfortable to you. Moreover, if you are a veteran developer who still struggles with the new Page Designer, you can set your preferences to use the Legacy Component View (pre-5 versions), while learning and assessing the merits of the new Page Designer—but bear in mind that as of APEX 5.1, this is a deprecated feature, so you are better off learning to use the new Page Designer.

SQL Workshop Module

The SQL Workshop module is an excellent manifestation of the declarative nature of the APEX IDE and its productivity enhancement features. Here you can deal with the database-related aspects of the developed APEX applications, while mostly using declarative wizards that free you from the need to remember the syntax of DDL statements or to compose SQL queries to browse and inspect various database objects (such as tables, indexes, triggers, sequences, and so on). Whenever the declarative resources are not enough to get you what you want, you can use manually composed SQL and PL/SQL code/scripts to achieve exactly what you need.

NOTE
The SQL Workshop is subject to the security privileges of the active schema and will not allow you to operate beyond the scope of these privileges. However, as it allows a direct interaction with the database, and this might not always be welcome (for novice and inexperience developers, for example), a Workspace administrator can restrict the access to this module through the developer Account Privileges. If the developer is not allowed access, the SQL Workshop will not be visible on the Workspace home page.

The home page for the SQL Workshop, shown in Figure 3-11, includes five large graphical icons that lead you to the various wizards, tools, and utilities of this module, which we'll briefly cover next. As you are dealing with database-related objects and actions, you can choose the active schema you want to work on (from those associated with the Workspace), and the home page will display a list of the Recently Created Tables and another list of Recent SQL Commands that you ran under this schema.

TIP
The sidebar at the lower-right of the home page shows the (productivity enhancer) Create Object tasks list. Use this to select the new database object you want to create and, with a single mouse click, go directly to the appropriate create wizard without needing to go through the Object Browser wizard first.

Let's review the other functionalities offered by the SQL Workshop module.

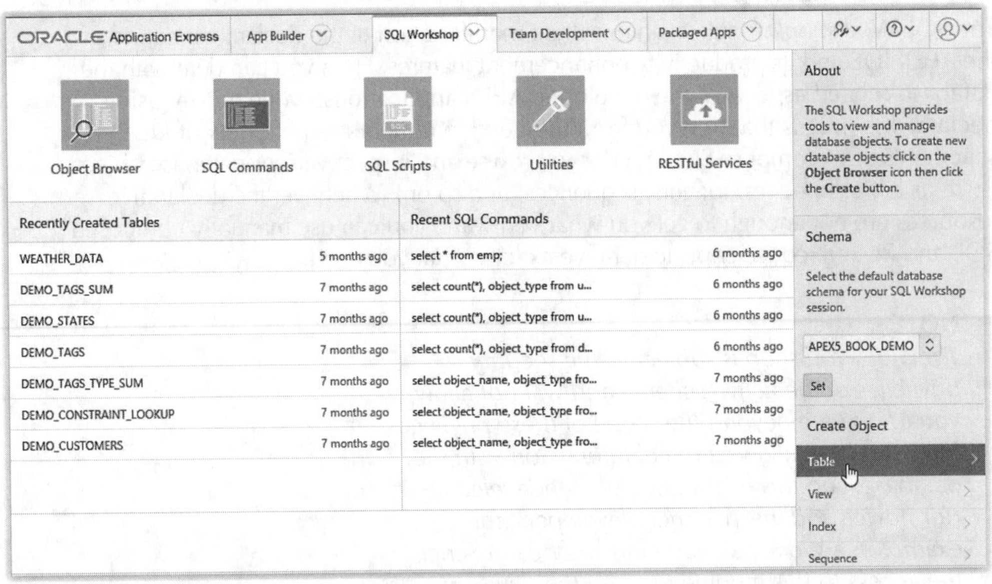

FIGURE 3-11. *The SQL Workshop home page*

Object Browser Wizard

Using this wizard, you can browse and inspect various database objects, their structures (including the SQL code), content (if relevant, such as for tables), and other features. You can use it to edit both the structure (such as add/modify/drop a column) and the data itself. (This is subject to the database rules. It will not allow you, for example, to lower a sequence value.) Figure 3-12 shows a typical display for a database table.

The Object Browser also includes a set of wizards that enable you to create new database objects; these are available by clicking on the Plus sign (Create) menu, just under the active schema name.

The Create Package wizard includes a useful productivity enhancer option for generating a package with DML methods on chosen table(s). It can save you a lot of tiresome manual SQL coding, but more importantly, its Update method includes an implementation of the optimistic locking algorithm, which the APEX engine also uses, to prevent lost updates in a multi-user environment. It's a simple solution to a complex issue (that is not mastered by many developers). Figure 3-13 shows the initial page of this wizard.

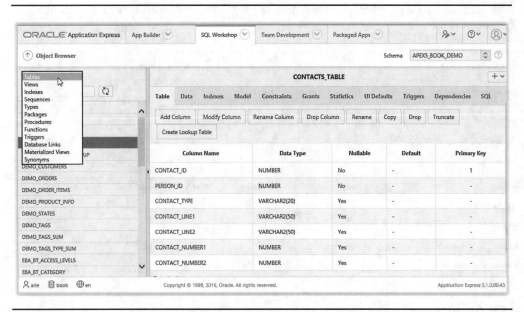

FIGURE 3-12. *A typical Object Browser display for a database table*

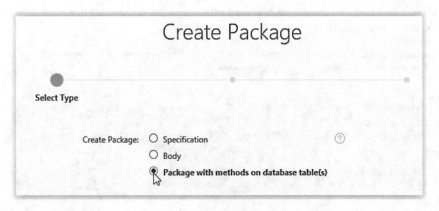

FIGURE 3-13. *The initial page for the Create Package wizard*

SQL Commands Wizard

Using this wizard, you can run SQL and PL/SQL snippets of code in a controlled environment. You can also check the Results of the running code, to examine its Explain scheme (a must for code optimization), as shown in the next illustration, and save code for future reruns, while maintaining a History repository of all recent code you ran.

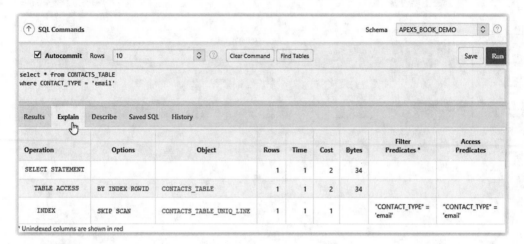

SQL Scripts

Use this tool to manage and track SQL scripts that were generated by other APEX wizards (such as deployment-related scripts from the Supporting Objects module, or DDL scripts such as the one in the example shown next). It provides a simple script editor that you can use to review and edit the wizard-generated scripts and to generate your own scripts manually.

Utilities

You can use an assortment of database-related utilities, shown in Figure 3-14, to help you load data into database tables using various resources, generate DDL scripts for database objects using reverse-engineering, work with multiple tables using a declarative Query Builder, and more.

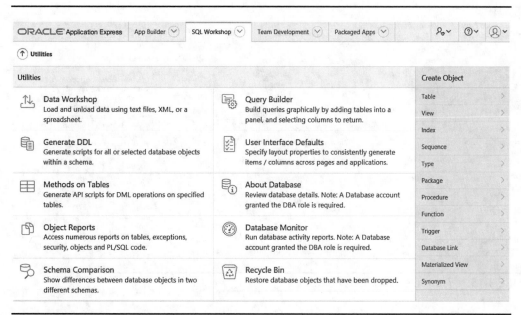

FIGURE 3-14. *The Utilities home page*

RESTful Services Wizard

Using this wizard, you can declaratively generate specifications of RESTful services that can be mapped to SQL and PL/SQL code. If you are going to use RESTful in your APEX application, this wizard can be of great help.

Team Development Module

One of the major drawbacks of the APEX IDE prior to APEX 4 was the lack of good and easy-to-use tools to manage and track the development process and its life cycle, especially when developing in a team is concerned. The APEX development team recognized this and devised a good and productive enhancer solution, the Team Development module.

The Team Development home page, shown in Figure 3-15, includes five large graphical icons that represent major elements and activities that are crucial to easy and accurate development cycle management.

Defining the various elements according to the screen display, from left to right, is the best practice to follow, because there are some hierarchical relationships between the elements. Begin with the leftmost, higher level perspective of the project Milestones, and continue toward the more itemized elements to the right. In some cases, the more detailed elements to the right have dependencies on higher level elements. For example, a Features definition includes association with a Milestone,

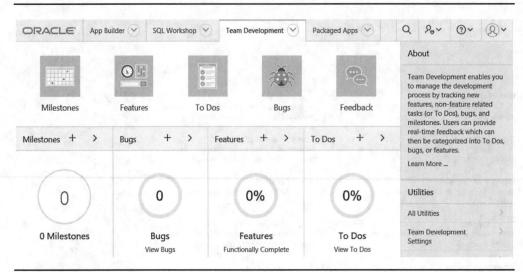

FIGURE 3-15.   *Team Development home page*

and a To Dos definition includes both a Features association and a Milestone that delimits its implementation time. If you are going to follow our application design recommendations in Chapter 2, you'll find that the Team Development tools help you to break down the High Level Design and the Detailed Design into action blocks that are easier to be assigned, implement, and track.

Every development project has its bugs during the development cycle. The Bugs tools help you document bugs, assign them to be fixed, and track the fixing process. The last tool, Feedback, helps you collect feedback from end users. The application users can be a valuable resource of comments, bugs, enhancement requests, and more. Using this tool, it's easy to track and document feedback and make the most of it.

TIP
A more detailed discussion of the Team Development capabilities is outside the scope of this book, but you are encouraged to explore it further and learn how it can help you with your development efforts. Moreover, don't be misled by its name. Although this module will be most effective for a team, it can also make your life as a single developer much easier and increase the quality level of your developed process and its final outcome.

Packaged Apps Module

In the Packaged Apps module, you can install, monitor, and administer packaged applications, such as those shown in Figure 3-16. These fully functional APEX applications were developed by the APEX development team and are included in the APEX distribution files.

In addition to using them as regular APEX applications according to their functionality (such as Survey Builder, Opportunity Tracker, Meeting Minutes, and others), these applications can serve as a high-level training resource for APEX development techniques. These applications reflect the accumulated experience and best practices of the APEX development team for new or more complex development issues such as the Universal Theme, data loading, the new Calendar, and much more.

Instance Administration Module

During the APEX installation process, an instance administrator is created, and this module is dedicated to its tasks. It has its own login URL (ending with …/apex_admin), but you can gain access to it by logging into the INTERNAL Workspace, which is also created during the APEX installation, using the credentials of the instance administrator.

As you can see in Figure 3-17, from the Instance Administration home page, this module enables the Instance administrator to create, provision, manage, and monitor various APEX resources on both the Instance and Workspace levels.

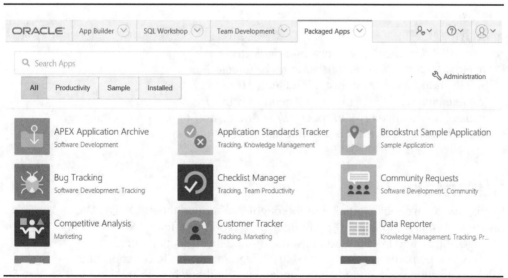

FIGURE 3-16. *Packaged Apps module*

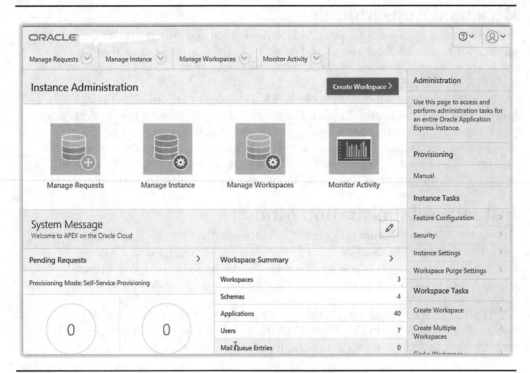

FIGURE 3-17. *Instance Administration home page*

NOTE
The APEX documentation includes a dedicated manual for the APEX administration tasks, Oracle Application Express Administration Guide. *This guide includes all the details you'll need to know if you are an Instance or Workspace administrator, and you are welcome to explore it, if relevant to your job.*

Summary

In this chapter, we took a quick (but thorough) tour around the APEX IDE. We reviewed its major modules—App Builder, SQL Workshop, Team Development, Packaged Apps, and Instance Administration—and their functionalities.

This tour prepared you for the next level: learning the basic concepts of the APEX application itself, including its fundamental building blocks and how to develop using them.

CHAPTER
4

APEX Applications:
Concepts and
Building Blocks

The Oracle Application Express environment—both the APEX IDE and the APEX applications themselves—have hierarchical characteristics. These are manifested in a series of logical containers, with hints to the real world, that contain and depend on each other in a hierarchical manner. In this chapter, we'll start at the top and review these containers, the concepts behind them, their role in the big picture of developing an APEX application, and how you create them. Then you'll see how to fill them according to your needs with the various prebuilt APEX building blocks.

The APEX Instance

The APEX Instance is the root container of the APEX hierarchical structure, and it is the logical result of the APEX installation process in the Oracle database. As mentioned in Chapter 1, each Oracle database or pluggable database (PDB) can hold only a single APEX Instance.

As part of the installation process, you create the Instance Administrator (by running the apxchpwd.sql script) and set the password. The Instance Administrator, usually called ADMIN, has its own APEX IDE module, Instance Administration, that enables it to perform its duties (discussed in Chapter 3).

The Instance Administrator creates the container on the next level of the APEX hierarchical structure, the Workspace. Each APEX instance can hold numerous Workspaces; a good example is the hosting APEX instance on apex.oracle.com, which holds tens of thousands of Workspaces, providing a great sandbox for anyone who wants to experience APEX, free of charge.

The APEX Workspace

The APEX Workspace is a logical container that holds all the APEX resources you will need during a development cycle, and it shares them with its users. An APEX Instance may include many Workspaces, but resource- and security-wise, they are separated from each other. We just mentioned the hosting site on apex.oracle.com; it includes many thousands of active Workspaces, whose owners can experience APEX development without interfering with others and without disclosing their secrets (applications and data).

Each Workspace has its own associated resources—available APEX IDE modules and preferences, database schema(s), APEX users, graphical themes, and more. When the Instance Administrator creates the Workspace using the Create Workspace task under the Instance Administration module (Figure 4-1), the admin is required to supply the Workspace name and optionally a Workspace ID. If a Workspace ID is not supplied, one will be automatically assigned by the APEX engine.

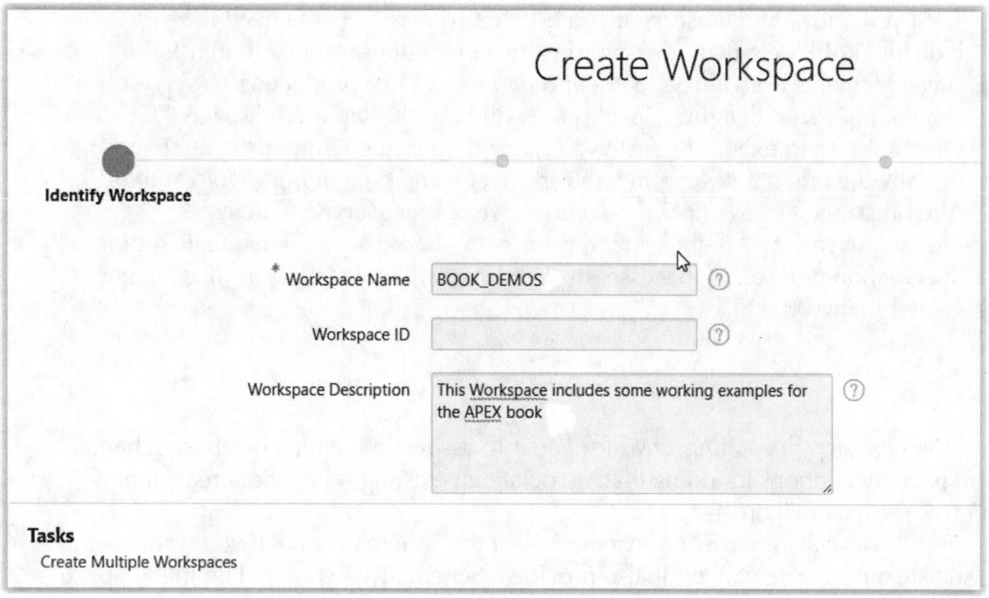

Create Workspace

Identify Workspace

* Workspace Name   BOOK_DEMOS ⑦

Workspace ID ⑦

Workspace Description   This Workspace includes some working examples for the APEX book ⑦

Tasks
Create Multiple Workspaces

FIGURE 4-1. *Entering a Workspace Name and ID in the Create Workspace task*

Workspace ID
The Workspace ID is an important behind-the-scenes factor if you want to share APEX elements among Workspaces on different APEX instances. Both the source and destination Workspaces must have identical Workspace IDs; otherwise, you'll get an error message similar to the following (in this case, an export of a single application page):

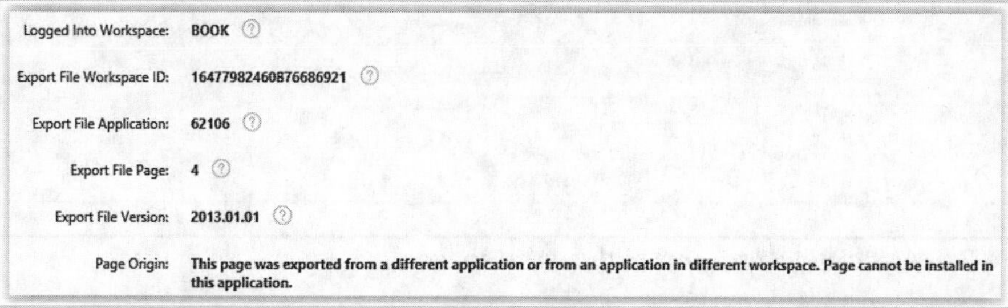

Logged Into Workspace:	**BOOK** ⑦
Export File Workspace ID:	**16477982460876686921** ⑦
Export File Application:	**62106** ⑦
Export File Page:	**4** ⑦
Export File Version:	**2013.01.01** ⑦
Page Origin:	**This page was exported from a different application or from an application in different workspace. Page cannot be installed in this application.**

(continued)

If you know, and most often you do, that you are going to need to share individual APEX elements among APEX instances (for example, to transfer single elements from a development server to a QA or production server), you should make sure that these Workspaces all have the same Workspace ID. One option is to export the first Workspace the Instance Administrator created (usually the original development Workspace), and then import it into another APEX instance (for example, from your development server to a client's production server). Another option is to set the Workspace ID manually during the creation process. In this case, the Workspace ID must be a positive integer greater than 100,000.

The next step in creating a Workspace is to associate it with a database schema. You have two options for doing that: associate an existing schema or create a new one, as shown in Figure 4-2.

If you associate an existing schema, select the Schema Name. If you want to associate a new schema, you'll also provide a Schema Password and an initial Space Quota of between 2 and 500 MB (which can be increased later).

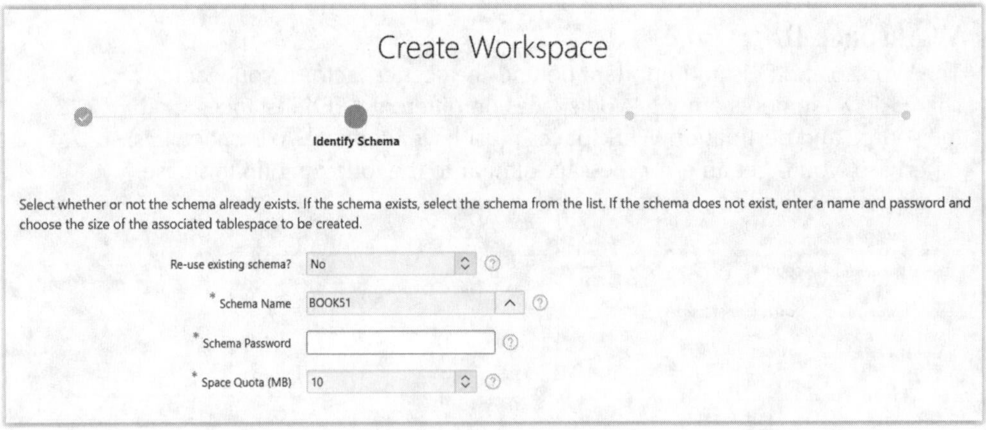

FIGURE 4-2. *Associating a schema with a Workspace*

NOTE
A Workspace can be associated with more than one schema. After the Workspace is created, the Instance Administrator can select the option Manage Workspace To Schema Assignments in the Manage Workspaces submodule of the Instance Administration module to associate any other existing schemas in the database to this Workspace.

As you are dealing with a new Workspace, you need to define its first user, which will be designated as the Workspace administrator. You can do it in the next screen, shown in Figure 4-3.

The last screen in the Create Workspace wizard is a summary display of what you've defined so far. If everything matches your intentions, click the Create Workspace button.

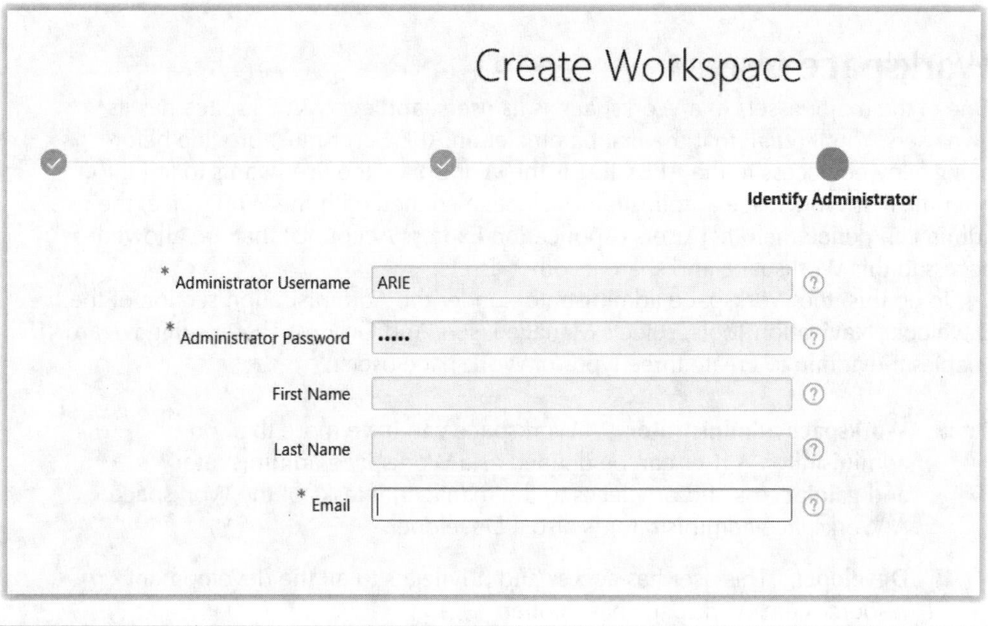

Create Workspace

Identify Administrator

* Administrator Username	ARIE
* Administrator Password	•••••
First Name	
Last Name	
* Email	

FIGURE 4-3.   *Designating the administrator*

TIP
APEX includes a Workspace provisioning mechanism that lets you automate parts of the process of creating a new Workspace by allowing you to submit a request for one. This mechanism should be enabled by the Instance Administrator and can be set to three levels of developer involvement: no involvement at all (the Instance Administrator manually creates the Workspace), developer request (by using a request link on the login page), and developer request with email verification (in which the developer needs to verify the Workspace request using a verification link received by email). A good example of this mechanism is the process of getting your own Workspace on apex.oracle. com, which was discussed on Chapter 3. You can read more about it in the Oracle Application Express Administration Guide.

Workspace Users

One of the major assets of a Workspace is its users, and every Workspace has its own users. You'll recall that the first parameter an APEX user must provide before being allowed access to the APEX IDE is the Workspace the user wants to log into. After the first Workspace administrator has been created with the Workspace, the admin can define the other users (Application Express Accounts) that are allowed access to this Workspace and share its other assets.

To do this, the Workspace administrator, under the Administration section of the Developer Navigation Tools, selects Manage Users And Groups. The ensuing wizard enables the admin to create three types of Workspace users:

- **Workspace administrator** A Workspace can have more than one administrator. A user can be defined as a Workspace administrator and gain access and privileges to the managerial tasks of the Workspace. A Workspace administrator is also a Developer.

- **Developer** This user has access and privileges to all the development resources the Workspace has to offer.

- **End user** This user doesn't have any development privileges, but can log into a developed APEX application that uses the Application Express Accounts scheme for authentication. End users can also run Websheets (which we'll discuss in the section "Websheet Application" later in the chapter) but cannot create them from scratch. End users are defined indirectly if the user is not defined as a Workspace administrator or a Developer.

APEX Applications

APEX Applications are the third level in the APEX environment hierarchy and the reason we are all here. APEX applications are assets of the Workspace. As such, identical applications (but with different IDs) can reside in different Workspaces on a single APEX Instance, without interfering with each other (unless the same database schema is associated with them, in which case, the applications share the same data).

To start creating an application, on the App Builder home page, click the Create icon to open the Create an Application wizard. As Figure 4-4 shows, you can create three types of your own developed applications and also be redirected to the Packaged Apps module, which was covered in Chapter 3.

Desktop Applications

APEX Desktop applications are the most feature-rich applications you can develop, and probably the most common types. The name might be a bit misleading, as you are not limited to creating applications for (classic) desktop machines only. These applications, especially when developed using responsive themes that are included in the APEX IDE, can easily run on a wide range of equipment, such as mobile computers, tablets, and even smartphones—although for smartphones, you can use a dedicated type.

After choosing the application type by clicking its icon, you provide the essential information for identifying the application and the APEX and database resources that will be available to it, as shown in Figure 4-5.

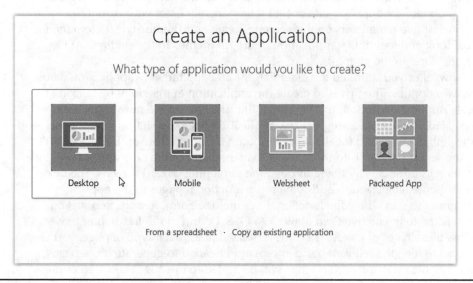

FIGURE 4-4. *Choose the type of application you want to create.*

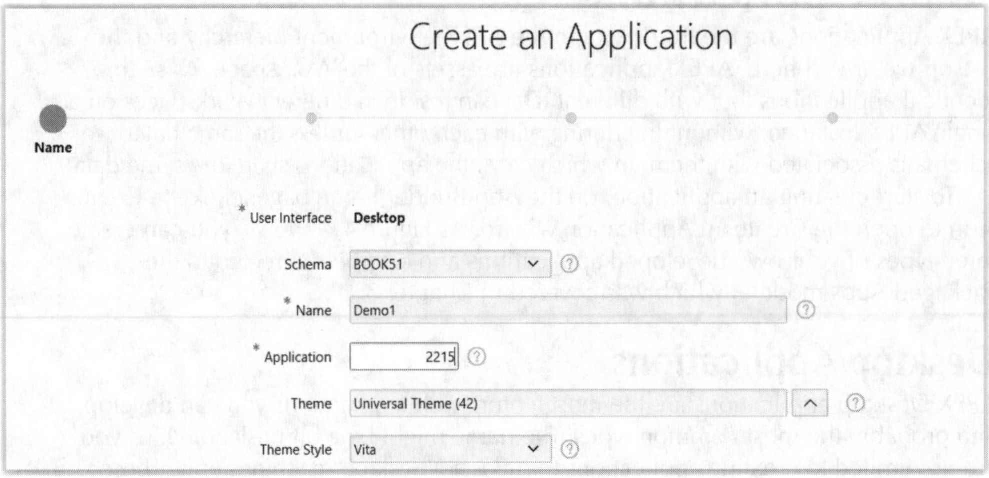

FIGURE 4-5. *Providing essential information for the application*

First, you assign a database schema to the application by selecting it from the list of schema(s) associated with the Workspace. Next, you enter the application Name, which contributes two letters to the compound (graphical) icon that identifies the application on the App Builder home page. The application ID (in the Application field) is a positive integer that uniquely identifies the application across the APEX Instance. To help avoid a collision with already existing IDs, the wizard suggests an appropriate valid ID. You can accept it or manually enter your own ID.

The last two parameters on this screen, Theme and Theme Style, determine the visual look and feel of the application (more on themes in the section "APEX Themes" later in the chapter).

Now, after you supplied the essentials for creating the new application, you have two options. The first is to create the application at this point by clicking the Create Application button. In this case, a thin skeleton of the new application will be created. It will hold a single blank application page, no shared components, and some globalization and localization attributes, based on the App Builder defaults.

The second option is to thicken the basic skeleton of the new application and fine-tune its attributes by going through the remaining wizard screens. The next screen then enables you to add some more functional pages to the application, right from the start. The page functionalities include Form, Report, Report And Form, Editable Interactive Grid (new to APEX 5.1), and more. In Chapter 6, we will discuss these types of pages. For now, let's say that for each type of page, you are required to feed the relevant basic information needed to generate these pages (such as table, SQL query), and they will be added to the application. Later on, you'll be able to edit these pages and fine-tune them to meet your needs.

Application ID

The application ID is a positive integer. The range 3000–9000 is excluded and reserved for internal use of the APEX IDE, which by itself is a collection of APEX applications that must have unique application IDs within the APEX instance.

While importing an APEX application into a Workspace, you can choose to Auto Assign New Application ID. This is a must if you are importing into a different Workspace on the same instance or if the original application ID collides with an existing application on another instance. You can also set the application ID manually by choosing Change Application ID, or if possible (unique ID–wise), you can retain the original application ID by selecting the option Reuse Application ID xxxx From Export File.

If the imported application contains a translated version(s), you must reuse the original application ID to preserve the translation functionality. This might be a problem across multiple instances. To preserve the uniqueness of the application ID, you should assign a "crazy" application ID to any translated application that you are going to deploy on different instances. I suggest you use at least a seven-digit number, with a random and "mad" digits order. Remember—there is no practical need to memorize an application ID, so you can go wild.

The Instance Administrator can set a minimum and maximum for the application ID range as part of the instance settings. This may be useful if your APEX environment includes more than one instance. By allocating a different application ID range to each instance, it becomes easier to port an entire Workspace to another instance, while keeping the original application IDs.

The next option the Create an Application wizard gives us is to Copy Shared Components From Another Application. If you already defined, in a previous application, shared components that you can reuse, copying them straight into the new application can save you valuable time and tedious work.

The wizard screen that follows enables you to define some specific application attributes, which can be especially handy if you want them to be different from the App Builder defaults. You can set the Authentication Scheme for the application, its primary Language, and, if it's a translated application, how to derive the UI language. You can also set various date- and time-related formats.

NOTE
Bear in mind that your current selections for the application attributes can be modified after the application is created.

The last screen of the wizard is a confirmation page, displaying a summary of all the wizard choices you made. If they match your intentions, click the Create Application button. If not, you can go back and fix any issues.

Mobile Applications

The Mobile application type is dedicated to applications for mobile devices, mainly smartphones. This type uses resources that are best equipped and optimized to deal with smaller screens, the relatively weaker processing power, and less running memory, which are typical for these devices. The theme associated with the Mobile type is better to handle specific operational characteristics, such as changes in the (page) orientation display and touchscreen events.

NOTE
Later in the chapter, we'll talk about APEX themes and elaborate more about the difference between legacy APEX themes, the responsive themes, and the Mobile Theme. This information should help you determine what type of application you should choose for various scenarios and target devices.

Wizard-wise, the Mobile application type includes the same options offered by the Desktop type; however, where theme is concerned, currently you can select only one out-of-the-box theme: Mobile (51).

TIP
Using the Mobile user interface, you can add mobile-oriented pages to a Desktop application and support both functionalities in a single application.

Application-Level Features and Shared Components

Each APEX application has features and attributes that are set and applied on the application level as part of the Shared Components, one of the major modules on the Application home page that we reviewed in Chapter 3.

These application-level features and attributes are classified into four major categories:

■ **Definition** Deals with major identification features, such as the application Name and Alias; behavioral features, such as Error Handling, Compatibility Mode (to previous APEX versions), Allow Feedback to users, and more; and availability features, such as whether the application will be available to APEX developers only or cannot be edited (for production application). This category also enables you to define your own, application-dedicated substitution strings. (We'll elaborate more about substitution strings in the "APEX Templates" section later in the chapter.)

■ **Security**   APEX applications can be made public or can be secured with required authentication. These security access features—Authentication, Authorization, (APEX) Session Management, and Session State Protection—are all set at the application level. Another security/performance option is to enable or disable the browser cache mechanism. (Security is a vast and important issue, and Chapter 10 covers it in detail.)

■ **Globalization**   You can develop the APEX application to use or to be translated into any language and locale the Oracle database supports. The Globalization and Localization attributes are set at the application level. Setting these attributes—date and time formats, and National Language Support (NLS)–related sorting attributes—should be considered best practice, because they become the application defaults and assure a consistent look and NLS behavior across the application.

Note that APEX 5.1 introduced a major globalization enhancement, declarative Right-To-Left support, within the Document Direction field, shown in Figure 4-6. If you are using the Universal Theme (42), you don't have to take any further actions to gain RTL support.

■ **User Interface**   This prebuilt set of attributes enable you, often in a declarative manner, to control the shape and look of the application pages, established links to (external) resources (such as JavaScript libraries from the Internet, specific JavaScript and CSS files), and fine-tune the built-in APEX elements Themes and Templates. Currently, APEX includes two user interfaces: Desktop and Mobile. A single application can use more than one user interface—it can have both a Desktop and a Mobile user interface; each includes a matching theme with its own (typical) login and home page. This means that a single application can support both the desktop and the mobile environments, and you can differentiate, easily and notably, between the various application pages and their orientation by using the appropriate user interface.

Websheet Applications

A Websheet is a very powerful type of application that enables you to delegate some of the APEX development capabilities to a power end user that is not necessarily an IT developer. This quick and fairly simple-to-use technology is packaged as a declarative wizard to make data, and data manipulation, more accessible.

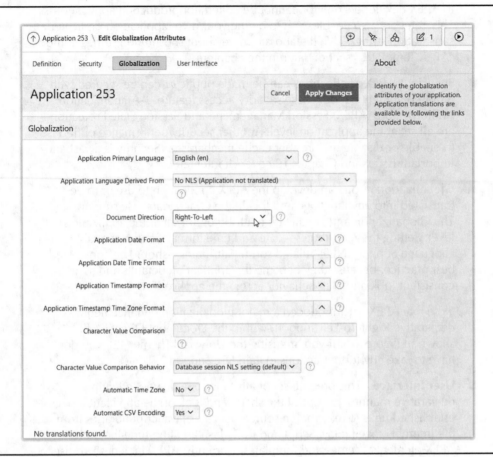

FIGURE 4-6. *Globalization attributes*

NOTE
Websheets are not supported under the APEX runtime environment.

Users can construct their own data structure in a Websheet application; they can devise plain input pages (including a data grid) and populate them manually or by uploading external structured or unstructured data files. They can build simple, yet dynamic and interactive, reports based on the data grid or (if allowed, privileges-wise) on the Workspace-associated schema objects (for example, tables and views). Users can share data structures and reports with others, while increasing collaboration by enabling users to annotate the data. And it's all available via a browser (no need to install anything), yet still uses the advantages of working in a secure environment (the user needs to authenticate) and other features that the database has to offer.

Many organizations are using various spreadsheets to collect information from their members (expense reports, project hours, and the like). Although spreadsheet software is very common, it was not necessarily designed to operate as a form replacement or to have database capabilities. The individual spreadsheet is usually not secured, and merging spreadsheets into an organization-level aggregated sheet can be a lot of work. Websheets are great candidates to replace spreadsheets, with a simple web application that enables users to work in a secure environment and enjoy database features that make collecting, aggregating, and displaying data much simpler and more productive.

Create a Websheet

The Websheet data and metadata are stored in a dedicated set of database objects with a name prefix of *APEX$_*. One of the instance preferences is whether Websheet objects will be created automatically for a new Workspace as part of its associated schema. If such objects were not created by default, a Workspace administrator can generate them at any time, as Figure 4-7 shows.

The Create Websheet wizard includes a single page (Figure 4-8). The first parameter to provide is the Websheet ID, which follows the same guiding rules as

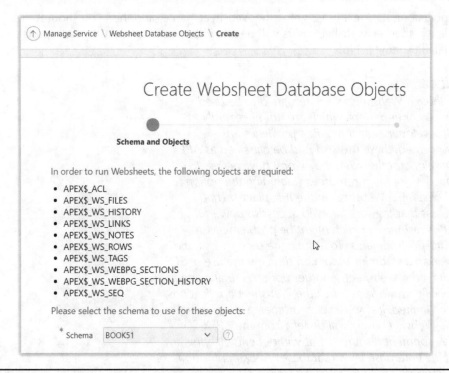

FIGURE 4-7. *Creating Websheet database objects*

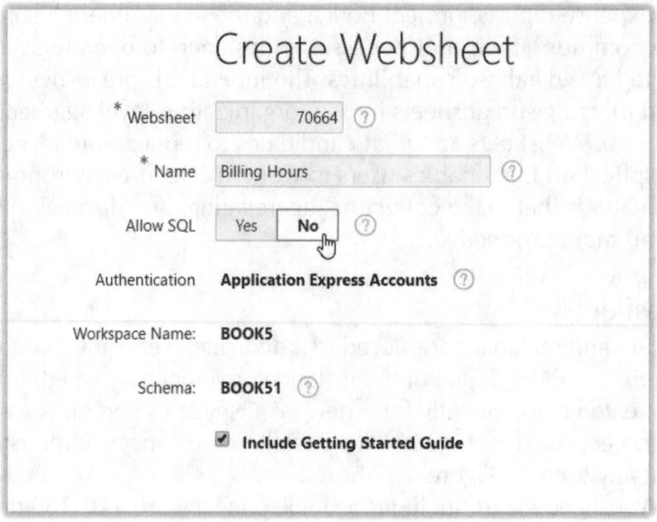

Create Websheet

* Websheet	70664	?
* Name	Billing Hours	?
Allow SQL	Yes **No**	?
Authentication	**Application Express Accounts**	?
Workspace Name:	**BOOK5**	
Schema:	**BOOK51** ?	
☑	**Include Getting Started Guide**	

FIGURE 4-8. *Create Websheet wizard*

the application ID. Next is assigning the websheet Name, and then you should decide whether the websheet users will be allowed to use SQL (mainly for reports). The default setting is No.

NOTE
Although Websheets were designed to be used by power end users, which are not necessarily IT developers, as far as APEX privileges are concerned, these users should be classified as APEX Developer; otherwise, they won't have access to any development resources (including the option of creating a Websheet in the first place). That means that they are allowed access to powerful APEX resources, which might be problematic in some environments. To reduce the security risk, the Workspace administrator can disallow the use of SQL within the Websheet. Another option is to allocate a specific Workspace for all the Websheet applications, with limited, if any, associated schemas. This way, the Websheet users will benefit from the APEX development resources, but without endangering any of the enterprise-level (database) APEX applications that reside on a separate Workspace.

The Create Websheet wizard screen displays three informative fields: Authentication, Workspace Name, and Schema that the websheet will be associated with. It also includes a default option, Include Getting Started Guide. This short guide, "Welcome to Websheets," is presented on the first page of the websheet and reviews some of the major features available to its users.

APEX Themes (Concepts)

The APEX theme is the next logical container in the hierarchical structure, although you can look at it as an element that actually encapsulates the APEX application and its components and is responsible for their look and feel.

An APEX theme is a collection of HTML, CSS, and JavaScript code, bundled and organized as APEX templates, which are classified according to APEX elements and functionalities. The templates are responsible for the look and feel of the assortment of elements that make up the APEX application, including the general layout skeleton of the application pages (such as sidebars, navigational aids, tabs, item positioning, and more).

APEX Themes: Evolution and Revolution

The APEX theme technology has been available from the start. Traditionally, every new APEX release added fresher and modern theme(s), which were mainly differentiated by their color palette (naturally, the most notable distinguishing feature), object style (for instance, rounded versus rectangle), and general positioning on the page. However, over time, some major changes have occurred regarding how the page elements are laid out on the page and how much the layout is responsive to the devices running the applications and their unique features (for example, large screen for desktop machines versus much smaller one for smartphones).

The APEX legacy themes (prior to APEX 4.0) based their layouts on HTML tables. This is an easy technique, as the positioning and justification of the page elements are based on the grid formed by the columns and rows of the table, which are very tangible. However, this advantage can also be considered a big disadvantage, as the layout might be deemed strict and inflexible. The evolution in the HTML world was to move to a layout based on DIV (**<div>**) elements, and APEX adopted this approach. DIV elements are much harder to position on page, because they don't have clear borders, and for the same reason, aligning the elements is not as straightforward as with a table. With DIVs, you need more excessive CSS support, but in overall look, they seem to consume less code but offer much more layout flexibility. As APEX developers, we shouldn't care too much about the higher complexity of the code, because the APEX engine, using the appropriate APEX templates, takes care of all that for us. We are left with the advantages of a smaller code footprint and a higher degree of flexibility (and responsiveness) in the layout process.

The next step in the APEX theme evolution occurred when a true responsive theme was introduced—Blue Responsive (25). This theme uses the Bootstrap framework, which bases its layout process on a DIV grid with 12 columns (and this is, of course, a very simplistic description but will suffice in our context).

TIP
Remember the 12 columns, because you'll encounter them later on. Layout decisions (for example, for APEX regions) will make much more sense.

Another new theme that was introduced around that time (with APEX 4.2) was the Mobile (51) theme, which started the era of mobile development in APEX. This theme was designed to develop dedicated mobile applications, mainly for smartphones. The theme was optimized to run on mobile devices, and it relies extensively on jQuery Mobile, A Touch-Optimized Web Framework.

Responsive Web Design

Responsive web design should take into account the media that runs the application, its features that have direct bearing on how the web pages are displayed, and the effect it has on their behavior and functionality. These features mainly include the screen size and resolution, which determine the effective screen space allocated for the application page display. A good responsive design adjusts the page layout according to the available display space, without impairing the user experience too much and without damaging the functionality of the page.

Old-school web designs didn't change the layout or size of the elements on a page. If the effective screen space was not enough (and we mainly deal with the screen width), a scrollbar was added, enabling the user to scroll to focus on the displayed content. However, the user experience was impaired, as most users didn't like to scroll the displayed content from side to side and found it annoying.

Responsive web design computes the effective display space, using the CSS3 media queries module (including the Media type and Media features attributes, which provide important information about the device resources available to be used) and adjust the proportions of the layout grid accordingly.

As a result, the page layout can be changed and the elements on the page can be repositioned and resized in a manner that will enable maximum display of content, in the most comfortable manner to the user (usually, by maintaining decent readable font size and input field width).

We can clearly see this behavior in the APEX-responsive themes. When the effective display space shrinks—not just when using mobile devices, but also when working with windows on a large screen—graphical icons (such as those on the home page of many APEX modules) are resized to be smaller; various input fields (APEX items) are resized; and noncrucial displayed information (for example, the logged-in username on the Developer navigation tools) is hidden. Moreover, depending on the effective width of the display area, the page layout may be changed, automatically, in a manner in which elements that were originally positioned side-by-side would be stacked on top of each other (for instance, page regions or the labels of the items).

The APEX Mobile Theme is a private case of responsive web design. As we mentioned, on top of the responsive behavior, this theme was optimized to be used on small mobile devices such as smartphones, and it offers specific solutions to their particular (hardware) characteristics.

The revolution in APEX themes came with the debut of the Universal Theme in APEX 5.0. This theme, which also uses the Bootstrap framework, presents a responsive, dynamic, and interactive web design behavior. Instead of introducing new theme(s), APEX 5.1 enhanced and extended the features and capabilities of the Universal Theme, and you can expect this trend to be continued in future releases.

NOTE
The Universal Theme is one of the more important new and productive features that APEX 5.x introduced. Chapter 8 is devoted entirely to this subject.

Choosing an APEX Theme

As of APEX 5.1, themes 1–26 and 50 are deprecated and considered legacy themes. This means that these themes will no longer be evolved in any way, and new features in future releases will not be tested on them. The Universal Theme (42) and the Mobile Theme (51) are the standard themes from APEX 5.1 onward, and new applications should be developed using only them.

TIP
If you want existing applications that use legacy themes to continue evolving alongside APEX, you should migrate them to the standard themes. You can find a tutorial about the migration options (and potential obstacles) in the following (public APEX) application: https://apex.oracle.com/pls/apex/ f?p=42:2000.

The best choice for an APEX theme depends on the nature of the application—enterprise-level comprehensive application or small and targeted one—and its intended audience—office workers equipped with desktops and big screens or on-the-move workers who need or prefer to run applications on smaller mobile devices. Hence, your first step should be to establish the nature and scope of the application and the hardware environment it will run on.

With APEX 5.x, the obvious choice for a new application is the Universal Theme (42). This is a responsive theme that has dynamic interactive features that enable the developer and the end user to shape and control the appearance of the application—for example, by using the Theme Roller and the Live Template Options. Furthermore, if your application needs to support some mobile functionalities, you can always add the Mobile UI to the default Desktop UI of the theme and enjoy both worlds. However, if you are going to develop a dedicated application for the mobile world that will run mainly on smartphones and tablets, you should consider the Mobile Theme (51), because on top of its responsive features, it can optimally handle the distinguished features (or lack of them) that are typical to these devices.

TIP
Before you choose to use the Universal Theme, check that the theme supports all the design and layout features that you need, especially if you are migrating from a legacy theme. For example, the current Universal Theme doesn't support two-level tab pages. It offers other layout solutions, however, so make sure they are applicable to your needs. Always remember that you can tweak existing templates, or add your own, to achieve what you want. You will read more details about that in Chapter 8.

APEX Templates

The APEX template is a logical container that bundles and organizes snippets of HTML code that the APEX engine uses while generating the rendering code of the APEX application page.

The final output of the APEX engine is HTML code that is sent to the client browser to be rendered. This HTML code includes links to external files such as CSS and JavaScript files, and it can also contain inline CSS and JavaScript statements. The template organizes this code in a generic and parameterized manner, enabling the APEX engine to reuse it, and still tailors it to a specific element instance, functionality, and appearance.

The APEX templates are classified according to APEX elements, such as page, region, label, button, and more. The element templates are classified according to functionalities, such as Login page, Interactive Report region, and Required label, and according to the appearance they generate, such as Right Side Column page, Optional – Above label, Text or Text with Icon button, and more.

Some of the template code is solely generated by the APEX engine, but some of it can be set by developers. The various Edit Template wizards display the template code, divided into relevant sections, according to functionality or location within the final page rendering code. For example, a Page template includes a Definition section, with fields for Header, Body, and Footer; it also includes a JavaScript section with fields that enable you to specify URLs to external JavaScript files or to include inline JavaScript code for Execute when Page Loads. On the other hand, the Definition section of a Label template includes relevant fields for the label's appearance, such as Before Label or Inline Help Template (new feature of APEX 5.1).

NOTE
As already mentioned, Chapter 8 is dedicated to a detailed discussion about themes and templates and how they serve us with the look and feel of the application. For now, bear in mind that if the out-of-the-box themes or templates don't fit all your application design and appearance needs, you can adapt them or create your own.

Substitution Strings

How do you make the APEX templates generic and parameterized? You need to use some sort of variables that can be set dynamically, according to the context you are working in. APEX uses *substitution strings*, variables that can be set by the APEX engine or by developers. Substitution strings are embedded into the template's code, and at runtime, the APEX engine substitutes their values with their current values.

The APEX engine has a long list of built-in substitution strings. Many of them are solely populated by the APEX engine itself, and some of them are populated with the content of relevant template fields. For example, in the Page template, the content of the Function and Global Variable Declaration field, which holds inline JavaScript code, is set into the **#TEMPLATE_JAVASCRIPT#** substitution string, which appears in the Footer field of that template. At runtime, when the APEX engine generates the page-rendering code, it substitutes **#TEMPLATE_JAVASCRIPT#** with the actual JavaScript code it holds.

Substitution strings are always referenced by an all uppercase name, and those associated with templates are enclosed by the number sign (#). Most templates include a substitution string information section that lists all the available substitution strings in the template.

Substitution strings are not limited to APEX templates. You can find a list of non-template–related substitution strings in the *App Builder User's Guide*. These substitution strings can be referenced using the *&NAME.* notation—a prefix ampersand sign (&) and a trailing period.

Substitution strings are a feature of the APEX engine, and as such, they must be used in code that is available to the APEX engine at runtime. Hence, you can use substitution strings with inline PL/SQL code, using the bind variable notation—a prefix colon sign (:). For example, you can use :APP_USER to get the name of the user running the APEX application. With external PL/SQL code (such as stored packages, functions, and procedures), you must use a built-in APEX function—V() for strings, and NV() for numbers—to get the value of the substitution string. For example, you can use **V('APP_USER')** or **NV('APP_ID')**.

NOTE
Although bind variables and function parameters are usually not case-sensitive, substitution strings are. When referencing them, you must always use all uppercase names.

TIP
Substitution strings will not be available directly to JavaScript code in external files, because those are not available to the APEX engine when it generates the page-rendering code. If you want to expose substitution strings to an external file JavaScript code, you can use the Function and Global Variable Declaration field, in the Page template, to assign the contents of the substitution string into a JavaScript global variable. Here's an example:
var app_user = '&APP_USER.';
As the assignment is part of inline code, the APEX engine can make the substitution, and because you defined a global variable, it will also be available to the JavaScript code in the external files linked to the application page.

APEX Pages

An APEX application is a collection of pages. A *page* is a logical container with a nod to the physical world. It's the basic application display unit that holds the APEX elements that support the content and functionality of the application, alongside elements that support operational and navigational actions. All these elements should be shaped and laid-out according to the actual display area available, and where mobile devices are concerned, it's often the physical smaller screen size. As mentioned earlier in the chapter, you can determine and control the page layout and its general look and feel by applying a page template, which in turn reflects the application theme (which, if you want to consider the physical world, should be a responsive APEX theme).

Each APEX application page has a lifecycle that comprises two major phases: page rendering and page processing. Each phase opens a database session for the duration of the dialog between the web server/listener and the database. In the page rendering phase, the HTML page code that was generated by the APEX engine in response to a client HTTP(S) request is sent from the database to the client browser to be rendered on screen. In the page processing phase, which starts when the user submits the page, the data from the submitted page is sent back to the database to be processed by the APEX engine. In between, other database sessions may be opened if Ajax request(s) are invoked by the page.

APEX Session vs. Database Session

You should not confuse an *APEX session* with a *database session*. An APEX session is a logic timeframe that starts when the user sends the initial APEX request—usually for the application home page (and if the application is secured, you'll be redirected to the application login page), but public pages (including the login page) also run within an active APEX session. The APEX session ends when the user logs out of the APEX application or the session is terminated by the APEX engine according to the Session Management parameters (which are part of the application-level parameters).

In the APEX context, a database session is a timeframe established for the very short time it takes HTTP(S), with the help of the web server/listener, to transport information between the client browser and the database, and vice versa. This means that the database session life span is a single HTTP(S) request/response.

We already mentioned that the APEX Session State is a mechanism that helps you overcome the stateless nature of a web application. Session State also helps you overcome some limitations the database session poses, such as the scope and life span of stored package variables—a single database session. For persistence, the APEX Session State is updated, automatically and transparently to the user, at least twice for every page—at the rendering phase and the processing phase (after page submit).

Each APEX page must be identified uniquely across the application with a Page Number ID, which is an integer value. The Create a Page wizard, which we'll discuss next, chooses the next available page number for you, but you can change it.

TIP
*The Page Number ID is a crucial factor in navigating (branching) around the APEX application. As such, it can be obtained, programmatically, by using the built-in substitution string APP_PAGE_ID. The APEX engine, automatically and transparently to the developer, also adds a hidden HTML item to every APEX page, with the **id** attribute of pFlowStepId, and the **value** attribute set to the page number. This makes the page number directly available to any JavaScript code running on the page.*

APEX Page Types

The Create a Page wizard (Figure 4-9) can be invoked from the APEX IDE application home page or from the Create option on the Page Designer toolbar. It includes various built-in APEX page types that are classified according to their main

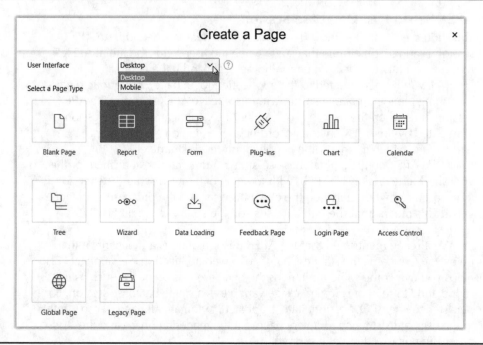

FIGURE 4-9. *The home page for the Create a Page wizard*

functionality. Some of these types, such as Form, Report, and Chart, include subtypes that enable you to target and refine the functionality of the page—for example, a form based on a database table or an SQL query; or how it handles and displays its data, such as single/double master detail page, classic report, or interactive grid.

After you select a page type, the Create a Page wizard adapts the upcoming screens to the selected page type, where you are required to supply relevant information. For example, in Figure 4-10, you can see the wizard screen for creating an (editable) interactive grid—an innovative feature introduced in APEX 5.1, which we will discuss in Chapter 6. This element can generate a data grid based on a database table or SQL query. Hence, and according to the Source Type you indicate, you must enter a database table or an SQL query. Other page types require information specific to them, such as start and ending dates for a calendar, target table for data loading, and more.

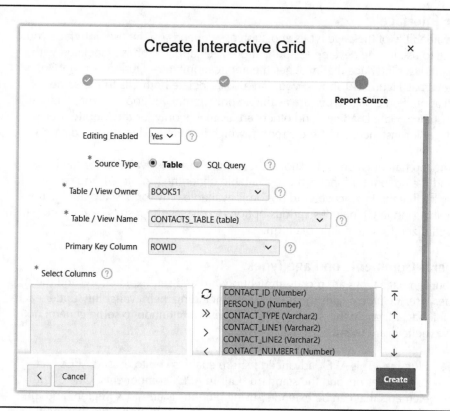

FIGURE 4-10. *Creating an interactive grid with the Create a Page wizard*

TIP
Using the Create a Page wizard, you can see various features of APEX in action. For example, Figure 4-10 shows a cascading select list—a secondary Table / View Name field that is populated using an Ajax call, based on the selected value in the primary Table / View Owner field. Furthermore, you can see some actions of hide/show fields based on the Source Type field. You can implement these elements and techniques in your own APEX applications.

After you create the page, the Create a Page wizard will redirect you to the Page Designer, where you can edit the page and fill it with the components it needs to perform its functionality.

User Interface

The availability of the page types and subtypes depends on the user interface you choose to use for the developed application. Each application is associated with a default User Interface that matches the application type—Desktop or Mobile. However, as Figure 4-9 shows, you can also associate both UIs to the same application. Some page types are available only in the Desktop user interface (for instance, Data Loading), and others are available only for the Mobile user interface (for instance, a List View report, which is optimized to display data on mobile devices).

The top half of Figure 4-11 shows the Report subtypes available for the Desktop UI, and the bottom half shows those available under the Mobile UI. You can see, for example, that the Interactive Grid option is available only for desktop applications, while the Mobile UI includes various options to display the results of a report, which are optimized for the mobile platform.

General Comments on Page Types

The built-in page types are mostly straightforward and self-explanatory, and the *App Builder User's Guide* details them very well, including their availability under each user interface. Ergo, in this section, we'll draw your attention to some general notes that we believe are useful:

- **Plug-ins** This APEX advanced feature enables you to extend APEX capabilities beyond the standard built-in APEX components. One of the elements that can be extended using plug-ins is an APEX Region, and the Plug-ins page type enables you to create an application page that includes a Region plug-in. However, if the developed application doesn't include any

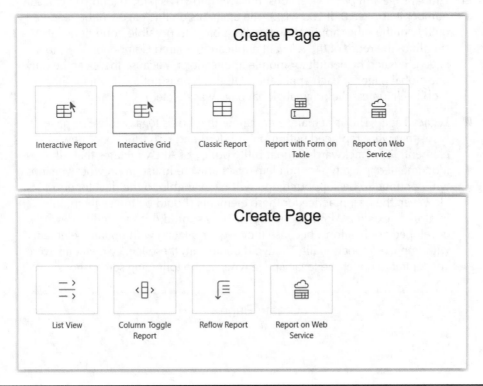

FIGURE 4-11. *The available Report subtypes under Desktop (top) and Mobile UIs*

Region plug-in, and you try to create a page using this page type, you'll see a message, "There are no plug-ins installed," even if the application includes plug-ins that are not region related.

- **Chart** APEX 5.1 uses Oracle JET charts, a component that is based on HTML5, CSS3, and JavaScript and will be supported only by modern browsers (per the official browser support policy of APEX, mentioned on Chapter 1). Existing AnyChart charts can be migrated to the new APEX 5.1 technology using the Upgrade Application wizard, which can be invoked from the Utilities option on the Page Designer toolbar.

- **Data Loading** As of APEX 5.1, you can use a single File Browse page item to upload multiple files, and their types can be restricted.

- **Access Control** A very simple security feature can easily be implemented with this page type. (More details in Chapter 10, which deals with APEX security features.)

■ **Global Page** In pre-5.x versions, this was known as page 0 (and you can still number it as page 0, if you wish). The elements on this page will be rendered on any of the other application pages (subject to possible conditions). It simplifies the reuse of the relevant application Shared Components. A global page is created by default for mobile applications. Because there can be only one global page for each application UI, this type is not available for the Mobile UI (unless the original global page was deleted).

■ **Legacy Page** This is actually a container that holds legacy (pre-5.x) page types that were replaced with more modern and rich functional new elements. The backward-compatibility policy of APEX dictates that all (documented) page types and elements that were in use in previous versions will continue to be supported and will be available to the developers. However, the best practice for these elements should be to use them only in already existing APEX applications. They should not be used in new developed applications, because they were replaced with updated elements with improved functionality. To avoid confusion, these legacy elements were concentrated under the legacy page type, as the following screenshot shows:

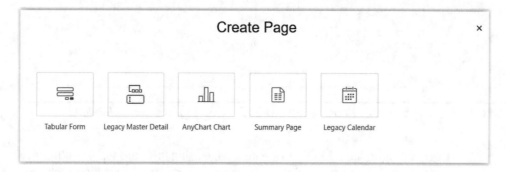

APEX Page Mode

In its recent (responsive) themes, APEX supports, out-of-the-box, three types of page modes: Normal, Modal Dialog, and Non-Modal Dialog, as shown next:

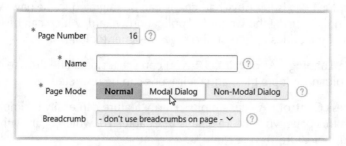

TIP
*(Advanced) To support the Modal Dialog page
mode, especially with the legacy themes, the
application theme must include a Modal Dialog
page template. If your (already existing) application
theme doesn't include such a template, you can
copy it from a theme that does contain it, such as
the Universal Theme (42). Make sure you activate
the copied template in the target theme, under the
Dialog Defaults tab, per the detailed instructions in
the* App Builder User's Guide.

Normal Page

The majority of the APEX application pages are rendered in the Normal page mode—a
regular window that opens and covers the entire display area, which can be resized
by the end user. This is indeed the normal standard window our browsers render by
default, and it usually deals with running an application main business logic task.

However, sometimes you need to deviate from the main course to complete
a task that will enable you to continue with your main mission or make it easier.
In some cases, the sequence of running things matters, and some tasks should
precede others. In these cases, the secondary task is being fired at a specific point
and should be completed before returning to the main course. (For example, under
certain scenarios, you must provide extra information that the main task depends
on, but for various reasons, you want to do it in a separate window for more clarity,
to differentiate and focus on a common denominator, or to avoid crowding the
main window.) In other cases, the sequence of running things is not that important,
and you can continue with your main task, regardless of the secondary one
(for example, applying search filters on a large dataset, which can make your
work simpler and faster, but you can also do without; extra information you should
provide, but without dependency ties to the main task). For the first type of cases,
you should use a Modal Dialog page mode, and for the other cases, you can use
the Non-Modal Dialog page mode.

Modal Dialog Page

A modal dialog page is a look-alike window that overlays the current window active
display area (viewport). It's a look-alike because it doesn't include any of the toolbars
that a normal browser window includes (such as navigation, menu, and URL address).
When a modal dialog page gains focus, its calling page is dimmed/grayed, and the
end user cannot shift the focus back to the calling page without closing the modal
page. APEX, of course, provides the means to do this properly by using dedicated
dynamic actions or a page process. These options also enable you, declaratively, to
pass/refresh data from the modal page to its parent page or to other application pages
(using a page branch process).

Note that you can control the appearance (dimensions) and some other features of the modal dialog through the Dialog section of the page (the APEX object), using the Property Editor, as the next illustration shows. The most common attributes to be used are probably those that enable you to determine whether the modal dialog is draggable and/or resizable.

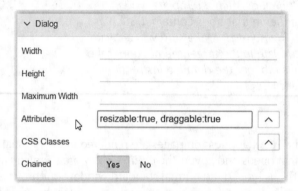

NOTE
You cannot run a modal dialog page directly from the Page Designer; you must invoke it from a parent page, which doesn't have to be a normal mode page. APEX enables you to branch from one modal page to another, as you can see in many App Builder wizards.

Non-Modal Dialog Page

This is actually a pop-up window that opens separately from the parent/calling window, and the end user can resize or minimize it. Unlike with the modal page, the calling page of the non-modal dialog page remains accessible in the background, and the user can shift focus between the non-modal dialog page and the page that invoked it.

APEX Regions

The next level of hierarchy in the APEX application model is the page Region, a logical container with tangible aspects in the physical world. The Region holds the APEX elements that you are placing on the application page, while setting clear (visible or invisible) landmarks for the page layout scheme. An example of a Static Content regions layout is shown in Figure 4-12.

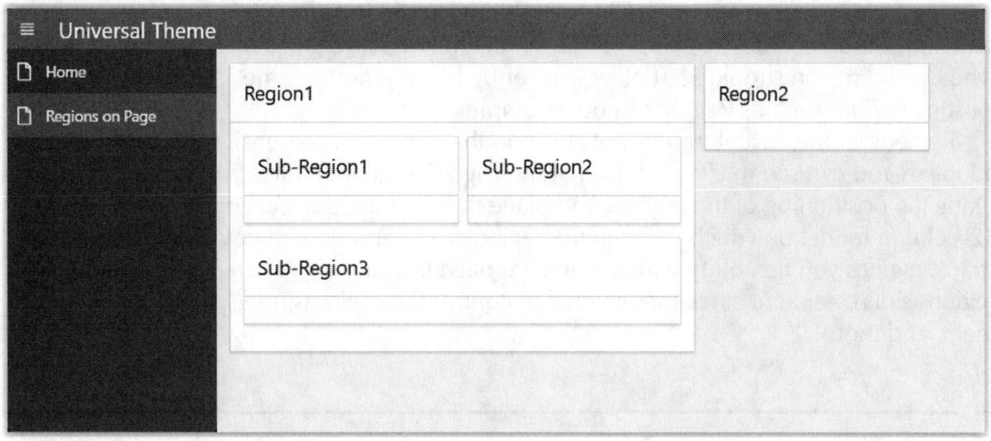

FIGURE 4-12. *Static Content regions layout*

Every APEX element on a page must belong to a specific region. The regions are classified according to the elements they can hold and their main functionality. For example, you should use the Static Content region for forms, and for reports, you can use several region options, such as Classic Report, Interactive Grid, or Interactive Report. For navigation purposes, you can use the Breadcrumb region, Region Display Selector, or the List. Other specific functional regions are Calendar, Chart, Map Chart, and the list goes on. Similar to the page types, the availability of the various regions is also dependent on the user interface you are implementing in the developed application—Desktop or Mobile.

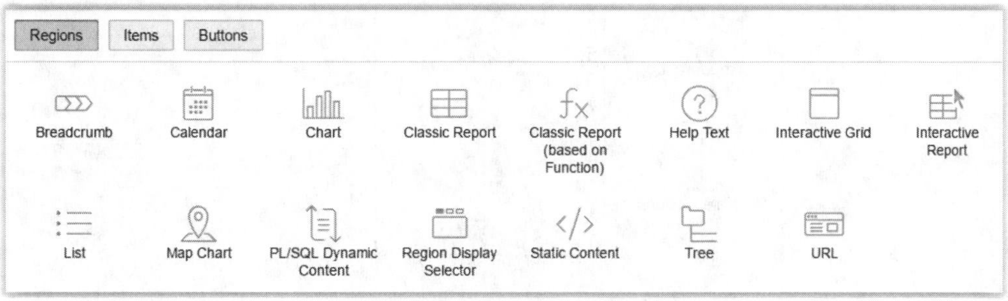

The actual layout is done with the Page Designer, and Figure 4-13 shows the relevant Layout section for one of the subregions shown in Figure 4-12. As you can see, this section enables you to set a Parent region (for subregions) and determine whether the region should Start New Row or be placed on the same row as an existing region (such as Region2 in our example).

Remember the 12-column layout skeleton that the APEX responsive themes adopted? You can see in Figure 4-13 that the Page Designer enables you to set and refine the positioning of the regions and place them on the page according to the 12-column model on which Column the region starts, and how many columns it spans. It gives you flexibility with the general page layout, as you can position the regions side-by-side or stack them; you can control their widths, the space between them, and more.

FIGURE 4-13. *A Page Designer section for Region layout*

TIP
*Although it's not mandatory, we usually give a
Title to a Region, using the Identification section
of the Region Property Editor. By default, the style
(appearance) of the title is determined by the region
template; however, it's useful to remember that the
Title field accepts HTML code, so you can style
the title as specifically as you want if the standard
(template base) style is unsuitable for your needs.
Moreover, this field also supports substitution strings,
which enable you to set dynamic titles, based on
available application data. For example, the following
Title field displays a dynamic title that includes the
user's full name, in red text:*

```
Expense Report - <span style="color:red;"> &USER_FULL_NAME.</span>
```

APEX Items

The most fundamental building blocks in the arsenal of APEX elements are the APEX items. These elements actually form the (interactive) interface between the end user and the APEX application; they are the means by which the user feeds data into the application, and in some cases, they display the application response to the end user (which doesn't have to be in the form of a report of some sort). APEX supports two levels of items: application-level items and page-level items.

APEX Application Items

The application items are nondisplayed variables you can use throughout the application, and when using Session State, they help you persist values you need to access across all the application pages or share with other active applications. Figure 4-14 shows the attributes you need to set for an application item.

First, enter a Name for the item using the naming rules we are going to specify shortly for the APEX page items (minus the naming convention prefix). The second mandatory parameter is the Scope of the application item. The default option is Application, which means that this item will be available only within the application in which it's defined. However, choosing a Global scope for the item allows you to share it with other applications that share the same APEX session with this application. The APEX IDE is a good example of such a scenario; it comprises several APEX applications, such as the major APEX IDE modules, that share a single APEX session, and it enables you, among other things, to navigate freely between the major IDE modules without performing a new login with each branch to a different module. It also allows these modules to share the values of global application items.

Application Item

Show All	Name	Security

Name

Application: **1263 Demo App1 (UT 42)** ⑦

* Name [   ] ⑦

* Scope [Application ⌄] ⑦
          Application
          Global

Security

Session State Protection [Restricted - May not be set from browser ⌄] ⑦
                          Unrestricted
                          Checksum Required - Application Level
                          Checksum Required - User Level
                          Checksum Required - Session Level
                          Restricted - May not be set from browser

Configuration

Build Option [   ]

Comments

Comments [   ]

FIGURE 4-14. *Setting attributes for an application item*

Next, set the Session State Protection rules that will apply to the application item. Although you are dealing with a nondisplayed item, its value can still be modified from the browser, and you should set the rules for allowing or forbidding it.

NOTE
Security is very important with any sort of application, especially when you are dealing with a web application. Chapter 10 is dedicated to security issues with APEX and includes detailed discussions about the various security options at your disposal, including Session State Protection.

APEX Page Items

The Page Designer, which we'll discuss in greater detail in the next chapter, enables you, declaratively, to define page items by generating all the basic HTML elements, such as text, select, hidden, radio/checkbox fields, and others alongside some compound elements specially devised for the APEX applications, by enhancing and expending the functionality of some basic HTML elements. These APEX compound elements include a date/color picker, Yes/No switch, multiselect shuttle item, and more. The full list of page item types is shown in Figure 4-15.

NOTE
The main purpose of most page items is to be submitted to the APEX engine to be processed and saved. As of APEX 5.1, the page-submitted data is being transferred to the APEX engine (database) using a JavaScript Object Notation (JSON) document. One of the notable perks of using this technique is that you are no longer limited by a maximum number of active APEX (input) Items per page (contrary to the recent limit of 200 active items per page and the legacy one of 100 items). However, be careful with this new freedom. Always remember that the application users should feel comfortable working with your application, and a crowded page might be intimidating and counterproductive, shifting focus from what is important.

Each APEX item has a list of attributes that define its functionality with regard to the APEX engine and the business logic, or that define the item's appearance and positioning with regard to the application page. Some of these attributes are shared across all the APEX items, such as the name of an item, how it is initialized, conditions for its participation/display on page, and more. Some items, mainly according to their functionality, include specific attributes for their type—for example, how to populate multiselect elements such as checkboxes, shuttle, and other items (by using static lists, or dynamic lists that are generated by querying the database); how to obtain displayed images; or the type of files the end user is allowed to upload. The Property Editor toggles the display mode (Show/Hide) of most of these specific item-related attributes according to their relevance to the item type you are editing.

In the upcoming sections, we'll concentrate on the concepts behind the various (page) item attributes, mainly with regard to the APEX engine, and how they define and influence the functionality of the item. In the next chapter, you'll learn how to set and manipulate page items and how to position them on the page using the Property Editor, which is part of the new Page Designer.

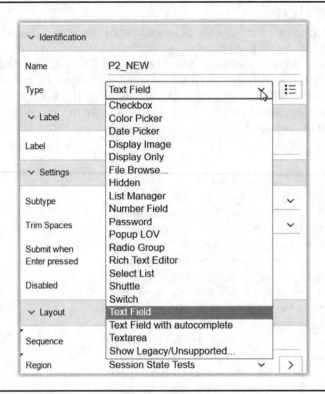

FIGURE 4-15. *Page item types supported by APEX*

Item Identification

Each APEX item must be identified uniquely across the application by an item name. As each APEX item is ultimately an Oracle database identifier, its name must adhere to the database identifiers naming rules—no spaces or new lines, and none of the characters & , . ' : + ? " ^. In addition, the item name must be in all uppercase letters (the Property Editor will take care of this for us) and should not exceed 30 bytes (for the English language, that means 30 characters).

TIP
The 30-byte limit enables you to use the item name with a bind variable notation (a colon (:) preceding the name) in SQL statements. Often you really need that while implementing the business logic of the application. Although the APEX engine will not issue an error message if you provide a longer name, you should avoid doing so.

Where the APEX engine is concerned, you can reference an item by using its name in the substitution string notation, *&ITEM_NAME.*, (an ampersand (&) as the name prefix and a period as its suffix). With SQL and PL/SQL code, you can reference an item by using the bind variable notation, *:ITEM_NAME* (no period).

TIP
Although bind variables are not case-sensitive, substitution strings are. To be on the safe side, the best practice is to use all uppercase letters whenever using an item name.

Moreover, the APEX engine uses the item name to identify uniquely the HTML item element on the page by assigning it to the **id** attribute. For example, if you named a Text type item P4_DEMO_NAME, the associated **<input>** tag would look similar to the following:

```
<input type="text" id="P4_DEMO_NAME" name="P4_DEMO_NAME" … />
```

This means that basic APEX items can be easily and directly referenced for Document Object Model (DOM) and JavaScript manipulations by using the native HTML **getElementById()** method; APEX even includes a built-in shorthand function, **$x**, with similar functionality (and it's documented in the *Oracle Application Express API Reference*, under the non-namespace JavaScript APIs section). As you can see from the code example, the item name is also being used with the **name** attribute. This is particularly useful with compound items such as radio groups and checkboxes, as you can collect all the related components of a specific item by using its name with the native HTML **getElementsByName()** method.

TIP
The APEX JavaScript APIs, which are documented in the Oracle Application Express API Reference, *include many JavaScript functions that use the page item name to gain access to its properties. For example, you can use the built-in JavaScript API function **apex.item("ITEM_NAME").getValue()** to retrieve the current displayed value of a page item— this is an equivalent version of the shorthand and popular **$v()** function. If you intend to use JavaScript in your applications, you are encouraged to review these APIs because they can make your developer life much easier and simpler.*

Naming Conventions The generic APEX item name format includes a prefix comprising the capital letter "P" and the page ID number, followed by an underscore, and then a meaningful name that should describe the item and help you identify it easily. For example, a name for a text item on page 4 should start with "P4_", followed by a meaningful description of the item, such as "FULL_NAME". This yields the item name **P4_FULL_NAME**. The prefix format should ensure the unique name of the item across the entire application pages.

The APEX engine also uses some derivatives of the item name, mainly with some suffixes. If you review typical source code of an APEX application page, you'll find HTML tags associated with the item (such as **<div>**, **<span>**, **<label>**, **<fieldset>**), with various attribute values that are based on the item name with suffixes like _ERROR_, _CONTAINER_, and _DISPLAY_. For items such as Radio Group or Checkbox, you can also see sequenced IDs like ITEM_NAME_0, ITEM_NAME_1, and so forth.

When you create a new item within the Page Designer, it will get a generic name of Px_NEW, where x represents the page number. For example, if you want to create a bunch of new items, one after another, on page 4 using the Page Designer drag-and-drop technique, these items will be named by default in sequence: P4_NEW_1, P4_NEW_2, and so forth. You can rename them more meaningfully after you finish the creation and positioning process.

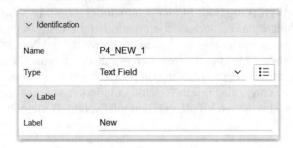

NOTE
*The APEX naming convention is just a suggestion. You can use whatever names you want, as long as you at least adhere to the database identifiers naming rules. Bear in mind, however, the use of the item name as the value of the HTML id attribute—as such, it also can be referenced by a CSS selector (**#id**). Hence, the item name should also comply with the naming rules in these cases. If you want to make your life easier, maintain pre-HTML5 compatibility, and avoid unnecessary escaping functions, keep it simple—start the item name with a letter [A–Z], and then continue with only letters, numbers, and the underscore sign. This is my personal best practice.*

Label, Settings, Layout, and Appearance

The attributes under these groups are mainly related to the application page and how the various items appear on it. Some of the attributes are item-type dependent and will be visible only when relevant to the specific item type you are editing. The following are some general notes with regard to the APEX engine and item functionality.

Label   Most page items have labels that should describe them and their content. The style and appearance of the label are set by a Label template and can include implied information—which could include, for example, that the item is required, by using a specific notation (such as a red asterisk) or color. Moreover, this field accepts HTML code and also supports substitution strings, so it enables you, in special cases, to generate a dynamic label and style it as you need. This should not be done regularly, however. If your general label styling needs are not met by the built-in label templates, you can, and should, create a template that works for you.

Subtype   This attribute pertains to text items and is HTML5 related, so it will be effective only on modern browsers that support HTML5. Its major functionality is to instruct virtual keyboards displayed on touchscreen devices to show the relevant keyboard to the subtype—such as a standard character keyboard or a numeric one, or a keyboard with a specific .com key—based on the level of support of the individual device running the application.

NOTE
*(Advanced) The APEX engine uses the matching subtype value—**text**, **email**, **tel**, or **url**—as the value of the type attribute for the item **<input>** element. As of APEX 5.1, with the Compatibility Mode set to 5.1 and above (which can be set in the Shared Components module, under the Application Definition Attributes), the client-side HTML5 constraint validation feature is supported. This means that if page validations are enabled to run prior to submitting the page, the relevant client-side HTML5 validations that match the item subtype will be run if your browser supports them. In any case, these client-side validations must not replace the server-side validations we'll discuss in Chapter 7.*

Submit When Enter Pressed   In some cases, most notably with search/filter fields, you want to submit the page immediately after keying your input, and the fastest way (because you are already using the keyboard) is simply to press ENTER. This attribute enables you, declaratively, to turn on this behavior.

Disabled This attribute disables the item, HTML-wise, which means that by HTML standard, the item will not be submitted so it will not be saved in Session State. However, if it's set to Yes, the Property Editor enables you to bypass the HTML standard by setting the Save Session State field to Yes.

TIP
*We'll return to this option with more detail as part of the **readonly** attribute discussion later in the chapter, where you'll learn about the visual and functional differences between a disabled item and a read-only item. This will help you choose the appropriate attribute to use.*

Sequence Each page item has a sequence that determines when it will be rendered, relative to the other page items on the page, when low sequences are rendered first.

TIP
Although the APEX engine will not raise an error if you assign the same sequence to more than one item on the same page, it may cause inconsistency in the appearance of the page, in case of exporting the application, and importing it to a different Workspace. Hence, best practice should be that each page item, definitely within the same region, has its own unique sequence.
In addition, if you relocate a page item using the Page Designer drag-and-drop technique, the APEX engine will adjust the sequence of the item and all the other items affected by the relocation to reflect the new page layout and rendering order.

Column CSS Classes, CSS Classes, and Column Attributes The theme and templates you chose to use in your application, and for the page items, determine their default appearance. However, you can change or fine-tune a default appearance by applying extra CSS classes or specific HTML style properties to a specific item. The content of these fields, under the Layout and Appearance groups, is injected into the container elements (**<div>**) that wrap the actual item element (usually an **<input>**). Hence, these properties, which can reference font, size, weight, color, and such, are inherited down and will affect all the item components, label and input field alike.

NOTE
You can choose to style only the input section of the item, and not its entire surrounding.

Format Mask   This attribute is applicable to number and date fields, which can be formatted to be displayed according to the application needs.

TIP
To maintain consistency of date and time appearance throughout the application pages, you should define the relevant Globalization attributes, under the application Shared Components. It may save you having to provide individual definitions at the item level.

Width   This attribute applies mostly to the various items that are based on a text field. It sets the width of the input field (the empty rectangle) allocated for the item on a page. It doesn't have to be identical to the actual length of the corresponding database object (if any), which can be smaller. Sometimes, because of layout and page symmetry considerations, you'll set the same width for items of different lengths because it looks better on screen.

This attribute doesn't apply to multiselect items such as checkboxes, radio groups, select lists, or shuttles. For these items, the width is determined mostly by the length of the options, and for checkboxes and radio groups, also by the number of columns you are using to list these options.

Value Placeholder   This is an HTML5-related attribute that is applicable to text-related items. It functions as an inline tooltip and will be displayed only if the field is (or becomes) empty.

Validation

In Chapter 7, we'll discuss how APEX enables you to validate your data after submitting a page (on the server side). Under the Validation group, the Property Editor enables you to define, simply and declaratively, two very basic and common client-side validations: Value Required and Maximum Length.

Value Required   In some cases, business logic dictates that an item is required, and as such, it must have a value. The Value Required attribute enables you to define an item as required, and that will make the APEX engine perform a NOT NULL validation on the item when the page is submitted. This will be done automatically and transparently by the APEX engine, without generating a visible validation action under the processing pane.

NOTE
If you are running APEX 5.1, with Compatibility Mode set to 5.1, on a modern browser that supports HTML5, the HTML5 client-side validation will be invoked prior to page submit. As mentioned, this is good only for improving the UI experience and must not replace the corresponding server-side validation.

In case of a NULL field, the APEX engine will raise a predefined error message in the following format: "#LABEL# must have some value." As you can see, the error message includes the label of the item, using a built-in substitution string.

TIP
*If, for any reason, you want to change the predefined error message, for example, to omit the item label or to style it differently, you can define your own. In the application Shared Components, under the Globalization group, select the Text Messages task and create a text message, **APEX.PAGE_ITEM_IS_ REQUIRED**, in the main language of the application, using the text you want. For example, the following would display your own error message phrase, and in boldface:*

```
#LABEL# - <span style="font-weight:bold;">item is required</span>
```

Maximum Length   This attribute sets the maximum number of characters the browser will allow you to enter into the field of the item. If this number is greater than the item's Width, the browser will (horizontally) scroll the input within the field. If the number is smaller, you will not be allowed to add any extra characters, even though it appears that you still have free (physical) space on the field.

NOTE
If the item represents an actual database object, this attribute should relate to the actual size of this object and must not exceed it. Using this attribute correctly will avoid runtime database errors such as "ORA-06502: PL/SQL: numeric or value error: character string buffer too small." When you're dealing with numbers, this attribute should take into account the characteristics and format of the number, such as scale, precision, decimal point, group separator, and plus/minus sign.

Advanced

The attributes under this group also have a strong impact on the appearance of items on the page, but they can also influence the page functionality. Following are some notes about these attributes:

CSS Classes, Custom Attributes, and Option HTML Attributes   These attributes specifically target the input section of the item. For example, the following code, in the Custom Attributes field, will display the content of the item input section in red:

```
style="color:red;"
```

This is also the field in which you attach HTML events to the item. This can be very useful for adding client-side (JavaScript) validations, which can provide an immediate feedback for the application users about their input, even before submitting the page. This can be used, for example, to verify a required length (for instance, nine digits for SSN); required format (for instance, digits only, phone or e-mail format, and such); valid dates (for example, alert about 31 days in 30-day months, using four digits for years, and such), and more. The following code will trigger a JavaScript function when a user leaves the current item:

```
onblur="validateItem(this);"
```

TIP
Bear in mind that HTML events can also be used with Dynamic Actions, using some degree of a declarative manner, mainly where syntax is concerned. After reading Chapter 9, which deals with Dynamic Actions, you can choose what method is best for you.

NOTE
As mentioned, client-side validations can improve the user experience, but they are not a replacement for server-side validations, which we'll discuss in Chapter 7. Client-side validations should be considered only as a "nice to have" feature.

In case of multiselect items, such as a checkbox or radio group, you can also style their options using the Option HTML Attributes field. The following attribute will display the options in boldface:

```
style="font-weight: bold;"
```

Note that this will not necessarily work, however, with the recent (responsive HTML5) themes, because those are using specific CSS classes to style the options, and these classes overcome inheritance. However, you can take advantage of the cascading principle (the first C in CSS) and define your own inline relevant CSS classes on the page level, and they will do the styling work for you. For example, with the Universal Theme, you can use code similar to the following to display checkbox or radio group options in boldface green text:

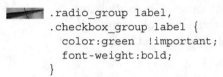

```
.radio_group label,
.checkbox_group label {
  color:green  !important;
  font-weight:bold;
}
```

Note that you need to use the **!important** keyword with the **color** property, because this property is specifically being used in the original (built-in) classes, and you want to make sure yours will take precedence.

Pre Text, Post Text   These attributes enable you to add a prefix and suffix to the input element of the item and can be used, for example, to add currency signs, unit notations (such as weights and measures), and such.

TIP
These fields also accept HTML code. For a long time, the Post Text field, holding an HTML button tag, was a simple option to generate a "button among items" that can fire JavaScript code. With recent versions, similar functionality can be achieved using Dynamic Actions (covered on Chapter 9), but it's not necessarily simpler to define or maintain, so you should choose what is best for you.

Warn On Unsaved Changes   On the page level of the Property Editor, you can use a mechanism that tracks changes to page items and warns the application users if they are trying to leave the page without saving those changes. You do this by setting the Warn On Unsaved Changes property to Yes. On the item level, this property enables you to determine which of the page items should be included in the change's tracking process, as, ultimately, not all items should be saved (for example, search/ filter items, temporary by nature items that are not associated with database objects, and such). You can instruct the tracking mechanism to follow the page default or to ignore changes on this particular item.

List Of Values (LOV)
This group, shown in Figure 4-16, is item-type dependent and will be visible only when relevant—items that include multiple options to be selected by the application user, such as Checkbox, Radio Group, Select List, Shuttle, Popup LOV, and List Manager.

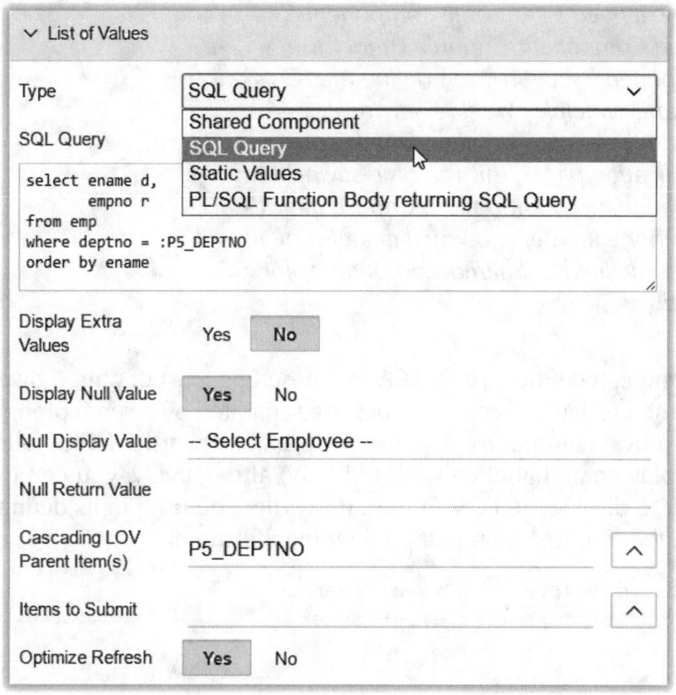

FIGURE 4-16. *The List Of Values (LOV) group*

The List Of Values comprises pairs of display values and return values. The display segment of the pair is what the user sees as the option to be selected, and the return part is the value submitted to the APEX engine, which is ultimately the item value, or in case of a multiselection item, a component of the value, which will include all the selected options.

NOTE
Most of the LOV-related items (Radio Group excluded) enable you to make more than a single value selection by setting the Allow Multi Selection property to Yes. If the returned value includes more than one selected value, it will be returned as a colon-delimited string. The exception is Popup LOV, which returns a comma-delimited string.

Now you need to decide the Type of the LOV, which determines how you are going to populate it. You can generate a Static Values list, which will include a fixed preset list of pairs of values, or you can generate a dynamic list based on a SQL query.

TIP
LOVs can be defined as reusable components in the Shared Components module (under the Other Components section). You define the LOVs using the same principles we'll review next, so if you repeatedly need to use the same LOV on various application pages, this is a time-saving and productivity enhancement option. Choose the Shared Component type, and you'll get a list of all the LOVs you defined as Shared Components for the application.

Static LOVs   You can define a static LOV by presetting a list of paired display and return values. The display and return values are separated by a semicolon, and each pair is separated by a comma. You can use the prefix keyword *STATIC*, followed by a colon, to display an alphabetically sorted LOV; alternatively, you can use the *STATIC2:* prefix to display the LOV in the same order you used in its definition. This code will yield the results shown in the following illustration:

```
STATIC:Red;Red,Yellow;Yellow,Green;Green
STATIC2:Red;Red,Yellow;Yellow,Green;Green
```

NOTE
(Advanced) Static LOVs cannot be translated using the APEX Translation mechanism. If your application needs to support multiple languages, you should use dynamic LOVs, which can be translated using the dynamic translations Utility.

Dynamic LOVs   Dynamic LOVs rely on SQL queries to generate the pairs of values that make up the LOV. The SQL **SELECT** statement must return only two columns: the first holds the displayed values and the second holds the returned ones. As you saw in Figure 4-16, you can use a static SQL Query or you can dynamically generate one, choosing the PL/SQL Function Body returning SQL Query type. This option gives you high flexibility in building the LOV the way you want.

In the following example, we added the item **P5_SORT_ORDER** (Figure 4-17), which enables the application user to sort the employee names displayed in a shuttle item, by returning the **ASC** or **DESC** keyword:

```
return 'select ename d, empno r from emp order by 1 ' || :P5_SORT_ORDER;
```

TIP
*Because you are dealing with a function body, your code must include a **return** statement. Moreover, if the function body is more complex and you need to use local variables, you can do that by using the PL/SQL anonymous block format, which includes the **DECLARE**, **BEGIN**, and **END** statements.*
*In addition, be aware of possible SQL injection scenarios when you are using page items fed by users in SQL statements. In the preceding example, you must validate that **P5_SORT_ORDER** contains only **ASC** or **DESC**. In general, it is your responsibility as a developer to prevent SQL injections; otherwise, your application and your data will be vulnerable.*

Cascading LOV Items   The last example is also a good demonstration of the cascading items principle. The way the list of displayed employees is built depends on the sorting order selected in the previous, or parent, item. In other scenarios, there may be so many possible options to display that you want to narrow down the list, while helping the users to easily locate what they are looking for. For example, if the user is trying to locate a street name, he can start by zooming in on a specific country or state, drill down to a particular city, and then the street. In each step, a more targeted list is built based on the user's previous selection(s).

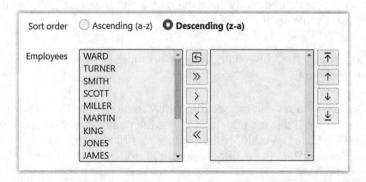

FIGURE 4-17.   *Sort order added to the application*

APEX fully supports a declarative definition of cascading LOV items; the LOV of an item is dependent upon the value of a parent item, and it is built at runtime using an Ajax call. Here are the properties you can use to define a cascading item(s):

■ **Cascading LOV Parent Item(s)**   This is the parent item for the current LOV. As you are dealing with a dynamic LOV, the **SELECT** statement should include this parent item in its **WHERE** clause (for example, the P5_DEPTNO item, in bind variable notation, in Figure 4-16). If the cascading chain includes more than one parent item (such as in the case of the street name), you can reference all the (higher level) participant parent items in a comma-delimited list. Whenever the value of these items is changed, each of the downstream cascading LOVs is being rebuilt, including empty LOVs, based on the changed value.

■ **Items To Submit**   The dependent LOV is being built by the APEX engine as part of an Ajax call. The server side needs access to the value(s) of the parent item(s), so those you named in the Cascading LOV Parent Item(s) field are automatically being saved into Session State. However, in some cases, the server side also needs access to other items that are not served directly as parent items, but are still relevant to the LOV building process (for example, the parent list includes product names and the cascading list includes possible package weights, which should be displayed according to a unit field—kg or pounds). You can name these items in this field and their values will also be saved in Session State every time one of the parent items is changed.

■ **Optimize Refresh**   A null value can be a legitimate and handled value of a parent item, and in this case, you should invoke the Ajax LOV building process for every value change in a parent item, regardless of null values, and set the Optimize Refresh property to No. In other cases, it's evident that a null value in a parent item yields empty (null) LOVs in all the downstream cascading items, and you can optimize the refresh process by not invoking the Ajax process and directly clear the relevant cascading LOVs. For these cases, you should set the property to Yes.

More LOV Properties   The LOV-related items have more unique properties dedicated only to them:

■ **Display Extra Values**   In the section "APEX Session State" a bit later in the chapter, we'll discuss how to initialize the page items, and you'll see that Session State is a major resource. It is possible that the value of a LOV item in Session State is no longer relevant (if, for example, the value was deleted from the list of valid options). In this case, if the Display Extra Values property is set to Yes, the non-valid (return) value will be displayed (as there is no valid matching display option). If this property is set to No, and the Session State value is not a valid one, the first option of the LOV is selected as the current value.

- **Display Null Value**   You can include a NULL option in the LOV by setting this property to Yes, and this option will be displayed first on the options list.

- **Null Display Value, Null Return Value**   If you enabled the previous property, you can set the displayed value that will represent NULL. As NULL is the first LOV option, this is the value the user will see first. You can also set a value that will represent the returned NULL value, or simply leave this property blank.

TIP
*Even if the value of the LOV item is required, you can still display a NULL value and use it to display a hint for the user—for example, a value similar to the following: -- **Select an employee's name** -- . If you defined the item to be required, the NOT NULL validation will issue an error message if the user does not select a non-null value (even if you set a tangible value to represent the returned NULL).*

Source
This group deals with a very primary and important task that's tightly related to the application business logic: generating the initialization value for the page item.

Source Type   APEX supports various sources, as Figure 4-18 shows, and you need to choose the Type based on the item characteristics and the application logic behind it: it's a single or multivalue item, it represents a database column, it holds a preset (static) value, or it is actually NULL from the start.

The following are the available source type options to initialize the page items:

- **Null**   Although this option appears last in the Type list, this is the default option, and it will set the initial value of the item to NULL.

- **Static Value**   This source type enables you to set an alphanumeric value as the initial value by revealing a Static Value field. You can use it to enter any static value you need, including zero (0), as the item initial value. However,

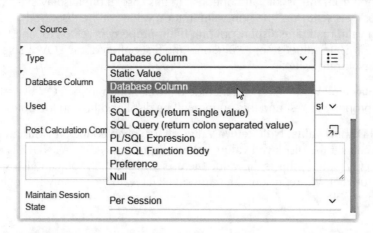

FIGURE 4-18. *Source types*

the Property Editor will not allow you to leave this field blank or to fill it with just a space character(s). If you need those, use the Null source type.

■ **Database Column**   This type associates the item with a database column, and selecting it reveals a Database Column field you should fill with the corresponding database column name, which is case-sensitive (usually, all uppercase).

NOTE
At this point, you enter only the column name, without referencing the table, which you specify as part of the page processes mentioned in the next paragraph. The Property Editor cannot verify the existence of such a column, so it is your responsibility, as developer, to enter the column name correctly.

You must use this type of source if you want the item to be included in the APEX built-in declarative data manipulation processes—the Automatic Row Fetch process, to initialize the item with a fetched value from a database column, or the Automatic Row Processing (DML) process, to apply **INSERT**, **UPDATE**, or **DELETE** actions to the item, after page submit. You will read more about this in Chapter 7, which deals with the built-in APEX processes.

- **Item**   The current item can be initialized with a value of any application- or page-level item, and not necessarily from the same page, as long as the source item was saved in Session State. Usually, this means that the source item was previously submitted during the present active APEX session.

- **SQL Query (return single value)**   You can select the initializing value using a SQL query that fetches a single value from a database table. Choosing this source type will reveal a SQL Query (Textarea) field, in which you'll enter the SQL query statement.

NOTE
*If the SQL query returns more than a single value,
only the first value will be used by the APEX engine.*

- **SQL Query (return colon separated value)**   With this source type you can initialize a multiselection item. The SQL Query field can hold a **SELECT** statement that fetches values from multiple rows. These will be concatenated by the APEX engine to a single colon-delimited string.

- **PL/SQL Expression**   Selecting this source type reveals a PL/SQL Expression field, in which you can enter a PL/SQL expression that yields a single value to be used as the item initializing value.

- **PL/SQL Function Body**   If a PL/SQL expression is not enough to produce the initializing value you need, this source type enables you to use a PL/SQL Function Body to return the value you need.

- **Preference**   APEX enables you, programmatically or with a dedicated page process, to save a user preference—a pair of preference name and value. The preferences are saved per user, across APEX sessions (that is, after being set, the preference will be available to you whenever the user is logged into the application). Selecting this source type reveals a Preference field, which enables you to name and fetch a specific preference and assign it to the item. (You can find more details about user preferences in Chapter 7, which deals with APEX computations and page processes that can be used to set and fetch the preferences.)

Source Used   After selecting the method of initializing the item value, you should instruct the APEX engine when to use it. You have two options—always use the selected source Type method to generate an initializing value, regardless of any previous values the item had during the present active APEX session, or use it only if the item was not initialized earlier. If the item was already assigned a value, and that value was submitted to the APEX engine and was saved in Session State, this will be the value to use, without reinvoking the source Type method.

APEX Session State

Earlier in the book, we mentioned Session State several times in various contexts. This is a good time to elaborate on this important concept and mechanism and help you see the influence it has on the value of APEX items.

Session State is a persistence mechanism that is managed by the APEX engine. It uses a database table in the APEX metadata schema to set or update values of the APEX application items constantly. Session State reflects and persists these values in different points in time, which we'll refer to as *Session State firing points*. Session State always pertains to a specific user and can be managed in two ways:

- **Per APEX session** The data is available throughout the entire APEX session but becomes stale and not usable when the APEX session is ended.

- **Per user, but across APEX sessions** The data is available to the users as long as they log into the application, regardless of the active APEX session (in a similar way to the user preferences). This is a simple and easy way, for example, to allow users to continue their work on the application exactly from where they ended it the last time.

We already mentioned Session State in the context of the stateless nature of the HTTP protocol, as the mechanism that helps you overcome it, and in a similar manner helps you overcome the life span of package variables (a database session, which in the APEX environment is very short and does not last throughout the APEX session). Having a database table that holds the values of the APEX items makes the values available to the APEX engine whenever it needs them, regardless of communication restrictions.

The Session State mechanism has several firing points. Some of them are fully automated and transparent to developers. Others involve manual coding, with some degree of declarative programming, and you can also manipulate Session State programmatically using APEX APIs.

The first, and probably the most notable, firing point is when an application page is submitted. Every submitted value on the page is saved into Session State (table), and only then the page processing phase begins, which, in turn, can also change Session State values as part of the second firing point.

Note that the page submit firing point is the only one that deals, automatically and transparently, with massive saves to Session State—all the submitted items on the page. All the other firing points are less generic and deal with pairs of specific items and their values.

The second firing point is not as targeted as the submit point, and it involves specific actions—setting or updating a value of an application- or page-level item, within an APEX computation or process. Whenever you are assigning a value to an item using a declarative computation or using the bind variable notation in PL/SQL code, the APEX engine updates the assigned value in Session State.

The third firing point is a page branch (which we'll discuss in Chapter 7). When you are branching from one page to another, or even self-branching to the same page, the branch action enables you, declaratively, to set item(s) value(s) in the target page. These values are saved in Session State, and as you'll see shortly, they can be used in the page rendering phase.

The fourth firing point, the **f?p** notation, is a manual manifestation of the third firing point—a manual branching/redirecting instruction. The **f?p** notation is part of the APEX URL. If you are familiar with the structure of a URL, you'll probably identify that you are dealing with a call to a function named f, passing it the p parameter—a colon-delimited string, where each segment represents a specific APEX element or functionality, based upon its location within the string. In this context, bear in mind that one of the segments enables you to name the items you want to save in Session State, and the adjacent segment enables you to list the corresponding values.

Dynamic Actions, which are thoroughly discussed in Chapter 9, also enable you to manipulate Session State values, especially as part of Ajax calls (in the APEX terminology, Execute PL/SQL Code). You can name the page items to submit: the page items that will be made available to the Ajax server side through Session State, and the items to return, which are values that were generated during the Ajax call and sent back to the client side. Those will be assigned to the corresponding page items, based on their Session State values.

Last, but not least, you can manipulate Session State programmatically. You can clear various portions of Session State, declaratively, using a dedicated page process, Clear Session State. It enables you to start clearing Session State for a single item on a page, going all the way up to clear Session State for the entire application. Moreover, the APEX APIs include some functions/ procedures to get and set Session State values. In this context, here are the most notable ones:

```
APEX_UTIL.SET_SESSION_STATE
APEX_UTIL.GET_SESSION_STATE
```

Now that you have a better understanding of Session State, it will be easier to understand the functionality of the source Used property. This property has two options:

- **Always, Replacing Any Existing Value In Session State**   This option actually tells the APEX engine to ignore any value the item has in Session State (if any), and always compute a new value, using the source Type method of the item. This option is the default for the Used property, and as of APEX 5.1, the required option (or a runtime error will be raised) for items with a Database Column type. Integrated with the Automatic Row Fetch process, the APEX engine will always initialize the item with a newly fetched value from the database and will not rely on any Session State value.

- **Only When Current Value In Session State Is Null**   Contrary to the first option, this option instructs the APEX engine to rely on the Session State value if one exists and ignore the source Type, which will be used only if the current Session State value for the item is NULL.

NOTE
Using the first option can lead to a scenario in which the on-screen displayed value of the item and its value in Session State are not the same, and this is a valid scenario. Bear in mind that using this option doesn't disable any Session State firing points. For example, in a page rendering phase, you can use a computation (included in the second firing point) to assign a value to an item. This value will be saved in Session State, but with a Used property of Always, it will not be displayed on screen, because with this option Session State values are ignored. Moreover, even though Session State is all about persistence, in the page rendering phase, the initializing values are actually being held in a temporary version of Session State. They will become persistent only after submitting the page. Going back to our example— an item with a displayed value different from the Session State value—at this point, if you reference the item using a bind variable notation, the APEX engine will use the displayed value and not the Session State value.

Confused? Yes, in some cases, the actual (referenced) value of an item can be set or used not as you expected. To help you resolve these scenarios, the Developer toolbar (which we reviewed in Chapter 3) includes the Session option. This opens a pop-up window displaying the current (real-time) Session State values, both at the application and page(s) levels. It's a great tool to use for a debugging session.

Post Calculation Computation   This property enables you to give the item displayed value a final tweak using a PL/SQL expression or by calling a PL/SQL function. Using the bind variable notation, you can reference the item itself or any other items in Session State. For example, the following code takes a value of a multiselect item (holding a list of available colors), which I hope you remember is a colon-delimited string, and replaces the colon with a comma and a space, making it more presentable on screen:

```
replace(:P4_AVAILABLE_COLORS,':',', ')
```

A stored value such as **Black:Navy:Red:Brown** will be displayed as Black, Navy, Red, Brown.

Maintain Session State   We already mentioned that Session State can be managed Per Session (APEX session), or Per User (across APEX sessions). This property enables you to set the appropriate management method for the underlying item.

Default

If the combination of the source Type and Used doesn't yield an initializing value that is not NULL, the Default type will be used to generate an item's value. You can leave this property unselected (and the item value will remain NULL), but if you selected a type—Static Value, PL/SQL Expression, or PL/SQL Function Body—it is required to provide the appropriate value or code.

Server-side Condition

On the APEX engine level, each page item can be conditioned to be rendered under specific terms that must be met; in order for the item to be rendered on page, the condition must be evaluated to be TRUE. The Property Editor enables you to do it declaratively, by providing you with a list of common conditions with matching parameters. If, however, the predefined conditions do not meet your needs, you can also define your own condition using SQL or PL/SQL expressions.

NOTE
You should use the predefined conditions whenever possible, not just because they are declarative and simpler, but mainly because they are more efficient and optimized for the APEX engine, which means they yield better performance for your application.

The list of predefined conditions includes the option Never (last on the list). With this condition, the item will never be rendered on page, but the APEX engine will still allocate it a database variable, which you can set and reference using the bind variable notation. Unlike the Hidden item type, which doesn't render on page but is included in the page HTML code, an item conditioned by Never will not be rendered and will not be included in the page HTML code. As such, it will be completely shielded from the application users and will be safer to use. The Never conditioned item acts similarly to an application item, but it will be defined on the page level, which should make it easier to understand its context and to maintain it. It is also good to remember the Never condition while running a debugging session. This condition is a quick and simple way to eliminate suspected APEX elements temporarily, while trying to pinpoint the source of a problem.

Read Only

This property enables you to conditionally define the item as read-only. It uses almost the same condition list as the Server-side Condition property is using, with the supplement of the Always condition.

Help

Things that are very clear to application developers are not always so clear to end users. The Help group enables you to define help instructions to the application users. Inline Help Text, a new attribute in APEX 5.1, enables you to display help text right below the item, as shown here:

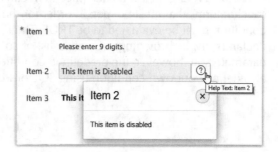

Read Only vs. Disabled

You already encountered the Disabled attribute (under the Settings group). So what is the difference between a Disabled item and a Read Only item? Well, the differences are both visual and functional.

Both attributes will not allow the user to change the item value, but a Disabled item retains the look and feel of an input element, while the Read Only item displays as regular text with some stylish features that depend on the application theme. In the following illustration, which was taken from an application using the Universal Theme, the Read Only item is being displayed in boldface. In some other APEX themes, it displays as normal text.

Item 1	This is a Text field
Item 2	This item is Disabled
Item 3	This item is Disabled (save Session State)
Item 4	**This item is Read-only**

Functionality-wise, according to the HTML standard, a Disabled item is not being submitted to the server (the APEX engine). As such, it cannot be saved in Session State. However, as you already saw, the Property Editor does give you the option to Save Session State. With this property set, the item is actually being defined (on the HTML level) as a Read Only item (using the HTML **readonly** attribute), but it still retains its appearance as an input item. The APEX engine explicitly defines on the page an extra hidden item, with the **readonly** attribute, which is being submitted as any other (nondisabled) items on page and being saved in Session State.

From this description, you can see that the APEX Read Only item and an HTML item with the **readonly** attribute are not the same. APEX implements the Read Only item as a compound object comprising several HTML elements. On the other hand, the HTML **readonly** attribute targets a specific **<input>** element.

Another functional difference between a Disabled item and a Read Only item is that a Disabled item is unclickable and therefore cannot get focus, which means it cannot invoke an HTML event. A Read Only item can get focus, however.

Finally, note that both Disabled and Read Only items can be manipulated using JavaScript (for example, with the built-in **$s()** function, to assign a new value).

The attribute accepts HTML code, so you can style your help as you want. For example, this code displays the inline help text in a navy blue color:

```
<span style="color:Navy;">Please enter 9 digits.</span>
```

The Help text attribute enables display of help text at the user's request. If this attribute is not left blank, the APEX engine will attach a small help icon adjacent to the input field. If the user clicks this icon, a pop-up window will be displayed with the content of this attribute, which can also be styled using HTML code.

Comments

Every APEX item has a Comment field. *Use it!* This property is more targeted than the (page level) Developer Comments and should be considered part of the application development documentation. Commenting is, of course, extra important if you are developing as part of a team, but you may find it extremely useful even if as a single developer. It is especially so with logic- and flow-related items (such as application items, the hidden items we use as flags, temp variables, and others). It's easy to guess the roles of items on screen, but it might be not so easy with the other items, more so over time. Their functionality may be very clear to you when you are deep into your code and all the logic is fresh in your mind. As time passes, and when members of the development team are being replaced by new ones, it might be much more complex and time-consuming to figure things out. Proper comments can save you time and effort when bringing in new developers or maintaining the application over time.

APEX Buttons

APEX buttons are page elements that have two major functionalities: they can invoke a specific action, such as submitting a page or triggering a Dynamic Action, and they can have navigational capabilities, such as redirecting to an application page. Use the Page Designer to create, define, and position the buttons on the page by setting the button properties in a similar manner to page items.

Button Properties

The appearance of a button (its shape, size, borders, color, and so on) and the way it renders on page (template base or legacy options such as HTML button) are theme- and template-dependent. As such, the button properties that are available may vary. However, as mentioned, since the Universal Theme is a standard theme for APEX 5.1, we will review the button features and properties under this theme. You'll need to use several major properties while defining button functionality and positioning it on a page.

Identification

The following properties identify the button on a page:

- **Button Name**   This name should uniquely identify the button on the page, and it must not include spaces, new lines, and the characters & , . ' : + ? " ^. Unlike the item name, the button name doesn't have to be uppercase. The generic names the Page Designer assigns to new buttons are New, New_1, and so forth.

- **Label**   This is the text that appears on the button.

The REQUEST Attribute

The APEX engine maintains a built-in attribute called **REQUEST**. When you click a button, the button name is automatically assigned to the **REQUEST** attribute. By default, the scope (life span) of the **REQUEST** value is the current Accept processing—the APEX actions (computations, validations, processes, and branches, which we'll discuss in Chapter 7) the APEX engine performs after a page submit. After the page branches to a new page (including self-branch) the **REQUEST** value is set to **NULL** automatically. However, if the Action property of the button involves redirecting to another application page (without submitting the current page), you are allowed to set the **REQUEST** value manually, and the APEX engine will assign it to the **REQUEST** of the redirected page. As such, the **REQUEST** value will also be available to the Show process of the page (its rendering phase).

The **REQUEST** value is very useful if you want to condition APEX actions with clicking a specific button. Note that the **REQUEST** value is case-sensitive, so a *Go* button and a *GO* button will not be evaluated the same way.

The Property Editor for these actions includes a Server-side Condition section with two **REQUEST**-related properties. The first, When Button Pressed, lists the names of all the buttons on the page, and their **REQUEST** value is used to identify if the clicked button is the one in the condition. The second property, Type, lists all the relevant APEX built-in conditions, including four **REQUEST** related conditions: Request = Value, Request != Value, Request is contained in Value, and Request is NOT contained in Value. In the same manner, you can also condition the rendering of page items and even the buttons themselves.

You can reference the **REQUEST** attribute by using the substitution string **&REQUEST.** (the trailing period is part of the name); the PL/SQL **V('REQUEST')** function; the **APEX_APPLICATION.G_REQUEST** global variable; or the bind variable notation **:REQUEST**. The value of **REQUEST** can also be available to you in JavaScript, if one was passed to the Show process during a branch action. The APEX engine embeds the **REQUEST** current value on the page using a hidden HTML item with the **id** of **pRequest**.

Layout

The following properties determine the position of the button on the page:

- **Sequence** The sequence number determines the order in which the button will be rendered on the page. With buttons in the same region and button position, the button with the lower sequence will be rendered first. Even though the APEX engine will not raise an error message if you assign the same sequence to more than one button in the same region, you should avoid doing so to insure consistency in the application appearance after export and import.

- **Region** Each button must belong to a specific region, and the button layout is determined by its structure (location, size, and borders).

- **Button Position** This property is responsible for the position of the item in the region to which it belongs. The relevant region templates include some predefined placeholders for buttons with specific functionalities, such as Copy, Edit, Create, Change, Delete, and more. Using the matching Button Position values, buttons can be positioned in these locations (regardless of their actual functionality).

A second group of possible locations places the buttons in a relative location to the upper and lower borders of the region:

- **Top Of Region, Below Region, Top And Bottom Of Region, and so on** With these positions, the Horizontal Alignment property is available, and you can align the button with the borders of the region.

- **Left Of Title and Right Of Title** Positions the item to the left or to the right of the region title.

- **Region Body** Veteran APEX developers know this as the "button among items." This position enables you to locate buttons next to existing page items, as you can see in the next illustration. With the Region Body position, you gain access to several more layout-related properties, such as Start New Row, Column, Column Span, and more. We'll review these properties as part of the page item layout properties discussion in the next chapter.

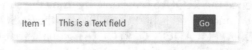

Appearance

The following properties are responsible for the look and feel of the button:

- **Button Template** The Universal Theme supports three major types of templates that shape the general appearance of the button: Text, Icon, and Text With Icon. The Text template generates the often-used plain button, similar to the left button in the following illustration. The Icon template enables you to generate a button with an icon for a label, similar to the middle button. The right button features the Text With Icon template, which is a merge of the first two template types.

- **Hot** This Yes/No property enables you to distinguish a specific button on the page by coloring its background (using the Curious Blue, #2D7BBB, color). Usually, this is the most important or most used button on the page, and you want to draw the user's attention to it. In the Page Designer, you can define more than one hot button per page, but doing so might defeat the original purpose of drawing the user's attention.

- **Template Options** This property opens a modal dialog where you can tweak some major attributes that control the appearance of the button, such as size, background color, space from other objects on page, and more.

- **CSS Classes** Use this property to apply your own classes to the button, if the default and declarative attributes are not sufficient to meet your needs.

- **Icon CSS Classes** If the template you chose supports icons, this property enables you to pick the icon-related classes for the icon you want to use. The first class is for the icon itself (from the default Icon library that is associated with the theme—Font Awesome or Font APEX). You can add extra classes that fine-tune the general appearance of the icon, such as Size, Animation, Rotate, Modifier, and Status. The Help tab for this property includes a link to the Universal Theme Sample Application (at https://apex .oracle.com/pls/apex/f?p=42:4000). This application includes an Icons module where you, declaratively, can choose and tweak the icon you need and copy and paste the related classes into the property field. For example, the following set of classes, which are separated by a space, relates to the exchange icon:

```
fa-exchange fa-3x fa-flip-horizontal fam-information fam-is-warning
```

Behavior

The properties of this section determine the functionality of the button.

Action   You can attach five basic actions to each button:

- **Submit Page**   Clicking a button with this action submits the page. The button will trigger the page Accept process; page items are saved to Session State, and the APEX engine performs all the actions you defined for the page processing phase, which we'll discuss thoroughly in Chapter 7. A button with this action has another property, Execute Validations. We already mentioned some of the client-side validations you can attach to page items, and in Chapter 7 we'll review the server-side validations. In this context, remember that you can instruct the APEX engine whether or not to execute the server-side validations, and with the application Compatibility Mode set to 5.1, also the client-side built-in validations. You will want to do that, for example, if the button is going to clear the page, delete a record on the database, or trigger a search action, while self-branching. Most of the page validations are not relevant to these actions, and you can waive them. Still, you can set specific validations to run anyway, using the Always Execute attribute.

- **Redirect To Page In This Application**   This action enables you to click the button and be redirected to another page in your application, without submitting the page. In this case, you need to set the Target property. Clicking this property opens a modal dialog, Link Builder – Target, which enables you, declaratively, to define the target page, set item values, clear Session State, manually set a **REQUEST** value (if relevant), and so on. Note that if you choose to clear Session State on the target page, and also set item values on this page, the APEX engine will first clear the current Session State of the page and then assign the new values to the page items.

- **Redirect To Page In A Different Application**   This action has the same functionality as the previous one, but the target page is in a different application and you need to provide the target application ID or alias.

- **Redirect To URL**   This property can hold a URL in the **f?p** notation. In pre-5.x versions, this action was very useful when you needed to exceed an APEX wizard's limitations (for example, passing up to three items to the target page; if you needed more, you had to construct the appropriate URL manually). With the Link Builder wizard, you no longer need to do that. Moreover, using the **javascript:** keyword, you can also use this action to trigger JavaScript code, although you can do the same using

Dynamic Actions (which is the preferable way). Note that for all the actions that involve redirection to a new page, you can use the Warn On Unsaved Changes properties to instruct the APEX engine not to check changes that have been made to item values on the page, or act according to the page default.

■ **Defined By Dynamic Action**   This action tells the APEX engine that the actual functionality of the button is set by a Dynamic Action, which we'll review in Chapter 9. Similar to the Submit Page action, the Execute Validations property is also available for this action.

Database Action   This property is relevant to the Page Submit action, on pages that include the built-in Automatic Row Processing (DML) process (which we'll discuss on Chapter 7). This process supports three DML actions in the database: Insert, Update, and Delete. However, the APEX engine must know which of the three it should perform. One way of doing this is to rely on the **REQUEST** value, and each DML action has some predetermined **REQUEST** values that are associated with it. (You can see the list in the Help tab for the Supported Operations property of the Automatic Row Processing (DML) process.) Another option is to associate the button explicitly with one of the DML actions by setting this property.

Advanced
This section includes two properties:

■ **Static ID**   This property enables you to assign a static ID to the HTML **id** attribute of the buttons. This gives you direct access and JavaScript manipulation options to the button element through the page DOM.

■ **Custom Attributes**   This property enables you to apply individual HTML attributes to the button. This is useful when you don't have an existing CSS class that can achieve what you need.

Server-side Condition
Buttons can be rendered on a page conditionally, and the Type property lists the available predefined conditions. The condition often depends on the button's functionality. For example, a save new record button should not be rendered if you are working on an existing record. It can be conditioned if Item is NULL, and the item is the one holding the primary key. In a similar manner, a delete button should be rendered only if Item is NOT NULL, and the item in this case is also the primary key holder.

Summary

In this chapter, we reviewed the basic APEX objects and elements and discussed the concepts behind them. We started at the root of the tree, with the APEX Instance, and climbed all the way up, through APEX Workspaces, which contain the APEX applications—Desktop, Mobile, and Websheets. Next, we discussed themes and templates and how they shape your application pages. These include APEX regions that hold the APEX items and buttons. In the next chapter, you'll get familiar with the Page Designer and how to use it to create and define various APEX objects we discussed and how to position them on the application page.

CHAPTER
5

The Page Designer

Good integrated development environments have traditionally been client-based software that require you to download the program to your local operating system (OS) and then install it. You then launch the program from the OS and connect to something, such as a database or web server, to commit and deploy your application changes. These IDEs all look similar—page structure on the left, a main canvas in the middle, and a property editor on the right. This model has worked for countless IDEs and is now the structure for APEX's Page Designer. APEX 5 with the Page Designer has provided a true IDE structure for building applications on the Web. As with all APEX versions, Page Designer is 100 percent browser-based with no client software to download.

Installing the Sample Database Application

Before we begin, you need to install the sample database application. This is easy to do—in fact, most default APEX installs already include this app. If it is installed, you can skip this section; if not, read on.

1. Click the Packaged Apps tab at the far right:

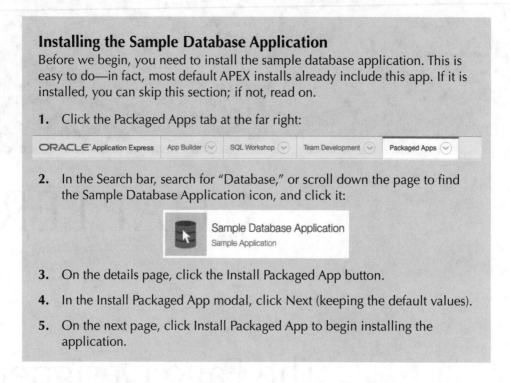

2. In the Search bar, search for "Database," or scroll down the page to find the Sample Database Application icon, and click it:

3. On the details page, click the Install Packaged App button.

4. In the Install Packaged App modal, click Next (keeping the default values).

5. On the next page, click Install Packaged App to begin installing the application.

Navigating the New Page Designer

Let's use the Sample Database Application to learn about the new Page Designer. Start by editing a page in the application.

1. Click the App Builder tab.

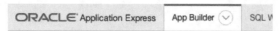

2. To see details for the Sample Database Application on the App Builder home page, click the application's name in the list view, or click the icon in the icon view. Both views are shown next:

3. Now let's open page 1 to start editing it. On the App Builder home page, click Page 1, Sample Database Application, in either the icon view or list view. Both views are shown in Figure 5-1.

FIGURE 5-1.   *Choose the Sample Database Application*

The Page Designer is one of the biggest changes in APEX 5. Those who have used previous versions of APEX may draw similarities between the Page Designer and the Tree View page developer in APEX 4.2. Figure 5-2 shows the Page Designer home page.

Let's start with a tour of the Page Designer.

The Toolbar

Near the top of the page, under the page tabs, is the Page Designer toolbar. At the far left is the Breadcrumb bar, shown next. Click the Application number to return to the details page. Click the up arrow to open the App Builder main page.

Application 740 \ **Page Designer**

Next is the Page Finder, where you can see the page you are currently on or easily navigate to other pages:

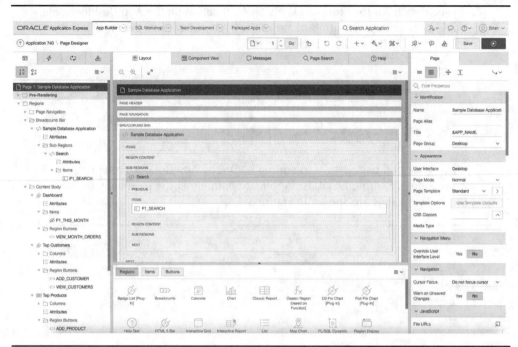

FIGURE 5-2. *The Page Designer home page*

There are three ways to open a page from the Page Finder:

- Click the page icon to open the Page Finder pop-up list of values (Figure 5-3), where you can use the page grouping tabs or the Search field to find and open the page you want.

- Click the page up or down arrow to move to the previous or next page, respectively.

- Enter the page number you want in the page number field and press ENTER/ RETURN or click Go.

Further to the right on the toolbar is a Lock button. Click this button to lock the page so that no other developers can make changes. This is very useful if your page is ready to move into production and you don't want other developers to make changes.

The next two buttons enable you to undo or redo changes you make on a page before the page has been saved:

Page Finder			⊗
Current User Interface	Current Group	All Pages	Recently Edited

🔍 Search ⟩

Page Number	Page Name	User Interface	Group
0	Page Zero	Desktop	Desktop
1	Sample Database Application	Desktop	Desktop
2	Customers	Desktop	Desktop
3	Products	Desktop	Desktop
4	Orders	Desktop	Desktop
5	Sales by Month	Desktop	Desktop
6	Product Details	Desktop	Desktop
7	Customer Details	Desktop	Desktop
8	Order Confirmation	Desktop	Desktop

FIGURE 5-3. *The Page Finder pop-up list of values*

Next is the plus icon. Click it to open the Create dropdown menu, where you can create pages, forms, and reports as well as page components such as regions and Team Development tasks.

Next is the Utilities dropdown menu:

From this menu, you can select the following actions:

- **Delete Page** Deletes the current page. A confirmation page asks you to be sure before the deletion occurs.

- **Advisor** Checks your application for security issues, programming errors, and best practices defined by the APEX team. After selecting this option, expand the Checks To Perform region to expose all the individual areas and components the page advisor will look for when running. Use the checkboxes next to specific items to add or remove them. After performing the page check, the advisor will present a results page outlining found issues, where on the page they are located, and why each particular component was flagged. This is a very useful tool to run on pages before sending them to production as well as a proactive way to check pages during development.

- **Caching** Indicates what pages and regions are currently being cached by APEX.

- **Attribute Dictionary** Quick link to the Attribute Dictionary.

- **History** Quick link to a report that displays recent modifications made to all the elements of the current page.

■ **Export** Quick link to export pages and page components on this page.

■ **Cross Page Utilities** Quick link to a group of utilities you can use to perform mass actions on multiple pages simultaneously, as well as a summary report of components used per page. Use these utilities to lock multiple pages at once, to delete multiple pages at once, and to grid edit multiple pages at once, changing various aspects such as security, name, template, and title.

■ **Application Utilities** Quick link to the Application Utilities page.

■ **Page Groups** Quick link to the Page Groups utility. Use page groups to group like pages together, or use them in conditional statements when building applications. (For example, use the PAGE_GROUP column on the APEX_APPLICATION_PAGES table.)

■ **Upgrade Application** Creates a report that helps you upgrade components after you upgrade your application from a previous version.

APEX Preferences and the Page Designer

A few options that you set in your APEX Preferences affect the Page Designer. To view these options, go to the Account Menu tab at the upper-right corner of the Page Designer home page. Click this tab to open the User information menu, shown next. Then click the Preferences button.

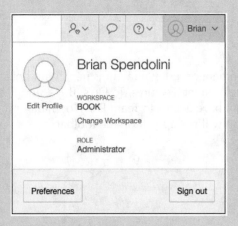

(Continued)

In the modal pop-up are three options that pertain to the Page Designer:

- **Enable Legacy Component View**   Enables the legacy Component View button in the Component view on the main canvas panel.
- **Run Application In New Window**   Applies only to developers using Mozilla Firefox and Microsoft Internet Explorer. When set to Yes, the default browser preferences are ignored and a new window always opens. When set to No, the runtime application opens in a new window or tab based on browser preferences.
- **Use Single Window To Run All Applications**   If set to Yes, each application you run from the App Builder will reuse a window or tab used for running the previous application. If set to No, each application you run will be opened in its own window or tab.

Next is the settings button, which you can use to change from a three-pane layout to a two-pane layout, or to reset the Page Designer layout. (The next section, "The Three Panes," discusses these panes.)

The Team Development dropdown menu is next, with links to all four major sections of Team Development: Features, To Do's, Bugs, and Feedback Entries. If your developers do not have access to Team Development or it was disabled in the Workspace, this button will not appear on the toolbar.

The next tool, the speech bubble with a plus sign, is the Developer Comments button. Hover over this button to see a tooltip indicating the number of comments made on this particular page.

Click this button to create a Developer Comment, Bug, or To Do in a modal window, as shown in Figure 5-4. Modal windows like this one don't require that you leave the page you're working on, which is very helpful if you are in the middle of creating or modifying page components and need to add a developer comment, bug, or to do item. Click the button, add your comment, and continue working without interrupting your workflow.

Next up on the toolbar is the Shared Components button. Click it to go straight to the Shared Components page. (You'll learn more about Shared Components in the upcoming chapters.)

The last two buttons on the toolbar are the Save and Save And Run buttons. Clicking the Save button saves all the changes you made to your page. Clicking the Save And Run button not only saves your page, but runs it, opening it in another browser window or tab or in the same window, depending on your APEX preferences. Use the Save button if you need to continue making changes or adding components to your page; use the Save and Run button if you want to see the changes in the application itself.

Create a Developer Comment, Bug or To Do   ×

Application	**740. Sample Database Application** ⑦
Page	1. Sample Database Applica ⌄ ⑦
* Type	Developer Comment ⌄ ⑦

Developer Comment Details

* Comment
```



```
⑦

Cancel   View Comments   Create

FIGURE 5-4. *Developer Comment modal*

The Save and Save And Run buttons can also help with productivity. When making multiple changes on multiple items in APEX 4.2, you had to visit multiple pages for each item. In APEX 5, you stay in the Page Designer, can make multiple changes on multiple items, and can then save all the changes at once using these two buttons.

The Three Panes

The Page Designer is divided into three panes, as labeled in Figure 5-5: Page Panels, Main Canvas, and the Property Editor. (The APEX documentation calls these the Left Pane, Central Pane, and Right Pane.)

NOTE
Separating each pane are window splitters that let you adjust the pane's width.

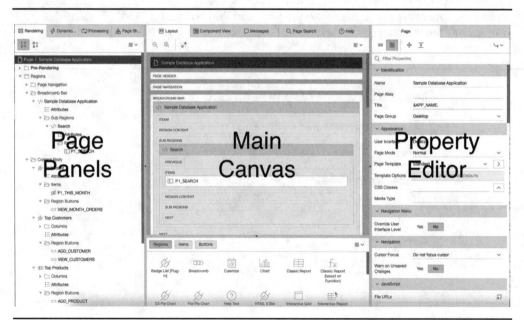

FIGURE 5-5. *The three panes of the Page Designer*

The Page Panels, or Left Pane

There are four page panels: the Rendering panel, the Dynamic Actions panel, the Processing panel, and the Page Shared Components panel, as shown next.

☰ Rendering	⚡ Dynamic Actions	⟳ Processing	⚙ Page Shared Components

The Rendering Panel The Rendering panel (Figure 5-6) is similar to the Tree View in APEX 4.2. It shows all the components, regions, and items on the current page.

Across the top of the Rendering panel are three buttons: the Group By Processing Order button, the Group By Component Type button, and the Menu button.

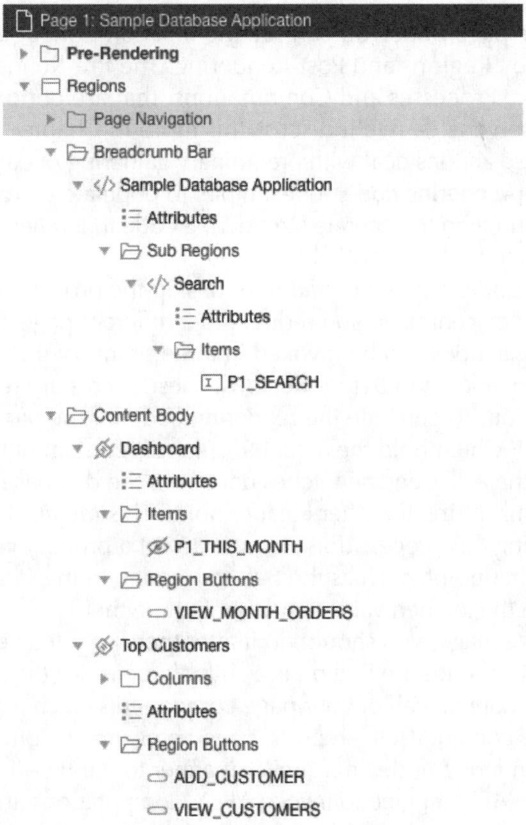

FIGURE 5-6. *The Rendering panel for the page*

- **Group By Processing Order**   Orders your page tree so that the processes and items that render first are displayed at the top of the list, with other components listed according to the order in which they'll be processed upon page rendering.

- **Group By Component Type**   Groups the page tree into component folders such as Regions, Buttons, and Page Items.

- **Menu**   Contains options to expand all of your tree folders to show all leaves and nodes or collapse the tree into the main tree nodes or folders.

Click the first button, Group By Processing Order, to take a closer look at the tree structure itself. For all pages, the current page is shown at the top:

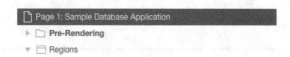

Directly under the page node you can see the first component group, Pre-Rendering, followed by Regions and Post-Rendering. The Pre-Rendering node contains APEX actions, Processes and Computations, that are performed by the APEX engine on the server side (we'll discuss this more in Chapter 7).

In our context, these actions deal with preliminary gathering of data that is needed for generating a proper rendering code, for example, to populate correctly the initial values of page items and then to generate a rendering code that reflects that. Another Pre-Rendering APEX action that is available to you is a Branch. You can instruct the APEX engine, usually under a certain condition, to skip the process of generating a rendering code for the current page and redirect to a different page altogether.

The Pre-Rendering actions can be invoked in three points of the rendering cycle: Before Header, After Header, and Before Regions. These points are related to the APEX engine preparations to generate the rendering code for the page HTML header and the page region(s), which hold the actual (displayed) content of the page. For example, by default, the APEX engine fetches data from the database in order to initialize the page items during the After Header point. This means that if you are interested in influencing this process (for example, to set a primary key value) you should do it in an earlier point, such as the Before Header. In the same manner, if you want to reference the fetched values and manipulate them prior to displaying them on the application page, you should do it after they were fetched but before rendering the region(s). The Before Region is a suitable point for that.

The Regions node contains all of your page components, such as navigation, breadcrumbs, and the content itself—reports, page items, and so on.

Lastly, the Post-Rendering node, in a similar manner to the Pre-Rendering node, enables us through the APEX engine to invoke APEX Computations and Processes that can interact and influence the rendering code of the page. This was generated during the previous stages and may include referencing the page HTML DOM itself.

The Post-Rendering actions can be invoked in three points, After Regions, Before Footer, and After Footer, the last of which is probably the most useful, as at this point generating the page HTML DOM is complete. For example, we can use the following PL/SQL code, within an APEX Process with an After Footer Point, to inject a JavaScript code that colors red negative values of a specific page item:

```
if :P3_BALANCE < 0 then
  htp.script('$x("P3_BALANCE").style.color = "red";');
end if;
```

Click the Group By Component Type button to reorder your page components. The first node under your main page node is the Regions node. Similar to the Regions node for Group By Processing Order, this node contains page navigation, breadcrumbs, and the content itself:

The Buttons node contains all the buttons on the page. Expand the node to see the buttons on the page grouped by region:

Click any of the button names, and the Main Canvas panel will update to indicate where that button is located on the page; in addition, the Property Editor will refresh to show details about that particular button. Click the VIEW_MONTH_ORDERS button under Dashboard to see how the Main Canvas and Property Editor refresh to show location and details:

The Page Items node is similar to the Buttons node—it groups all the items according to the region they belong to. Click Page Items, and then click P1_SEARCH under the Search region. The Main Canvas and Property Editor update to show location and details:

The Dynamic Actions Panel The next panel in the Page Panels is the Dynamic Actions panel:

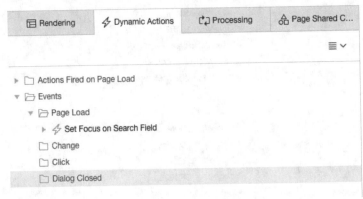

The Dynamic Actions toolbar contains only the Menu toolbar button. Listed within the panel are two main nodes for page 1 of the Sample Database Application: Actions Fired On Page Load and Events.

Dynamic Actions are covered fully in Chapter 9; for now, just know that they are event handlers based on a JavaScript framework built into APEX. These event handlers can be created without your having to write a single line of code and can fire or run at various points in your page. Dynamic Actions listed under Actions Fired On Page Load usually deal with preparing the page for the user. The Dynamic Action on page 1 of the Sample Database Application sets the cursor within the search field on the page when the page loads or renders. This is helpful—the user who comes to the page doesn't have to use the mouse to click into this field, because the cursor is already there, so the user can begin typing immediately.

The Events node deals with all other Dynamic Action firing points. The sample application has only one event (Set Focus On Search Field), which you can see under the Page Load node. Other types of events are Click events (a user clicks a page element), Change events (the value of a page element changes), Key events (a set of keyboard events such as key presses and releases), and Mouse events (mouse enters and mouse leaves).

You can also create Dynamic Actions in this panel by right-clicking any top-level node or subnode to open the Create Dynamic Action pop-up menu:

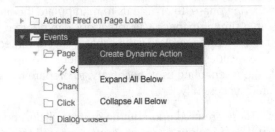

You can also edit and add or delete existing Dynamic Actions by right-clicking an existing action to open a pop-up menu:

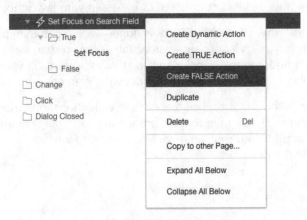

The Processing Panel   The Processing panel, shown next, contains all the page processing on your page. Where Dynamic Actions contain client-side processing, the Processing panel contains server-side or database processing.

These processes are divided into subcategories that indicate when the processes will run on your page. If you click the Group By Component Type button at the top of the panel, you'll see that processing is divided into four component types: Computations, Validations, Processes, and Branches:

- **Computations**   We mentioned earlier that Computations can be used during the page rendering phase, to enable us to manipulate the initial values of page items. In a similar manner, Computations can be used in the Processing phase to enable us to manipulate values that were submitted by the page or to generate new values based on submitted values. Computations are fired before Validations, enabling us, if necessary, to prepare the submitted values to be validated successfully.

- **Validations**   These are fired upon button or item clicks and are used to check for valid data in your pages or forms. (We will talk more about Validations in Chapter 7; as a best practice, data validation must be enforced at the database level. Client-side data validations are helpful for instant user feedback but can be circumvented or bypassed with JavaScript blockers.)

- **Processes**   This is where the work is done—where you manipulate data, call web services, clear or set session state, or even send e-mails. Processes, like other nodes in this panel, can run at various points in your page and will probably be the most popular processing elements you use.

- **Branches**   You can associate branches to validations, processes, and page submits. These components branch the user to a specific point in your application. You can branch to a page, to a procedure, or even an external URL.

Page Shared Components Panel   In the Page Shared Components panel, you can view, edit, and create Shared Components. Right-click a component name to create a new component or edit an existing one.

⊞ Rendering	⚡ Dynamic Actions	⌷ Processing	⚙ Page Shared Components

≡ ˅

▸ ☐ Navigation Menu
▸ ☐ Navigation Bar
   ☐ Lists of Values
▸ ☐ Lists
   ☐ Authorizations
   ☐ Build Options
   ☐ Data Load Tables
   ☐ Web Service References
▸ ☐ Breadcrumbs
▸ ☐ Templates

The Main Canvas, or Central Pane

The Main Canvas, or Central Pane, includes five tabs: Layout, Component View, Messages, Page Search, and Help.

Layout Tab   The Layout tab (Figure 5-7) is a visual representation of the regions, items, and buttons that make up an APEX page. We will use the Layout tab extensively in later chapters, but know that you can select multiple items, drag-and-drop, delete, and edit any component as well as hover over a particular component to see more information.

Across the top of the Layout tab is a toolbar. Two particular buttons to keep in mind (from left to right) are the Expand button and the Layout Menu button, shown next:

Clicking the Expand button expands the Layout tab to take up the entire Page Designer window. It moves the right and left window splitters fully out to the right and left sides of the web page.

Clicking the Layout Menu button lets you decide and customize what content is shown on the canvas. For example, you can hide legacy APEX positions, hide empty positions, hide global elements, as well as hide page components such as buttons and items. To make a specific region fill the Layout pane, select the region in the Main Canvas. Then click the Layout Menu button and select Display From Here.

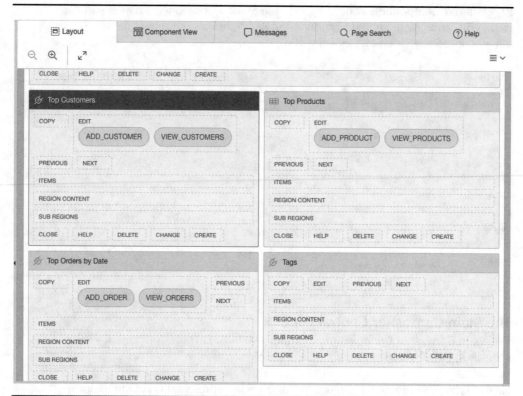

FIGURE 5-7. *The Layout tab*

The selected region fills the Layout pane. To restore the view, click the Layout Menu button and select Display From Page. Alternatively, you can right-click a region and select the same menu choices.

At the bottom of the Layout Canvas is the Gallery panel (Figure 5-8), where you can quickly select Regions, Items, and Buttons and drag-and-drop them onto your Canvas. Hover the mouse over any component of the Gallery to see a tooltip with information about that particular component.

Component View Tab   The Component View lays out the page in sections and lists the components in those sections. For users of APEX 4.2 and earlier, this view will look familiar. Click any component or region to work with that component's properties in the Property Editor (Figure 5-9).

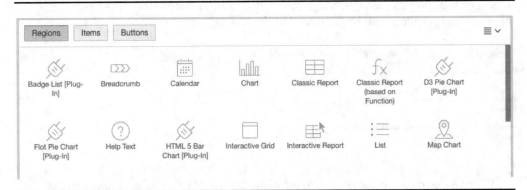

FIGURE 5-8. *The Gallery panel*

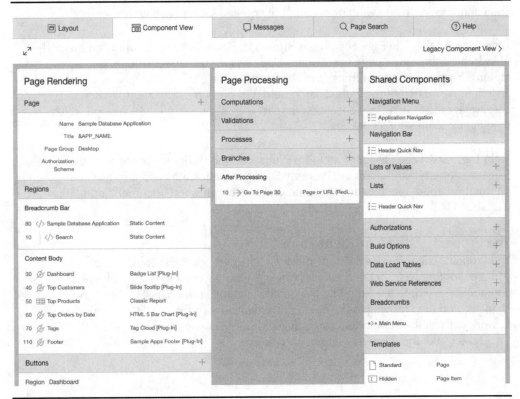

FIGURE 5-9. *The Component View*

Messages Tab When you're editing and creating components in the Page Designer, all errors and warnings will be presented in the Messages tab:

🖹 Layout	🔲 Component View	💬 Messages ③	🔍 Page Search	⑦ Help
Process → New → Source → PL/SQL Code Is required!				
Validation → New → Error → Error Message Is required!				
Validation → New → Validation → PL/SQL Expression Is required!				

When an element on the page is in error, the Messages tab displays a small circle indicating that errors were found. The Messages tab indicates two types of messages: errors (indicated in red) and warnings (indicated in yellow). Selecting an error or warning message displays the associated attribute in the appropriate color in the Property Editor on the right and will pull cursor focus directly to the errant property. You cannot save a page with errors on it, but you can save a page with warnings.

Page Search Tab The Page Search tab, shown in Figure 5-10, is an ultra-fast method of searching through a page's metadata. Use this tab to search through items, regions, buttons, report columns, and Dynamic Actions, to name a few. To use Page Search, enter search terms in the Search field and press RETURN/ENTER. To match the case, select the Match Case checkbox, and to search for a regular expression, select the Regular Expression checkbox.

Help Tab The Page Designer includes Help for every Property Editor attribute. Select a property attribute in the Property Editor and click the Help tab. You'll see information about the item and, in some cases, examples and documentation links (Figure 5-11).

The Property Editor, or Right Pane

The Property Editor (Figure 5-12) displays all attributes for the current component you are working with. In previous versions of APEX, you had to work with one component at a time, clicking into the details, making your changes, saving the changes, and then moving to the next component. The Property Editor enables you to work with all the components on a page without leaving the page.

At the top of the Property Editor is the toolbar:

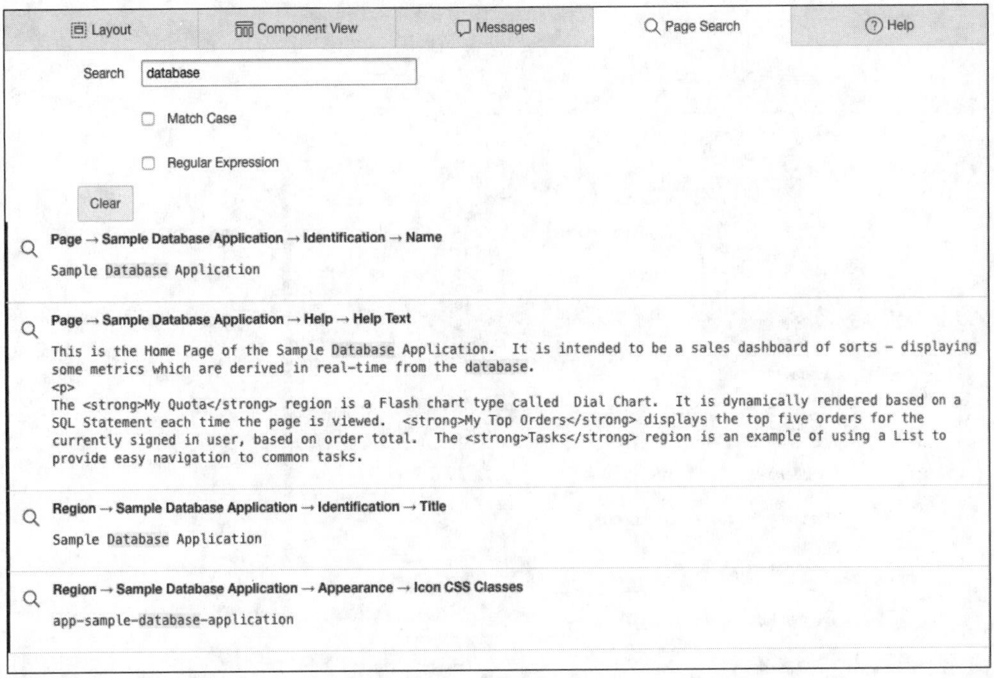

⧉ Layout	▥ Component View	▢ Messages	◷ Page Search	⑦ Help

Search database

☐ Match Case

☐ Regular Expression

Clear

◷ **Page → Sample Database Application → Identification → Name**

Sample Database Application

◷ **Page → Sample Database Application → Help → Help Text**

This is the Home Page of the Sample Database Application. It is intended to be a sales dashboard of sorts – displaying some metrics which are derived in real-time from the database.
<p>
The My Quota region is a Flash chart type called Dial Chart. It is dynamically rendered based on a SQL Statement each time the page is viewed. My Top Orders displays the top five orders for the currently signed in user, based on order total. The Tasks region is an example of using a List to provide easy navigation to common tasks.

◷ **Region → Sample Database Application → Identification → Title**

Sample Database Application

◷ **Region → Sample Database Application → Appearance → Icon CSS Classes**

app-sample-database-application

FIGURE 5-10. *The Page Search tab*

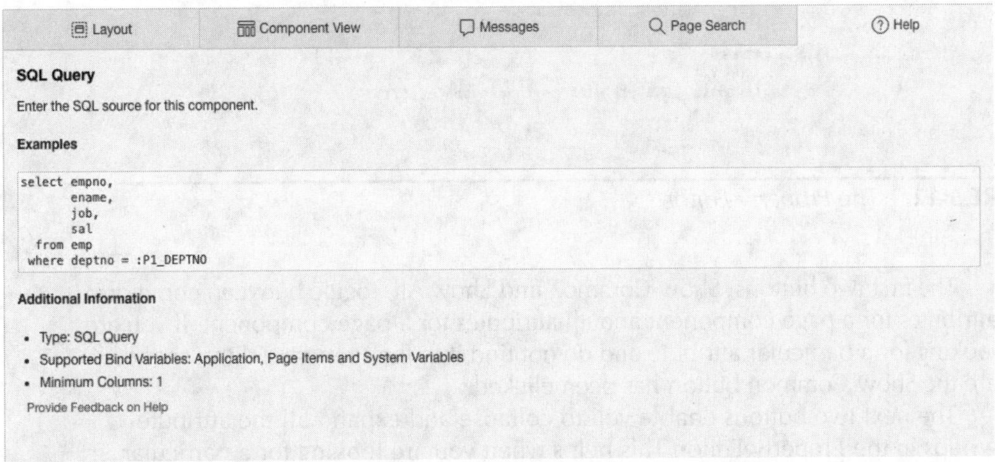

⧉ Layout	▥ Component View	▢ Messages	◷ Page Search	⑦ Help

SQL Query

Enter the SQL source for this component.

Examples

```
select empno,
       ename,
       job,
       sal
  from emp
 where deptno = :P1_DEPTNO
```

Additional Information

- Type: SQL Query
- Supported Bind Variables: Application, Page Items and System Variables
- Minimum Columns: 1

Provide Feedback on Help

FIGURE 5-11. *The Help tab showing information about an SQL Query*

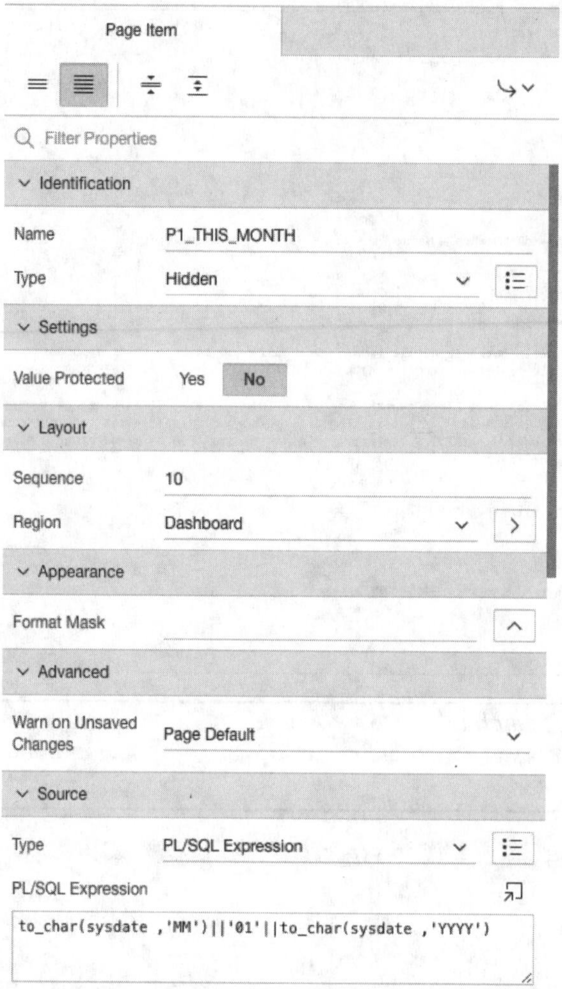

Page Item		

≡ ▤ ÷ ⊥ ↳⌄

🔍 Filter Properties

∨ Identification

Name	P1_THIS_MONTH	
Type	Hidden	⌄ ☰

∨ Settings

Value Protected	Yes **No**	

∨ Layout

Sequence	10	
Region	Dashboard	⌄ ＞

∨ Appearance

Format Mask		⌃

∨ Advanced

Warn on Unsaved Changes	Page Default	⌄

∨ Source

Type	PL/SQL Expression	⌄ ☰
PL/SQL Expression		⤢

```
to_char(sysdate ,'MM')||'01'||to_char(sysdate ,'YYYY')
```

FIGURE 5-12. *The Property Editor*

The first two buttons, Show Common and Show All, toggle between common attributes for a page component and all attributes for a page component. If you are looking for a particular attribute and do not find it in the Property Editor, chances are the Show Common button has been clicked.

The next two buttons enable you to collapse and expand all the attribute groups in the Property Editor. This helps when you are looking for a particular property group.

When clicked, the Go To Group button, the last button on the toolbar, shows a dropdown menu, where you can quickly move to an attribute group without scrolling in the Property Editor. Click the attribute group in the Go To Group menu and you'll go directly to the attributes in that group.

An alternative way to find the exact property you are looking for is to use the Property Search field at the top of the Property Editor, shown in Figure 5-13. Start typing text in this field and the property list will change dynamically to highlight items containing that particular search string.

Under the toolbar are the component attributes, where you can set attributes for your page components without having to leave the page. Here you can set attribute values, choose display conditions, or use the code editor for SQL, PL/SQL, JavaScript, and HTML code.

The Property Editor also lets you work with multiple items at the same time. You can select two or more items in either the Rendering panel or the Main Canvas, and the Property Editor will show all the common properties, enabling you to edit multiple items in a single update.

Also, when editing multiple items at the same time, if a blue triangle, or delta, appears next to the item you chose, it means that a property is different between two or more components. The Property Editor cannot show the individual values, so it shows a blank field and the blue delta. Note that if you change the value in this text field, it will be applied to all the components selected.

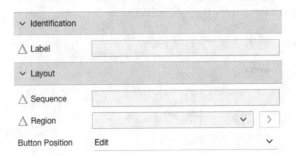

NOTE
In previous versions of APEX (4.2 and earlier), you could edit only one item or component at a time. The multiple item edit page helped in version 4.2 but was not as nearly as useful as the Page Designer.

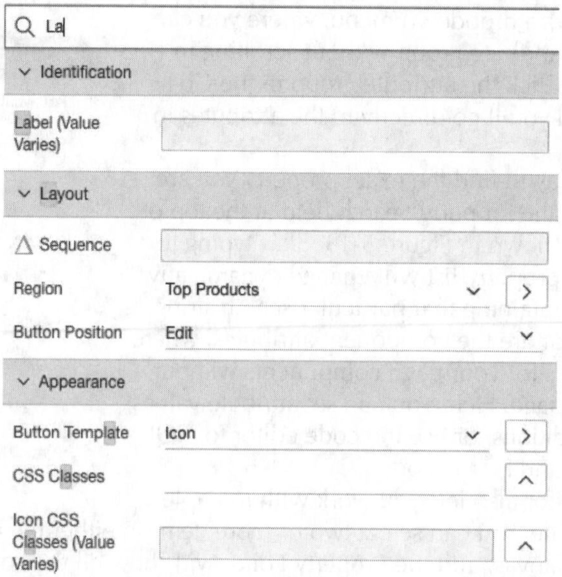

FIGURE 5-13. *Entering criteria in the Property Search field*

As you edit a property, when a change is made, a small blue earmark is displayed at the upper left of that property, as shown next. This helps you keep track of changes you have made to components if you're making multiple changes.

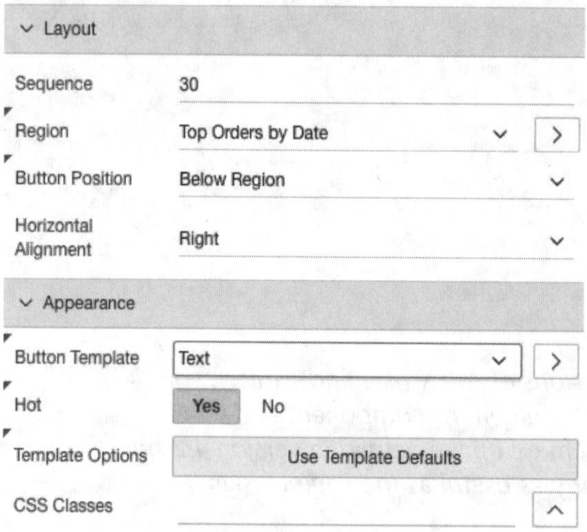

Laying Out Items on a Page

Now that you are versed in the Page Designer operational aspects, let's examine some of the functionalities it offers and the concepts behind them.

As you will see in Chapter 6, APEX wizards can be a great help in creating form pages that are based on a database table/view, or even an SQL query or PL/SQL stored procedure. The APEX wizards help us create all the page items that correspond with the columns of the table/view or SQL query, or the parameters of the stored procedure, and will position them on the application page in a single column layout.

Most often, however, these are not the only page items you will need, so the Page Designer enables you to create more APEX items manually and position them on the application page, as you need. In Chapter 4, we reviewed the most common properties that define APEX items, mainly with regard to the APEX engine—create, identify, initialize (according to the item type and functionality), major appearance and functional characteristics, rendering conditions, help content, and so on. Ultimately, you want to put these items on your application page, and the Page Designer is here to help.

You have two options to create new page items: you can use a context-sensitive menu, or use drag-and-drop.

To use a context-sensitive menu, right-click the Items/Page Items node (depends on your grouping view) in the Rendering pane, and choose Create Page Item. A new (Text Field) item will be created and named according to the naming conventions specified in the previous chapter while discussing the APEX page items, and it will be positioned on a new row, just below the current last item on the page. Using the Property Editor, if needed, you can change the default item type to the item type you need, and you can also change its default location on the page using the layout properties we'll discuss in a moment.

The second option uses a drag-and-drop technology both to create and position a new item in a single step. The Page Designer enables you to drag a specific item type from the Items gallery and drop it into an available location on the Layout canvas. After choosing the item type from the gallery, as you begin dragging it toward the Layout canvas, all the potential eligible rows to accept the new item are colored yellow. While you hover your mouse over these rows, a more specific available item location on the row will be colored in a darker yellow, meaning that you can drop the new item at that location. The Property Editor will be populated with properties that reflect the new item type and location, and you will be able to fine-tune them as you need.

Layout Properties

The Property Editor for a page item includes a Layout section with properties that enable you to fine-tune the appearance and location of the item on the application page. Following are the major properties.

Sequence

Every page item has a sequence number, as discussed in Chapter 4. In our current context, the sequence determines the location of the item on the page, relative to the other items. An item with a higher sequence will be rendered after items with lower sequence numbers. When you are using the drag-and-drop technique to position or reposition an item on the Layout canvas, the Property Editor will automatically update the item sequence to reflect its current location, and, if necessary, for example, if the item is relocated among existing items, all the other related sequences will be updated accordingly.

Region

Every APEX item resides in an APEX region, and this property enables you to associate the item with the region to which it belongs. From reading Chapter 4, you know that APEX regions don't have to be stacked on one another, and you can spread them to exploit the full width of the page (screen). However, while doing this, you might encounter alignment problems with the various items scattered on the page; using the region's layout can help with that, as the alignment/justification arithmetic for positioning the items is done in relation to the region borders.

Start New Row

By default, a new item occupies a new row, but you already know that you can change that and position the new item beside an existing one. In this case, this property should be set to No.

NOTE
The following properties use the term "column" but may refer to two different types of columns, depends on the APEX theme you are using. If you are working with the (APEX 5.x) standard/responsive themes, the term "column" refers to the Bootstrap 12-column layout model. If, however, you are working with legacy (non-responsive) APEX themes, the column is one of the layout table columns that these themes use.

Column

This property enables you to fine-tune the location of the item on a page, based on the layout grid your theme uses (Bootstrap-based, or HTML table). Its default value is Automatic, and if you are using a standard theme, this means that the Page Designer will automatically allocate the first available location on the page, taking into account the Start New Row property, and optimally justify the items across the page. In case of a legacy theme, the next available column in the layout table will be used, also with accordance to the Start New Row property.

If the automatic layout doesn't meet your page design needs, or you want to gain more control over the item location, you can set the column number manually by choosing the appropriate value from the select list. If you are working with a standard theme, the options are 1–12, in accordance with the Bootstrap layout model; for legacy themes, you can choose 1–20 (as HTML layout tables can include more than 12 columns, this depends on how many side-by-side items you want to position, each in its own column). When you're working with a standard theme, using a specific column number offers you a higher degree of flexibility in positioning items on the same row, including better control over the gap between the items, as shown in the following illustration. These layouts are much more difficult to achieve with legacy themes, as empty HTML table columns occupied minimum space.

Column Span, Label Column Span

Working with standard themes, these properties offer you better control over the overall width of the item element—label and input field. If the item spans insufficient columns to occupy its width fully, internal scrolling will be implemented in the input field. Where the label is concerned, the number of columns can determine, for example, whether the label will occupy a single row (if it can span enough columns to hold all of it) or the label will be broken into more than a single row (if it can span fewer columns).

Using manual settings with the column-related properties, instead of their default values, might lead to some layout conflicts, such as overload elements that were set to occupy the same location or were not allocated enough columns (page space).

In these cases, a runtime error message will be raised, as shown next, with details about the layout conflict (and some technical information that is available to the APEX developers only). You must resolve the conflict by manually changing the offending values to continue and successfully render the application page.

Label of Page Item **P48_T1** cannot be rendered as the label column span grid setting for this page item is invalid. It is set to be displayed with a **Label Column Span of 2**. This is not supported as the page item itself only has **2 Column(s)** available.

Contact your application administrator.

Technical Info (only visible for developers)

1. is_internal_error: true

NOTE
You'll be able to implement the concepts of application page layout and practice them hands-on, in Chapter 8, which deals with the powerful Universal Theme. The chapter thoroughly reviews what APEX offers to help you craft a powerful modern UI for your APEX application.

Keyboard Shortcuts

APEX 5 introduces keyboard shortcuts that can be used across the App Builder on various pages. Table 5-1 shows these shortcuts.

Page	Keys	Action
Page Designer, Layout	CTRL-ALT-D	Display from here
Page Designer, Layout	CTRL-ALT-T	Display from page
Page Designer	ALT-2	Go to Dynamic Actions
Page Designer	ALT-9	Go to Gallery buttons
Page Designer	ALT-8	Go to Gallery items
Page Designer	ALT-7	Go to Gallery regions
Page Designer	ALT-5	Go to layout
Page Designer	ALT-F1	Go to Help
Page Designer	CTRL-F1	Go to messages
Page Designer	ALT-4	Go to page Shared Components
Page Designer	ALT-3	Go to processing
Page Designer	ALT-6	Go to Property Editor
Page Designer	ALT-1	Go to rendering
Page Designer	ALT-SHIFT-F1	List keyboard shortcuts
Page Designer	CTRL-ALT-F	Page search
Page Designer	CTRL-Y	Redo
Page Designer	ALT-F11	Restore/expand
Page Designer	CTRL-ALT-S	Save
Page Designer	CTRL-ALT-R	Save and run page
Page Designer	CTRL-ALT-E	Toggle hide empty positions
Page Designer	CTRL-Z	Undo
Page Designer with focus anywhere that has a context menu	SHIFT-F10, CONTEXT MENU key	Open context menu
Page Designer Layout Gallery and Icon List in wizards	ARROW keys	Move selection
Page Designer Property Editor with focus on a group heading	UP/DOWN ARROW keys	Move to previous/next group

TABLE 5-1. *App Builder Keyboard Shortcuts (Continues)*

Page	Keys	Action
Page Designer Property Editor with focus on a group heading	HOME/END keys	Move to first/last group
Page Designer Property Editor with focus on a group heading	LEFT/RIGHT ARROW keys, ENTER, SPACE	Expand or collapse group
Page Designer with focus on any tab	ARROW keys	Select previous/next tab
Focus on a splitter handle	ARROW keys	Move splitter
Focus on a splitter handle	ENTER	Expand or collapse splitter (if supported by splitter)
On pages that have a splitter	CTRL-F6	Move to next splitter
On pages that have a splitter	CTRL-SHIFT-F6	Move to previous splitter
Focus on any field with a (?) help icon	ALT-F1	Open field Help dialog
Focus on a field Help dialog	ALT-F6	Move focus back to field without closing dialog
Focus in any dialog	ESC	Close dialog
Any page, focus on region display selector tabs	ARROW keys	Select previous/next tab
SQL commands	CTRL-ENTER	Run current command
Code editor	CTRL-Z	Undo
Code editor	CTRL-SHIFT-Z	Redo
Code editor	CTRL-F	Find
Code editor	CTRL-SHIFT-F	Replace
Code editor with focus in find field	UP/DOWN ARROW keys	Find previous/next instance
Code editor	CTRL-SPACE	Auto complete (when available)
Code editor	ALT-F6	Leave code editor and go to next tab stop
Code editor	ALT-SHIFT-F6	Leave code editor and go to previous tab stop

TABLE 5-1. *App Builder Keyboard Shortcuts (Continued)*

Summary

In this chapter, we reviewed the Page Designer, one of the most important innovations of APEX 5.x. This tool was designed to ease the work of APEX developers and increase their productivity by employing the latest technologies in the web development arena.

We reviewed the Page Designer structure and operational features and targeted one of its most common and important tasks—laying out the APEX items on the application page—by reviewing the concepts behind it. In the next chapter, we'll discuss the APEX wizards, and you'll see that many of the Page Designer tasks can be done automatically using these wizards, which makes developer life much easier.

CHAPTER
6

APEX Wizards

Any application framework or tool should be easy to get started with and easy to use. It cannot contain nested levels of hidden complexity that force beginners to learn a process that's more appropriate for experienced users. It cannot require client tools as well as web tools that overlap in functionality but still require the user to use both. Elements such as these alienate inexperienced users, resulting in their deciding that the platform is too difficult to use. Luckily for us, the Oracle Application Express team has included *wizards*, guided pages that instruct the user on creating applications and components without needing to know a line of code, digging into complex functions, or being forced to use multiple toolsets. Let's jump right in and use the application wizard to create our first APEX application.

The Application Wizard

You now know the development parts of APEX and how you can use them in theory, so let's put that knowledge into practice. We'll start by creating a desktop application. We have the database components of our Contacts application ready to go, so we can build upon them.

Start by opening the App Builder tab in APEX if you're not already there. Then click the Create button. Both the App Build tab and Create button are seen in Figure 6-1.

On the Create An Application page (Figure 6-2), you'll see the types of applications you can build:

- **Desktop** These applications are targeted for larger screens such as desktop or laptop screens and large tablets.

- **Mobile** These applications are targeted for smaller screens on smartphones and tablets. This type of application uses jQuery Mobile for its UI framework.

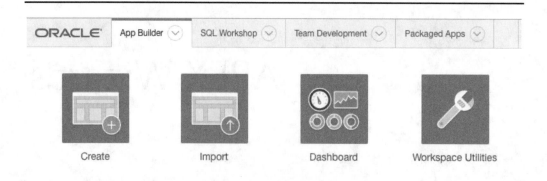

FIGURE 6-1. *The Application Builder home page*

- **Websheet** These applications are interactive pages that combine text, images, and data. They are highly dynamic and don't have as much complexity behind them as desktop and mobile applications do. Though limited in functionality, websheets provide rich UI controls and the ability to add annotations such as files, notes, and tags.

- **Packaged App** Oracle APEX comes with many premade applications from which you can choose. Packaged applications set up the application and the database objects for you and provide a fully functional application. These are also great for learning by dissecting the code to see how the applications work.

Two more options are also available on the Create An Application page:

- **From A Spreadsheet** You can create an application from a spreadsheet. Application Express will read the spreadsheet, create a table from it, enter the data into the database, and then create a form and report on this new table.

- **Copy An Existing Application** This option enables you to copy an existing application that is in this workspace.

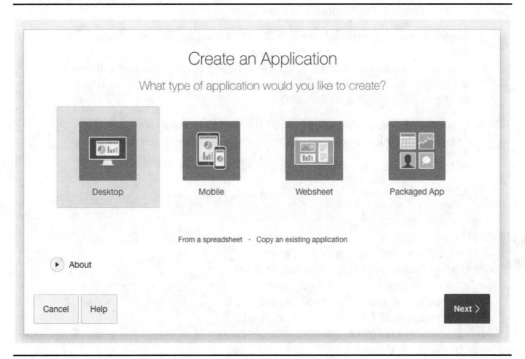

FIGURE 6-2. *Create An Application page*

Next, click the Desktop button to launch the Create an Application wizard.

Finding Help

Need help with a component in APEX? Click the question mark icons that appear next to components and fields in APEX to get help and information about the items. Pressing ALT-F1 on your keyboard will also bring up help for components and form items.

You have some choices to make on the first page of the Create an Application wizard.

1. For User Interface, Desktop is already selected, because you chose this option on the Create An Application page.

2. For Schema, choose the database schema upon which this application is going to be built. Choose the schema we previously set up when we created our workspace. For this book, we used APEX5_BOOK_DEMO. You will see this referenced through this book, but know that your schema may be different.

3. For the Name, enter **Contacts in the Cloud**.

4. For the Application field, leave the default ID setting. This number, or application ID, is an automatically generated number that is assigned when you create an application, or it can be assigned by the developer. If you were to assign an application ID of an existing application, APEX would alert you and ask for a different ID.

5. Leave the Theme setting at Universal Theme (42)—the default—and for Theme Style, select Vita (if not automatically selected) from the list.

   At this point, your page should look similar to Figure 6-3.

6. After checking your values, click Next to move on.

NOTE
To the left of the Next button is the Create Application button, which lets you take a shortcut and create the application without continuing on with the rest of the wizard. We will use the Create an Application wizard in this book, but know that you can click this button to create the application without using the wizard.

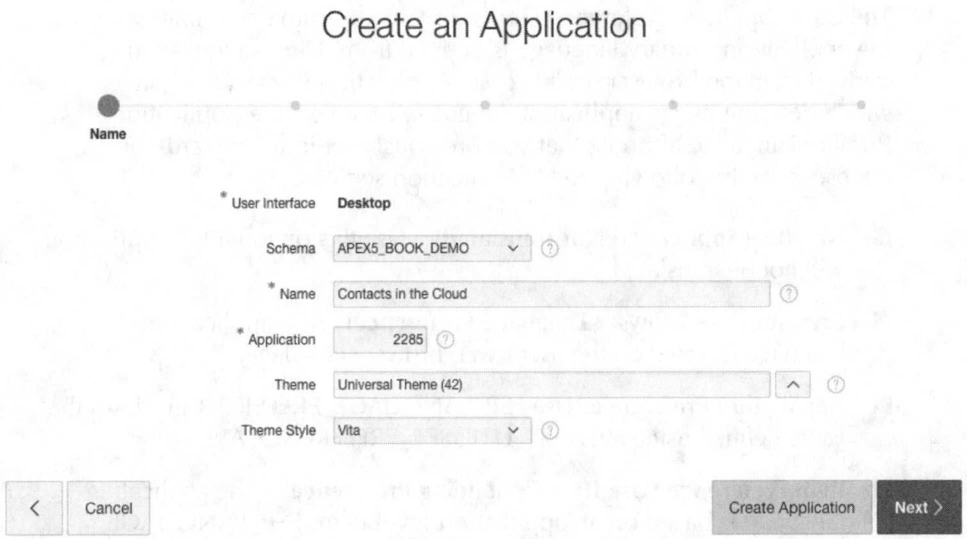

Create an Application

FIGURE 6-3. *The first page of the Create an Application wizard*

Control the Wizard Size

You can move and resize any wizard modal. See the scroll bar on the right of the wizard modal? You can drag it up a bit higher in your browser window and then drag the lower-right corner to make the modal bigger.

7. The next step of the wizard is the Pages step, where you can add multiple pages and page types. For this exercise, you'll be creating your pages at a later stage, so keep the default Home page and click Next.

8. Shared components are commonly used application items that you can predefine and share across multiple applications. This ensures consistency across items such as selection lists, navigation bars, security elements, and database objects. There are no predefined shared components, so leave Shared Components set to No and then click Next.

9. The Attributes step is an important step in the wizard. Here you can define authentication, or how a user logs into the application; language; and date formats. For Authentication Scheme, multiple authentication schemes are available (which we will go over in Chapter 10). For this application, use the default setting, Application Express Accounts.

10. For the Language attribute, keep the default of English (en). This language attribute is used as the base language from which all translations will come.

11. The User Language Preference Derived From attribute determines where the application primary language is derived from. Choose the language derived from the browser (in this case, Application Primary Language, which determines the application language based on the Application Primary Language attribute that you previously set in the wizard), or choose from the following APEX application settings:

- **No NLS (Application Not Translated)** Use this option if the application will not be translated.

- **Browser (Use Browser Language Preference)** The application language is based on the user's web browser language.

- **Application Preference (Use FSP_LANGUAGE_PREFERENCE)** Uses the value defined using the APEX_UTIL.SET_PREFERENCE API.

- **Item Preference (Use Item Containing Preference)** The application language is based on an application-level item, FSP_LANGUAGE_ PREFERENCE.

- **Session** The application language is derived from the session setting. This can be set via either the APEX_UTIL.SET_SESSION_LANG procedure or the **p_lang** parameter of the F procedure in the URL.

12. Also on this page are four date and time formats for various date types. By setting these formats here, developers and users all see the same format. Developers no longer have to set the date formats in reports or forms; the application will use this default format across all pages. For this application, choose the Date Format of DD-MON-YYYY. Enter this manually or click the up arrow next to the field and select 12-JAN-2004. Leave the rest blank. The wizard should now look similar to Figure 6-4. Check your values and click Next.

13. The last step of the wizard is a confirmation or review page. Here you can double-check all the major attributes of your application, such as ID, Name, Language, and Authentication Scheme. Also of note is the Parsing Schema. This is the database user or schema that the application will be built upon. We set this up when creating a workspace, but you could change it if you had multiple schemas associated with a workspace. It should be set to the schema you previously chose.

14. After you are satisfied with all the values, click the Create Application button.

Create an Application

Attributes

Authentication Scheme	Application Express Accounts ⌄ ⑦
Language	English (en) ⌄ ⑦
User Language Preference Derived From	Application Primary Language ⌄ ⑦
Date Format	DD-MON-YYYY ⌃ ⑦
Date Time Format	⌃ ⑦
Timestamp Format	⌃ ⑦
Timestamp Time Zone Format	⌃ ⑦

< Cancel   Next >

FIGURE 6-4.   *The application attributes*

Congratulations! You have just created an APEX application. You should now see the App Builder home page, with the page you added in the wizard (Home) and a login page. Run the application by clicking the Run Application button:

Run Application

Next, you'll see a login page. Remember that you selected Application Express Accounts for your authentication. Enter the username and password we created when setting up the workspace. Then click Login. Welcome to your Contacts in the Cloud application!

The Report Region

Nice page, but it's a bit empty. Let's create a report on the PERSONS table.

1. On the Developer toolbar at the bottom of the page, click Edit Page 1.

2. In the Page Designer Rendering panel on the left, right-click Regions and select Create Region to create a new region, called New, under the Content Body node (Figure 6-5).

3. The New region should already be selected, so turn your attention to the right side of the page and the Region Property tab. Start by finding the Identification property group.

4. In the Title field, enter **My Contacts**.

5. Change the Type to Classic Report by choosing it from the list. The Identification property group should now look like the following:

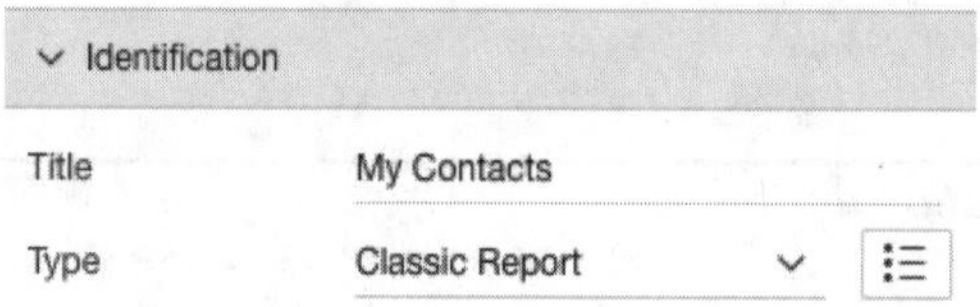

⌄ Identification		
Title	My Contacts	
Type	Classic Report ⌄	☰

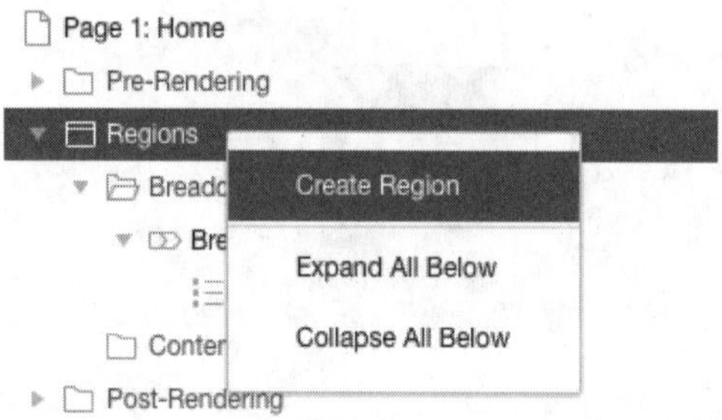

- 📄 Page 1: Home
  - ▸ 🗀 Pre-Rendering
  - ▾ ▤ Regions
    - ▾ 🗁 Bread‹   **Create Region**
      - ▾ ⬭ Bre
        - ☰   **Expand All Below**
      - 🗀 Conter   **Collapse All Below**
  - ▸ 🗀 Post-Rendering

FIGURE 6-5. *Create a region*

Just below the Identification property group is the Source property group. The SQL Query property should have a red X next to it, as shown here. This indicates that this property is in error—you need to add some values.

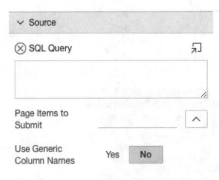

6. Click the pop-out icon (the arrow pointing to a box) at the upper-right to open the Code Editor – SQL Query. Here you can build a SQL statement without knowing how to write SQL code. On the toolbar across the top of the Code Editor is a hammer icon, shown next. Click the hammer icon to start the Query Builder.

7. On the left side of the Query Builder is a list of the tables in your workspace. Click PERSONS_TABLE to display this table with its columns and data types, as shown in Figure 6-6.

8. Click the checkbox next to the columns that have them. As you click each checkbox, the column is added to the bottom section of the page. Once you have added all the columns, click the Return button at the upper-right corner of the page. After returning to the Code Editor modal, you'll see that the SQL has been pregenerated for you. The SQL should look like the following:

```
select PERSONS_TABLE.PERSON_ID as PERSON_ID,
    PERSONS_TABLE.PERSON_TYPE as PERSON_TYPE,
    PERSONS_TABLE.PERSON_PREFIX as PERSON_PREFIX,
    PERSONS_TABLE.PERSON_FIRST_NAME as PERSON_FIRST_NAME,
    PERSONS_TABLE.PERSON_MIDDLE_NAME as PERSON_MIDDLE_NAME,
    PERSONS_TABLE.PERSON_LAST_NAME as PERSON_LAST_NAME,
    PERSONS_TABLE.PERSON_BIRTHDAY as PERSON_BIRTHDAY,
    PERSONS_TABLE.PERSON_NOTES as PERSON_NOTES
 from PERSONS_TABLE PERSONS_TABLE
```

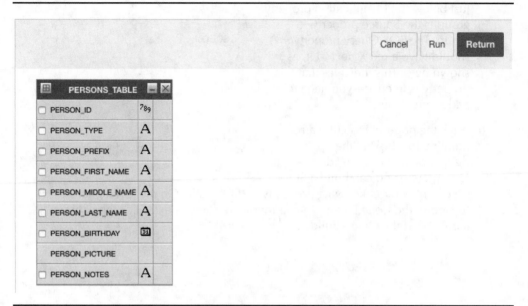

FIGURE 6-6. *The PERSONS_TABLE in the Query Builder*

9. Click OK on the lower-right corner of the Code Editor modal. This will remove the error from the SQL Query property.

10. Back on the left side of the Page Designer in the Rendering panel, click the Attributes node under My Contacts.

11. Look on the right at the Property Editor, Attributes tab. These properties dictate how the report will behave, while the Property Editor for the actual region will dictate how the region will render. While still looking at the report attributes, scroll down to the Pagination property group, shown next:

12. Here, you can set the type of pagination for your report. You have many options to choose from. For the Type property, select Row Ranges X To Y (With Next And Previous Links). This type will display the current set of rows you are looking at.

For example, if you set your Number Of Rows property (from the Layout attributes group) to 15, your pagination will be 1–15, 16–30, and so on. If you chose the type X To Y Of Z, the display format would look like this: 1–15 of 300. The only downside to this is that the database has to perform two queries: one query to know the row set you are on and a second query to get how many total rows there are. Depending on the table and total rows, this could be a very expensive query, hindering performance. Another popular pagination scheme is Search Engine. It sets pagination as page numbers for how many pages of results you get.

13. Display Position will set the position of the pagination. There are various options, such as right or left, top or bottom, or even both on top and bottom. For this report, leave the default of Bottom – Right.

14. For the Partial Page Refresh property, choose Yes. This will refresh only the report region. (If you set this attribute to No, the refreshes affect the entire page, causing a page reload.)

15. Under the Pagination property group is the Messages property group, where you can define custom messages when you have no data found or too many rows are found. In the When No Data Found message area, enter **No Contacts Found**, as shown next:

Note: Scroll down through the properties and you'll see many familiar properties that you saw in the Report wizard, such as Break Formatting.

16. Back in the Rendering panel, expand the Columns folder above Attributes and click PERSON_TYPE.

17. On the right side in the Property Editor, in the Column tab, you can see the properties for a column. Find the Heading property group and look at the Heading property. You see it is Person type, from our table. APEX altered our column heading, PERSON_TYPE, by capitalizing only the first letter and pulling out the underscore.

18. Now you should change the rest of the column headings as shown in the following table. You can do this quickly by clicking the item in the Rendering panel and then changing the Heading property:

Change This Heading	To This
PERSON_PREFIX	Name Prefix
PERSON_FIRST_NAME	First Name
PERSON_MIDDLE_NAME	Middle Name
PERSON_LAST_NAME	Last Name
PERSON_BIRTHDAY	Birthday
PERSON_NOTES	Notes

19. Just before you save and run the page, click PERSON_TYPE and scroll down in the Property Editor (or use the Go To Group dropdown) and find the Sorting property group. You can manually set sorting on a column as well as the sorting order. The sorting order is the order in which the report will sort your data. Set the PERSON_TYPE sort order to 1, PERSON_LAST_NAME to 2 (remember to click PERSON_LAST_NAME to bring up the Column properties for that specific column), resulting in all the types being sorted first, then the last names, and so on.

20. Finally, click the Save button on the upper-right corner of the Page Designer and then click the Save And Run Page button next to it on the right. You can now see the changes you made in the report.

The Form Wizard

Now that we've created a report on the PERSONS table, our next step is to create a form for entering and editing PERSONS data. We start by creating a new page.

1. On the Developer toolbar, click Edit Page 1 to open the Page Designer.

2. In the upper-right corner, click the Create menu (the + sign) and select Page:

3. In the Create Page wizard, because we want to build a new page that includes a form, click Form.

Select a Page Type

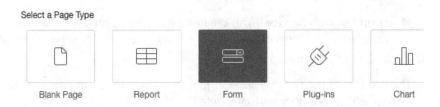

4. Before we can create a form, we need to choose the type of form we need for entering contacts in our application, as shown in Figure 6-7.

Let's go over a few of these form types:

■ **Report With Form On Table** This form creates two pages: a form in which to insert, update, and delete data, as well as a report that contains the data from the table that the form is on.

■ **Form On A Table** This option creates a form on a database table or view and lets the user insert, update, or delete a row of data at a time.

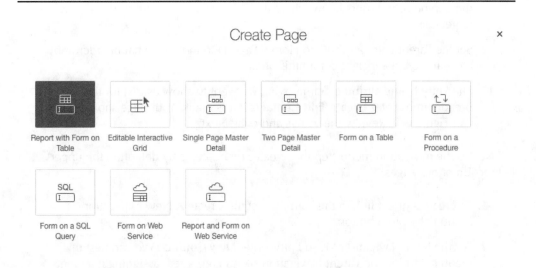

FIGURE 6-7. *Form Page options*

- **Form On A Procedure** This type of form uses a stored procedure for its page elements. It is best used when there is specific logic in the stored procedure for inserting or updating data.

- **Form On Web Service** This creates a form based on a web service definition. The items of this form correspond to the web service's inputs.

5. Click Form On A Table.

6. The first step of the Create Form On Table wizard is to set up Page Attributes. Leave the Page Number set to the default value of 2.

7. For Page Name, enter **Create/Edit Contacts**. This page name will appear on the top of the browser window as well as anywhere in the page template that references this attribute.

8. For Page Mode, leave the default value of Normal. This attribute defines the behavior of this page, whether it will be a regular APEX page, a page in a modal window, or a pop-up page.

9. For Branch Here On Submit, enter **1** so that our app will go back to the report after submitting our form.

10. The Cancel And Go To Page attribute dictates where we go if we cancel out of the form. Enter **1** for this attribute.

11. For Breadcrumb, select Breadcrumb for the value. Having breadcrumbs in the app helps the users know where they are, how they got there, and how to get back.

12. Set the Parent Entry attribute to Home (Page 1) to indicate what breadcrumb we want to appear right before this one.

13. The Entry Name attribute defines what we want to show as text for this breadcrumb. Enter **Create/Edit Contacts** if it is blank. Your page should look like Figure 6-8. Review the values and click Next.

Next is the navigation menu step that creates menu items by default in the upper left section of our pages.

1. To create a direct link to this form, select the Create A New Navigation Menu Entry radio button.

2. For the New Navigation Menu Entry, enter **New Contact**. We can nest this menu control in the Parent Navigation Menu Entry area, assigning it a menu hierarchy. Leave No Parent Selected and then click Next.

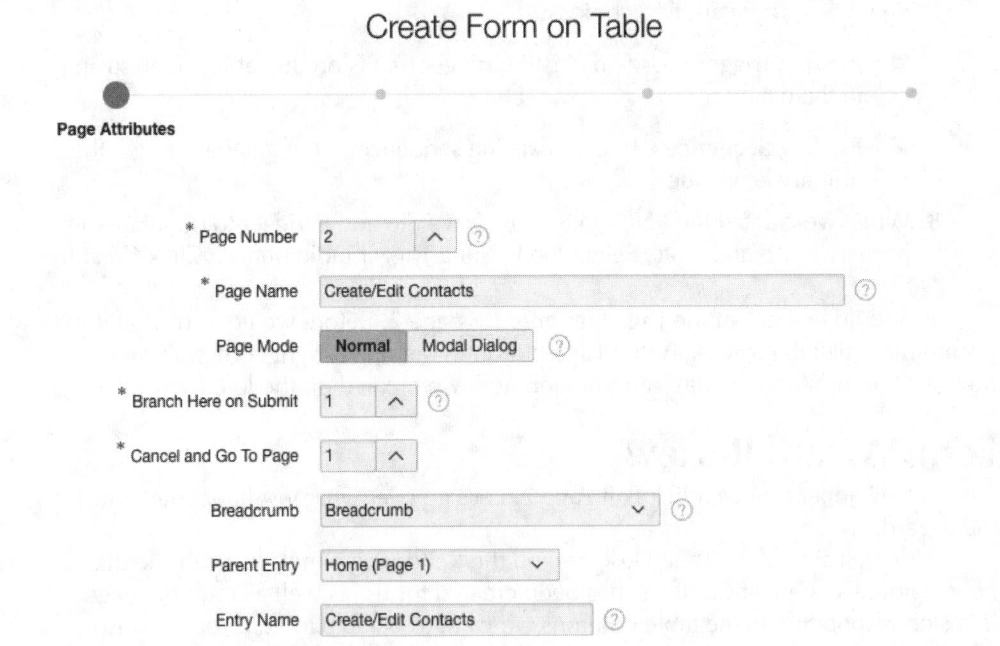

Create Form on Table

Page Attributes

* Page Number	2
* Page Name	Create/Edit Contacts
Page Mode	**Normal** Modal Dialog
* Branch Here on Submit	1
* Cancel and Go To Page	1
Breadcrumb	Breadcrumb
Parent Entry	Home (Page 1)
Entry Name	Create/Edit Contacts

FIGURE 6-8. *Create Form on Table Page Attributes*

3. Now choose the table or view you want the form to be based on. We want it based on the PERSONS table, so for Table / View Owner select the schema you used to create this application on if it's not already selected. For Table / View Name, select PERSONS_TABLE.

4. We want all the columns of the table, so leave them selected and then click Next. APEX should have prepopulated all the columns of the table.

5. Next, we choose a primary key for our form; this is how the database knows what row we want to edit. There are two choices:

- **Managed by Database(ROWD)**   Uses the ROWID pseudo column to identify rows to update and delete

- **Select Primary Key Column(s)**   Uses the database table's primary key to identify rows to update and delete

6. Select the Select Primary Key Column(s) radio button. You'll see two dropdown lists, from which you can choose up to two primary keys. For the first Primary Key Column, choose PERSON_ID (Number) if it's not already selected. You can ignore the second Primary Key Column entry.

7. APEX now needs to know how we will provide this value when creating new rows. There are two choices:

- **Existing Trigger**   Use an existing trigger that is on the table we are using in the database.

- **Existing Sequence**   Use an existing sequence in the database to get the primary key value.

8. When we created the PERSONS_TABLE, we did add a trigger to populate the primary key of the table. Select the Existing Trigger radio button. Click Create.

You should be back at the Page Designer for page 2. Before we go into what the wizard did, click the Save And Run Page button in the upper-right corner. You can now see the form and the navigation menu item we created on the left.

Form Wizard Review

On the Developer toolbar, click Edit Page 2. Let's go over what just happened with the wizard.

On the left side of the Page Designer, on the Rendering panel, you can see that a new region, Create/Edit Contacts, has been created for us, as well as multiple page items corresponding to the table columns we want to be able to edit. You can also see that four buttons have been created and placed just below these items. If you mouse over a button or item, you can see some basic information about that item, as shown next:

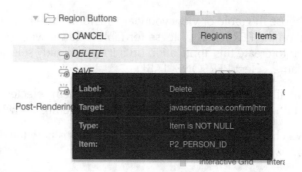

Now click the Processing tab, shown in Figure 6-9, to show the Processing panel.

FIGURE 6-9.   *The Processing tab*

In the Processing panel, you can see the row processing procedure as well as the page branch we created. Click Process Row Of PERSONS_TABLE and look at the Property Editor on the right side of the Page Designer. Under Identification, you'll see Name and Type. Notice the Type, which is Automatic Row Processing (DML). This type of process will insert, update, and delete from our PERSONS table without you needing to write any code—APEX handles it all for you. The Automatic Row Processing process also handles database read consistency.

Database Read Consistency

Database read consistency ensures that users see a consistent view of the data. This includes all changes made not only by the user working with the data, but changes, or committed transactions, made by other users in the system.

Under the Settings attribute group is our table name and primary key, but APEX has also created a page item, P2_PERSON_ID, to store the value of the primary key. Also in Settings (just under the attribute Runtime Where Clause), notice that we have the ability to return the primary key value of a new row into a page or application item. This would be useful if we needed that value for a follow-up page or a custom PL/SQL procedure.

Scrolling down in the Property Editor, just before the Execution Options attribute group, you'll see the Supported Operations. Here we can control what database operations a user can perform with this form.

Continuing down the right panel is Success Message, which is displayed when the row is successfully inserted, deleted, or updated. If there is an issue with an update, insert, or delete, the Error Message will display a user-friendly message and maybe some debugging info. To help with error messages, APEX provides two built-in options:

- **#SQLERRM_TEXT#**   Text of error message without the error number

- **#SQLERRM#**   Complete error message

When an error does occur, APEX will substitute the # enclosed strings with the proper SQL error message.

On the right side of the page, in the Process panel, below the Process Row procedure, click the Reset Page process shown in Figure 6-10.

Then, in the Property Editor's Process tab, in the Identification section, under Type, you can see that this is a Clear Session State process. This resets all the values at various levels of the application. The level of reset values is determined by the Type attribute under Settings. The type used on this page is Clear All Items On The Current Page, which does exactly that—clears all the page items and resets them to NULL.

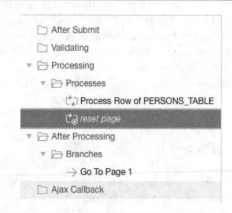

FIGURE 6-10. *Choosing the Reset Page process*

We can clear session state at various levels:

- Clear All Items On The Current Page

- Clear All Items On Page(s)

- Clear Items

- Clear Current Session

- Clear Current Application

- Clear Applications

Customizing a Report

Now let's link our report page to our form page.

1. Click the down arrow of the page selector on the top of the Page Designer, shown next, to go to page 1.

2. On the left side in the Rendering panel (you may have to open the Rendering panel), navigate to the Content Body folder and the My Contacts report region under that. If it is not expanded, click to expand and see the Columns

tree node. Open this folder, and you should see all the report columns in the My Contacts report, as shown next.

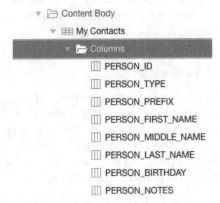

3. Click the PERSON_ID column. On the right side of the Page Designer, the Property Editor, Column tab is shown. Here you can see all the properties of a report column, just as you did earlier in the chapter.

4. Change the column Type to Link. In the Property Editor, the Link property group will be displayed.

5. We need to rename the column Heading from PERSON_ID to Edit, making the report a bit more user friendly. In the Property Editor, find the Heading property group, and for the Heading Property, change Person Id to Edit.

6. For the Target property, click No Link Defined:

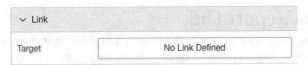

7. In the Link Builder – Target modal dialog, you'll define the type of column link. Under Target, you can choose several Type options:

- Page In This Application

- Page In A Different Application

- URL (External To APEX)

Select Page In This Application.

8. For the Page property, click the up-pointing arrow to the right of the field and choose page 2. You'll be returned to the Link Builder – Target modal, where "2" will be shown for the Page property.

9. Next, we need to pass the Person ID to page 2 so that we can query the database for that user and get the details. (APEX also created a Fetch Process on page 2 for us.) This will enable us to view, edit, or delete the data for a particular person. Under Set Items, click the arrow next to the Name field and choose P2_PERSON_ID.

10. Click the arrow next to the Value field and choose PERSON_ID. You'll see #PERSON_ID# in the Value field.

11. Lastly, we want to reset the session for page 2 when clicking this link, to ensure that no leftover data remains in the form from a previous person ID. Under Clear Session State, for the Clear Cache property, enter **2**, or click the arrow and select 2. The Link Builder – Target modal should resemble Figure 6-11. (Note that the Reset Pagination option would reset a report's pagination to the first set of data. Ignore this option for now.)

12. Double-check your values and click OK.

We now have a linked column in our Contacts report. Just below the Target property we used is the Link Text property; it should show an error status, indicated by the red X icon, because the text of the link must be either static text, a column value, or an image. For Link Text, click the arrow and choose apex-edit-pencil.png to add an edit icon (the little pencil) in place of our person ID in the report. Clicking this icon will allow us to edit the contact information.

To see our changes in the report, click the Save button at the upper-right of the Page Designer and then click the Save And Run Page button. You'll see the report, in which the Person ID column is replaced with an Edit column that contains pencil icons (Figure 6-12).

Testing the Report Link

Let's test the link to the form. Click one of the pencil icons in the report to open the Edit Contact page with the contact's details in our form. Here you can edit any field and save the changes or completely delete a contact from the database.

How did all this information land on the Edit Contact page? When we created the report, the form wizard created the fetch row from the PERSONS_TABLE procedure in the page for us. APEX automatically handles fetching the data into the form, updating the database with your changes, and removing any record, all automatically—there's no need for you to know SQL or PL/SQL to make these changes. This demonstrates the power of APEX and its wizards.

Now let's create a button on the report page to enable us to link to the empty form, just as we can from the navigation menu.

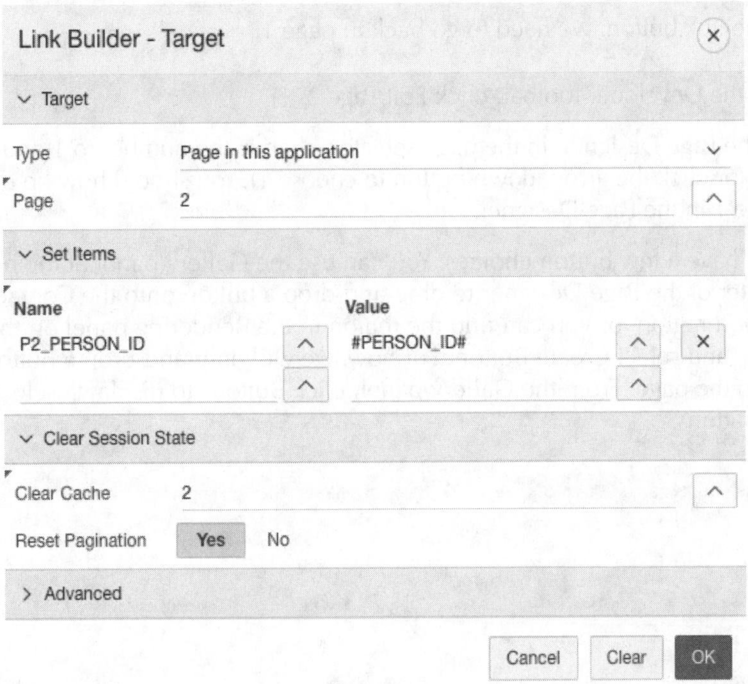

Link Builder - Target

Target

Type	Page in this application
Page	2

Set Items

Name	Value
P2_PERSON_ID	#PERSON_ID#

Clear Session State

Clear Cache	2

Reset Pagination **Yes** No

> Advanced

Cancel   Clear   OK

FIGURE 6-11. *Selected options in the Link Builder – Target modal*

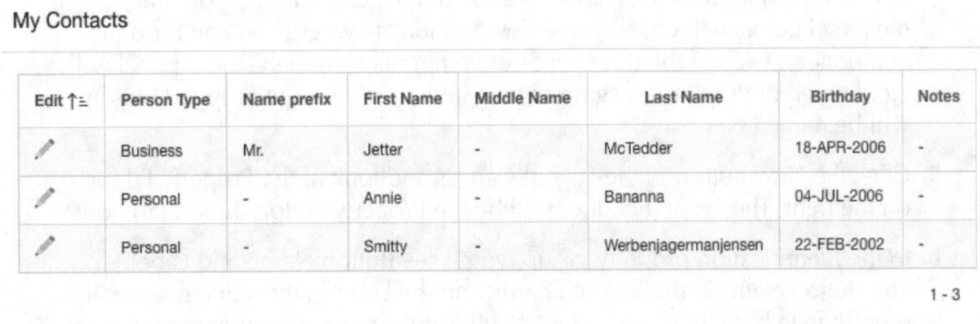

My Contacts

Edit ↑≥	Person Type	Name prefix	First Name	Middle Name	Last Name	Birthday	Notes
✏	Business	Mr.	Jetter	-	McTedder	18-APR-2006	-
✏	Personal	-	Annie	-	Bananna	04-JUL-2006	-
✏	Personal	-	Smitty	-	Werbenjagermanjensen	22-FEB-2002	-

1 - 3

FIGURE 6-12. *Edit icons in the leftmost column*

Creating a Button

To create the link button, we need to go back to page 1.

1. On the Developer toolbar, click Edit Page 2.

2. In the Page Designer, in the page selector, change the number to 1 and click Go (or click the arrow down button to choose 1). You should now be on page 1 in the Page Designer.

3. You have a few button choices. You can use the Gallery panel at the bottom center of the Page Designer to drag-and-drop a button onto the Contacts Report region, or you can find the region in the Rendering panel on the left side, and select Create Button. For now, we will drag-and-drop a button onto the page. From the Gallery panel, click Buttons to display a selection of buttons:

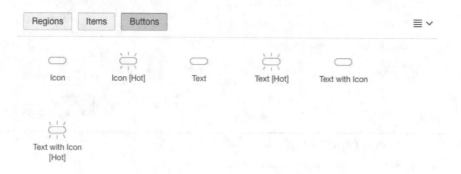

4. Drag-and-drop the Text With Icon [Hot] button onto the My Contacts Report region in the Create area, as shown in Figure 6-13. As you drag, the panel colors will change to yellow to indicate where you can drop the component. Each of the three types of components in the Gallery panel will yield different drop areas, again highlighted in yellow. The dropped button will be named New.

5. Click the New button in the Layout Canvas and look at the Property Editor on the right. The Property Editor will be the Property Editor, Button tab now.

6. In the Identification property group, you'll see Button Name and Label. The Button Name is the internal name and the Label is the value users will see. Change both to New Contact. You'll see an error. Button names cannot contain spaces, but labels can.

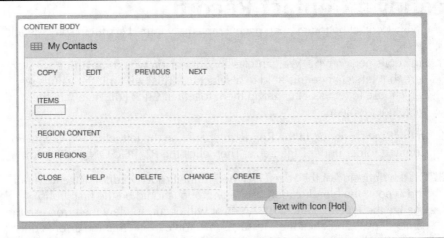

FIGURE 6-13.   *Dropping the button on the Create area*

7. To fix this error, change the Name field to NEW_CONTACT. Once the value is changed and you leave the field, the error will no longer be present and APEX will change Label to New Contact.

8. Next we need to determine the button behavior. In the Property Editor, scroll down to the Behavior property group. The Action property shows the following options:

   - ■   Submit Page
   - ■   Redirect To Page In This Application
   - ■   Redirect To Page In Different Application
   - ■   Redirect To URL
   - ■   Defined By Dynamic Action

9. Select Redirect To Page In This Application, and you will see the Target property display with an error.

10. Click the No Link Defined button to return to the Link Builder – Target modal.

11. Enter **2** for the Page property and **2** for the Clear Cache property, and then click OK. Save your work by clicking Save and then click Save And Run Page. On the lower-right of our report is our new contact button.

Creating a Contact Record

Click the New Contact button to open page 2, an empty form. Let's fill in some details.

1. First up is person type. We can classify our person type as anything we want here, but let's change this field to a select list. This will limit the values we can choose to let us better group them together. Click Edit Page 2 in the Developer toolbar.

2. In the Page Designer, in the Rendering panel on the left, click the Create/Edit Contacts folder under Page Items. Then click the P2_PERSON_TYPE item.

3. On the right side of the Page Designer, in the Property Editor, Page Item tab, find Type in the Identification property group (should be the first group). Change the Type to Select List. An error will occur. To view the error, use the center canvas and click the Messages tab. You can see that the error is due to the fact that our P2_PERSON_TYPE item needs a List of Values Type. To fix this error we can either scroll down the Property Editor – Page Item for P2_PERSON_TYPE or click the error message in the Messages Canvas.

4. Once you find the error, change the Type in the List Of Values property group to Static Values. This should prefill the Static Values attribute like so:

   ```
   STATIC:Display1;Return1,Display2;Return2
   ```

5. Save the changes and rerun the form.

You can see that the Person Type field is now a dropdown select list with two values, Display1 and Display2, as well as a blank value for NULL.

A static list of values is simple to create. You separate the display and return values with a semicolon (;), and the different sets of values are separated with a comma (,).

Let's create a static list of values for Person Type. We first need to decide on what values we want. We can group our contacts with the following types: Personal, Business, and Family. To generate our static list of values, we can construct it in the following way:

```
STATIC:Personal;Personal,Business;Business,Family;Family
```

1. Click Edit Page 2 in the Developer toolbar.

2. Click the P2_PERSON_TYPE item.

3. In the List Of Values property group, shown in Figure 6-14, for Static Values, enter **STATIC:Personal;Personal,Business;Business,Family;Family**.

4. For the Display Extra Values property, click No.

5. For the Display Null Value, click Yes.

6. For the Null Display Value, enter **-- Select Contact Type --**. Setting the Null Display Value gets rid of the empty space at the top of the select list and replaces it with a value of our choice to represent NULL. The List Of Values property group should look like Figure 6-14.

Lists of values can also be derived using the following methods:

■ **Shared component** A static list of values or SQL query list of values that is predefined at the application level, not the page item level. This enables us to reuse this list of values across the application in multiple places.

■ **SQL query** Derived by selecting the display and return values from a table in the database. The format is the following, with *d* being the display value and *r* being the return value:

```
select value1 d, value 2 r
from table X;
```

■ **PL/SQL function body returning SQL query** This dynamic list of values is based on the SQL query returned by the PL/SQL function body you enter here.

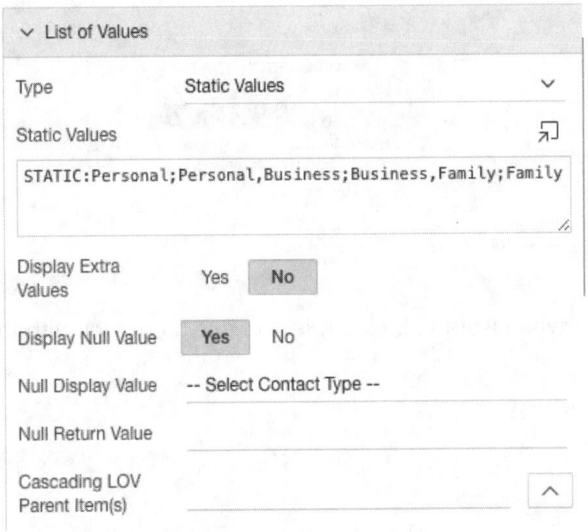

FIGURE 6-14. *The List Of Values property group*

Changing the label for an item is just as easy: In the Page Designer, Property Editor – Page Item, find the Label group and the Label property. It shows Person Type as the Label, but let's change it to Type: click in the text field and enter **Type**.

We can change the labels of all the items in this form to more user-friendly values. To switch quickly between items, you can either click the item names on the left side of the Page Designer in the Rendering panel or click the items on the Grid Layout Canvas in the middle of the page. As you click the items, on the right side of the Property Editor, Page Item tab, the properties change. You can quickly change the label of each item.

Let's change the form items' values as follows:

Change From	Change To
Person Prefix	Name Prefix
Person First Name	First Name
Person Middle Name	Middle Name
Person Last Name	Last Name
Person Birthday	Birthday
Person Picture	Picture
Person Notes	Notes

Save and run the page. You can select the values you just entered to group your contacts, as shown next:

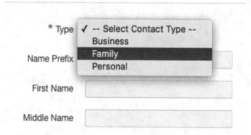

With the contact type List of Values set, let's create a contact with the following values:

Contact Type: Business

Prefix: Mr.

First Name: Kenny

Middle Name: M

Last Name: Mah

Birthday: 14-Nov-1975 (Note that we can enter this text or click the calendar icon for a pop-up calendar and select the date this way.)

Picture: (Upload a picture of your choice. Use file formats such as .jpg, .png, and .gif.)

Notes: Kenny is the CEO of the Kenny Mah Science Institute.

Once these values are set in the form, click the Create button. The row should be inserted and you should see the newly created row back on the My Contacts Report page. We are not going to do much with the person picture, but just know that we can store images in the database and later display them in reports.

Creating Interactive Reports

Let's go back to page 1, the Home page, and take a closer look at the report. We can either click the Home menu item at the upper-left of our application page to get to page 1, or we can change pages in the Page Designer to page 1 and look at the page from there. Once on page 1, you'll notice a few things about this report: We can't search easily or format this report. Also, it's not clear how we would download this report in multiple formats. All this can be determined by changing the report type.

You could click Edit Page 1 on the Developer toolbar to start. But before you click that link, let's try a shortcut to edit this report:

1. On the Developer toolbar, click Quick Edit. The page will dim and your cursor will become a plus sign.

2. Move your mouse over the report name and a blue box will surround the report. Click the box to open the Page Designer with the Contacts Report in focus. You can use Quick Edit to edit any page component quickly, without having to click the Edit Page X link, using the Rendering panel or Grid Layout, and finding the component you want to edit.

3. On the right side of the Page Designer, Property Editor, Region tab, look in the Identification property group. Change the Type property from Classic Report to Interactive Report.

4. Save and run the page. The report should look a bit different, with the main difference being a toolbar and search field above the report, as shown in Figure 6-15.

Person id	Person type	Person prefix	Person first name	Person middle name	Person last name	Person birthday	Person notes
1	Business	Mr.	Jetter	-	McTedder	18-APR-2006	-
2	Personal	-	Annie	-	Bananna	04-JUL-2006	-
3	Personal	-	Smitty	-	Werbenjagermanjensen	22-FEB-2002	-
4	Business	Mr.	Kenny	M	Mah	14-NOV-1975	Kenny is the CEO of the Kenny Mah Science Institute.

1 - 4

FIGURE 6-15. *The interactive report with the search field and toolbar*

Column Headings

At any time in an interactive report, you can click a column heading to bring up a sorting and value pop-up, where you can sort in ascending or descending order, hide the column, or set a control break on this column.

Click the Person Type heading, shown next, to see all the unique values included in this column. We can click a particular value and instantly create a column filter on that value. By typing in the Filter text field, we can quickly filter on a custom value in that column, again creating a column filter.

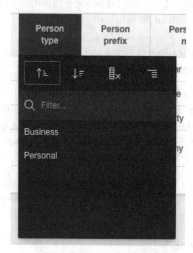

Reports Toolbar

By using interactive reports, users can customize and tailor reports exactly how they want to see them. Interactive reports offer powerful filtering and analytical functions that don't require you to know how to code SQL. Users can download the report into the format of their choosing, schedule a report to have it delivered to them via e-mail at a particular time, or save their customizations to share with other users. As a developer, you can specify which of these options is available to the end user through the Page Designer.

Search Bar

Let's start with the interactive report Search bar.

By typing a phrase or keyword in the text field, you can search a report and find all occurrences of the phrase or keyword.

Enter **Jetter** in the Search field and click the Go button. The report instantly filters to the Jetter McTedder contact row. Just under the Search bar is a down-pointing arrow. Click that arrow to reveal your filters if they are not already open:

Here are a few key options of note:

- **Checkbox** If selected, this checkbox applies the filter to our report; if unchecked, it removes the filter. Uncheck the checkbox and all the rows return in the report. Click the checkbox to select it and apply the filter.

- **The filter itself** In our case, Row Text Contains 'Jetter', which tells us that this filter will return any row with the text match of Jetter.

- **X icon** Hovering your cursor over this changes the icon to a red X with a "Remove Filter" tooltip. Clicking the X will delete the filter—this is different from the checkbox, because upon clicking the X, the filter will be completely removed, not just turned off.

■ **Magnifying glass** Click this icon to reveal a dropdown containing all the columns in your report:

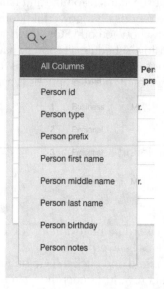

You can use the Magnifying glass dropdown list to make column-specific searches, or column filters.

1. Click Person Prefix, and the text box displays the phrase "Search: Person prefix". This alerts the user that this text search is going to be performed only in that column.

2. Type **Jetter** in the text box and click Go, and unlike our last search where it found a row, no rows will be returned, because "Jetter" does not occur in the Person Prefix column. In the filter field, you can see that a filter is applied to the report but it is slightly different from the previous one. The filter icon is green and not blue as before, and the text is a link:

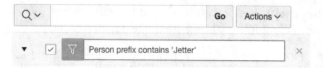

3. Click the text to open the Filter modal window (Figure 6-16). You can see the structure of a column filter (which will be discussed later in the chapter). For now, just know that you can get to this Filter modal window by clicking the text of a column filter.

4. Close the modal by clicking Cancel, and remove the column filter by clicking the X to the right of the filter field.

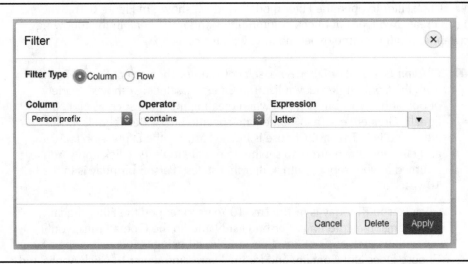

FIGURE 6-16. *The Filter modal window*

Actions Button

Finally, to the right of the Search bar is an Actions button. Click the button to access a menu that includes number of actions you can perform on an interactive report.

Select Columns   In the Filter modal window, click Column to open the Select Columns modal window, shown next, where you can shuttle around columns you want to view in the report. By using the shuttle controls or double-clicking, you can move columns to display or not to display in the report.

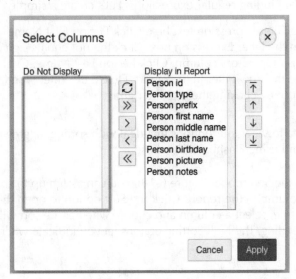

Filter   Click Filter to open the Filter modal window, shown in Figure 6-16, where you can create two types of filters: column filters and row filters. In the following paragraphs, you'll do some experimenting with filters.

- ***Column filters***   For Filter Type, select Column. Then select Person Birthday from the Column dropdown list. The Operator select list shows a variety of operations you can perform when creating the filter, such as Not Null, Equals, Greater/Less Than, some date-specific filters, Between, Is In The Next, and Is In The last. Choose Is In The Last. Set the Expression to 10 and click the down arrow to set the time scale to Years. Click apply. You're returned to your report, with a filter that states "Person birthday is in the last 10 years".

  Click Person Birthday Is In The Last 10 Years to reopen the Filter modal, and change the column to Person First Name. In the Operator list, you'll see options such as Contains, Like, and In, all being text-specific operators. Choose Does Not Contain, and for the Expression, enter **tt**. Click Apply, and the report will be filtered to show all rows where the First Name does not contain *tt*, as stated in the filter First Name Does Not Contain 'tt'. Note that when you're defining the filter, the dropdown list on the Expression field contains previous searches you have done, with the Search bar making it easy to set up filters that you previously ran.

  Row filters   For Filter Type, click Row. In the Row Filter Builder, shown in Figure 6-17, you can compare data across rows rather than columns. Scroll down or expand the modal to view the area below the Filter Expression text box. Column names are represented with alphabetic characters. On the right are functions or operators we can use. Scroll through the list to see the choices, including regular expressions. Let's create a simple filter.

  Clear the Filter Expression text box. Click Person First Name, and a letter is placed in the Filter Expression box. Click the not equals sign (!=) from the Functions / Operators column. Click Person Last Name. Click Apply, and you'll see the Row Filter in the report. Delete this filter when you are done trying it out by clicking the X to the right.

Data   Click Data to view four options that deal with sorting, aggregation, computations, and using Flashback Database.

- **Sort**   In the Sort modal (Figure 6-18), you can assign up to six sorting rules to any column in the report. Click the Sort option to open the modal. To create a rule, select a column and choose whether the sort will be Ascending or Descending. The Null Sorting options let you indicate where you want

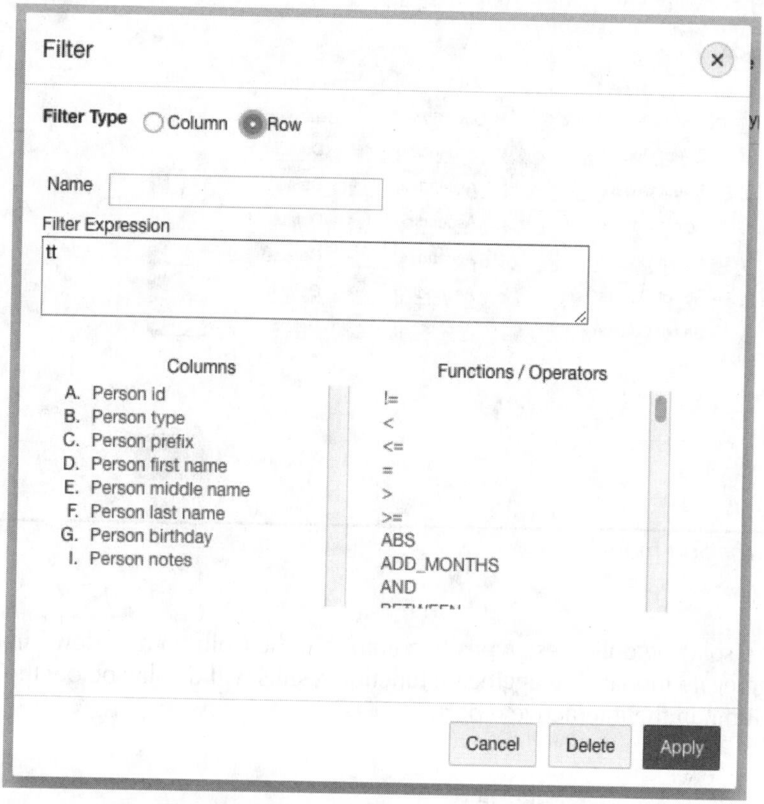

Filter ⊗

Filter Type ○ Column ●Row

Name [   ]

Filter Expression

[tt   ]

Columns	Functions / Operators
A. Person id	!=
B. Person type	<
C. Person prefix	<=
D. Person first name	=
E. Person middle name	>
F. Person last name	>=
G. Person birthday	ABS
I. Person notes	ADD_MONTHS
	AND

[Cancel] [Delete] [Apply]

FIGURE 6-17. *Row Filter Builder*

NULL values to be placed: Always First or Always Last. For example, if you were sorting on the Middle Name column, there might not be a value for every contact. In that case, you could choose to have all the NULL values show first in the report, and then contacts that have a value for Middle Name, or you could have all the contacts with no middle names be sorted last and start with contacts with middle names. When a sort is on a column, it will be indicated with an icon just below the text of the header.

■ **Aggregate** In the Aggregate modal, you can choose to see existing aggregations or create a new one. These options enable you to perform mathematical computations against a column. For Function, you can choose from the following: Sum, Average, Count, Count Distinct, Minimum, Maximum, and Median. Being mathematical functions, the column to which you apply the aggregate must be of the Number type. APEX helps with this

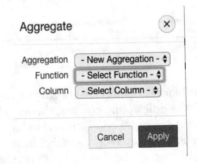

FIGURE 6-18. *The Sort modal*

by displaying only these types of columns in the Column dropdown in the Aggregate modal. The aggregate function results will display below the column in the interactive report.

- **Compute** The Compute modal (Figure 6-19) looks similar to the Row Filter modal, sharing a similar column and function interface. The options here enable you to create columns in the report based on a computation you define. You can create a new column that adds or subtracts dates, create new values by concatenating existing values, or create a complex mathematical statement. For this report, combine the First Name, Middle Name, and Last Name columns into a single column titled Full Name.

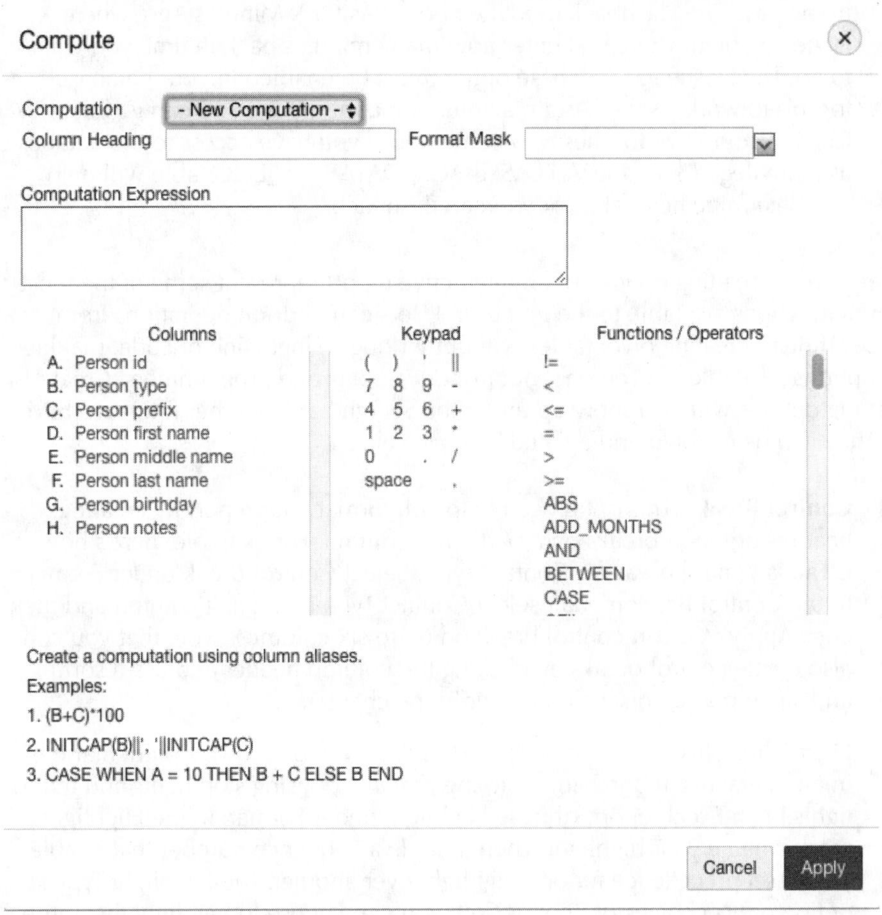

Compute ⊗

Computation | - New Computation - ⬦ |

Column Heading | [   ]   Format Mask | [   ] ▾ |

Computation Expression

[   ]

Columns	Keypad	Functions / Operators

Columns

A. Person id
B. Person type
C. Person prefix
D. Person first name
E. Person middle name
F. Person last name
G. Person birthday
H. Person notes

Keypad

( ) ' ||
7 8 9 -
4 5 6 +
1 2 3 *
0 . /
space ,

Functions / Operators

!=
<
<=
=
>
>=
ABS
ADD_MONTHS
AND
BETWEEN
CASE

Create a computation using column aliases.

Examples:

1. (B+C)*100
2. INITCAP(B)||', '||INITCAP(C)
3. CASE WHEN A = 10 THEN B + C ELSE B END

| Cancel | Apply |

FIGURE 6-19. *Compute modal*

In the Computation Expression text box, enter the following expression or something similar:

D ||' '|| E ||' '|| F

(The double pipes [||] in SQL indicate a concatenate.)

Note that new columns you create will not show up under the Search bar, as do other formatting options. To edit a compute column, either click the column header and then click the compute icon (additional calculator icon on the right) or bring up the Compute modal under the Format option in the Actions menu.

■ **Flashback** This action lets you query data as it existed at a particular time in the past. The Flashback modal will offer As Of X Minutes Ago, where X is the text field where you enter how many minutes back in time you want to go. The Flashback Database option must be enabled in your database for this to work, as well as a maximum amount of time you can go back. Consult your DBA for these exact metrics. If you have access to the database as a privileged user, the V$FLASHBACK_DATABASE_LOG table will help you determine how far back you can flashback.

Format The formatting options of an interactive report represent some of the most powerful functions available to the end user. Users can perform operations from simple sorting to creating pivot tables without writing a single line of code, making these options available to everyone, not just developers and programmers. Created formatting options will also show up under the Search bar like other filters we have seen. They can be enabled and deleted here as well.

■ **Control Break** This option can help you format your report by creating headers or report breaks on a particular column. For example, here's how to create a control break on Contact Type: Select Control Break under Format. In the Control Break modal, select Contact Type in the first column and then click Apply. You can control break on up to six columns. Note that you can also create control breaks by clicking the column header and use a sorting and value pop-up discussed earlier in the chapter.

■ **Highlight** This option lets you change the color of a row or particular cell in an interactive report, similar to the practice of using stop lights and traffic lights in an Excel report. Choose Highlight under Format. In the Highlight modal, name your highlight. Then include a Sequence number that enables you to set precedence for one highlight over another. The Highlight Type option offers choices of Row or Cell: you can choose to highlight the entire row if the filter matches or just the individual cell.

The next two options are the color choices for the highlight: Color Of The Background of the highlight and Color Of The Text. APEX provides some clickable choices in the format of [yellow][green][blue][orange][red]. Clicking those options will prefill the HTML color field. You can also create custom color choices by clicking the small up arrow next to the color field to open the custom color chooser, where you can select any color you want by sliding the color bar or increasing or decreasing the RGB values.

Finally, the Expression Builder Or Highlight Condition lets you choose the column, the operator, and expression condition you want to highlight. Click the Apply button when you're done to see your work in the report. An example of highlighting is shown in Figure 6-20.

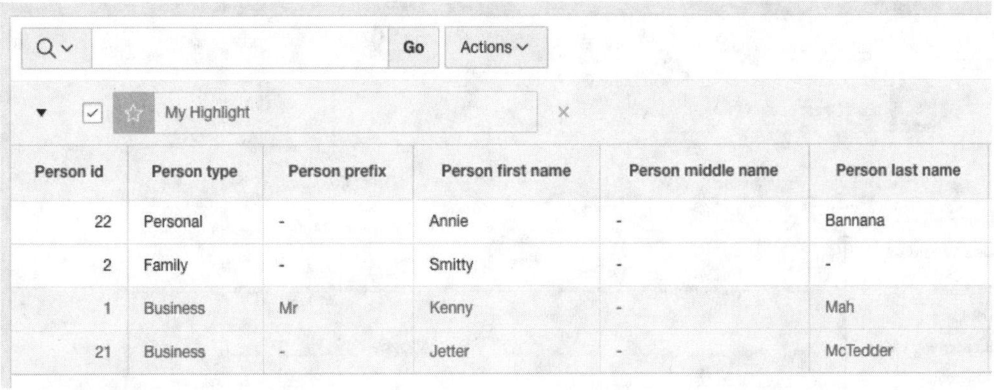

Person id	Person type	Person prefix	Person first name	Person middle name	Person last name
22	Personal	-	Annie	-	Bannana
2	Family	-	Smitty	-	-
1	Business	Mr	Kenny	-	Mah
21	Business	-	Jetter	-	McTedder

FIGURE 6-20. *Highlighting*

■ **Rows Per Page** This Action menu item enables you to determine how many results are shown in the report before pagination occurs. To change the number, hover your cursor over the option and select a new number by clicking it.

Chart You can create bar, line, and pie charts in an interactive report. These charts can be viewed in any HTML5-compliant browser and do not need the Adobe Flash Player to view. Once you have created a chart, you can toggle between the data view and chart view by clicking the icons at the top of the modal next to the Search bar, as shown in Figure 6-21. While in the chart view, under the Search bar, you can click the down arrow to expand the Filter area and then click the Edit Chart text to make changes or delete the chart. Hover the mouse over charts to see the actual values of the data represented. Figure 6-21 shows an example that uses a bar chart to show a count of APEX items that have changed in the last day. You can view four chart types: vertical bar, horizontal bar, pie, or line chart.

Group By The Group By icon is located near the Search bar. Using the Group By formatting option, you can group data by one or more columns and then add aggregate functions on top of that data. In the Group By modal window (Figure 6-22), you can group by a single column, or, by clicking the linked text Add Group By Column, you can group on multiple columns. The same goes for the aggregate functions—a single line is presented, but you can add more by clicking the linked text. The resulting Group By formatting will be presented in a new report, similar to a chart. While in the Group By report, under the Search bar, you can expand the Filter area and click the Edit Group By link to make changes or delete the report.

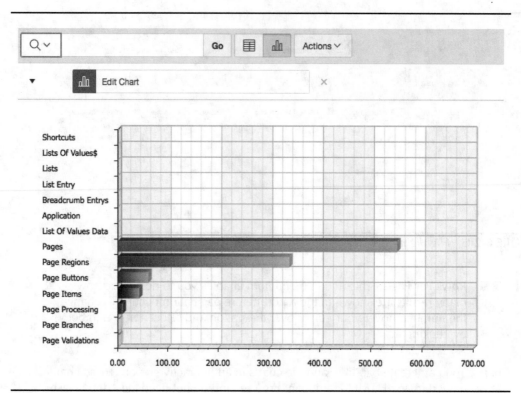

FIGURE 6-21. *APEX charts*

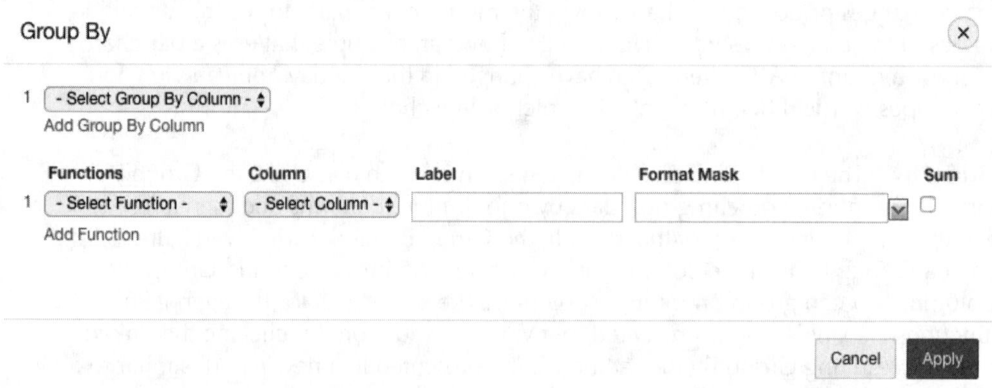

Group By ⊗

1 [- Select Group By Column - ♦]
Add Group By Column

Functions	Column	Label	Format Mask	Sum
1 [- Select Function - ♦]	[- Select Column - ♦]	[ ]	[ ] ⌄	☐

Add Function

Cancel   Apply

FIGURE 6-22. *The Group By modal*

Pivot New to APEX 5, the Pivot format option enables you to pivot rows into columns. The pivot function used to be a very difficult SQL query to write, making it unavailable to all but skilled developers. APEX puts the power of the pivot function into the hands of business users, so they can create powerful reports without having to ask for help from a DBA or developer. The Pivot modal asks the user to first choose the columns on which to pivot, then the columns to display as rows, and finally the columns to aggregate along with the mathematical function to be performed. The resulting Pivot report is presented in a new report page. While in the Pivot report, under the Search bar, you can expand the Filter area and click Edit Pivot to make changes or delete the report. In Figure 6-23, in an orders report from the APEX database sample packaged application, the order month rows have been pivoted to columns to create a sum of orders created by each customer per month. This report was created completely with the Pivot function in APEX and no DBA or developer was needed.

Save Report The Save Report action (under the Report option) enables users and developers to save the current version of the report for public and private use. As a developer, you can create multiple versions of the report and set them as either a default report or a named report. Users see the default report as soon as they view the page with the interactive report, and the named report is a report that users can

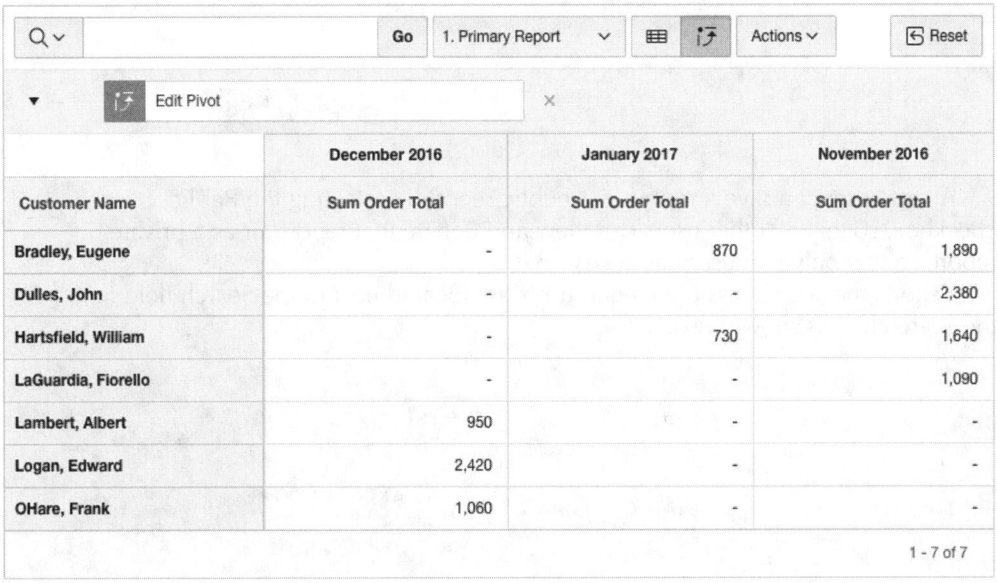

Customer Name	December 2016 Sum Order Total	January 2017 Sum Order Total	November 2016 Sum Order Total
Bradley, Eugene	-	870	1,890
Dulles, John	-	-	2,380
Hartsfield, William	-	730	1,640
LaGuardia, Fiorello	-	-	1,090
Lambert, Albert	950	-	-
Logan, Edward	2,420	-	-
OHare, Frank	1,060	-	-

1 - 7 of 7

FIGURE 6-23. *A Pivot report*

choose from a dropdown list on the toolbar. If a named report is not chosen, users will see the default report when viewing an interactive report. Here's the developer user's Save Report modal:

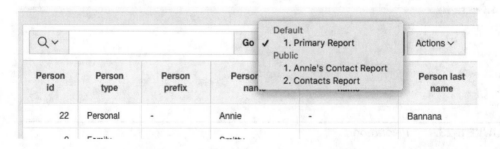

Here's the end user's Save Report modal:

An end user can save a report as a public report by selecting the Public checkbox, so that all other users can view and update that report, or as a private report, so that only that user has access to it.

Reports that are accessible by end users are located next to the Search field in the Search bar, as shown next:

To delete saved reports, open the filter dropdown under the Search bar and click Remove Report X. You'll see a confirmation box where you can confirm you want to delete this report.

Reset   Use the Reset action to reset the report back to its default state; note that you'll lose all unsaved formatting options. The Reset modal will prompt you to make sure you want to perform a reset. Upon clicking Apply, the report will be reset. The default state of the report is defined by a developer, as discussed in the "Save Report" section earlier in this chapter.

Download   Click the Download action in an interactive report to view six download formats: CSV, HTML, Email, XLS, PDF, and RTF. (More on why XLS and RTF may not be seen will be discussed later in the chapter.)

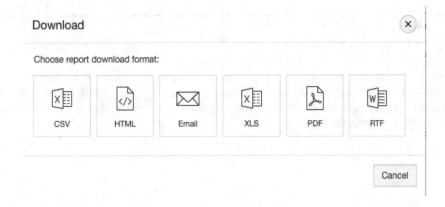

NOTE
In these data files, break formatting and highlighting will not be preserved on download.

Click the Email option to e-mail an HTML version of the report. Although the HTML version does not maintain break formatting or highlighting, it does include a Search box you can use to search and limit your dataset in the HTML page, as shown in Figure 6-24. The PDF download does not maintain break formatting or highlighting, but it can be created without any additional software or plug-ins.

Subscription   The Subscription action enables users to e-mail an interactive report in HTML format (break formatting and highlighting are not retained) on a scheduled time basis. The Subscription modal, shown next, includes fields for a single or

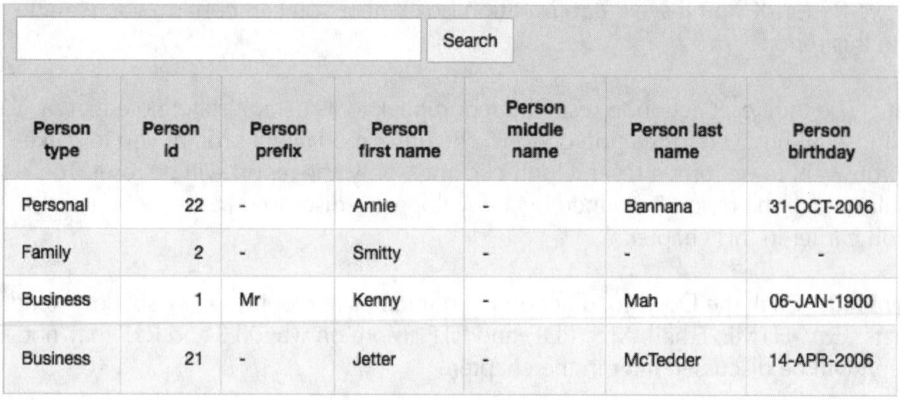

Person type	Person id	Person prefix	Person first name	Person middle name	Person last name	Person birthday
Personal	22	-	Annie	-	Bannana	31-OCT-2006
Family	2	-	Smitty	-	-	-
Business	1	Mr	Kenny	-	Mah	06-JAN-1900
Business	21	-	Jetter	-	McTedder	14-APR-2006

FIGURE 6-24. *A sample HTML report with a Search bar*

multiple e-mail addresses (comma separated), a subject line for the e-mail and time frames—Daily, Weekly, and Monthly—along with starting and ending dates. If these fields are empty, the subscription will run indefinitely. To edit or delete a subscription, click the Subscription action item.

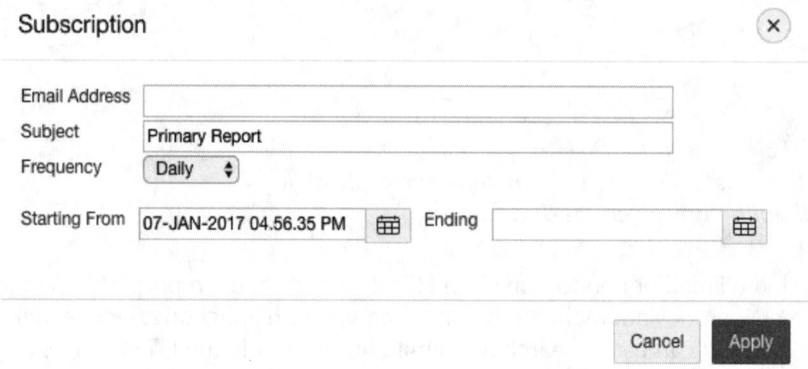

Subscription

Email Address	
Subject	Primary Report
Frequency	Daily
Starting From	07-JAN-2017 04.56.35 PM
Ending	

Cancel   Apply

Help   Clicking the Help action brings up the interactive report's Help page, where you can find help and descriptions for all aspects of an interactive report. There is also a link to the *Application Express End User's Guide.*

Behind the Interactive Report Properties

Now let's take a look at some of the available options for interactive reports behind the scenes.

In the Page Designer, click the Attributes folder under the My Contacts report. Then move your attention to the Property Editor, Attributes tab, and click the Show All button at the top of the Property Editor.

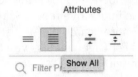

You'll see every property for a particular component, not only the common ones. Here are some of the more important properties you can set for interactive reports:

- **Link Property Group, Link Column** This property automatically creates a link in the report that brings the user to a custom page, similar to what we have in our linked form.

- **Link to Single Row View** This link brings you to a special read-only form that displays the data for the row you are viewing. It does not create a new page, but uses the interactive report region to display this single row view.

- **Exclude Link Column** Choose this option to leave out the link column with the value.

Using the Link Column option, let's create a link to our form.

1. Change the value of Link Column to Link to Custom Target.

2. Click the No Link Defined button in the Target Property.

3. In the Link Builder modal, set Page to **2**.

4. In the Set Items section, use the pop-up List Of Values (LOV) to set Name to **P2_PERSON_ID**.

5. In the Value property, use the pop-up LOV to set it to PERSON_ID, which will display as #PERSON_ID#.

6. In the Clear Session State section, set the Clear Cache property to **2**.

7. Click OK. The link to our form has been restored in an interactive report.

Scroll down a bit in the Property Editor and find the Pagination property, which is part of every report, regardless of type. Here you can set where the pagination will display on a report and the range. There are less options in an interactive report, because the number of rows per page is an interactive report option in the Actions menu.

In the Messages property group, you can define custom messages if, for example, the report cannot find data or the report returns more rows than the maximum set.

One of the more important property groups is the Search Bar group (Figure 6-25). You can define what parts of the interactive report Search bar you want exposed to end users. You can restrict the entire Search bar or just components of it. The last property here, Maximum Rows Per Page, enables you to restrict the maximum number of rows that pagination will allow.

In the Actions Menu property group, you can restrict every aspect of the Actions menu or remove the Actions button entirely.

In the Download property group, you can restrict what types of files the end user is able to download. Two options require Oracle BI Publisher to work: XLS and RTF. (The Integration between Oracle APEX and BI Publisher is not discussed in this book.) Below the Download Formats property are some options for the CSV format. By default, CSV files are comma separated, but the CSV Separator property lets you override this. With the CSV Enclosed By property, you can override how the CSVs are enclosed, which, by default, use double quotes. The last property under the

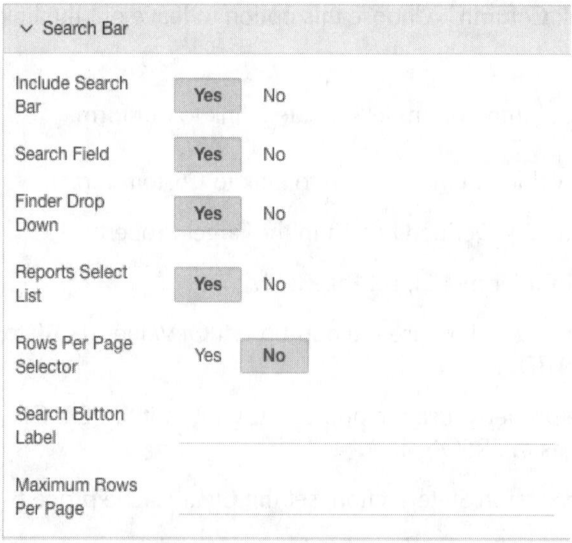

FIGURE 6-25. *Search Bar properties*

Download group is Filename. You can change the default name of the file the user gets when clicking one of the download options. By default, the filename will be the name of the report.

Finally, in the Performance property group, Maximum Rows To Process lets you limit the number of total results a report will produce. By default, it is set to 1000000, which is a bit large and may cause performance problems. This value should be evaluated for your particular report and set accordingly.

Behind the Interactive Report Columns

In the Page Designer's Rendering panel, above the Attributes folder, is the Columns folder. Expand that folder and click PERSON_PREFIX. Then look at the Property Editor, Column tab. Just as the Attributes folder contains multiple properties for customizing the interactive report's functionality, similar options here can affect individual columns, enabling you to get down to a granular level for interactive report customization.

Scroll down the Property Editor to the Enable Users To property group (Figure 6-26).

Here are many options to apply to a particular column. You can limit the user's formatting, column sorting, and views and selections options. By hiding the column with the Hide property, the column will not only be unavailable for any of the actions, but it will no longer appear on the report at all. This action does not merely move the column from the Selected Columns from the Display In Report to the Do Not Display side, but it makes the column completely unavailable.

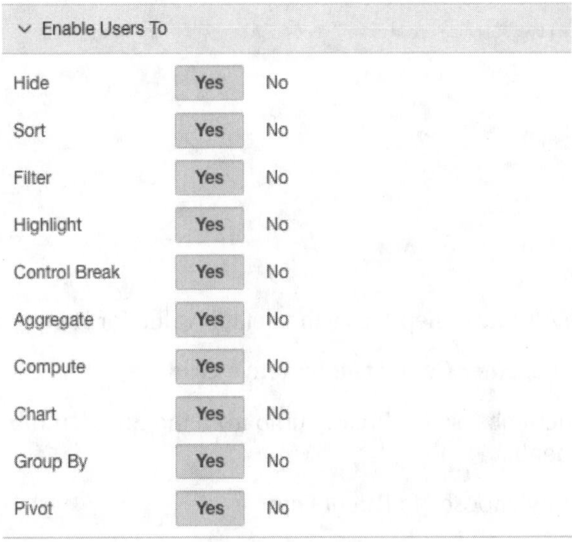

FIGURE 6-26. *Enable Users To properties*

Interactive Grids

You can continue to add contacts with your single form, but wouldn't it be much easier to be able to add multiple contacts in a single form? How about combining the power of an interactive report with the form you use to manipulate data? Enter the interactive grid, a hybrid type of form and report that enables you to update, insert, and delete multiple rows of data at a single time, just like a spreadsheet. The interactive grid can also be used for reporting, with most of the rich features of an interactive report. This feature is new with Application Express 5.1.

Create an Interactive Grid

To create an interactive grid, follow these steps:

1. In the Page Designer, click the Create dropdown menu and select Page.

2. In the Create Page wizard, choose Form and then click Next.

3. Choose Editable Interactive Grid, as shown next:

4. For the Page Attributes step, leave the default value for Page Number.

5. For Page Name, enter **Contacts Interactive Grid**.

6. To use breadcrumbs, select Breadcrumb from the Breadcrumb field dropdown menu.

7. For Parent Entry choose No Parent Entry.

8. For Entry Name, enter **Contacts Interactive Grid** if this is not filled in for you. Your page should look similar to Figure 6-27.

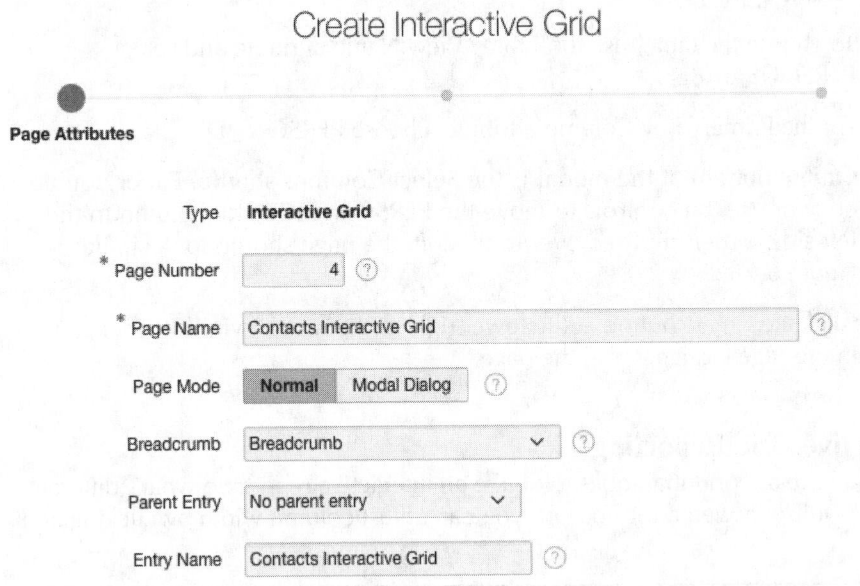

Create Interactive Grid

Page Attributes

Type	**Interactive Grid**
* Page Number	4 (?)
* Page Name	Contacts Interactive Grid (?)
Page Mode	**Normal** Modal Dialog (?)
Breadcrumb	Breadcrumb ⌄ (?)
Parent Entry	No parent entry ⌄
Entry Name	Contacts Interactive Grid (?)

FIGURE 6-27.   *Interactive grid Page Attributes*

9. Click Next.

10. Next, you'll set up the Navigation menu. You can link this interactive grid page to the navigation pane on the left of all of your pages, just as you did with forms and reports, to switch quickly to the editable grid without creating any special navigation or buttons. Select the radio button next to Create A New Navigation Menu Entry.

11. In the New Navigation Menu Entry field, enter **Contacts Interactive Grid**.

12. For Parent Menu Control, leave it set at the default value of – No Parent Selected –.

13. Click Next to move to the next step.

14. In the Report Source step, you'll choose a table or editable view you want this interactive grid to use. For Editing Enabled, choose whether you want to edit this grid or not. Set this to Yes.

15. For Source Type, ensure that the radio button next to Table is selected.

16. The Table / View Owner select list should be set to the schema you created for this application.

17. To choose the table, use the Table / View Name attribute and select PERSONS_TABLE.

18. For the Primary Key Column attribute, choose PERSON_ID.

19. On the bottom of the modal is the Select Columns shuttle. Either double-click or use the controls to move the PERSON_PICTURE column to the left side. When shuttled over to the left, the page should look similar to Figure 6-28.

20. Click the Create button at the lower right of the modal window. Then, back in the Page Designer, run the page.

Interactive Grid Reporting

Now you have a report that looks a lot like an interactive report. So what's different about it? Quick answer: a lot. To start, you can adjust column width by clicking and

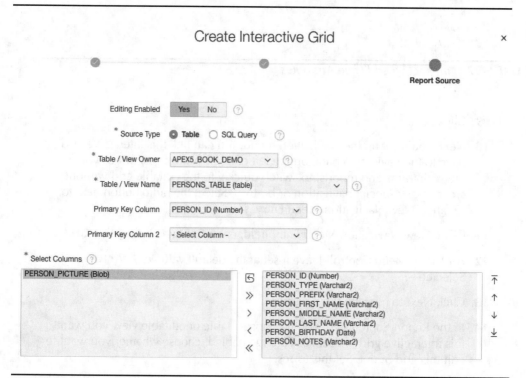

FIGURE 6-28. *The Report Source step to create an interactive grid*

dragging the column. When you hover over a column's left or right side, the cursor will change to a two-sided arrow icon, as shown in the next illustration. Click and drag the column to make it wider or narrower. You can also change the width by pressing CTRL-LEFT ARROW or CTRL-RIGHT ARROW (CTRL-CMD-LEFT ARROW or CTRL-CMD-RIGHT ARROW on a Mac) when the column header has keyboard focus by hovering your mouse on the left side of the column.

Person First Name	✛Pers
Annie	-

You can also reorder columns in the interactive grid by dragging and dropping the column header to another location, as shown next. Or, by using the keyboard while a column header is in focus, press SHIFT-RIGHT ARROW or SHIFT-LEFT ARROW to move the column to the right or left, respectively. You no longer need to use the Column submenu to reorder columns.

	Person First Name	Person Middle Name
-	Annie	Person Prefix
-	Smitty	-
Mr.	Kenny	M
Mr.	Jetter	-

Column sorting has also been enhanced by adding ascending/descending buttons in the column header, as shown next. Or you can use the keyboard when the header is in focus and press ALT-UP KEY or ALT-DOWN KEY to move the column up or down, respectively. Interactive grids will also let you do a multicolumn sort by SHIFT-clicking the headers.

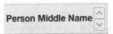

You can sort a column using the arrows in the header. To do a multicolumn sort, SHIFT-click the sort arrow in a column header. You'll see a tiny number in each column that indicates its order, as shown in the next illustration. Continue the multicolumn sort by SHIFT-clicking another column header's sort arrows. The following illustration shows a three-column sort:

Person First Name ↓₌¹	Person Middle Name ↑₌²	Person Last Name ↓₌³
Smitty		Werbeniggermanignang

Another welcome and popular enhancement in interactive grids and interactive reports is sticky, or frozen, headers and footers. Sticky headers stay on the top of a report if you are scrolling down past the visible bottom of the report. In the past, the header would scroll up and out of sight. Sticky footers stay at the bottom of the report as you scroll.

The Column Header Menu   You can click a column header to see a pop-up menu that includes several popular options, which are represented across the top as four icons with a Filter and Select list:

- **Control Break**   Click the first icon on the left to control break your report on that particular column instantly, rather than using the Actions button.

- **Aggregate (summation symbol)**   Click to bring up the Aggregation modal, where you can create column aggregations.

- **Column Freeze (snowflake)**   Click to freeze columns and prevent them from being moved.

- **Hide (column stack and x)**   Click to hide columns.

Column Groups   The interactive grid can create column groups, custom groupings of like columns that will display under a single higher level column. This column grouping can also be dragged and dropped, taking all members of the column group with it.

To create a column group, follow these steps:

1. Edit the page.

2. On the left side of the Page Designer, find the Attributes folder under the Interactive Grid region. Expand the Attributes folder and right-click the Column Groups node and select Create Column Group.

3. On the right side in the Column Groups property panel is a Heading
section. For Heading, enter the name of the column group:

∨ Heading	
Heading	Name
Alternative Label	

Now you can assign the column group to one or more columns:

1. On the left side of the Page Designer, under the Interactive Grid region, expand
the Columns node.

2. Click PERSON_PREFIX and then SHIFT-click PERSON_LAST_NAME to select
all four columns.

3. On the right side, in the Column Property tab, find the Group property in
the Layout property group. (Find it quickly using the Property Search box
and entering **group**.)

4. In the select list, choose Name. The Use Group For attribute appears. You can
use this grouping for the regular report or the single row view.

5. Leave the default of Both and save and run the page.

You'll see the four columns grouped under the Name heading group, as
shown here:

Name			
Person Prefix	**Person First Name**	**Person Middle Name**	**Person Last Name**
Mr.	Jetter	-	McTedder
-	Annie	-	Bananna

NOTE
*If you move a column out of the group by click-
dragging it in the report, the column header will
retain the grouping. This is especially useful because
it enables you to use the column groups to add
context to the column names.*

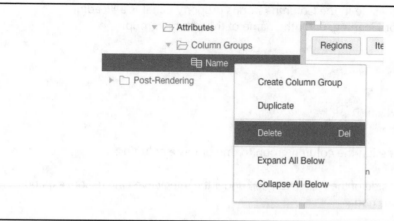

FIGURE 6-29. *Deleting a column group*

You can edit the page and delete the column group by right-clicking the column group name in the Rendering panel in Page Designer and choosing Delete (Figure 6-29).

The Interactive Grid Toolbar

The interactive grid toolbar, shown next, is similar to that of interactive reports. Run the page to take a look at the interactive grid toolbar.

Starting on the left, the column search selection dropdown menu, Search bar, and Go button serve purposes similar to the same buttons in an interactive report. Next are the Grid and Create Chart options that are available after you create a chart.

The Actions menu is missing some options found on the interactive reports menu. Let's go over what the Actions menu offers for interactive grids.

Columns

Choosing Columns will bring up the Columns modal window, where you can show or hide columns, reorder columns, or set the column width in pixels (Figure 6-30). These modal windows will be used going forward for many of the interactive grid options.

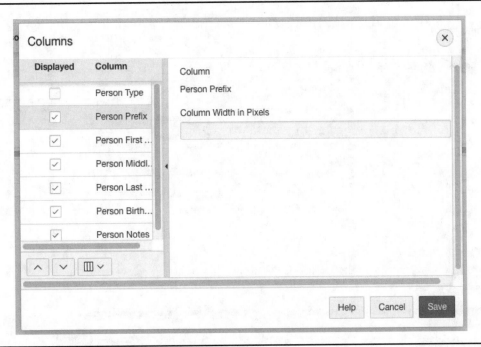

FIGURE 6-30. *The Columns modal window*

This new format enables you to work with multiple complex options and actions in a single place, maximizing productivity.

Filter

Click Filter to open the Filters modal window (Figure 6-31), where you can choose from two types of filters: Row and Column. Row and column filters work just as they did in interactive reports, except you can work with multiple filters of different types all from this modal.

Data

The options found in the Data submenu enable you to sort and aggregate data as well as flashback to a previous point in the database to look at the data from that point in time. The Data submenu contains the following options:

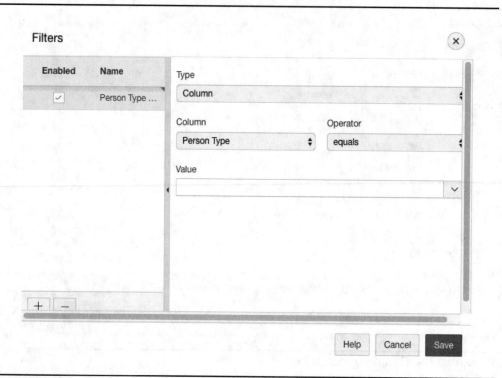

FIGURE 6-31. *The Filters modal window*

Sort   This option enables you to create column sorts on your data (Figure 6-32). This is similar to creating a sort by clicking the column headers, but it gives you a canvas to create them all in one place. You can also dictate how you treat nulls in your sorts using this modal; this option is not available by clicking the column headers.

Aggregate   As with interactive reports, you can use this option to run aggregation functions on your data. New for interactive grids is the Aggregation modal, where you can work with multiple aggregations at the same time (Figure 6-33). In addition, you can have a grand total displayed by checking the Show Overall Value checkbox, and the functions are filtered based on the column type; in interactive reports, the columns are filtered based on functions.

Refresh   This option repopulates the interactive grid with the most current data from the database.

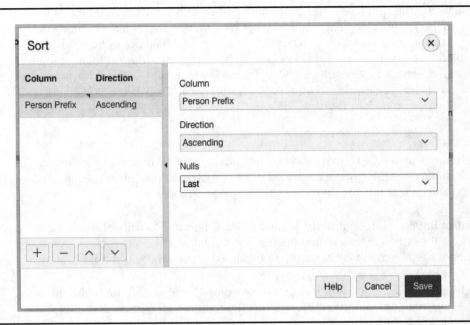

FIGURE 6-32. *The Sort modal*

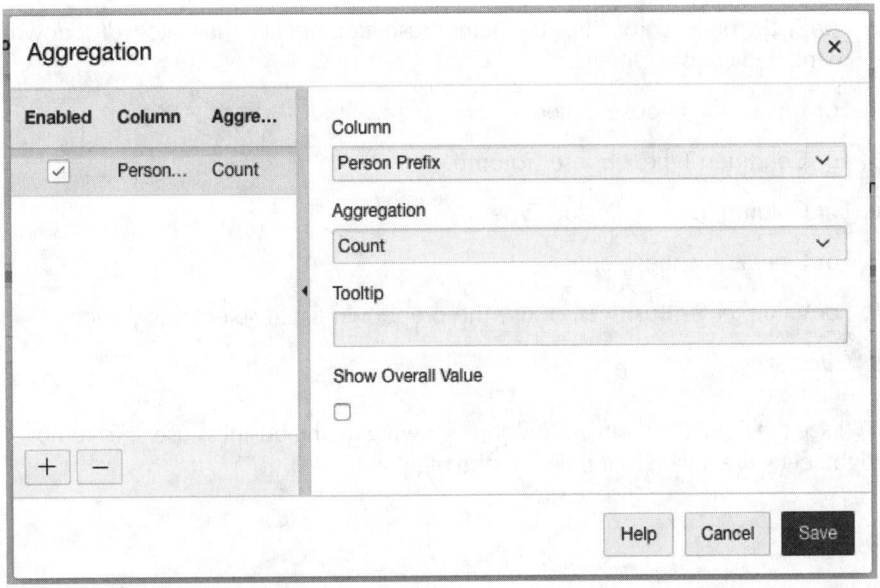

FIGURE 6-33. *The Aggregation modal*

Flashback   This option lets you query data as it existed at a particular time in the past. In the Flashback modal, you can enter how many minutes back in time you want to go in the Minutes Ago text field. (Note that the Flashback option must be enabled in your database for this to work, along with a maximum amount of time you can flashback to. Consult your DBA for these exact metrics. If you have access to the database as a privileged user, the V$FLASHBACK_DATABASE_LOG table will help you determine how far back you can flashback.)

Format

The options under the Format submenu let you add control breaks or highlighting to your interactive grid to make the report more readable or highlight a specific data point. The Format submenu contains the following options:

Control Breaks   The Control Break modal offers the same functionality you have by clicking the option in the column header. The modal window lets you work with multiple page breaks at the same time as well as dictate how you sort null values.

Highlights   This option will let you create colored row or column highlights based upon a particular data rule. In the Highlight modal (Figure 6-34), let's create a highlight.

1. For Name, enter **Person Type**.

2. For Highlight, keep the default selection, Row. We are going to highlight rows.

3. For Background Color, click the paint brush icon or click the Colors dropdown menu and choose Orange

4. For Text Color, choose Green.

5. For Condition Type, choose Column.

6. For Column, choose Person Type.

7. For Operator, choose equals.

8. For Value, enter **Business**, or use the dropdown list to select this value.

9. Click Save.

You'll see the highlighting in your report, showing all the business users. To remove a highlight, click the X icon to the right of the highlight.

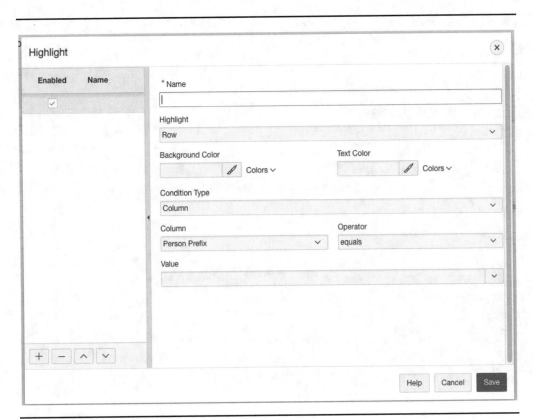

FIGURE 6-34. *The Highlight modal*

Chart

Select Chart to work in the Chart modal (Figure 6-35), where you can choose the chart type, labels, data, and attributes for the chart. The charts used in the interactive grid and in APEX 5.1 are the new Oracle JET Data Visualizations, HTML5-compliant charts that work on any device in any browser.

Report Settings

Report Settings has grouped the save report options with the reset and delete options that were in the Actions menu in interactive reports. It also shows several options:

Save   The Save option saves the interactive grid as your default report view. No longer is there a modal for this, stating whether we want this to be our default view; it's now just a simple Save option.

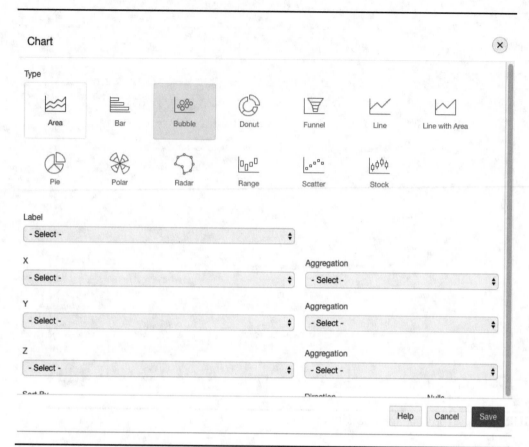

FIGURE 6-35. *The Chart modal*

Save As　The Save As option functions like the old Save Report option. In this modal, you can save the report as a Public (if enabled, this is similar to interactive reports: from the Page Designer, choose the Attributes node and then view the Enable Users To property group), Primary, Private, or Alternate report. New in the interactive grid is the Alternate report type. With this report, you can add another layer of security by using APEX authorization to control who can access it.

Reset　The Reset option returns the report to its previous saved or default state.

Delete　Use the Delete option to delete saved reports.

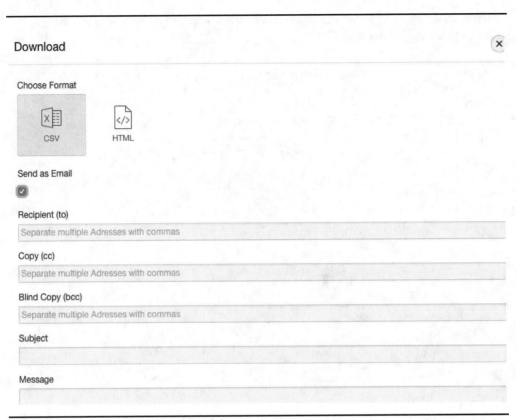

FIGURE 6-36. *The Download modal*

Download
In the Download modal (Figure 6-36), you can download the report in either CSV or HTML format. You can also e-mail this report to one or many recipient addresses.

Help
Choosing the Help option launches the interactive grid Help modal, with a summary of how to use interactive grids.

Row Actions Menu
The Row Actions menu, shown next, is located at the right of the checkbox for each row in an interactive grid. Use these actions to perform the following: view the row

in single row view, add a row, duplicate rows, delete rows, refresh rows, or revert changes to abandon your edits:

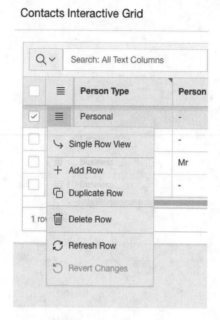

Add Row

Selecting Add Row adds a blank row in your interactive grid. It enables you to create a new row without having to use a form. You can also add a row by pressing ALT-INSERT on the keyboard when working in the interactive grid. Or you can use the Add Row button on the interactive grid toolbar.

Duplicate Row

Use this option to duplicate one or more rows. Click Row Actions next to the row you want duplicated and then select Duplicate Row. Once selected, that row is duplicated.

Delete Row

Click Row Actions next to the row you want duplicated and then select Delete Row. The row does not disappear from the table but appears with the strikethrough font (shown next). The row will not be deleted from the database until you save the changes.

| Business | Mr | Kenny | - | Mah | 06-JAN-1900 |

Refresh Row and Revert Changes

The Refresh Row option refreshes the selected row, refreshing the data in the interactive grid. If you change the data in a particular cell, you can revert that change with the Revert Change option. This option will revert only the changes made to the selected row, not the entire table. Note that this will undo all changes to the row, not just the latest change.

Edit and Save Buttons

Click the Edit button to put the grid into edit mode. Click the Save button to save your data changes.

Other Features of Interactive Grids

Many powerful properties of interactive grids can be used to offer security, to speed up page loads, and to return data faster. To see these properties, edit the page and open the Attributes node under the interactive grid in the Rendering panel on the left side of Page Designer.

On the right, in the Attributes property tab, find the Edit Authorization property group, shown next. Using these properties, you can set security on add, update, and delete functionality of an interactive grid. Based on who the user is and what rights she has, you can secure the various actions of the interactive grid.

The next property group is Performance, with the Lazy Loading property. If set to Yes, this property will load the page, components on the page, and the interactive grid. While the page is loading, APEX, in a separate process, will fetch the data. This prevents the end user from seeing a blank white page while APEX is fetching the data and presents the user with a fully rendered page with a processing spinner over the data section.

The Pagination property group, shown next, offers some new features for creating a better experience for the end user viewing large sets of data:

The Type property has two options:

- **Page**   The first rows will be displayed based on the number specified in the Rows Per Page formatting option. If there are additional rows, APEX will add traditional pagination controls in the report footer.

- **Scroll**   This provides the user with a single page of data to fill the specified height of the interactive grid. As the user scrolls down the report, additional rows are displayed, displaying more data from the server on demand.

The Toolbar property group determines whether the toolbar is shown to end users. You can also control whether the Save and Reset buttons are shown, to allow or disallow them to commit changes to the database by saving. Lastly, you can change the label of the Add Row button, calling it whatever you want.

Editing Data with the Interactive Grid

Back in the interactive grid (run the page if you're still in the Page Designer), double-click any cell of the grid to see a prompt and change data within that cell. Let's change the middle name of one of our contacts.

Double-click a cell and enter **Banannakins**, as shown next. Click the Save button on the toolbar. The data is not changed in the database.

Jetter	-	McTedder
Annie	Banannakins	Bananna
Smitty	-	Werbenjagermanjensen

While you are still in the cell, you can easily move around the grid using the keyboard ARROW keys once you are no longer editing the cell. Press the ESC key to exit edit mode. The cell will still be highlighted but not editable. You can now move around the grid using the ARROW keys. When you find a cell you want to edit, press ENTER or RETURN.

If you want to navigate the grid while still in edit mode, press TAB to move one cell to the right, or press SHIFT-TAB to move one cell to the left.

Press ENTER or RETURN while in edit mode to move down one cell, and press SHIFT-ENTER or SHIFT-RETURN to move up one cell.

NOTE
*Here are some housekeeping rules around data
changes and saving. All edits are local until you click
the Save button. If you attempt to leave the page
with unsaved edits, you will see a warning pop-up.
You will also see this warning if you attempt to
change filters or sorting while you have unsaved
changes. Caution! Those actions will reset the data
and you will lose any edits you have made.
Pagination, however, will not cause you to lose edits.*

Once the data in a cell is changed, a small blue earmark will be displayed in the
upper-right corner of the cell, as shown here. This lets you know which cells have
changed data. Click the Save button, and your changes will
be saved to the database and the blue earmark will be
removed from the cell.

Interactive Grid Validations

An interactive grid also can include validations for data editing and entry:

1. Edit the page.

2. On the left side of the Page Designer, expand the Columns node under your
Interactive Grid region in the Rendering panel.

3. Click PERSON_FIRST_NAME, and then go to the right in the Property Editor,
Column tab.

4. In the Validation property group, change the Value Required property to Yes.
Then save and run the page.

∨ Validation		
Value Required	Yes	No
Maximum Length	50	characters

5. In the grid, choose any contact and erase his or her first name. Instantly,
you'll see that this cell is in error:

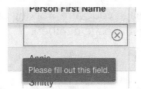

6. Click Save and a pop-up will tell you to correct all the errors before you can save. You'll also see a red earmark in the upper-right corner of the column header. This also indicates that this column cannot be null.

7. To revert back to the original values, use the Row Actions to select Revert Changes for the row on which you erased the first name.

Advanced Interactive Grid Options

You can edit a person type field with freeform text. Let's change that from freeform text to a select list, just as you did on your form.

1. Start by editing the page.

2. Click the Shared Components icon at the upper right of the toolbar in Page Designer. Instead of having to enter the same string of text for a static LOV each time, we can create a reusable select list.

3. On the Shared Components page, click List Of Values in the Other Components group.

4. Click the Create button to start the Create List Of Values modal wizard.

5. On the first step of the wizard, choose From Scratch and then click Next.

6. Name the list of values **Person Type** and keep the Type set to Static.

7. Using the Dynamic option, you can create a list of values based on a SQL statement, so you can add and remove values at the database level, rather than changing static text each time.

8. Select the radio button for Static and click Next.

9. Fill out the table using the following values:

Display Value	Return Value
Personal	Personal
Business	Business
Family	Family

10. Your page should look like Figure 6-37. Click the Create List Of Values button. You should see your list of values in the report.

11. Go back and edit the page you were working on (upper right on the toolbar, click the Edit icon with the page number).

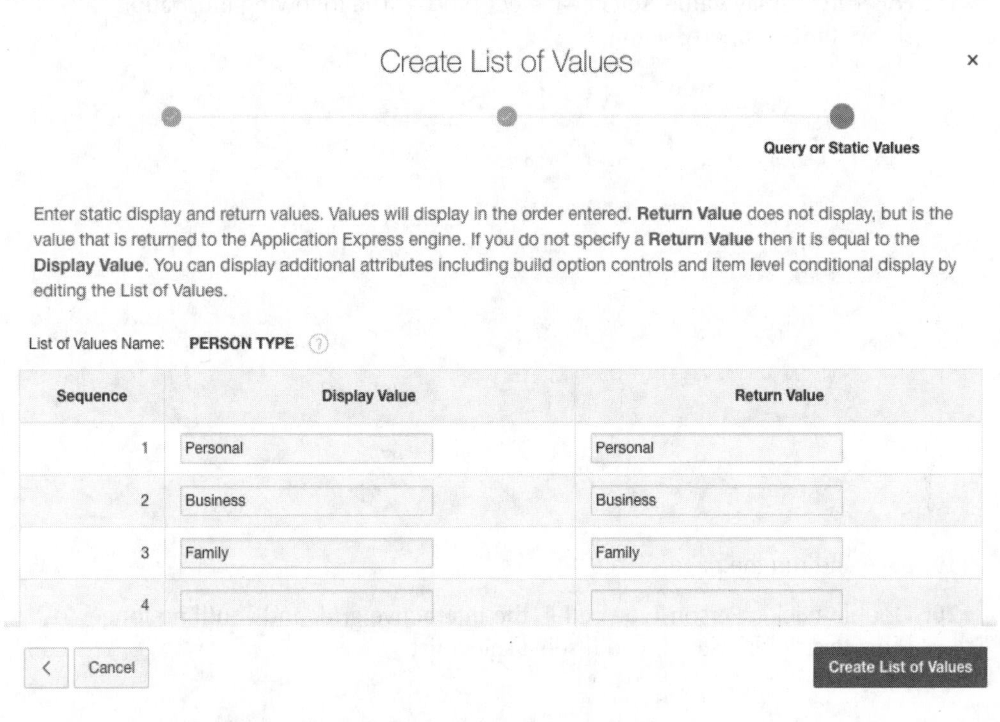

Create List of Values ✕

Query or Static Values

Enter static display and return values. Values will display in the order entered. **Return Value** does not display, but is the value that is returned to the Application Express engine. If you do not specify a **Return Value** then it is equal to the **Display Value**. You can display additional attributes including build option controls and item level conditional display by editing the List of Values.

List of Values Name: **PERSON TYPE**   (?)

Sequence	Display Value	Return Value
1	Personal	Personal
2	Business	Business
3	Family	Family
4		

| < | Cancel | **Create List of Values** |

FIGURE 6-37.   *Create List Of Values modal, static values grid*

12. Back in the Page Designer, set the PERSON_TYPE column in the Interactive Grid region to a select list. Expand the Columns folder under the Contacts interactive grid region.

13. Click PERSON_TYPE.

14. On the right, in the Properties panel – Column, change the Type in the Identification property group to Select List.

15. Now in the List Of Values property group, change the Type to Shared Component, and change the List of Values to PERSON TYPE.

16. For Display Extra Values, select No.

17. For Display Null Value, select Yes.

18. For Null Display Value, select -- Select Type --. The following illustration shows these property settings:

19. Save and run the page.

20. Double-click a Person Type cell in the interactive grid, and you'll no longer see a text field; instead, you'll see a select list:

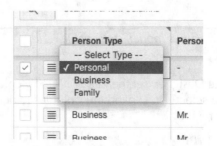

Allowed Row Operations Column

Interactive grids offer the ability to protect data from updates. By using the Allowed Row Operations Column attribute, you can limit the operations on that row. The attribute is set to a column in your table. This column can also be a virtual column, made up in the SQL query. The values this attribute is expecting are as follows:

■ **U** Row can be updated.

■ **D** Row can be deleted.

■ **UD**   Row can be updated or deleted.

■ **NULL**   Row cannot be edited.

Let's add some SQL to your page to create this virtual column.

1. Back in the Page Designer, click the Interactive Grid region and look at the property panel.

2. In the Source property group, find the SQL Query property. The SQL should look like the following:

```
select PERSON_ID,
       PERSON_TYPE,
       PERSON_PREFIX,
       PERSON_FIRST_NAME,
       PERSON_MIDDLE_NAME,
       PERSON_LAST_NAME,
       PERSON_BIRTHDAY,
       PERSON_NOTES
from PERSONS_TABLE
```

3. You need to add this virtual column, so either add the extra lines or copy and paste to replace the SQL in the SQL Query attribute:

```
select PERSON_ID,
       PERSON_TYPE,
       PERSON_PREFIX,
       PERSON_FIRST_NAME,
       PERSON_MIDDLE_NAME,
       PERSON_LAST_NAME,
       PERSON_BIRTHDAY,
       PERSON_NOTES,
       case when PERSON_TYPE = 'Family'
               then 'UD'
            when PERSON_TYPE = 'Business'
               then 'D'
            else null end CTRL
   from PERSONS_TABLE
```

4. Save the page. You'll see a CTRL column on the left in the Columns node.

5. Click the column, and in the Properties panel on the right, find the Source property group.

6. Change the Query Only attribute to Yes, as shown next. This change tells APEX not to try and commit this row on an insert or update because it's only a virtual column and not an actual one on the table.

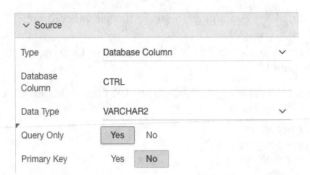

7. Time to tell this interactive grid to use this column in edit mode. Click the Attributes node.

8. On the Properties panel on the right, Edit property group, for the Allowed Row Operations Column, set the attribute to CTRL.

9. Save and run the page.

10. Now when you edit the grid, you are restricted by this column. If any contact is of type Personal, the row is grayed out and you cannot edit or delete it. Family types are also grayed, but you can delete those rows:

Master Detail Form and User Interface Defaults

We need to create a report that has our contacts and links to a form about each contact, and we need a way to add multiple addresses to this contact. Or, better yet, with APEX 5.1, we need two interactive grids that are linked. We can accomplish all this with a single wizard to create a master detail form.

Creating a Master Detail Form

Let's create the master detail form:

1. Edit the page if not already in the Page Designer.

2. From the Create dropdown menu (the + sign) on the toolbar, select Page.

3. In the Create Page modal, select Form. Then click Next.

4. On the Create Page modal, select Single Page Master Detail:

Create Page

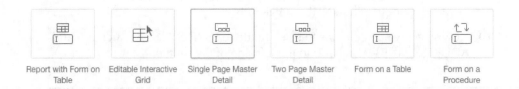

| Report with Form on Table | Editable Interactive Grid | Single Page Master Detail | Two Page Master Detail | Form on a Table | Form on a Procedure |

5. For the first step of the Create Master Detail wizard, choose a page number and name. Set the Page Number to **10** and the Page Name to **Contacts Master Detail**.

6. Keep the Page Mode to Normal and for the Breadcrumbs select list, choose Breadcrumb. Leave the rest of the entries set to their defaults. Then click the Next button.

7. For the Navigation Menu step of the wizard, set the Navigation Preference to Create A New Navigation Menu Entry. For the New Navigation Menu Entry, enter **Contacts Master Detail** if not already entered by default.

8. For Parent Navigation Menu Entry, choose – No Parent Selected –. Then click Next.

9. The Master Source step of the wizard defines your master table. For Master Region Title, enter **My Contacts**.

10. For Table / View Owner, use the schema you used when creating the workspace.

11. For the Table / View Name, choose PERSONS_TABLE (table).

12. For the Primary Key Column attribute, choose PERSON_ID (Number).

13. In the Select Columns area at the bottom of the modal, move PERSON_
    PICTURE (Blob) to the left side of the shuttle. The modal should look like
    Figure 6-38. Click Next.

14. The Detail Source step is next. For the Detail Region Title, enter **Addresses**.

15. Now choose a related table. APEX will help by showing only tables that
    have a foreign key reference to your master table. Select the Yes button for
    the Show Only Related Tables radio button.

16. The Table / View Name select list should have two tables in it. Select
    ADDRESS_TABLE.

17. For Primary Key Column, select ADDRESS_ID (Number).

18. You need to define the Master/Detail relationship in the Master Detail Foreign
    Key field. Choose PERSON_ID -> PERSON_ID.

19. Now select which columns to use. Shuttle ADDRESS_LINE2 (Varchar2) and
    ADDRESS_LINE3 (Varchar2) to the left side of the shuttle.

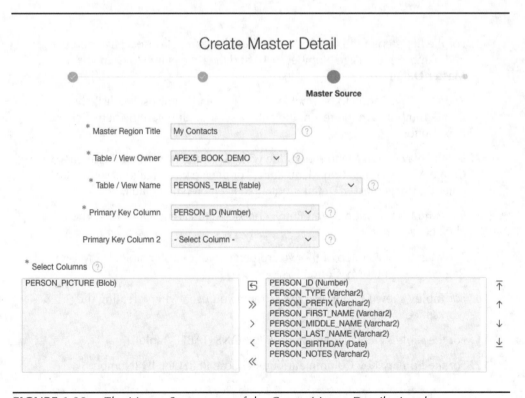

FIGURE 6-38. *The Master Source step of the Create Master Detail wizard*

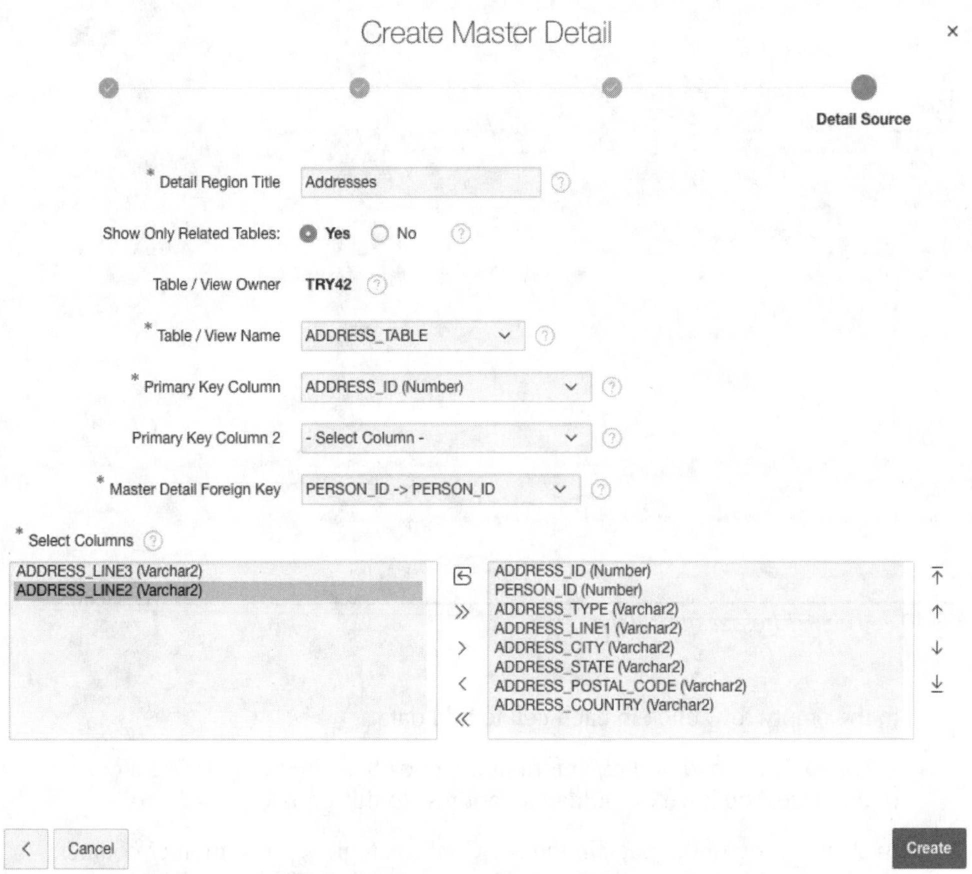

FIGURE 6-39. *The Detail Source step of the Create Master Detail wizard*

20. When your modal window looks like Figure 6-39, click the Create button. Once back in the Page Designer, run the page.

Your master detail report's Addresses interactive grid is shown at the bottom section of the page (Figure 6-40).

You can click a row in the My Contacts region to see the Addresses interactive grid refresh. Let's try this out:

1. Click any contact.

2. In the Addresses interactive grid, click the Add Row button if an empty row has not been created already.

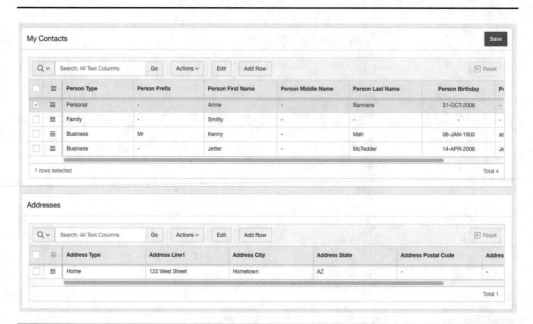

FIGURE 6-40. *The Addresses interactive grid*

3. In the empty row, click in each cell to add data.

4. Once you've added address information, click Save in the upper-right corner of the page. You have just added an address to this contact.

5. Back at the top of the page in the My Contacts region, click another contact. Once the Addresses interactive grid has refreshed, no addresses are shown. Go back and click the contact you created an address for and after the refresh you will see the address.

As you can see, master detail forms can combine multiple steps in one wizard with great functionality.

As you did with the other interactive grid earlier in this chapter, you can make the Address Type cell a select list. Let's create a List of Values for the Address Type. You'll use a shared component that you'll access in a different way.

1. Edit the page, and in the Page Designer, on the left side, click the Page Shared Components panel.

2. Right-click the List of Values node and select Create:

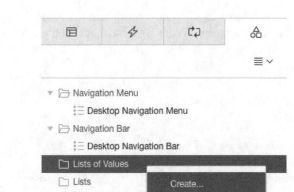

3. In the Create List Of Values modal, select From Scratch and then click Next.

4. Name the List Of Values **Address Type** and for Type, choose Static. Then click Next.

5. The last page of the Create List Of Values modal is the values grid. Use the following values:

Display Value	Return Value
Residential	Residential
Business	Business

6. Once the grid is filled in, click Create List Of Values in the lower right.

7. Back in the Page Designer, look at the Rendering panel on the left (you may have to select it because we were using the Shared Component panel), and find the Addresses node under Content Body.

8. Expand the Columns folder and click on ADDRESS_TYPE.

9. On the right side, in the Property Editor, Column tab, change the Type from Text Field to Select List in the Identification property group.

10. An error will pop up, telling you to choose your Type in the List of Values property group. Choose Shared Component and then, for List of Values, choose the ADDRESS TYPE shared component.

11. Set Display Extra Values to No and set the Null Display Value to -- Select Type --.

12. Save your work and run the page.

13. Add a row to the Addresses interactive grid, and the Address Type column is now a select list, shown next. When you have added the address you want, click Save.

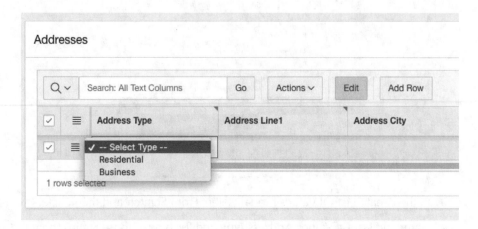

User Interface Defaults for a Table

Remember that you had to change the names of your form and report columns multiple times. You can create a *user interface default* for this, so that when you use the Contacts table in any page in your APEX application, it uses the labels for the columns you define.

To do this, follow these steps:

1. From the Page Designer main toolbar at the top of the page, click SQL Workshop.

2. Click the Utilities button, and then click the User Interface Defaults item, shown next. (A shortcut to get to User Interface Defaults is to use the dropdown menu on the SQL Workshop tab. Just click the \/ icon on the right of the tab and navigate to Utilities | User Interface Defaults.)

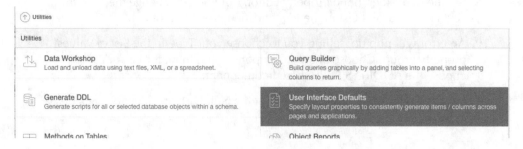

3. This page is the Dashboard report. Click the Table Dictionary tab, as shown next:

4. Find and click the PERSONS_TABLE.

5. In the Create Table Dictionary Defaults page, click the Create Defaults button.

6. On the Table Dictionary report, you should now see the PERSONS_TABLE in the report with a Yes in the Defaults Exist column. Click PERSONS_TABLE in the report to open the Table and Column Properties report, shown in Figure 6-41.

7. In this report, you can click the column names and change the column label as you wish. To start, click PERSON_TYPE, and in the next form, change the Label to Type, as shown in Figure 6-42.

You can see from the Column Defaults page that you can control many aspects of how this column will render throughout your application. We are going to change only a few values, but remember the options you have here for future use.

↑ Utilities \ User Interface Defaults \ Table Dictionary \ Table and Column Properties

Schema: **BOOK** ⑦   Object Name: **PERSONS_TABLE** ⑦   Object: **1 of 1**

Form Region Title: **Persons Table** ⑦   Report Region Title: **Persons Table** ⑦   Object Exists: **No** ⑦   Edit Table Defaults

Column Name	Sequence ↑≡	Label	Column Group	Alignment	Display In Report	Display In Form	Required	Help Length
PERSON_ID	1	Person Id	-	Right	✓	✓	✓	-
PERSON_TYPE	2	Person Type	-	Left	✓	✓	✓	-
PERSON_PREFIX	3	Person Prefix	-	Left	✓	✓	-	-
PERSON_FIRST_NAME	4	Person First Name	-	Left	✓	✓	-	-
PERSON_MIDDLE_NAME	5	Person Middle Name	-	Left	✓	✓	-	-
PERSON_LAST_NAME	6	Person Last Name	-	Left	✓	✓	✓	-
PERSON_BIRTHDAY	7	Person Birthday	-	Left	✓	✓	-	-
PERSON_PICTURE	8	Person Picture	-	Left	✓	✓	-	-
PERSON_NOTES	9	Person Notes	-	Left	✓	✓	-	-

FIGURE 6-41.   *The Table and Column Properties report*

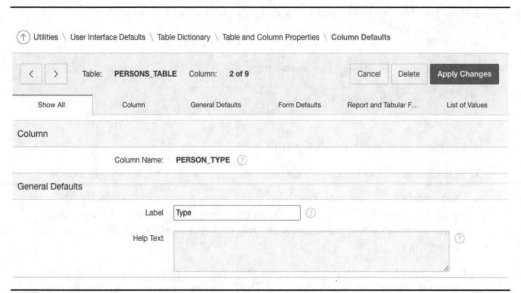

FIGURE 6-42. *Changing the PERSON_TYPE column label*

8. In the Form Defaults section on the same page, change Display As to Select List.

9. Scroll to the bottom of the form, find the List Of Values section, and click the Create Static List Of Values button. Use the following values in the Create Static List Of Values page:

Display Value	Return Value
Personal	Personal
Business	Business
Family	Family

10. After the grid is filled out, click Create at the bottom of the page.

11. In the Edit Static List Of Values page, you can change the sequence and double-check your values. When you're done, click Cancel.

12. Back on the PERSON_TYPE page, click the Apply Changes button at the upper right.

13. Change the labels for the rest of the columns. To go through all the columns quickly, you can use the left and right navigation arrows on the upper left of the column details page.

Change the labels as follows:

Change From	Change To
Person Prefix	Name Prefix
Person First Name	First Name
Person Middle Name	Middle Name
Person Last Name	Last Name
Person Birthday	Birthday
Person Picture	Picture
Person Notes	Notes

14. Once your labels are set, click the Edit Table Defaults button in the upper right.

15. Now you can change the display name used for report and form regions that use this table. Change both the Form Region Title and Report Region Title fields to My Contacts. Then click Apply Changes.

Now when you're creating a form or report on the PERSONS_TABLE, APEX will check the table dictionary for the existence of any user interface defaults. Creating user interface defaults will also ensure consistent column names across applications and developers. Developers no longer need to worry about what a column will be called in a report; it can be controlled from the table dictionary in the user interface defaults.

View Existing User Interface Defaults

You can see what user interface defaults are on a table in the SQL Workshop Object Browser. From the workspace, click SQL Workshop, and then Object Browser. Find and select your table in the list on the left. In the main panel on the right, click the UI Defaults tab to see all the user interface defaults for this table.

Summary

You have just created powerful forms and reports on multiple tables. You were able to insert data, update existing data, and delete data you didn't want. You linked reports and forms, searched through data in a report, and downloaded that report in multiple formats. You also used the powerful new interactive grids, which enabled spreadsheet-type experiences in a web browser working on real database data.

All this functionality helps you create a powerful application that can be used by multiple users. Not a single line of code needs to be written, and not once do you have to go to a command prompt to run some script or DBA-specific task, compile a JAR or library, or stage code to a remove server. The APEX wizards guide you through building forms and reports in a declarative way, so you don't need to know obscure database terms or technology.

This is the power of Oracle Application Express.

CHAPTER
7

Computations, Validations, Processes, and Branches

Oracle Application Express gives you a complete set of tools to use on your pages to work with data at the page level or database level. In this chapter, we will review computations, validations, processes, and branches. These programmatic elements will prove to be invaluable when you're building applications.

Computations

When building an application, you may sometimes want to set items to a particular value, or just before submitting a value to the database, you may want to alter that value for a specific reason. APEX enables you to compute these item values with *page computations*. You can create these computations at either the page level or the application level. For example, a page-level computation could compute sales tax upon order submission, and an application-level computation could set the user's preferred language, currency, or data format. Let's look at the types of computations available.

Computation Types

When creating a computation, you need to think about how you are going to get or compute the value. Will the value need to reference data in the database? Will the value be set from another item or from an application item? APEX lets you choose from several types of computations:

- **Static Value** Set to the text entered into Static Value Item Property.

- **Item** Set the item to the value held in session state for a particular Item.

- **SQL Query (return single value)** Set to the first value returned from a SQL Query entered in the SQL Query property for the computation.

- **SQL Query (return colon separated value)** Set to a single colon separated value, which concatenates each row value, returned from the SQL Query property for the computation.

- **SQL Expression** Set to the value that results from a SQL Expression entered. Examples would be sysdate, upper('a'), or even a case statement.

- **PL/SQL Expression** Set to the value that results from executing the PL/SQL Expression entered.

- **PL/SQL Function Body** Set to the value returned from the PL/SQL Function Body entered.

- **Preference** Set to the value of the Preference entered. You can use User Preferences here.

User Preferences

User preferences store data that is specific to a single user. The preferences persist across sessions, so any time a user logs in, regardless of session time or day, these preferences still apply. User preference settings include what tab to start on in a tabbed region, how many rows of a report to display, if a hide/show region is open or closed, and a preferred format for data types. These user preferences are stored in the database and will not expire unless explicitly told to do so. User preferences can also be used in computations, validations, and conditions.

To set or reference user preferences programmatically, use the APEX_UTIL PL/SQL API. For setting preferences, use the APEX_UTIL.SET_PREFERENCE procedure. To get or reference the value of a user preference, use the API function APEX_UTIL.GET_PREFERENCE. You may also remove a preference with the APEX_UTIL.REMOVE_PREFERENCE PL/SQL API.

Page Execution Points

Computations (and processes, discussed later in the chapter) can fire or occur at various points in your application. This is important, because if you are referencing Session State in this computation, depending on the execution point, that state may or may not be set yet. The execution point might even occur on login or based on JavaScript. The following are the execution points for computations and processes:

■ **New Session** The computations or processes occur when a user creates a new APEX session. New sessions can be created on login or created declaratively.

■ **Before Header** The processes or computations occur before a page is rendered. Good for fetching or computing data before the page is loaded. This processing point also occurs before any HTML is rendered.

■ **After Header** The processes or computations will occur after the page template header is rendered. Items set at the application instance or before header level can be referenced here.

■ **Before Regions** The processes or computations will occur before any of the content body regions are rendered. Processes or computations here may reference any page items set in the header regions or application-level items.

■ **After Regions** The processes or computations will occur after the content body regions are rendered. Processes or computations occurring here may reference any page items set in the Header, Application, and Region levels of the application. Remember that setting item values here that have been rendered in any of the previous points will not change the displayed value on the page—in fact, it will change the value in session but not on the page.

■ **Before Footer**   The processes or computations will occur before the page template footer is rendered. You can use this to compute or process any information that will be in the footer region such as page terms of service, dates, or HTML links.

■ **After Footer**   The processes or computations will occur after the page template footer is rendered. This is not a good place for processes or computations, because the page is already loaded. Perhaps use this region for a process that logs user, environment, or visitation timestamp information.

■ **After Submit**   The processes and computations fire after the page has been submitted. This is a good place to set items to return to the page or to pass to another page.

■ **Processing**   The processes and computations fire during page processing.

■ **AJAX Callback**   The process or computation runs when the application asks for it to be run. May be requested by a page process or dynamic action.

Creating a Computation

Let's create a computation on our main Contacts in the Cloud application. This computation will concatenate the first, middle, and last names into a display-only item on the page. Start by running the application, logging in, and editing any contact record.

1. Edit the page by clicking Edit Page 2 in the Developer toolbar at the bottom of the page.

2. In the Page Designer, Rendering panel, right-click the Create/Edit Contacts region node and select Create Page Item, as shown next:

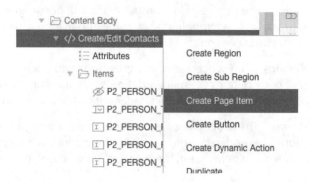

3. The new page item will appear at the bottom of the expanded Items node and will be called P2_NEW. Click P2_NEW, and look on the right of the page in the Page Item properties panel.

4. In the Identification property group, change the Name to **P2_PERSON_FULL_NAME**.

5. Set the Type to Display Only.

6. In the Label property group, for the Label property, enter **Full Name**. The two property groups should look like this:

7. This item was created referencing a database column, but we have no Full Name column on the table. We can fix this in the Source property group, by setting the Type property to Null, as shown next:

8. In the Rendering panel, drag the P2_PERSON_FULL_NAME item to just below P2_PERSON_TYPE and above P2_PERSON_PREFIX:

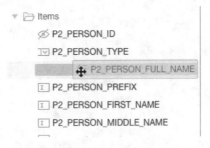

9. Now you'll create the computation itself. Right-click P2_PERSON_FULL_
   NAME and select Create Computation:

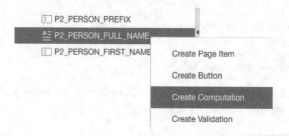

10. In the Rendering panel, the new computation is displayed in two places,
    as shown in Figure 7-1. Both are red highlighted and appear with a red X,
    indicating an error.

FIGURE 7-1. *The newly created computation*

11. On the right of the Page Designer, in the Computation properties panel, find the Identification property group. Set the Item Name (if not already set) property by either entering the text **P2_PERSON_FULL_NAME** or clicking on the pop-up LOV and selecting P2_PERSON_FULL_NAME. This sets the computation on that particular item.

12. Just below the Identification property group is the Execution Options property group. Here, set the Point property to Before Header.

13. In the Computation property group just below that, set the Type to PL/SQL Expression and enter the following into the PL/SQL Expression text field:

```
:P2_PERSON_PREFIX||' '||:P2_PERSON_FIRST_NAME||' '|| :P2_PERSON_
MIDDLE_NAME||' '||:P2_PERSON_LAST_NAME
```

These property groups should look similar to the following:

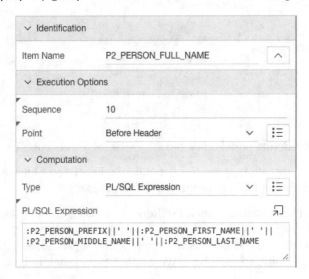

14. Save and run the page.

NOTE
If you no longer are editing a contact, you can go back to the home page and select a contact to be returned to the contact editing page.

On the page, you'll see your new item, but no value. The values for all the names in the form are there, but the computed value for the new item isn't. Why is this? Let's find out.

1. On the Developer toolbar, click edit page 2. In the Page Designer, in the Rendering panel, Pre-Rendering node, you see the Before Header node that contains the computation. Just below that is the After Header node and the row fetch for getting the values of the items and filling the form (shown next). The computation ran before there was data in the items, so it was not able to set the new item value.

2. In the Rendering panel, click the P2_PERSON_FULL_NAME computation.

3. In the Computation properties panel, in the Execution Options property group, change the Point property to After Header.

4. Back in the Rendering panel, Pre-Rendering node, you can see the computation is now in the After Header node but still occurring before the row fetch. Computations will happen before processes in the same execution point, so even here, we would have a blank full name.

5. Finally change Point to Before Regions. Now the computation occurs after the row fetch, as shown next, so you should see the full name in the new item.

Page 2: Create/Edit Contacts
▼ 🗁 **Pre-Rendering**
　🗀 Before Header
　▼ 🗁 After Header
　　▼ 🗁 Processes
　　　⌐ Fetch Row from PERSONS_TABLE
　▼ 🗁 Before Regions
　　▼ 🗁 Computations
　　　P2_PERSON_FULL_NAME

Save and run the page to see the full name showing for this new item, as shown next:

* Type	Business
Full Name	**Mr. Jetter McTedder**
Name Prefix	Mr.
First Name	Jetter

You can also set this value before the row fetch:

1. Edit the page and select the computation by clicking it.

2. In the Property Editor, find the Execution option and set Point to Before Header.

3. In the Computation property group, change the Type to SQL Query (Return Single Value).

4. For the SQL Query property, enter the following:

```
select person_prefix ||' '|| person_first_name ||' '|| person_
middle_name ||' '|| person_last_name person_full_name from
persons_table where person_id = :P2_PERSON_ID
```

When you're done, the Properties should look like the following, and the computation will again appear in the Before Header node in the Pre-Rendering section.

Execution Options	
Sequence	10
Point	Before Header
Computation	
Type	SQL Query (return single value)
SQL Query	

```
select person_prefix ||' '|| person_first_name ||' '||
person_middle_name ||' '|| person_last_name
person_full_name from persons_table where person_id =
:P2_PERSON_ID
.
```

Save and run the page. You should see the full name value in the new item. This is because the value comes from the database and APEX is not waiting for the page to render and the row fetch to happen.

Computations can also perform calculations, such as a date arithmetic—for example, they can determine how old a record is in the database or perform numeric calculations such as sales tax on an order.

Validations

Validations are very important for enforcing data consistency across your application. You can create validations on the client side with JavaScript, but those can be bypassed by browser plug-ins. For this reason, you want to enforce data consistency at not only the browser/client level, but at the database level as well.

Oracle Application Express has three types or levels of validation: on an item, a page, and an interactive grid. Let's start by creating an item-level validation.

Item-Level Validation

To create an item-level validation, start in the Page Designer on page 2, the create/edit form.

In the Rendering panel on the left side of the page, click P2_PERSON_MIDDLE_NAME.

On the right side, in the Property Editor, find the Validation attribute group. You can easily make this a required value so that the user must enter a middle name by changing the Value Required property to Yes, as shown next. With APEX 5.1, not only is this validation done on the server side, but it's also done on the client side with instant feedback, and no need to wait for a page submit. We are going to create a special validation, so keep Value Required set to No.

Item Value Required Property

APEX enables you to make items on the page required on form submission. All you need to do is change the Value Required property in the Validation attribute group to Yes. This is a very simple way to ensure data quality and consistency. This check is also done at the database level, so users cannot circumvent it at the browser level as they can with JavaScript blockers. When creating forms on tables, APEX will look at not null columns and automatically set this value to Yes for you on the corresponding form item fields.

So, what if you wanted to have the middle name required only when the person's prefix was entered? You can create this conditional item-level validation:

1. Right-click P2_PERSON_MIDDLE_NAME and select Create Validation, as shown next:

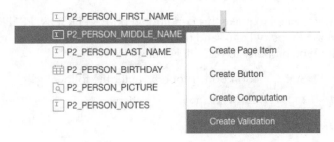

2. In the Validation property editor on the right side, in the Identification property group, Name field, enter **Middle Name Required**.

3. For the Validation property group, Type property, select Item is NOT NULL.

4. If Item is not already filled in for you with the value P2_PERSON_MIDDLE_NAME, click the pop-up list of values in the Item property and select P2_PERSON_MIDDLE_NAME. The Identification and Validation property groups should now look similar to Figure 7-2.

FIGURE 7-2.   *Setting up the item validation*

5. In the Error property group, for the Error Message property, enter the following text:

```
#LABEL# must have a value if entering a Name Prefix.
```

The #LABEL# substitution string will use the label of the item you used in the Validation property group earlier.

6. Lastly, you need to make this conditional on P2_PERSON_PREFIX. Scroll down the Property Editor and find the Server-side Condition property group. Set the Type property to PL/SQL Function Body.

7. In the PL/SQL Function Body property, enter the following:

```
if :P2_PERSON_PREFIX is not null then

   return true;
else
   return false;
end if;
```

The Error and Server-side Condition property groups should look like those shown in Figure 7-3. (Note that you can use the When Button Pressed property if you want this validation to occur only when a particular button is pressed.)

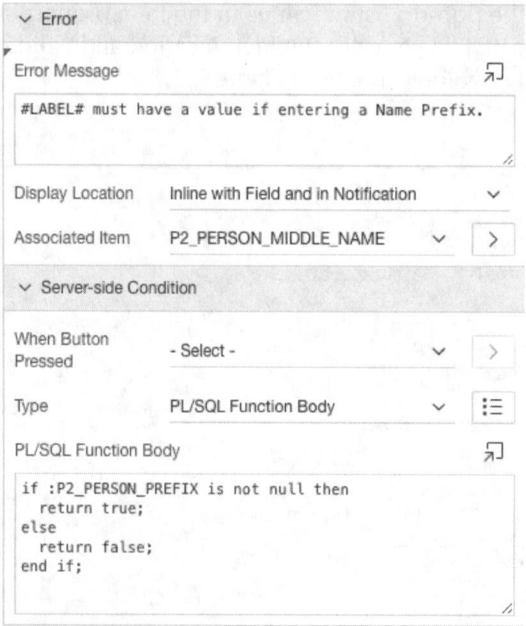

FIGURE 7-3. *The Error and Server-side Condition property groups*

Save and run your page. To test this validation, include a value in the Name Prefix form item and leave the Middle Name form item blank. Then click Apply Changes. An error should appear on the top of the page, as shown next:

> **1 error has occurred**   ×
>
> ⚠   • Middle Name must have a value if entering a Name Prefix.

You will also see an error on the Middle Name item itself:

First Name	Jetter
Middle Name	

Middle Name must have a value if entering a Name Prefix.

* Last Name	McTedder

Page-Level Validation

Use page-level validations to work with multiple page items to create a single validation. These validations can be quite complex blocks of PL/SQL code or simple function comparisons. The example we'll create will compare the contact's first, middle, and last names to ensure that we don't enter in the same name for all three. Again, this is not the most complex of validations, but it will show you that you can work with multiple page items in a single validation instead of a single item as you did previously.

1. In the Page Designer for page 2, start in the Processing panel (Figure 7-4).

2. Right-click Validating and select Create Validation.

3. On the right side of the Page Designer, Validations property panel, Identification property group, for the Name property, enter **Name Quality Check**.

4. In the Validation property group, change the Type property to PL/SQL Function Body (returning Boolean).

5. For the PL/SQL Function Body Returning Boolean property, enter the following:

```
if :P2_PERSON_FIRST_NAME = :P2_PERSON_MIDDLE_NAME and :P2_PERSON_
FIRST_NAME = :P2_PERSON_LAST_NAME then
    return false;
else
    return true;
end if;
```

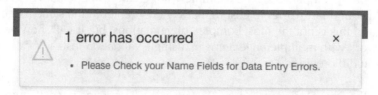

FIGURE 7-4. *Creating a validation in the Processing panel*

6. Lastly, in the Error property group, Error attribute, enter the following Error Message:

```
Please Check your Name Fields for Data Entry Errors.
```

Your property groups should match those shown in Figure 7-5.

Now save and run your page. Either edit an existing contact or create a new one, and if you put the same name in for first, middle, and last, you will see the new page error as soon as you attempt to save this record:

> ⚠ **1 error has occurred**   ✕
>
> • Please Check your Name Fields for Data Entry Errors.

Interactive Grid Validations

For the next type of validation, we need to switch to the Contacts Editable Interactive Grid page we created. Remember back in Chapter 6 that we did a not null validation by setting the Value Required property to Yes. Let's create a more complex validation on an interactive grid that will take multiple aspects into consideration. We are going to create a grid-level validation that will use multiple columns in the validation.

1. You need to edit the Contacts Interactive Grid page, so find this page in the App Builder and click the page icon to open the Page Designer—or, if you're already in the Page Designer, use the page selector at the top of the toolbar to edit the Contacts Interactive Grid page.

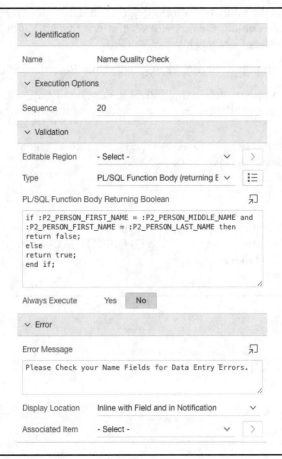

FIGURE 7-5. *Page-level validation values*

2. Right-click the Contacts Interactive Grid node in the Rendering panel on the left and select Create Validation. A validation named New is created.

3. On the right, in the Property Editor, choose the type of validation you want. In the Identification property group, for the Name property enter **Birthday**.

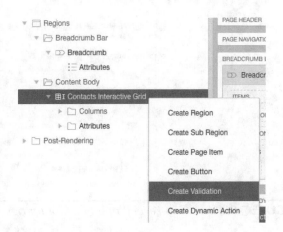

4. Below that, in the Validation property group, the first property, Editable Region, should contain the name of your interactive grid. If not, use the select list to select Contacts Interactive Grid.

5. For the Type property, choose, PL/SQL Function (Returning Error Text).

6. For the next property, now named PL/SQL Function Body Returning Error Text, create your validation. In the text area, enter the following code:

```
begin
    if :PERSON_TYPE = 'Family' and :PERSON_BIRTHDAY is null then
        return 'Please Enter a Birthday';
    end if;
    return null;
end;
```

7. Below the Validation property group is the Error property group. Set the Associated Column property to PERSON_BIRTHDAY. The Property Editor should now look like Figure 7-6.

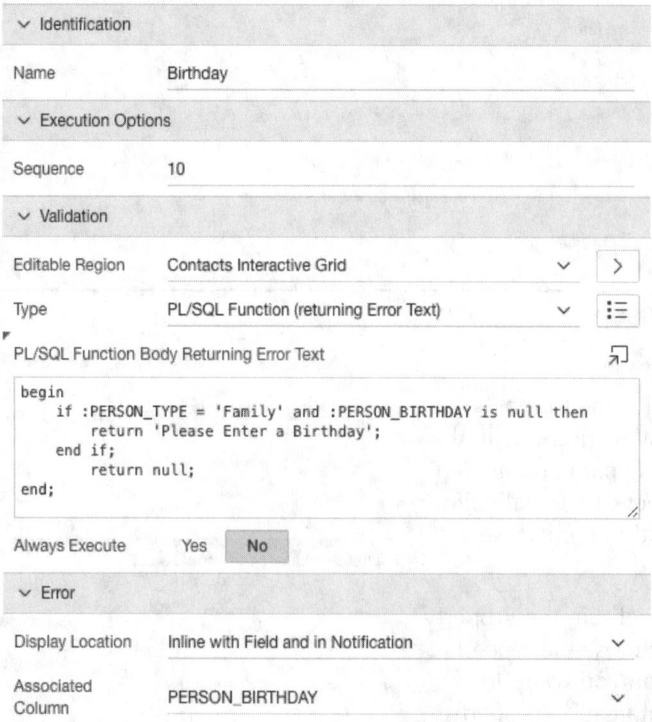

∨ Identification	
Name	Birthday
∨ Execution Options	
Sequence	10
∨ Validation	
Editable Region	Contacts Interactive Grid
Type	PL/SQL Function (returning Error Text)

PL/SQL Function Body Returning Error Text

```
begin
    if :PERSON_TYPE = 'Family' and :PERSON_BIRTHDAY is null then
        return 'Please Enter a Birthday';
    end if;
        return null;
end;
```

Always Execute	Yes **No**
∨ Error	
Display Location	Inline with Field and in Notification
Associated Column	PERSON_BIRTHDAY

FIGURE 7-6.   *The Grid-Level Property Editor for our validation*

8. Save and run this page.

9. Click the Add Row button and create a contact of type Family.

10. Enter the cells for Person First Name, Person Middle Name, and Person Last Name in the interactive grid but leave Person Birthday empty.

11. Click the Save button. You will see an error on the upper-right of the page, and the Person Birthday cell is outlined in red with a red X. This validation has prevented you from entering a Family contact without a birthday.

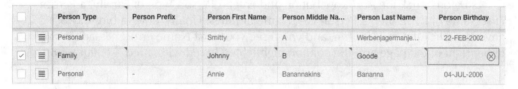

		Person Type	Person Prefix	Person First Name	Person Middle Na...	Person Last Name	Person Birthday
☐	≡	Personal	-	Smitty	A	Werbenjagermanje...	22-FEB-2002
✓	≡	Family		Johnny	B	Goode	⊗
☐	≡	Personal	-	Annie	Banannakins	Bananna	04-JUL-2006

12. In the PL/SQL statement, you included bind variables for the columns you referenced in the format :COLUMN_NAME. You can use the format to reference any columns in your interactive grid when creating complex validation that go beyond an "is null" check as you did just now.

13. Enter a birthday for this contact and save the row.

Now you'll create a column-level validation and see how you can reference the column name in an error message.

1. Edit this page, and on the Rendering panel on the left, right-click the column PERSON_FIRST_NAME under the Columns node in the Contacts Interactive Grid region. Then select Create Validation.

2. Back on the right of the page, in the Property Editor for your new validation, change the Name property in the Identification property group to Valid First Name.

3. In the Validation property group, look at the Type property. Click that select list and see all the validation types APEX provides. Use the select list to choose Column Is Alphanumeric. This validation type will pass if the value in the PERSON_FIRST_NAME cell contains only letters and numbers. It will fail if you try to use special characters.

4. In the Error property group, you see the Error Message has defaulted to "#COLUMN_HEADER# must have a value."

5. You can reference the column header here with the substitution string #COLUMN_HEADER# in your error message text. This substitution string will be replaced with the column header upon the validation failing. One of the advantages of this is that you can change the column header at a later date, and this error message with automatically use the new value. Change the Validation Error Message to **#COLUMN_HEADER# cannot contain special characters.**

The Validation Property Editor should look like Figure 7-7. Save and Run the page. As before, click the Add Row button and enter a Person Type of **Family**, a Person First Name of **!!!!!!**, then a Person Last Name of **Jones**. Finally, enter a birthday of any date. Click the Save button, and you'll see your First Name error message in the upper right of the page and the column highlighted in red with a red X (Figure 7-8).

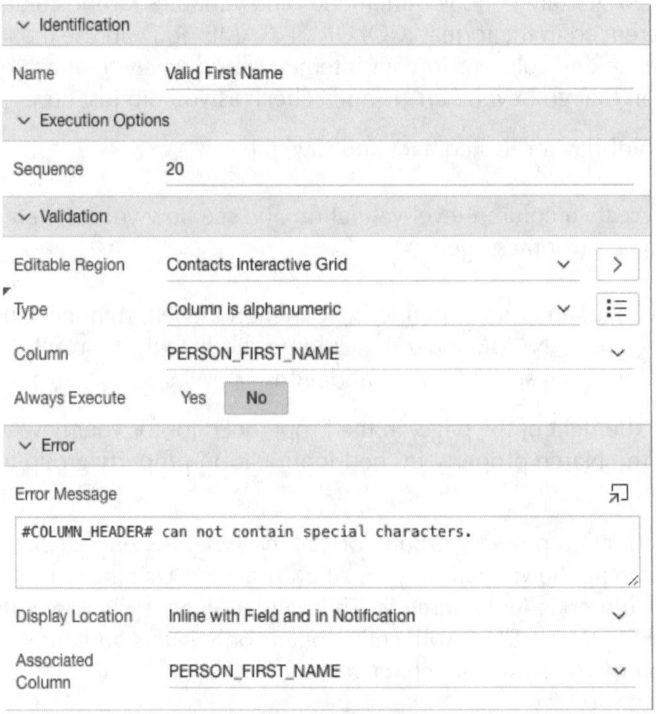

FIGURE 7-7. *The Person First Name column validation*

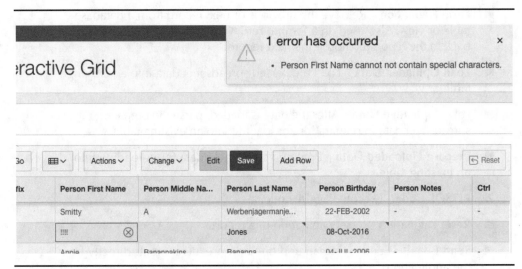

FIGURE 7-8. *The Person First Name column validation in the interactive grid*

Processes

You use processes to work with data and the database—to fetch, update, insert, and delete data from the database. You can also use processes to alter the Session State of the APEX application. As you will see, page processes can run at specific points in your page flow, such as at rendering or submission.

Process Types

A number of process types are available in APEX 5.1. You can use these process types to work with data from the database, update and insert data via tabular forms, alter Session State, and control how your reports paginate:

- **Automatic Row Fetch** Retrieve records from a single database table or view. Used to populate form items with a source of Type Database Column.

- **Automatic Row Processing (DML)** Insert, update, or delete records into a single database table or updateable view. Also used to work with form items with a source of Type Database Column. The attributes of this process and the Automatic Row Fetch process should correlate.

- **Clear Session State** Clear Session State stored within Application Express.

- **Close Dialog** Close the current modal or non-modal dialog page.

- **Form Pagination**   Retrieve the previous or next record from a database table or view. Also used on a form to retrieve records without having to go back to the report to choose the next record.

- **Load Uploaded Data**   Load the parsed spreadsheet data into an existing table or view.

- **Parse Uploaded Data**   After the data is loaded, parse the prepared spreadsheet data in preparation for loading into an existing table.

- **Prepare Uploaded Data**   Prepare spreadsheet data for uploading into an existing table.

- **PL/SQL Code**   Execute PL/SQL code.

- **Reset Pagination**   Reset pagination of a report.

- **Send E-Mail**   Send an e-mail and one or more attachments directly from the application.

- **Interactive Grid**   Automatic Row Processing (DML).

- **User Preferences**   Set User Preferences for the end user.

- **Web Service**   Consume a web service.

NOTE
Depending on your application, you may see an additional process type called Plug-ins. These display as <My Plug-in> [Plug-in] and will be shown only if you have previously installed or have plug-ins configured for your application.

Optimistic Locking

When you use the automatic row fetch process that's created when building APEX forms for fetching data, it employs optimistic row locking. APEX creates a checksum or hash of the data in the row, so when you attempt to update that record, APEX quickly creates that hash again and compares it to the original one. If it's the same, APEX updates the row. If the hash differs, APEX throws an error alerting the user that the data in the row has changed.

Working with Processes

You have already used some process points while building your application. You have used After Submit for processing contacts as well as After Header for fetching data into your create/edit form. You'll find that the Before Header, After Header, and After Submit processing points are the most popular points that are used quite often in building your applications.

We are going to create a process that will insert a row into a table every time a user views a contact. We will then display that data and time to the user.

Start by editing page 2, the entry form. We'll first create a new table to hold this information using the SQL Workshop.

1. Click the down arrow to the right of the SQL Workshop tab in the Page Designer, and then click SQL Commands, as shown next:

2. Enter the following SQL command into the Worksheet. Then click the Run button at the upper right.

```
create table contact_last_viewed (user_name varchar2(100),
contact_id number, view_date timestamp);
```

On the bottom of the page, in the Results tab, you should see the message "Table created." You have now created the table you will use for your view data.

3. Go back and edit page 2. Navigate back to the App Builder by clicking the App Builder tab. In the App Builder, click your application from the report, and then click Page 2 (Create/Edit Contacts).

4. In the Processing tab, on the left side of the Page Designer, right-click the Processing node and select Create Process:

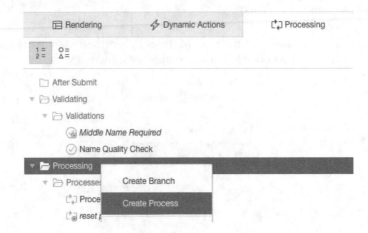

5. On the right side of the Page Designer, in the Process property panel and the Identification property group, change the Name property from New to Insert View Info.

6. The Type property will be PL/SQL Code (use the select list if it's not already preselected).

7. In the Source property group, for the PL/SQL Code field, enter the following:

```
insert into contact_last_viewed (user_name, contact_id, view_
date) values (:APP_USER, :P2_PERSON_ID, systimestamp);
```

8. In the Execution Options property group, just below the Source property group, set the Point property to After Footer. Why use the After Footer point? If we used a processing point before we fetched the row, we would update the row to the current date and never see the date from the database.

9. Set the Run Process property to Once Per Page Visit to ensure that the process runs each time the page is visited. The Process properties for your process should look like Figure 7-9.

10. Now you can add a display only page item to show this date and time. On the left side of Page Designer, click the Rendering tab.

FIGURE 7-9. *The Process properties for the Insert View Info process*

11. Right-click the Create/Edit Contacts node and select Create Page Item.

12. In the Page Item property panel on the right, in the Identification property group, for the Name property enter **P2_LAST_VIEWED**.

13. Set the Type property to Display Only.

14. For the Label property in the Label property group, enter **Last Viewed On**. The Identification and Label property groups should look like this:

15. Scroll down to the Source property group and set the Type property to Null. Now you need to create a computation to fill this item with data.

16. This process is not only going to guide you through creation, but you are going to pull from your computation knowledge you gained earlier as well. On the left side of the Page Designer, right-click P2_LAST_VIEWED and select Create Computation. The Computation has already applied itself to the P2_LAST_VIEWED item and all you need to do is set the value. You should also see the Computation property panel highlighting an error on the right side of the Page Designer.

17. The SQL Query property should be in error. Enter the following into the SQL Query property in the Computation property group:

```
select max(to_char(view_date, 'Mon DD YYYY HH24:MI')) view_date
from contact_last_viewed
where contact_id = :P2_PERSON_ID and user_name = :APP_USER group
by user_name, contact_id;
```

This SQL is selecting the last date viewed for this contact and formatting it into a very readable format. You will also filter this result by using the :APP_USER application item. This item is an application-level APEX item that you can use to reference the person who is logged on at this time. In this case, you want to see the last viewed date for us, not for someone else who is using the application.

18. Let's also add a condition so that this computation runs only when you are looking at a contact and not creating a new one. Find the Server-side Condition property group and set the Type property to Item Is NOT NULL.

19. Set the Item property to P2_PERSON_ID, either by entering the text or using the pop-up LOV to the right of the property field.

20. Save the page and change the page to Page 1 (home) using the page selector at the top of the Page Designer. Run page 1.

21. In the report, select any contact and click the edit icon.

22. On the following page you should see your new item but no value. Refresh/ reload the page and a date and time formatted in a readable fashion should be displayed:

Last Viewed On   **Oct 08 2016 17:03**

Branches

In Chapter 6, you created *branches*, instructions to link to a specific page, procedure, or URL after a given page is submitted. You created a branch from the Behavior property group for buttons or links. Using the Link Builder, you can create branches in your APEX applications. As with other APEX items, branches can have conditions.

Branch Execution Points

Branches can occur at points other than when a user clicks a button or link. Branches can be applied to just about any point in a page's processing order, such as at the following page points:

- **After Submit**   Branching occurs before computations, validations, or processing. This type of branch can be used for a Cancel button.

- **Validation**   Branching occurs after computations, but before validations or processing. For example, suppose a user was working in an order form and upon submitting it, a computation ran to check stock. If no stock remained, the user could be branched to a stock refresh request form rather than seeing an error saying no stock was available.

- **Processing**   Branching occurs after computations and validations, but before processing. For this option, you could have a computation that would check whether a user was able to update a particular row or piece of data. If the validation failed, the user would be branched to a particular page, such as an access grant form.

- **After Processing**   Branching occurs after computations, validations, and processing. We have been using this option in our application. It can be used with Submit or Create buttons, for example.

- **Before Header**   Branching occurs before a page is rendered. For example, if a user needs to fill out a profile before using an application, the branch detects this and takes the user to a profile page.

Branches do not always have to link to a page in an application. They can branch to an external URL as well as to a procedure.

Branch Types

Branches are divided into two categories: redirect branches and show only branches.

- **Redirect Branches** The resulting branched page is an actual URL. If a user were to refresh the page, the page would refresh without issue and retain context. For example, after submitting a form, you are redirected to a report showing the new row. This report page has an actual URL you can see.

- **Show Only Branches** These branched pages show within the existing page, and there is no direct URL. The resulting URL is wwv_flow.accept, not a traditional APEX URL.

TIP
Oracle recommends that you use redirect branches to provide a better end user experience rather than show only.

You can use the following branch types:

- **Page or URL** This is the branch type used when defining target links. You supply a page number and items to set, and indicate whether you want to reset pagination and clear the cache.

- **URL Identified by Item** With this branch, you can redirect the user to a page based on a page item. This item can be computed or calculated based on page logic or application logic. You could, for example, branch the item to a page you just came from, so that you could easily return to the page by accessing the stored branch value.

- **Function Returning a URL** This branch gets its URL based on a function written in PL/SQL. This branch type is very useful; you can dynamically create the branch target on any data you choose.

- **PL/SQL Procedure** Use a PL/SQL stored procedure to create the branch dynamically.

- **Page Processing {not common}** This is an interesting branch that enables you to redirect a user to the processing section of a page but not the page itself. This would enable you to reuse some page processing logic on another page without actually being on that page.

Creating Branches

Let's put some of these branches into practice. We'll start by creating a new page so that we can experiment with the various branch types.

1. In the Page Designer, create a new page. From the Create dropdown, select Page.

2. In the Create A Page modal, select Blank Page.

3. On the first page of the Create Page wizard, keep all the defaults, except in the Name field, enter **Branches**. Then click Next.

4. Now to create a new navigation menu for this page: click Create A New Navigation Menu Entry. This new entry should default to Branches. Keep the Parent Navigation Menu Entry set to – No Parent Selected –. Your modal page should look like Figure 7-10. Click Next.

5. On the final page of the modal, click Finish.

Create a Blank Page

Navigation Menu

Navigation Preference	○ Do not associate this page with a navigation menu entry ⑦
	◉ **Create a new navigation menu entry**
	○ Identify an existing navigation menu entry for this page
* New Navigation Menu Entry	Branches ⑦
Parent Navigation Menu Entry	- No parent selected - ⑦
	Home
	New Contact
	Contacts Interactive Grid
	Contacts Master Detail
	Security Administration

FIGURE 7-10. *Creating a Branches navigation menu*

Now you have a new page on which to create new branches. Let's start with a Before Header branch.

1. In the Page Designer, find and expand the Pre-Rendering node. Right-click Before Header and select Create Branch:

2. In the Property panel on the right, in the Identification property group, enter **Before Header Branch** for the Name property.

3. In the Behavior property group, set the Type to Page or URL (Redirect).

4. Click the No Link Defined button for the Target property.

5. In the Link Builder modal, set the Page property to 1. Then click OK. The Branch Properties should look like those in Figure 7-11.

6. Now save and run the page. You will be instantly redirected to page 1.

    Want to try that again? Click the navigation menu item on the left and it will happen again. You can see that using this branch combined with a condition can make for a very powerful asset in your APEX toolbox.

7. Go back and edit your branch page, and select Before Header Branch to change the type of branch.

8. In the Property panel, in the Behavior property group, change Type to Function Returning A Page (Show Only).

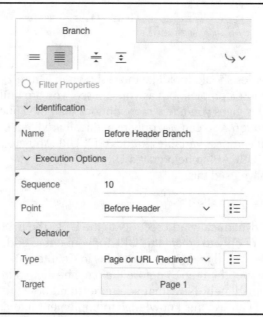

FIGURE 7-11. *Our Before Header branch properties*

9. In the PL/SQL Function Body field, enter the following:

```
if :APP_USER is not null then
    return '1';
else
    return '2';
end if;
```

10. Save and run the page, and you are instantly redirected to page 1 again.

Using a PL/SQL function, you can add some logic into your page branching to augment a condition you can put on the branch itself. You can dynamically control where the redirect goes based on variables we define.

1. Go back and edit this page, and look at the properties for this branch. Change the Type to Function Returning A URL (Redirect).

2. In the PL/SQL Function Body property, enter the following code:

```
if :APP_USER is not null then
    return APEX_UTIL.PREPARE_URL(
        p_url => 'f?p=' || :APP_ID||':2:'||:APP_SESSION||':::::P2_PERSON_ID:1',
        p_checksum_type => 'SESSION');
else
```

```
return APEX_UTIL.PREPARE_URL(
    p_url => 'f?p=' || :APP_ID || ':101:'||:APP_SESSION||':::::',
    p_checksum_type => 'SESSION');
end if;
```

Your branch properties should look like those shown in Figure 7-12.

This code is a bit more complex, but as you can see, you are building the URL from the ground up. This gives you a few more options than the Function Returning A Page (Show Only) option. You can not only dynamically redirect based on PL/SQL logic, but you can add and pass variables in the APEX URL. You are using the APEX_UTIL.PREPARE_URL API to help craft a URL.

You could easily have used this:

```
return 'f?p=&APP_ID.:1:&SESSION.';
```

But then you couldn't dynamically add security to the URL. The **p_checksum_type** parameter tells APEX not only to create this URL for you, but to add security on the URL so it's tamperproof. You'll read more about this in Chapter 10.

In this section, you put the branch before the page header so that you could see how it worked immediately. Now that you understand how the different types of branches work, you can use this knowledge to implement branches in your applications.

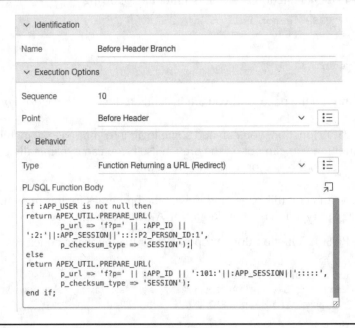

FIGURE 7-12.   *Function Returning A URL (Redirect) properties*

Summary

The programmatic elements of APEX enable you to work with data beyond a report or form. You can compute values of page items in your forms or application items in an app, manipulating the data to suit your needs. You can also ensure that data is being entered into your application correctly, providing consistency and helping to remove erroneous entries.

APEX also lets you control the flow of data in and out of your database. These elements also can occur at various points in an application, giving you flexibility regarding when and what data you want to work with.

Lastly, branches let you dynamically control page flow throughout your application with a variety of methods. All this functionality is available right in the Page Designer, and most of it can be created in an easy and declarative way.

CHAPTER
8

Crafting a Powerful UI

Business applications don't have to be ugly. All day long we work with bland and drab applications that, although functional, use the same color pallet as old curtains. For years, APEX has included stylish themes in various colors, with some being responsive to various screen sizes. You can use themes to add color and style to what could have been another gray-and-yellow business app. APEX 5 has taken it a step further by making themes and templates easier to use. No longer do you have to be an HTML/CSS expert to change some of the most used attributes of a template. And the Universal Theme brings the ability to alter the very foundation of templates into the end users' hands. Throw the new Theme Roller on top of this newfound ease and anyone can create good looking, powerful UIs with little effort.

Themes and Templates

APEX themes contain a collection of templates that you can use for just about every component in the user interface. From the page itself, to the item labels, themes provide everything you need to add color and styling to your application.

Selecting a theme is a very easy process that we will walk through right now. To start, in the App Builder, select your Contacts in the Cloud app. On the application home page, click Shared Components.

In the middle of the Shared Components page is the User Interface panel, which shows three options: User Interface Attributes, Themes, and Templates.

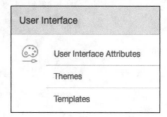

User Interface Attributes

Click User Interface Attributes to see a list of all your user interfaces. You can edit all the UIs on this page or add a new one, such as a Mobile UI, by clicking the Add User Interface button. You can also click the Edit icon (the pencil icon) to edit this particular user interface via the User Interface details page, or click the theme or theme style name to see respective detail pages, where you can edit the theme itself.

User Interfaces						Add User Interface >
Name	**Type**	**Default**	**Auto Detect**	**Global Page**	**Theme**	**Theme Style**
Desktop	🖥	✓			Universal Theme - 42	Vita

User Interface Details Page

Click the Edit icon for the Desktop UI to open the User Interface details page. We are now on the User Interface details page.

Identification Section   In the Identification section, shown next, you can change the UI's Display Name and the Sequence, which determines the display sequence of this UI in the previous page in the User Interfaces list.

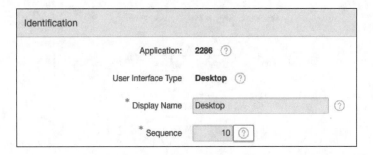

Attributes Section   Several settings are offered in the Attributes section (shown in Figure 8-1):

- ■ **Auto Detect**   If enabled (Yes), the user will be redirected to the corresponding login page or home page. Select Yes when you have multiple types of themes, such as a mobile and a desktop theme, so that mobile users go to the Mobile UI and the desktop users go to the Desktop UI.

- ■ **Default**   Sets this UI as the application default UI if you have multiple UIs of the same type (multiple Desktop or Mobile UIs).

- ■ **Enable End Users To Choose Theme Style**   Allows users to change the Theme Style of the application. Only Public theme styles can be accessed by users.

- ■ **Home URL and Login URL**   Dictate the corresponding pages for users to log into and where users are redirected to for the home page after login. By default, the Home URL is page 1, but you can change this here.

- ■ **Theme Style**   This is based on the read-only Theme attribute just above it. We will go over theme styles later in this chapter in the "Styles" section.

- ■ **Global Page**   Shows what page, if any, in your application is set as the global page, or master page (usually page 0, but it can be set to any page here).

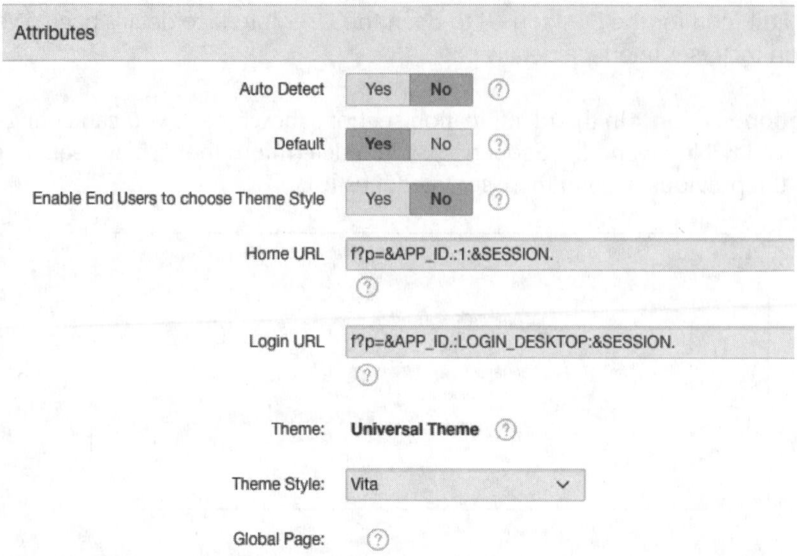

Attributes		
Auto Detect	Yes **No** ⑦	
Default	**Yes** No ⑦	
Enable End Users to choose Theme Style	Yes **No** ⑦	
Home URL	f?p=&APP_ID.:1:&SESSION. ⑦	
Login URL	f?p=&APP_ID.:LOGIN_DESKTOP:&SESSION. ⑦	
Theme:	**Universal Theme** ⑦	
Theme Style:	Vita ⌄	
Global Page:	⑦	

FIGURE 8-1. *The Attributes section*

Navigation Menu and Navigation Bar Sections   The Navigation Menu and Navigation Bar sections (Figure 8-2) control those particular UI elements and do not dictate when one is used over the other.

Following are the attributes in the Navigation Menu section:

■ **Navigation Menu List**   Choose which navigation menu to use as the default for the application.

■ **Position**   Choose where the default navigation menu list is positioned on the page. The Navigation Menu List and Position attributes work together—for example, if you choose a traditional navigation tab bar, Bar Menu List, choose the Top position so that the bar appears across the top of your application. Use the Side position to locate the navigation menu on the left side of the page, as we have used in previous chapters. Setting the Position attribute to Side will render the navigation menu list template in the **#SIDE_GLOBAL_NAVIGATION_LIST#** position in your page template; setting the Position attribute to Top will render the navigation menu list template in the **#TOP_GLOBAL_NAVIGATION_LIST#** position.

■ **List Template**   Change the template for your navigation list.

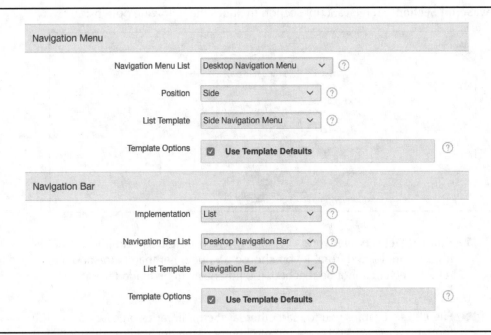

FIGURE 8-2. *The Navigation Menu and Navigation Bar sections*

■ **Template Options**   This attribute will change based on the template options set for the List Template you choose. We will discuss Template Options later in this chapter in the section "Templates"; for now, change the template values and see how the Template Options change, but don't save your changes yet.

The attributes in the Navigation Bar section are similar to those of the Navigation Menu section, but they use the legacy components from earlier APEX versions.

■ **Implementation**   Setting the value to Classic will render the navigation bar as a classic navigation bar in the **#NAVIGATION_BAR#** position. Setting it to List will render the navigation bar as a list, using the selected list and list template in the **#NAVIGATION_BAR#** position.

■ **Navigation Bar List**   Choose the List you want to use. This List of Values (LOV) includes all the lists in your application.

■ **List Template**   Works just as it did for the Navigation Menu section. Select a template for your list and the Template Options will refresh to reflect your choice.

JavaScript Section   The JavaScript section includes the following options:

JavaScript	
Content Delivery Network	None (use Web Server) ⌄ ⑦
File URLs	
	⑦
Include Legacy Javascript	Yes **No** ⑦
Include jQuery Migrate	Yes **No** ⑦

- **Content Delivery Network**   Choose where your jQuery and jQuery Mobile libraries are loaded from. If you choose a value other than None and the remote server cannot be reached, the libraries will be loaded from the local server.

- **File URLs**   Enables you to load other JavaScript libraries on every page. The format is a regular URL for a remote library or the /local_directory/fileName .js format for local files. You can also use a few substitution strings: **#MIN#** to include .min or **#MIN_DIRECTORY#** to include minified/ in your file URL. For example, here we use both:

```
/mycooljs/#MIN_DIRECTORY#main#MIN#.js
```

Here's the output:

```
/mycooljs/minified/main.min.js
```

Or you can use conditional statements for a situation such as early versions of Internet Explorer:

```
[if IE]
    /myuncooljs/ie.js
[endif]
```

- **Include Legacy JavaScript**   Set this to Yes if you are importing an app created in an older version of APEX or using an older theme. This attribute will include all the legacy JavaScript libraries in each of your pages. If you are using a newer theme or the Universal Theme, set this to No to increase the speed of page rendering (less scripts to load).

- **Include jQuery Migrate**   Set this to Yes to include the jQuery Migrate plug-in on all your pages. This attribute is best used when you have imported an application that uses jQuery APIs from versions previous to 1.9. This plug-in will preserve the functionality of the depreciated APIs. If no jQuery uses APIs from older versions, set this to No to reduce the overall size of the JavaScript files loaded.

Cascading Style Sheets Section Similar to the JavaScript File URLs attribute, the Cascading Style Sheets section, shown next, contains the same attribute, and the same rules apply here as well as a few new ones.

Cascading Style Sheets	
File URLs	

The substitution string **#MIN#** to include .min or **#MIN_DIRECTORY#** to include minified/ in your file URL both apply here as well as conditional statements (for your IE 6 users). The File URLs attribute can also use conditional media queries, such as this:

```
[media="only screen and (max-device-width: 480px)"]/mymobilecss/mobile.css
```

Use the Application Version substitution string **#APP_VERSION#** to include the application's version in the file URL:

```
/mycoolcss/main.css?version=#APP_VERSION#
```

Concatenated File Section A concatenated file comprises multiple CSS or JavaScript files concatenated into one single file. Using a concatenated file greatly speeds up page load times. To use this, you must have the concatenated file precreated and staged on a server. You cannot create files from this section.

To create the reference to this file, click the Create Concatenated File button to open the Create/Edit Concatenated File modal window (Figure 8-3).

- **Concatenated File URL** Reference the location of your file.

- **Single File URLs** Enter all the individual file URLs for which a concatenated file should be loaded instead. The list of files in the text box must be separated by return characters, rather than commas, semicolons, or spaces. Here's an example:

```
#APP_IMAGES#js/core.min.js?version=#APP_VERSION#
#APP_IMAGES#js/search.min.js
#APP_IMAGES#js/morecoolscript.min.js
```

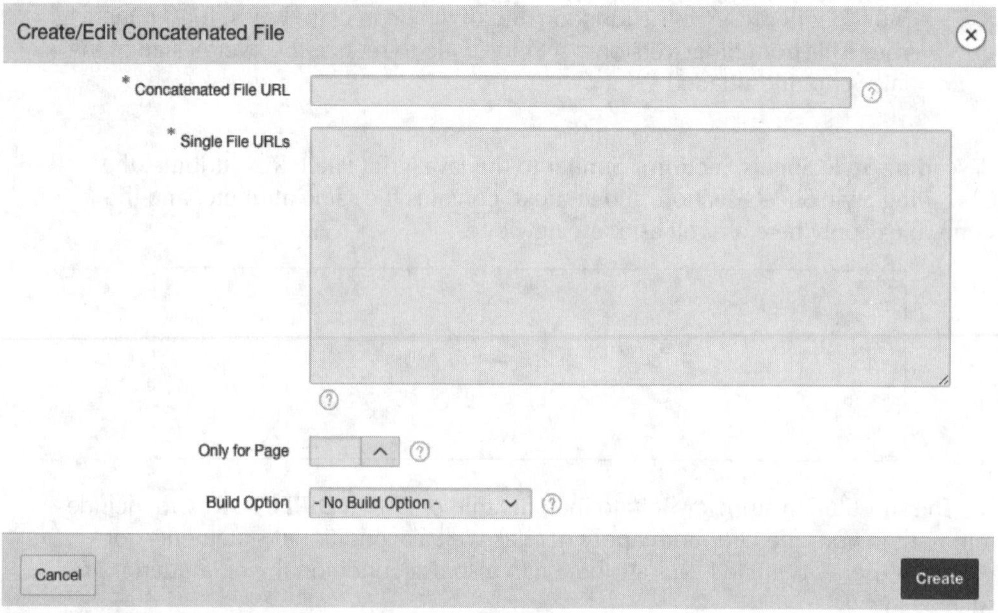

Create/Edit Concatenated File ⊗

| * Concatenated File URL | | ⑦ |

* Single File URLs

⑦

Only for Page [   ] ∧ ⑦

Build Option [- No Build Option - ⌄] ⑦

Cancel   Create

FIGURE 8-3. *Create/Edit Concatenated File modal*

- **Only For Page**   Choose a particular page that this will run on. Leave it blank if you want it to run on all pages.

- **Build Option**   Discussed in detail in Chapter 11, these allow you to restrict components when exporting or importing your applications.

Click Create to create a reference, and click Cancel if you do not need to create a reference at this time.

NOTE
User interface defaults for the Mobile theme are very similar to those for the Desktop theme, except the Mobile theme includes only a Navigation Menu section, not a Navigation Bar section.

When you're done looking over the User Interface details for a Desktop UI, click the Cancel button, or, if you have made changes, click the Apply Changes button.
Back on the User Interface attributes page are several more sections containing UI attributes (Figure 8-4).

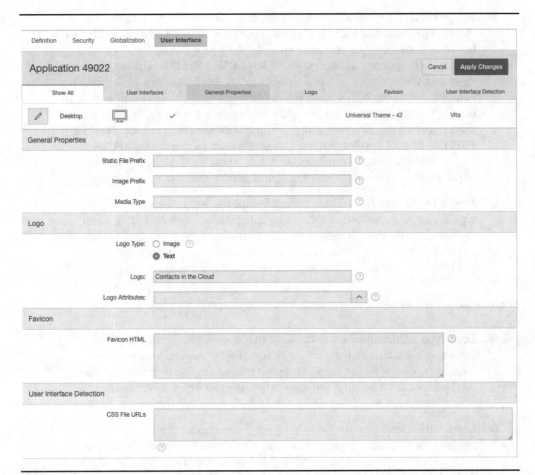

FIGURE 8-4. *User Interface attributes*

General Properties Section The General Properties section includes the following attributes:

- **Static File Prefix** Set the prefix substituted for **#APP_IMAGES#**. Suppose, for example, you have all of your application images in a directory on your web server. Using the substitution string **#APP_IMAGES#**, you can automatically point to that directory at application runtime. Setting it to a directory such as /myFiles/ would append this to the hostname of the current server. If your server was named http://apex.mycompany.com/, then upon runtime, **#APP_IMAGES#** would be set to http://apex.mycompany.com/myFiles/. You can also set **#APP_IMAGES#** to be a fully qualified hostname and directory if the static files are on a separate server.

- **Image Prefix**   Override the virtual directory where APEX's images are stored. During installation, the virtual path is usually set to /i/, but this can be overridden here. As you saw with the Static File Prefix, the /i/ can be used within your application with the **#IMAGE_PREFIX#** substitution string. Even though /i/ is easy to type, it's not always the best option. Imagine, for example, that your application moves through multiple environments from development to production. For security reasons, on the production server, the default image directory is /myCompany/images/. If you used **#IMAGE_ PREFIX#** in your application, no changes would be needed; you could just update the Image Prefix attribute. But if you used /i/ throughout your application, you would have to find and update every occurrence of /i/.

- **Media Type**   This is a two-part identifier for file formats on the Internet, a type and a subtype, and one or more optional parameters. If both the page-level and application-level values for Media Type are set to NULL, the value of text/HTML is used for both. Note that the Media Type attribute is used in the Content-Type HTTP header when rendering the page.

Logo Section   The Logo section contains the following attributes:

- **Logo Type**   Control whether the logo that appears at the upper-left of your application page is an image or text. If you use an image for the logo, provide the image name and path if needed. The format would be /myLogoImages/logo.gif if the logo is local to the APEX server of the full URL if remote. If you use Text for the Logo Type, enter the text of the logo.

- **Logo Attributes**   Use the pop-up select list to choose some prebuilt attributes for text and image logos. You can also set your own attributes, such as **width="100"** or **height="200"** for an image and **color="#FF0000"** or **font-size="20"** for text logos. Note that your template must contain the **#LOGO#** substitution string for this to work.

Favicon Section   The Favicon section lets you provide a custom favicon HTML for your application. A favicon is an icon that appears on browser tabs or in the URL section of the browser. An example favicon for the APEX builder pages is shown here:

To include a favicon, your page template must include the **#FAVICONS#** substitution string.

User Interface Detection Section   The User Interface Detection section includes one attribute, CSS File URLs. Here you can provide APEX with additional CSS files to load when the page or application loads; these CSS files work at an application level, not at the specific UI level.

You can also use media queries:

```
[media="only screen and (max-device-width: 480px)"]/myCompanyCSS/mobile.css
```

Or use conditional statements in case a user chooses a specific or unsupported browser:

```
[if IE 6]
    /myCompanyCSS/ie6.css
[endif]
```

Or use certain substitution strings such as **#MIN#** to include .min, **#MIN_DIRECTORY#** to include minified/ in your file URL, and **#APP_VERSION#** if you want to include the application's version in the file URL. The app version is taken from the application properties page. This

```
/myCompanyCSS/#MIN_DIRECTORY#file#MIN#.css
```

would output

```
/myCompanyCSS/minified/file.min.css
```

And this

```
/myCompanyCSS/main.css?version=#APP_VERSION#
```

would output

```
/myCompanyCSS/main.css?version=12.1.2.4
```

Themes

You can manage themes for your application or use multiple themes in your application, but only one can be active at a time. If your app has both a Desktop and Mobile UI, an active theme can be created for each.

Create / Edit Theme Page

To create or edit a theme, on the User Interface panel, click Themes. Then click the Universal Theme – 42 link to open the Create / Edit Theme page, which shows the interworkings of this theme.

Name Section   The Name section on the top of the page (Figure 8-5) is an informational report about the theme, including Theme Number, Name, and Navigation Type.

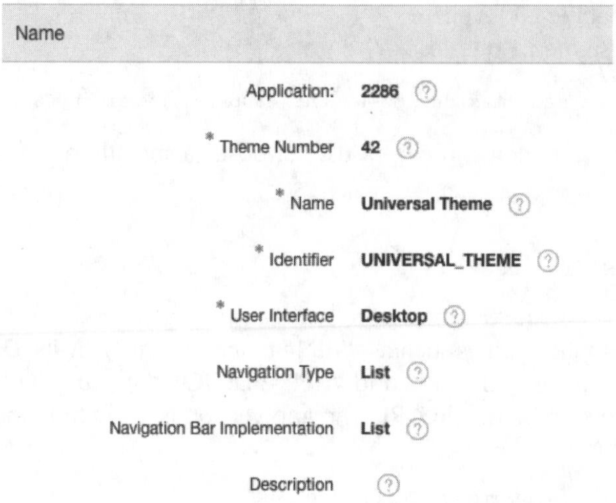

Name		
Application:	**2286** ⑦	
* Theme Number	**42** ⑦	
* Name	**Universal Theme** ⑦	
* Identifier	**UNIVERSAL_THEME** ⑦	
* User Interface	**Desktop** ⑦	
Navigation Type	**List** ⑦	
Navigation Bar Implementation	**List** ⑦	
Description	⑦	

FIGURE 8-5.   *The theme details in the Name section*

Theme Subscription Section   When creating applications, you often use many common UI elements. In the Theme Subscription section, you can develop the common theme elements in one application and use them from any number of other applications by subscribing to a *master theme*. If you make any changes to that master theme, you can have them cascade down into your subscribed theme. Subscribed templates are read-only to prevent changes that are not in the master theme and to prevent themes from going out of sync. The Subscribed To Standard Theme attribute will note any theme to which this particular theme is subscribed.

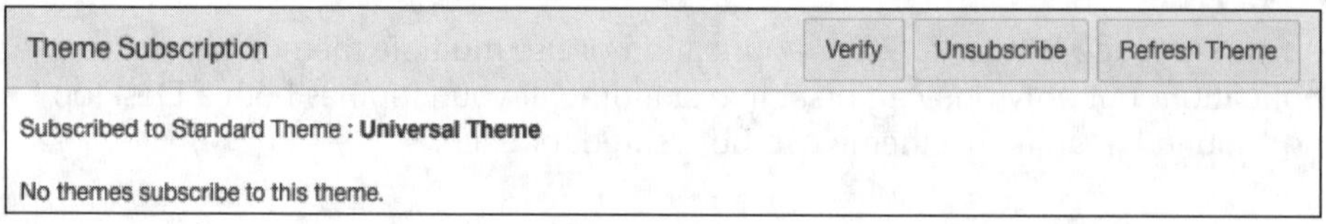

Theme Subscription		Verify	Unsubscribe	Refresh Theme
Subscribed to Standard Theme : **Universal Theme**				
No themes subscribe to this theme.				

To the right of this section are three or four buttons, depending on whether this is a master theme or a subscribed to theme:

- **Verify**   Click this button to open the Verify Theme Subscription modal, which displays the name and number of the master application and theme as well as the name and number of the subscribing application and theme.

Clinking the Verify button shows us the Subscription Status Report, a report detailing the templates in your theme, including those that need to be resynched to the master. If your theme needs to be synched, you will see a Refresh Theme button. If no templates need to be refreshed, an OK button is displayed. Click OK or Cancel to close this modal.

- **Unsubscribe** Click to unsubscribe from the master theme. This is useful if you want this theme to be independent—or perhaps to be used as a master theme itself.

- **Refresh Theme** Click to sync all the templates with the master, just as you can with the Verify Theme Subscription modal. If this theme has subscribing themes, the Publish Theme button will be shown.

- **Publish Theme** Click this button to push all changes from the master theme to the subscribing themes. If you want to push the changes to a subset of the subscribing themes, go to the individual theme's details page and click the Refresh Theme button.

Component Defaults, Region Defaults, and Dialog Defaults Sections In the Component Defaults, Region Defaults, and Dialog Defaults sections, you can choose a default template for specific components in your APEX application. The template set on this page is used by default when you create particular items or regions. Leaving a component blank will result in the developer being asked to choose a template upon component creation. At creation time, a developer may use another template for a component, but setting it here allows for uniformity across your applications.

Global Template Options are template options that are used across all templates of that particular class. You'll learn more about template options and global template options in the "Templates" section later in this chapter.

Icons Section New in Application Express in 5.1 is the Icons section (Figure 8-6), which includes several attributes:

- **Library** Choose from two built-in icon libraries: Font Awesome and Font APEX. Font APEX is a font library of icons specifically created to fit with the aesthetics of the Universal Theme and overall APEX look and feel and the preferred choice.

- **Customer Library File URLs** Enter the URL for a custom icon library.

- **Custom Classes** Specify a comma-delimited list of CSS classes that will be listed in the picker for Region and Button Icon CSS Classes within the Page Designer.

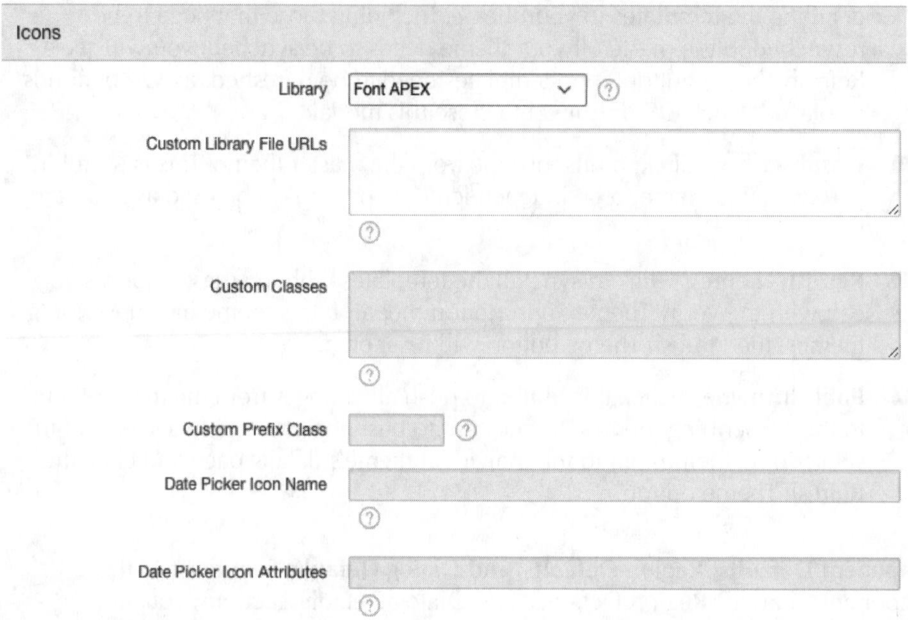

FIGURE 8-6. *The Icons section*

- **Custom Prefix Class**   At runtime, prefix the icon CSS classes defined for regions, buttons, and lists. The prefix will be applied if they are not using a class of the icon library. Adding this custom prefix to the imported icon library will help you avoid class naming collisions.

- **Date Picker Icon Name and Date Picker Icon Attrributes**   Define customer date picker icons and icon attributes.

Styles Section   In the Styles section, you can choose a current style for your application created with the Theme Roller. The Theme Roller is covered in detail later in this chapter in its own section, but it's important to note that after you create and save a new style with the Theme Roller, it will be displayed here where you can switch to it. The style used for the application is indicated by a checkmark in the Is Current column. To change to another style, click the style you want; then, on the Theme Styles page, select Yes for the Is Current attribute. Then click Apply Changes.

Click the Add Style button. Then, on the next page, enter a name for your Style. For the File URLs attribute, enter the URL reference from the previous page, usually in the form of #THEME_IMAGES#your_uploaded_style_file.css. Then click Create and that style will be available for use.

Files Section   All the custom styles created with Theme Roller are stored as files and can be downloaded in the Files section. Note, if you do not have any customer themes, this section will be empty.

If you do have a customer theme or create one and return to the section, click the File Name Link in the Files Report to view the details. When viewing the details, you have the option of deleting the file or downloading it. The option to download is also available in the Files Report as a Download link. If you have a customer theme roller file from another application or from a completely different system you previously downloaded, you can click the Upload File button to upload CSS file for Theme Roller here.

Once you upload a Theme Roller CSS file, you will see the new file in the Files report as well as a Reference URL to that file. Use that Reference URL when adding a new Theme Roller style to your application.

Theme Tasks

Click Cancel to leave the Theme details page.

Back on the Themes main report page is a list of various tasks you can perform around themes such as copy, delete, and import/export. The import/export tasks are especially valuable if you have a corporate theme developed in another system and need to import or export it for a particular application.

Templates

All themes are made up of a collection of templates. Templates dictate how individual components are rendered. They consist of HTML, CSS, and APEX substitution strings. Let's take a closer look at some templates.

Back in the User Interface section, click Templates to open the Templates report. This interactive report will show all the templates in all of the themes within your current application. Look across the top in the subtab section to see the following reports that you can view:

- **Templates**   Show all the templates for all your themes in an interactive report. Use this report to view and change any template.

- **Subscription**   This report displays subscribing templates in your applications. You can refresh these templates by selecting the checkboxes and then clicking Refresh. Any changes in the master will be included in the subscribed templates.

- **Publish**   This report shows templates that can be subscribed to. You can also select the checkboxes and click the Publish button to publish changes in these templates to be inherited by the subscribed templates.

- **Utilization** This report page shows which templates are used in the current application. It is divided into template types and provides information on the template name, the theme, and a number link in the Reference Column that brings you to a subreport that shows the specific page and component that uses that template.

- **History** This report shows recent changes made to Page and Region Templates in this application.

At the upper right of the Templates report are two buttons, Reset and Create. Click the Reset button to reset the interactive report; click Create to create a new template. (We will explore the Create button later in the section "Creating a Template.") A Templates report includes lots of information and several columns.

- **Type** Indicates the type of template used. Just about every component of APEX can have a template (Shuttles and Trees are two exceptions), so you'll see duplicate types such as Page, List, Button, and Breadcrumb.

- **Name** This is simply the name of the template.

- **Subscribed From and Subscribers** Indicates what the particular theme is subscribed to and how many subscribers are using that particular template. This is important when you're making changes to templates with multiple subscribers. The changes you make in the master will roll down those other templates when refreshed.

- **References** Indicates how many components in your application are using that particular template. The number is also a link, and clicking it will open a subreport that contains the exact page, region, and item using that template.

- **Updated and Updated By** Indicates who made a change to a template and when this change was made.

- **Default** Indicates whether this template is the default template for that component in this theme. Remember that you can set this in the Theme details page.

- **Theme** Shows the number of the theme used, such as 42, the Universal Theme.

- **Copy** Click this icon to copy the template.

Let's look at the Page template and the attributes it includes. We'll start by filtering this report.

In the Search text field for the interactive report, enter **Row text contains 'standard'** and press RETURN/ENTER. You'll then see a filtered report, where you can easily find the Standard page template (shown in Figure 8-7).

Click the Standard page template link in the Name column. (Note that if this is a template that is being subscribed to and not the master template, some of the following options will be either locked or disabled.)

The Template details page includes several sections.

Name Section   The Name section (Figure 8-8) includes several attributes:

- **Name and Theme**   Shows the page template type and theme.

- **Template Class**   Helps identify a specific use for the template and helps when you're moving from one theme to another by matching like classes in the new theme to the template classes in the old theme.

- **Translatable**   Select this checkbox if this particular template contains text strings that require translation.

- **Template Type**   Either Normal Page or Dialog Page. Specifies how the page is rendered and used in an application.

Row text contains 'standard'

Type

Type : Page

Name	Identifier	Subscribed From	Subscribers	References	Updated	Updated By	Default	Theme	Copy
Standard	STANDARD	Theme		2			✓	42	🗍

Type : Region

Name	Identifier	Subscribed From	Subscribers	References	Updated	Updated By	Default	Theme	Copy
Standard	STANDARD	Theme		8			✓	42	🗍

Type : Report

Name	Identifier	Subscribed From	Subscribers	References	Updated	Updated By	Default	Theme	Copy
Standard	STANDARD	Theme		2			✓	42	🗍

FIGURE 8-7.   *A report showing the Standard page template*

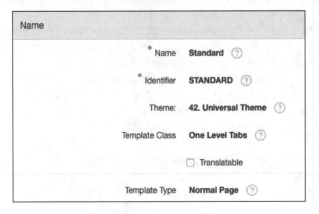

FIGURE 8-8. *The template Name section*

NOTE
With the Universal Theme, the Template Class and the Translatable checkbox are locked. To unlock them, you would need to unsubscribe the theme. If you needed to do this in the future, you would go back to the Theme details page, Theme Subscription section, and click the Unsubscribe button. The APEX development team recommends you do not do this (so please don't). In keeping the Universal Theme subscribed and locked, you can easily move to the latest Universal Theme with no issues.

Subscription Section   The Subscription section includes the following:

- **Reference Master Template From**   Choose a master template from the pop-up list of values.

- **Refresh checkbox**   Once subscribed, you can refresh from the master automatically by selecting this checkbox.

The Reference Master Template From option and Refresh checkbox are available only if the template is unsubscribed. APEX will also tell you this template is unsubscribed to a master template: "This is the 'master' copy of this template."

Template Options Section   New to APEX 5 are Template Options (Figure 8-9).

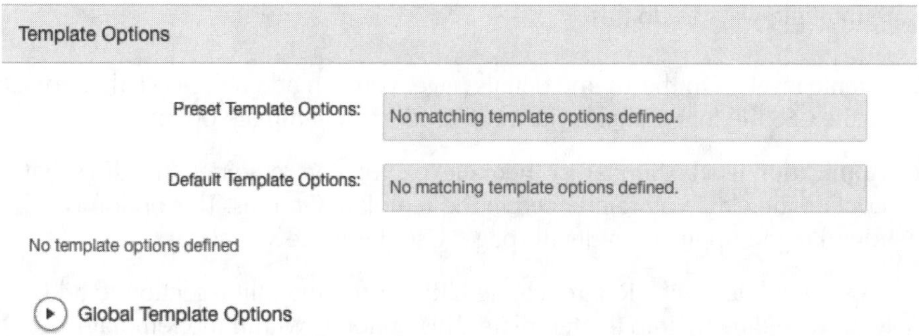

Template Options

Preset Template Options: No matching template options defined.

Default Template Options: No matching template options defined.

No template options defined

(▶) Global Template Options

FIGURE 8-9. *Template Options section*

Use the Template Options section to create CSS modifiers for the specific template you are working with. Add options such as borders, padding, icons, colors, and size, and they will be easily accessible from the Page Designer. Each template option corresponds to one or more CSS class names that are inserted in the template in place of the **#REGION_CSS_CLASSES#** substitution string when the template is rendered at runtime. Theme CSS files define rules that use these class names in selectors to control the look of the template markup.

In previous versions of APEX (4.2.1), you could add classes to instances of templates using the CSS Classes or Custom CSS Classes attribute, but this required somehow documenting the available classes in the theme. Template options bring all of this together in a single declarative UI. The following template types can have template options:

- Page
- Region
- Report
- Breadcrumb
- List
- Button
- Label

NOTE
We will use Template Options in our application when we examine how the Universal Theme is controlled with the Page Designer.

If you're using template options, you will need to define the CSS class used. There are multiple ways to do this.

- **Theme level**   On the Theme details page, you can add a file URL that points to the CSS file that contains the class used in the template option.

- **Application level**   Similar to Theme level, you can reference file URLs that contain the class you referenced in the Template Options. This option is found in the Application details page, User Interface subtab.

- **Page template level**   Reference file URLs or use the inline section to add your style directly into the template. This option is within the Template details page for a page template.

- **Page level**   In the Page Designer, when you're looking at the attributes for a page, scroll down to the CSS section, where you can reference file URLs or add inline CSS.

NOTE
File URL locations can be on remote web servers, or you can reference files uploaded to APEX.

Global Template Options, at the bottom of this section, are used across all templates of the same type. These Global Template Options can also be created in the Theme details page.

Definition Section   The Definition section contains all the HTML code that makes up the template itself. Depending on the type of template you are viewing, the subsections in the Definition area will differ.

Page Template options are Header, Body, and Footer. Click the Help icon next to each of these options to see an example of how you can create this section of the template plus all the substitution strings you can use.

A more comprehensive list of all the substitution strings used in this particular template is also displayed at the bottom of this page. This expanded list contains the string name, where it should go in a template, and a short description. Of note are **#REGION_POSITION_01#** through **#REGION_POSITION_08#**. These are the main substitution strings in a page template where you can place regions (form, report, static) as well as items and components. Also displayed are specific substitution strings that you can place in your templates for navigation areas as well as success, error, and validation messages.

JavaScript Section   The JavaScript section of this page template enables you to link file URLs or include direct inline JavaScript code. The file URLs will be placed in the **#TEMPLATE_JAVASCRIPT#** substitution string in the page template, and the inline JavaScript code will be placed in the **#GENERATED_JAVASCRIPT#** substitution string in the page template. Use the Function and Global Variable Declaration for JavaScript functions and variables that will be used in your template, and use the Execute When Page Loads section for JavaScript that needs to be run as soon as your page loads in the browser.

Cascading Style Sheet Section   Similar to the JavaScript section is the Cascading Style Sheet section. The only difference here is that both the CSS File URLs and the inline code will be placed into one substitution string, **#TEMPLATE_CSS#**. When the template type is a Dialog Page, the JavaScript section includes fields for entering code for initializing (opening), closing, and canceling a dialog.

Subtemplate Section   In the Subtemplate section, you can finely tune and customize many of the smaller and/or nested sections in a template. You can customize the success message, the navigation bar, navigation bar entry, and the notification definitions. If using the older tab navigation in your application, the Image Based Tab attributes section lets you set images for active and inactive tabs.

Grid Layout Section   Grid Layout or Layout controls how regions are aligned within a particular section of a template. For the Grid Layout Type, you can choose from HTML Tables, Fixed Number Of Column, or Variable Number Of Columns. Using HTML tables will require just one attribute to be filled in, Region Table Attributes. Set the cell padding, cell spacing, and width of your HTML tables. HTML tables are a good way to display data, but a fixed or variable column layout gives you much more flexibility. It is recommended that when using the Universal Theme, you leave the options of this section at the default settings. When using Fixed Number Of Column or Variable Number Of Columns, along with the many other options, you also have three template sections for the grid layout (Container, Row, and Column) as well as a JavaScript Debug Code section for providing additional layout help with the Show Grid and Hide Grid buttons on the Developer toolbar.

Display Points Section   Display Points (Figure 8-10) give you more control than ever over your page template region positions.

You can give readable names to the various **#REGION_POSITION#** substitution strings in the page template. This enables you to alter or create new page templates with specific uses for the region positions. Previous to APEX 5, this functionality did not exist, and you had to guess as to what region position was used in custom templates. For example, in a two-column layout, you can now use a name such as "smaller column" to the region you assign to the smaller column, so that when positioning page components, you can easily find this region position. You can also define whether that particular region position is Grid Layout–enabled by selecting the Grid Support checkbox. You can also limit the number of columns with Maximum Fixed Grid Columns. Lastly, the New Row checkbox dictates whether or not this Region Position can be placed on a new row.

Display Points					Delete	Add Row
	Name ↑≟	Template Substitution	Grid Support	Maximum Fixed Grid Columns		New Row
☐	Before Navigation Bar	REGION_POSITION_08	☐			☐
☐	Breadcrumb Bar	REGION_POSITION_01	☐			☑
☐	Content Body	BODY	☑	12		☑
☐	Footer	REGION_POSITION_05	☑	12		☑
☐	Inline Dialogs	REGION_POSITION_04	☑	12		☑
☐	Page Header	REGION_POSITION_07	☐			☑
☐	Page Navigation	REGION_POSITION_06	☐			☑

1 - 7

Breadcrumb Display Point **Page Template Region Position 1** ⓘ

Sidebar Display Point ⓘ

FIGURE 8-10. *Display Points section*

Dialog Section   In the Dialog section, you define how large this page template will display in a modal dialog by default. This is used with the Modal Dialog Page template. The attributes set here will be overridden by attributes set at the page level.

NOTE
When using a Desktop template, it's best to use pixel lengths such as 500px, and when using a Mobile template, use percentages.

APEX embeds modal dialogs in iFrames. The Allow Embed In Frame attribute controls how this page will be rendered if it is a modal dialog. This option works with the application-level security option Embed In Frames. For example, setting the application-level attribute Embed In Frames to Deny and checking Modal Dialog For Allow Embed In Frame will instead use the value Allow From Same Origin for Embed In Frames when displaying dialog pages that use this template. This will ensure that modal templates render correctly. Each attribute set here, except for Allow Embed In Frame, has a corresponding substitution string (**#DIALOG_WIDTH#, #DIALOG_HEIGHT#, and #DIALOG_MAX_WIDTH#**).
The Error Page Template Control allows for customization of the error notification area.

Comments Section   Use the Comments section to leave helpful information about the template and any changes that were made for future reference.

Substitution Strings Section   The Substitution Strings section details all the substitution strings that are used within templates to reference component values.

This report details substitution string usage for this template and is a super handy reference when you're using template substitution strings.

Creating a Template

This section will guide you through the process of creating or copying a template.

1. On the Application home page, click Shared Components. Then open the Templates page.

2. Click the Create button in the upper right to launch the Create Template wizard.

3. Under Template Type (Figure 8-11), click Label.

4. The next step asks if you want to create a template from scratch or use a copy of an existing template. Choose to make a copy of an Existing Template, and then choose from what application you want to copy the Label Template.

5. Click Next. Then choose the theme you want to copy from and the theme you want to copy to.

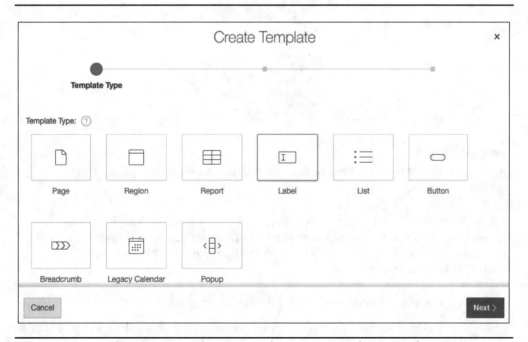

FIGURE 8-11. *Choosing a template type in the Create Template wizard*

6. You'll then see all the Label templates (per your choice in step 3) that you can copy.

7. To copy a Label template, change the Copy? select list from No to Yes, and enter the name of your new template in the To Name text field.

8. Click the Copy Label Templates button at the bottom of the page.

If you chose From Scratch in step 4, you are asked to enter a Template Name, choose a Theme, and select the Template Class to which it belongs, as shown next. Remember that template classes identify a specific use for the template you are creating and can help when you're switching themes. To create a template, choose the Template Class that best fits the intended use of this template. Once the template is created, you can fill in the details, starting with the bare minimum.

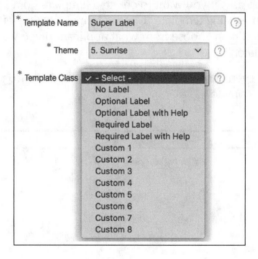

Template Tasks

On the right side of the Templates page (on the Shared Components page, select Templates) are various tasks.

Replace Templates   Select Replace Templates In This Application With Templates From Another Application to replace as many templates as you want with templates from another application, using a grid edit page. There are two options regarding which templates to replace:

- **Replace**   Copies the template definition from your application

- **Replace / Subscribe**   Copies the templates from your application and adds a subscription

Once you choose what templates are being replaced or subscribed, click the Replace Templates button at the bottom of the page.

View Page Template Region Position   Select View Page Template Region Position Utilization Task and APEX will create a helpful report that tells you what template is used in what region on a page and how many times it's used in that region. This is handy if you are looking to make a change and checking to see what is affected. The report does not go down to the page level but stays at the application level.

Theme Reports   Select Theme Reports to open the Reports subtab on the Themes page. This report gives you a breakdown of all the templates and template types in your application across all themes.

Replace Templates   Use the Replace Templates task to swap out one template with another globally in your application.

Unsubscribe Templates   Select this task to mass unsubscribe template types. Choose the theme and template type(s) and click the Unsubscribe button.

Creating a Theme

To create a theme, on the Shared Components page, User Interface section, select Themes. Click the Create button to launch the Create Theme wizard (Figure 8-12).

FIGURE 8-12.   *Create Theme wizard*

Start by choosing one of the following options:

- **From The Repository**   Choose from more than 26 precreated themes.

- **As A Copy From Another Application**   Have you built or customized a theme in another application in the same workspace? Copy it with this option.

- **From Scratch**   Start with a bare-bones template and build from there.

- **From Export**   Have a theme export you downloaded, bought, or created? Import it here.

From the Repository   Choose From The Repository, and the next step is to choose the User Interface Type: Add User Interface or Desktop. Choose Add A User Interface to add a Mobile UI or Desktop UI. The next page will provide you with Theme choices. For the Desktop UI, choose from among several precreated themes, including the Universal Theme. For Mobile, a single Mobile theme (Theme 51) is available. Select a theme and click Next; then click Create. That theme will now be displayed in the Theme Report for you to switch to.

As A Copy From Another Application   Choose As A Copy From Another Application, and the Copy Theme wizard will guide you through selecting an application from which to copy the theme.

1. Choose the Application from which you want to copy the theme.

2. Choose the name of the theme you want to copy from.

3. Provide this theme a new ID number. (Numbers 1–100 are reserved for APEX's built-in themes.)

4. Subscribe the theme. Choose Yes, and any changes made in the original theme in the original application will apply to this theme when you click the Refresh button on the Theme details page.

5. Once the page is filled out, as shown next, click Next.

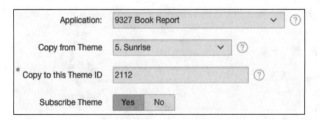

6. On the next page, click Copy Theme. The theme will now be included in your Theme report and you will see the parent application number in the Subscribed From column.

From Scratch   Choose From Scratch to open the Create Theme form.

1. In the Theme Number field, give the theme a number.

2. In the Name field, enter a theme name.

3. Choose what type of User Interface you want to start with, Desktop or Mobile.

4. For Navigation Type, choose either List or Tabs. Tabs were used in previous versions of APEX but have since been replaced with List navigation, a much more flexible option. Use tabs if you are using legacy themes (every theme except for Universal and Mobile).

5. For Navigation Bar Implementation, choose either List or Classic. List uses a list template, and Classic uses markup from subtemplates in the Page template. The List option is a much more flexible choice.

6. Add a Description, and then click the Create button to see your new theme in the report.

From Export   Choosing the last option, From Export, launches the Import wizard, where you are asked to upload the theme export file.

1. The File Type Of Theme Export has already been preselected for you. Once uploaded, click Next to start the import process.

2. The File Import Confirmation page confirms that the file has been successfully imported. Click Next to see the Install Theme step.

3. Click the Install Theme button to start this process. The Install Into Application option has defaulted to the current application you are working in. You can change this to another application if you want before clicking the Install Theme button. Once installed, this theme is available to be chosen from the Theme report.

Switching Themes

Back on the main Theme report page are three task buttons, shown next:

- ■ **Reset**   Reset the Interactive Report for Themes back to its original state.

- ■ **Switch Theme**   Change to a different theme; note that you must have more than one theme in your application to use this option.

- ■ **Create**   Create a new theme from scratch or choose a precreated theme from the repository.

1. Click the Switch Theme button to launch the Theme Switch wizard to help with the process.

2. On the first page, choose which theme is currently active and which theme you want to move to. As shown next, the Currently Active Theme is 5, Sunrise, and we're switching to the Universal Theme, 42.

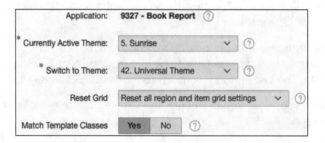

3. Next, choose a Reset Grid option; this gets a bit complex. The grid setting in a page defines the positioning of regions and items. Regions may be positioned next to each other horizontally; items can be positioned next to each other on the same row in a form. Resetting the grid will set all regions and items horizontally, thus preparing for the following situations when theme switching:

- ■ When switching from a table-based Grid Layout, as in Theme 26, to a DIV-based layout, such as the one in the Universal Theme, any fixed positioned regions need to be reset, so you would select the Reset Fixed Region Positions option.

- ■ When switching themes that contain the same type of Grid Layout, select the Keep Current Region And Item Grid Settings option.

- ■ When switching from an older theme (non-Grid Layout theme) to the new Universal Theme, select the Reset All Region And Item Grid Settings option. Be warned, however, that all previous region and item positions will be lost in the switch.

4. Choose a Match Template Classes option to attempt to match the template class of the old theme to the new theme. When creating or using a template, it can be assigned a class, which will aid in theme switching.

   Note that if you attempt to switch from a theme that uses list-based navigation to a theme that uses tab-based navigation, you will see the following message: "1 error has occurred. This application cannot be converted to a theme using tab-based navigation, as it uses list-based navigation." You will see this error when attempting to go from Theme 42 to Theme 5.

5. The next step of the Theme Switch wizard is Verify Compatibility, with a list of Theme Templates and the corresponding match in the new theme (shown in Figure 8-13). The matching is done based on template class. The Status column tells you whether a match has been found, no match has been found, or multiple matches have been found. When no or multiple matches are found, you can choose a template from a select list that best fits the new theme.

6. The last step is the Confirmation page. Click the Switch Theme button to move to your new theme. Once switched, in the Theme report, you will see an asterisk (*) next to the current theme and a checkmark in the Is Current column, as shown here.

Name	User Interface	Is Current
Orange - 8	Desktop	
Universal Theme - 42 *	Desktop	✓

Template Type ↑=	From Template	To Template	Status
Breadcrumb	Breadcrumb Menu	Breadcrumb ⬍	✓
Button	Button	Text ⬍	✓
Label	Optional with help	Optional ⬍	No matching class
Page	Printer Friendly	Standard ⬍	No matching class
	Login	Login ⬍	✓

FIGURE 8-13. *Template compatibility report*

Using the Universal Theme in Your Application

With APEX 5 comes one of the biggest enhancements to APEX, the Universal Theme. As you learned from the previous discussions about themes and templates, using themes can get a bit complex. Going into a template's definitions and changing some HTML or CSS to get a border on a region is a lot to ask from someone who has never used these programming languages.

The Universal Theme is an HTML5-based theme that uses template options to change the look, feel, and behavior of an application. You don't even need to know CSS to alter the Universal Theme. The APEX development team has included a Universal Theme sample application you can install and use as a visual aid for the next part of this chapter.

Pages

The Universal Theme provides some template options through Page Templates and Navigation placement choices. To take a closer look, let's edit Page 1 of our application.

In the Rendering panel in the Page Designer, click Page 1: Home. Then, on the Page Properties tab, find the Appearance property group.

Appearance Property Group

First is the Page Template attribute, where you can choose from among multiple layouts for your page. The Theme Default is selected (set in the Theme details page, mentioned previously), but you can change the template by selecting a new one from the select list. The page templates available with the Universal Theme enable you to alter the column layout of your pages. Choose a two-column layout with a large column or region on the left and a smaller sidebar on the right, or choose the exact opposite of that. You can also choose a three-column layout, Left And Right Side Columns, which includes a column on the left and a collapsible column on the right, as shown in Figure 8-14. These page templates are also responsive, meaning they will flex and rearrange content based on the screen size of the browser or device—very useful for mobile and tablet devices.

Next is a Template Options property, where you can enable the template options in the Page Template details. All the template options can be enabled or disabled by selecting a checkbox, or you can choose a value from a select list. Click the Use Template Defaults button to bring up the Template Options modal window. The button will be disabled if there are no Template Options to choose from. In Figure 8-14, this button is disabled, but we will use this button extensively in the coming sections.

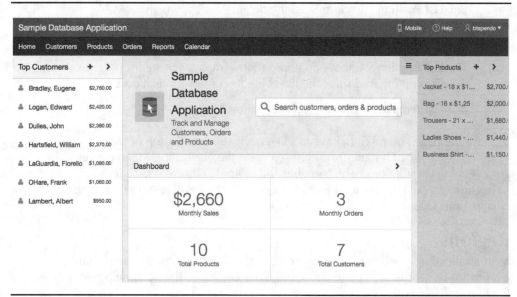

FIGURE 8-14.   *Three-column page layout with top navigation*

Navigation Menu Property Group

The Navigation Menu property group is just below the Appearance property group. The theme dictates what navigation style your pages are going to use based on the Navigation Menu List Position property on the Theme details page.

    The first property in the Navigation Menu group is Override User Interface Level. When you select Yes, you can alter all the navigation elements for this page. Click Yes to see what you can change:

- ■ **List**   Choose one of several options: Do Not Show Navigation Menu List (hides the navigation on the page), Desktop Navigation Bar, and Desktop Navigation Menu. Select Desktop Navigation Menu to see three more properties: List Position, List Template, and Template options:

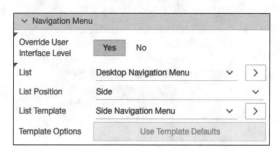

- **List Position**   Choose Side, the default, or Top, which looks like the traditional tab layout in previous versions of APEX (though it's a list template, not APEX tabs).

- **List Position**   Choose an appropriate template for the list position. Choose Top to display the list at the top of the application.

- **List Template**   Choose Top Navigation Menu.

Save the page and run it to have tab-like navigation on the top of the page.

Back in the Page Designer, your last setting in the Navigation Menu property group is Template Options, which enable you to apply custom CSS styles to your list navigation, if available. Set the Override User Interface Level to No to reset the changes and save the change.

Regions

Most applications include regions—whether they are reports, static, or specialized regions, APEX 5 brings template options and the Universal Theme to help customize the look and feel with ease.

To try out some of these regions, let's create a new blank page.

1. In the Page Designer, click the Create dropdown menu and select Page.

2. On the first page of the Create Page wizard, click Blank Page.

3. On the first page of the Create Blank Page wizard, keep the default page number, and for Name, enter **My Regions**.

4. Set the Page mode to Normal. Leave Breadcrumbs unselected. Click Next.

5. On the Navigation Menu step, select the Create A New Navigation Menu Entry radio button, and then click Next.

6. On the Confirm page, click the Finish button at the lower right of the modal window.

7. Back in the Page Designer, in the Rendering panel, click the Content Body node under the Regions node and select Create Region, as shown next:

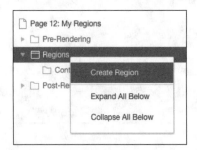

A new region will be displayed on the Canvas in the middle of the Page Designer. Feel free to create a new page for each of the following regions. This will ensure that you have a library of pages with different regions you can refer back to later or experiment with.

Standard Region

Let's create a standard region:

1. In the Page Designer, Rendering panel, click your new region.

2. In the Region properties panel on the right, find the Appearance properties group. The template we are using for this region is the Standard Region template.

3. Click the User Template Defaults button in the Template Options property.

4. In the Template Options modal (Figure 8-15), you'll see several options:

   ■ **Body Height** Set a fixed height for your region, or have it stretch based upon the content in it by selecting Auto – Default.

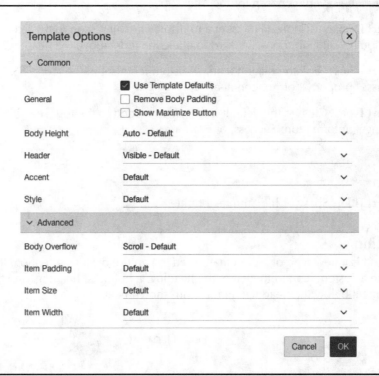

FIGURE 8-15. *The Template Options modal for a standard region*

- **Header**   Choose whether to show, hide, or hide the header with accessibility.

- **Accent and Style**   Change the look and feel of the region.

- **Body Overflow**   Control how the region will behave if the contents are larger than the region's size. You can choose to hide the overflow or have a scroll bar appear to scroll through the overflow.

5. Click OK to close the Template Options modal.

Alert Region

Let's set an alert region:

Back in the Page Designer Region properties, change the Template property to Alert Region. This type of region includes an icon to the left of the heading that can indicate one of four different alert severities: Danger, Information, Success, or Warning.

Click the User Template Defaults button; then, in the Template Options modal, choose several options:

- **General**   The Highlight Background checkbox will shade the region to match the severity chosen for the Alter Type.

- **Alert Display**   Choose Horizontal to display the alert icon to the left of the region heading or choose Wizard to place the icon above the heading.

- **Alert Icons**   Use the default icon, a custom icon (set in the Icon CSS Classes property), or no icon at all.

- **Alert Type**   Change the default icon to correspond to the four severities: Danger, Information, Success, or Warning.

- **Alert Title**   Show or hide the region title.

Hero Region

A hero region is a new type of region that's used to capture or draw attention. It renders with a custom icon to the left of the heading, a boldface heading, and the region's content below the heading; all three are shown next:

New in APEX 5.1 are two hero region styles:

- **Featured**   Increases the size of the icon and text and centers and stacks the larger icon and text and layers or stacks them (shown in the middle illustration).

- **Stacked Featured**   Features large icon on top, with larger main text under that and subtext on the third layer (at far right).

Buttons Container Region

A buttons container region, shown next, is a great way to organize multiple buttons neatly in a single region. The buttons container has no heading but multiple button placement regions. There are no specific template options for the buttons container.

Carousel Region

The carousel region is also new in APEX 5. In this region, you can cycle through content in subregions. Let's create a carousel region:

1. Change the Template in the Property Editor, Appearance property group, to Carousel Container in your test region.

2. Back in the Rendering panel on the left, right-click your Carousel Region and choose Create Sub Region—these are the content subregions that will be cycled through.

3. Do this twice to create two subregions.

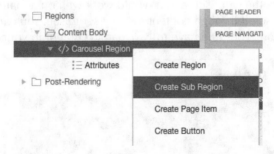

4. Click your first subregion. On the right in the Region Properties tab, for the Title property of the first subregion, enter **Slide 1**.

5. In the Source property group, set the Text Property to Slide 1.

6. In the Appearance property group, change the Template to Blank With Attributes.

7. For the CSS Classes property, enter the following: **u-Color-4-BG--bg u-Color-4-FG--txt h200**

8. Either in the Rendering panel or on the main Canvas, select the next subregion. In the Region Properties tab on the right, for the Title property, enter **Slide 2**.

9. In the Source property group, set the Text property to Slide 2.

10. In the Appearance property group, change the Template to Blank With Attributes.

11. For the CSS Classes property, enter the following: **u-Color-7-BG--bg u-Color-5-FG--txt h200**

12. Back in the Page Designer or on the main Canvas, select the main Carousel region and look over in the Region Property tab on the right.

13. Set the Title to **My Carousel**.

14. For the Template Options property, click the Use Template Defaults button.

15. Start with the Timer option. Setting this attribute to something other than No Timer will automatically change to the next subregion in that specified amount of time.

16. For the Animation attribute, the content can change with these three animation types: Slide, Fade, or Spin. Experiment with all three to see which one you like best.

17. Once you have selected the template options and click OK in the modal, save and run your page to see the carousel in action.

As you can see, the carousel region would work well on a main page where you can automatically scroll through content for the user to see. You can even set the subregions to Report Types and have truly dynamic content in your carousel!

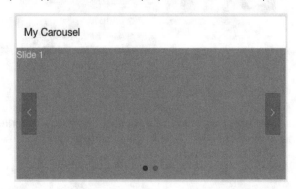

Wizard Region

We have been working with wizards throughout this book. APEX gives us the ability to create a custom wizard just like the ones we have used.

1. Start in the Page Designer and click the Create dropdown (plus sign menu) and select Page.

2. In the Create a Page wizard, select Wizard:

Tree   Wizard   Data Loading

3. On the first page of the wizard, for the Wizard Name attribute, name the wizard My Wizard.

4. Set the Create This Number Of Pages to 3. This will create three wizard steps.

5. For Page Mode, set to Modal Dialog. This will create a pop-up type of wizard, rather than a full-page one. (Just like the wizard you are working with now.)

6. Once done, click Next.

7. For the Navigation Menu step, select **Do not associate this page with a navigation menu entry** if not already selected and then click Next.

8. On the last step of the wizard, we can select the page numbers we wish to have for the wizard steps, the page names, and also how many items we want to have automatically created for us. Leave these defaults and click Create.

9. We are now back in the Page Designer. We need to go to create a blank page so that we can launch this wizard. Again, use the Create dropdown menu and select page.

10. Select Blank Page in the Create a Page wizard.

11. Name the page "Launch Wizard," leave the defaults for the rest of the attributes, and click Next.

12. On the Navigation Menu step, click the radio button next to Create A New Navigation Menu Entry. Then click Next.

13. Click Finish on the final step of the modal.

14. Now in the Page Designer, right-click the content body node in the Rendering panel on the left and select Create Region.

15. Right-click on this New region node and select Create Button (we will be going over buttons later in this chapter).

16. In the Button Property Panel on the right, find the Behavior property group and using the select list, select Redirect to a Page In This Application for the Action property.

17. The Target property will be in error. Click the No Target Defined button to bring up the Link Builder – Target modal.

18. Click the pop-up LOV button for the page attribute and select the first page of your wizard. Then click OK to close the modal.

19. Save and run the page.

20. On the page click the New button. Upon clicking this button, the first step of your wizard will appear in a modal.

Wizards are very useful in guiding your users along a path that helps with directions or data entry. We see that APEX, using a wizard, helps us to create a wizard.

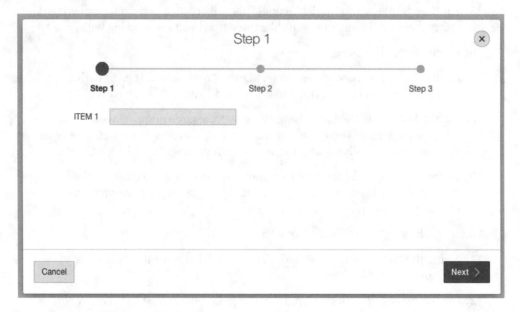

Title Bar Region

A title bar region is used for breadcrumbs, page titles, or primary actions. This region has a single template option that is unique, called Region Title. With this option, you can place either breadcrumbs, by choosing the Use Current Breadcrumb Entry value, or the page title, by choosing the Use Region Title value. Upon your selecting and saving a value, the region will automatically place the selected component in the region for you, with no additional code needed. This region would work well on the top of a page to give breadcrumbs a very professional and unique look, as shown in the following illustration. Best results are achieved when placing this region in the Breadcrumbs section of a page.

Lists

Another set of templates that have been overhauled in APEX 5 are lists. The Universal Theme provides more list types and uses than ever before. There are so many, in fact, that to do lists justice, we will create a new page in our application.

Creating a Badge List

Let's start by creating a new badge list. Badge lists are useful for displaying a region with important statistics or summary information.

1. In the Page Designer, click the Create dropdown menu and select Page.

2. Keep the User Interface set to Desktop and select Blank Page.

3. Name the page **My Lists** and keep the other defaults for this step. Then click Next.

4. On the Navigation Menu step, select the Create A New Navigation Menu Entry radio button and click Next.

5. In the Confirm step, click Finish. You now have a blank page to work with.

6. In the Page Designer, click the Shared Component icon:

7. To the left of the Shared Components page in the Navigation group, click Lists.

8. Click the Create button to start the Create List wizard.

9. Select From Scratch and then click Next.

10. On the Name and Type step, enter a name for the list, **My Static List**, and for Type, select Static. Then click Next.

11. For the Query or Static Values step, enter five random values for List Entry Label. You can leave the values for Target Page ID or custom URL empty. Then click Next.

12. On the Confirm step, for the attribute Create List Regions?, select Create List Region On Current Page. A few more attributes will be displayed.

13. For Region Position, select Page Template Body; for Region Template, select Standard; and for List Template, select Badge List. The final page of the modal should look like Figure 8-16.

14. Click Create List. Then click the Run button at the upper right to run the page.

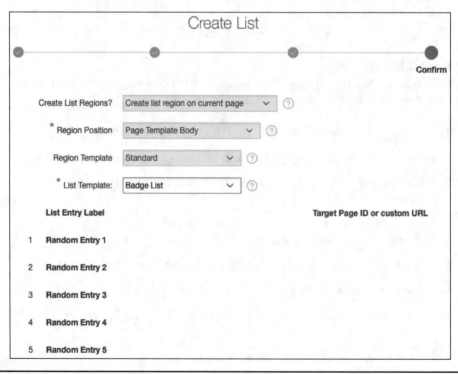

FIGURE 8-16. *The Confirm modal page of Create List*

A Wealth of List Attributes

The List Entry page, or the page where you can edit or create a list item, includes a wealth of attributes. Here are a few of the major ones that you can use in template options and the Universal Theme:

- **Parent List Entry** Nest list items as children. With the Menu Bar template, you can nest multiple levels of list items to create a cascading menu that expands out as you navigate down. Each lower child level of the menu is indicated with a right-facing arrow icon.

- **Image/Class Attribute** Add icons to your lists in the List Entry details page. Select the list entry you want to add an icon to and use the pop-up LOV on the details page, Image/Class attribute.

- **User Defined Attributes** Use these entries for Card templates. The Body Text region in the Card templates is taken from the User Defined Attributes section's first two attributes. (Note that these user-defined attributes are used in other list templates for particular functionality, and they are not specific to the Card templates.)

- **List Template Attributes** Confused about which User Defined Attribute does what? APEX has you covered. Click the List Template Attributes button in the User Defined Attributes section to bring up a modal region, the List Template Attribute Description. Here you can select a theme and a list template to get a description of what User Defined Attributes actually do and mean.

Now you have created a vertically aligned list of badges. You can change the look and feel of your badge list with template options.

1. Edit this page, and in the Rendering panel on the left, find the Attributes node under our List Region named My Static List.

2. In the Attributes tab on the right, click the None Selected button in the Template Options property.

3. Notice the first option in the General section. The Responsive checkbox will cause your badge list to react to different screen sizes, changing the layout to be readable on smaller screens. (You can see this in a desktop browser by resizing the browser window to various sizes.)

4. Next, you can change the layout of your badges with the Layout attribute. You can have them aligned in a grid of up to five columns, have them stacked, or even span them horizontally.

5. You can change the size of your badges with the Badge Size attribute to make them very large or quite small. Experiment with the options and run the page. Badge lists are very useful counters as well.

To display text in the badge, you need to edit the list itself. You can do this back in the Shared Components page. Once you edit your list and select the entry you want to work with, use the User Defined Attribute 1 (**#A01#** in the template) on the List Entry details page, shown next, to have the counter display a value, as shown in the second illustration.

User Defined Attributes

Substitution strings #A01# - #A10# are optional attributes within a list template, which can be used to reference list ent Attributes to view a more meaningful description of the substitution strings in use in the list templates available in the c

☐ Translatable

1. HI

My Static List - Badges

(HI)   ( )   ( )

Random Entry 1   Random Entry 2   Random Entry 3

Creating a Cards List

Back in the Page Designer, in the Rendering panel, find the Attributes node and change the List Template property to Cards. Click the Use Template Defaults button next to the Template Options property. The Cards template displays your list as cards where you control the size, style, and layout.

In the General section, we have Apply Theme Colors. This option will give your cards some colors that match your current theme. The color will be used in the card depending on the following options in the section.

In the Template Options modal are three options for Style: Compact, Basic, and Featured. These style options change the size of your cards from smallest (Compact) to largest (Featured).

■ **Icons**   Choose whether you want to display icons, initials, or just text (No Icon) in your cards. Remember that icons can be added via the List Entry details page, Image/Class attribute.

■ **Layout**   Similar to badges, where you can place the cards in columns or span them horizontally.

■ **Body Text**   Takes the User Defined Attributes from the List Entry details page and places the text in the card based on how many lines you choose for the attribute.

■ **Animation**   When hovering the mouse over the card, have it fill with color or raise up slightly.

Here is a sample of a static list using the Cards template:

Creating List Tabs

Tabs in APEX have had a rough ride. With APEX 5, we move from legacy tabs to list tabs. Before version 5, if you wanted to move to list tabs, you had to code and set it up yourself. APEX 5 and the Universal Theme provide a Tab template for lists. Let's create a list tab:

1. In Page Designer, click the Attributes node under the My Static Lists Region in the Rendering panel on the left.

2. In the Attributes tab, change the List Template to Tabs.

3. Click the Use Template Defaults button to open the Template Options modal and several options:

   ■ **Size**   Set the value to Small, Default, or Large, and the text size will change based on your selection, with the tab size changing as well.

   ■ **Style**   The Default style displays tabs as text links. The Simple style provides a background color change as you mouse over the tab. The Pill style encapsulates your tabs into a tab bar and provides a hover-over background color change effect as well.

- **Icon**   Choose no Icons, icons that sit above the text (Above Label), and icons that align with the tab text (Inline With Label). (Note that if you choose the Pill style, icons will always be displayed above the label and not inline, even if you select this option here.)

- **Layout**   The Default value keeps tabs together based on label length. The Fill Labels value spans the tabs horizontally to fill all available space in a row.

The following illustration shows an example of tabs in the Pill style, with icons set to Above Label and Layout set to Fill Labels.

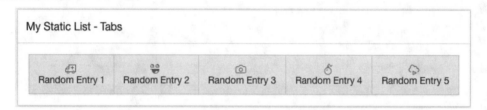

Creating Media Lists

Media lists are common design patterns for lists. A media list aligns list entries in a (usually) vertically stacked fashion and can contain an icon, badge, heading, and description.

1. In the Page Designer, in the List Attributes tab, change the List Template to Media List.

2. Click the User Template Defaults button to bring up the Template Options modal. You can see several of the major options as checkboxes in the General section:

   - **Show Icons, Show Description, and Show Badges**   Checking these options will include them in your media list only if you first uncheck the User Template Defaults checkbox.

   - **Apply Theme Colors**   Choose this checkbox to color your badges in colors similar to those used in your current theme.

   - **Size**   Control the size of the icon: Default or Large.

   - **Layout**   Stack your entries in multiple columns or horizontally.

Media lists work very well as user task lists and are used throughout APEX. A static list in the Media List template is shown next:

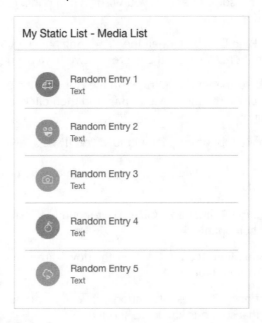

Creating a Menu Bar

Menu bars are useful for navigation as well as for providing advanced interaction with your applications. Placing a list in a menu bar requires that you create a parent-child relationship among list items. Let's alter the static list we used in the previous examples to create nested options for this parent-child relationship.

1. First, let's edit our list. From the Page Designer, you have a few options to edit the list: You can click the Shared Components icon in the upper tool bar. You can also edit your list from the Shared Components panel on the left side of the Page Designer. Or, from the Rendering panel, click the Shared Components tab to bring up the Shared Components panel.

2. Expand the List node and find your List. Right-click the list and select Edit.

3. On the List details page, click the Create Entry button in the upper right.

4. For the Parent List Entry attribute, select a parent value.

5. Enter a name for the List Entry Label attribute.

6. In the Target Section, set the Target Type to No Target.

7. Click the Create List Entry button in the upper right.

8. Create as many sublist items as you wish. When done, click the Edit Page icon at the upper right.

9. Back in the Page Designer, open the Rendering panel if it's not already open. Click the Attributes node for the list region we have been working with.

10. In the Attributes panel on the right, in the Appearance property group, change the List Template to Menu Bar, and then click the Use Template Defaults button.

11. In the Template Options modal window, you'll see a few checkbox options:

   - **Behave Like Tab**   Highlights the current menu item you are on, similar to an active tab

   - **Enable Slide Animation**   Gives your menu lists a smooth dropdown effect when opening

   - **Show Sub Menu Icons**   Controls the down-arrow icon shown after the menu bar item label

   - **Add Actions**   Enables integration between menu items and the actions facility that supports keyboard shortcuts

   Select Enable Slide Animation, and then save and run the page.

12. You will see a tabular menu with submenu options where you created child list items. Click the down arrow in the menu item, and the subitems will appear with a smooth dropdown effect.

NOTE
*To see the full content of the menu list, you may need to go into the Template Options of the region and set Body Height to 640px, or set the CSS Classes attribute in the Appearance property group to **i-h240**.*

TIP
There is a shortcut to reach the Shared Components panel for your list. Look at the List properties in the Source property group of the List Properties tab. You'll see a button with a right-facing arrow (Go To List). Click that button to bring you to the desired place in the Shared Components tree.

You can also create list items that are children of children. You can do this in the List details page (back in step 1): For the Parent List Entry attribute, select a child as the parent. This will create a menu list item similar to this:

Creating Show Sub Menu Icons and Using Add Actions

Show Sub Menu Icons and Add Actions are powerful and complex components. The following section will take a close technical look at these two template options and how best to use them.

Show Sub Menu Icons   In a traditional desktop menu bar, when you click a list item, a select list drops down. APEX menus, however, provide four possibilities after clicking:

- ■ **Case 1**   If the list item has no target and does have subitems, then clicking anywhere on the item will drop down the menu.

- ■ **Case 2**   If the list item has a target and subitems, then clicking the label will redirect to the target, but clicking the down arrow will drop down the menu.

- ■ **Case 3**   If the list item has a target but no subitems, then clicking it anywhere will redirect to the target, and there is no dropdown menu.

- ■ **Case 4**   Here there are no target and no subitems—you should avoid this.

Split menus always show a down arrow. The Show Sub Menu Icons checkbox controls what happens in case 1. If the Show Sub Menu Icons checkbox is checked, then normal case 1 menus will always have a down-arrow icon. If it is not checked, normal menus will not have a down-arrow icon unless the menu bar includes one or more action items (case 3 or 4). The Show Sub Menu Icons checkbox should always be unchecked unless all your menus are the normal case and you want them to have a down-arrow icon.

Add Actions   This option enables integration between menu items and the actions facility that supports keyboard shortcuts. You may have noticed the keyboard shortcut capability in the Page Designer, such as the shortcut ALT-F11. Press this combination and notice how the Expand/Restore icon button and Grid Layout menu item are all kept in sync. That is the power of actions.

Using this option requires that you do a little extra work.

NOTE
If you are using APEX 5.1 or higher, you can skip this following step that manually adds a JavaScript library to the page.

You must include actions.js on any page that has a menu with this option checked. Add #IMAGE_PREFIX#libraries/apex/#MIN_DIRECTORY#actions#MIN#.js to the page, app, or possibly theme as appropriate.

To use this on the page we are working on, look at the Property panel. Click the highest level node in the Rendering panel, usually called Page X: PAGE_NAME where X is the page number we are on and PAGE_NAME is the name of the current page. In the Page Properties tab on the right, find the JavaScript Properties group and add

   #IMAGE_PREFIX#libraries/apex/#MIN_DIRECTORY#actions#MIN#.js

to the File URLs property.

We also need to make sure that the Add Actions template option is checked regardless of whether we're using APEX version 5.0 or 5.1. To do this, in the Rendering panel in the Page Designer, click the Attributes node under your list region. Click the Use Template Defaults button next to the Template Options property. Then ensure that the Add Actions checkbox is checked. Once checked and the modal closed, save the page.

These steps give you the ability to add keyboard shortcuts to menu items. Let's add some actions now. We need to add a few pieces of code to the static list we previously created.

1. Start by editing the static list using any of the methods described in this chapter (Shared Components or Shared Components tab).

2. Next, on the List details page, edit any sub or child entry; in this sample list, we called it Sub Random Entry 1. Your sub entry or child list may be named something different.

3. To use these actions, you need to set three attributes. In the Target section, set the Target Type to URL; the URL Target is where you'll input your JavaScript code. Enter

   javascript:alert('Hi there');

   in the URL Target section.

4. In the User Defined Attributes section (scroll to the bottom of the page), for 1 (A01), enter an alphanumeric identifier for the action such as "actionHiThere".

5. And for 5 (A05), add a shortcut key combination. For this sample, use
ALT+SHIFT+M.

6. Once done, click Apply Changes in the upper right of the page.

Now run the page again, and if all goes well, when you drop down the menu
you will see the shortcut key listed in the menu item as in the following image; also
pressing that key combination on the page will invoke that menu item action
(assuming that the key isn't used by the browser or OS).

Attaching Actions to Buttons

Once you have added actions.js on your page, you can also attach actions to
buttons. Define your actions in the menu list, giving them an ID in the User
Defined Attributes section, 1 (A01); a shortcut key in 5 (A05); and optionally
a title in 4 (A04). Then define an action button by creating a normal APEX
button and giving it CSS class **js-actionButton** and Custom Attribute **data-
action="actionHiThere"** where the value of the attribute is the action ID
value in A01. Set the button behavior to Defined By Dynamic Action, just so
it doesn't submit the page. Now the menu item, the button, and the keyboard
keypresses all do the same thing. This is just the beginning of what you can
do with actions. More advanced stuff would require a little more JavaScript.

Creating Links List

Links lists can be used for a variety of purposes. You can use them for task actions
linking to pages within your APEX application, use them to list external pages, and
even nest sublists. Let's create a links list, starting with changing the List template in
the Page Designer.

1. Edit your Lists page and click the Attributes node under your list region in
the Rendering panel on the left side of the page.

2. On the right side of the Page Designer, in the Attributes tab, find List
Template and change its value to Links List.

3. Click the User Template Defaults button to bring up the Template options. Let's start with the General section:

■ **Show Badges** Shows any badges you have entered as User Attributes on your List details page. The Badge will appear to the right of the list.

■ **Show Right Arrow** Places an arrow to the right of your list.

■ **Disable Text Wrapping** Truncates link text so it does not wrap down to a second line.

■ **Style** This option has two values. The Default option renders the links list as text with horizontal lines separating items. The link color is blue in the default Universal Template. The Actions style renders the list in black text with no horizontal lines separating the items, giving it a more task-based look and feel rather than a list of links.

■ **Display Icons** You have three choices: No Icons omits any icons from your links list. For All Items will show icons not only for top-level items, but for your sublevel items as well. For Top Level Items Only will omit the icons on sublists and show them on your top-level list items only.

Figure 8-17 shows an example of a links list.

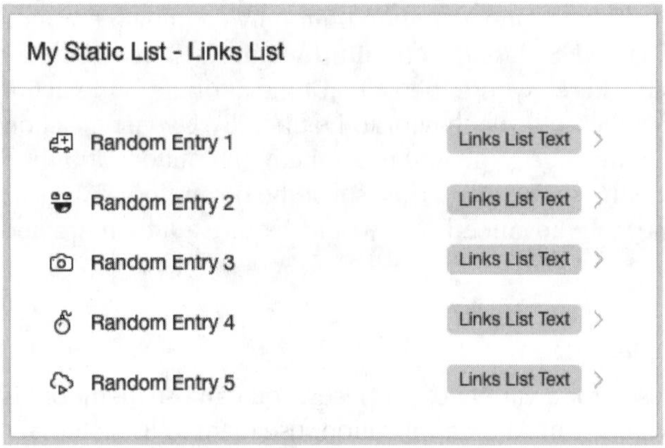

FIGURE 8-17. *Links list example*

Reports

Next up are template options for reports. To learn about these options, it's easiest to create a new page with a report on it, so you can experiment. Let's get started:

1. In the Page Designer, click the Create dropdown menu and select Page.

2. In the Create Page wizard, select Report, and then Classic Report.

3. In the first step of the Create Classic Report wizard, enter the name of the page: **My Report**. Leave the rest of the default settings and click Next.

4. For the Navigation Menu, select Create A New Navigation Menu and then click Next.

5. In the Report Source step, make sure that for Source Type, the Table radio button is selected.

6. For Table / View Owner, use the Schema you created when creating the workspace.

7. Choose the PERSONS_TABLE for the Table / View Name and use all the columns except PERSON_PICTURE. Once your page looks similar to the following, click Create.

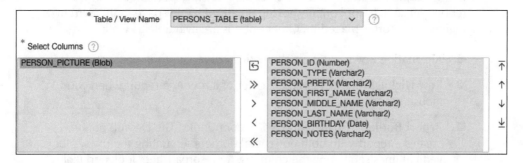

8. In the Page Designer, in the Rendering panel, find the Report 1 region and click the Attributes node (Figure 8-18).

9. On the right side in the Attributes tab, in the Appearance property group, you'll see that Template Type is set to Theme. You have two options here: Theme and Predefined. Theme lets you choose templates that are within the current theme you are using—in this case, the Universal Theme. Predefined templates are templates you can use regardless of theme. There are four predefined templates—two visual (HTML and a Vertical display) and two that allow you to download the report in XML or CSV formats. Let's work with the Theme template type.

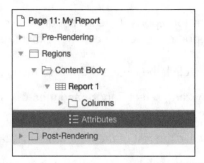

FIGURE 8-18. *The Attributes node under My Report*

Create the Table Report

Now let's work with the report template and template options.

1. If not already selected, for the Template property, choose Standard.

2. For the Template Options property, click the Use Template Defaults button.

3. In the Template Options modal, select the Stretch Report checkbox; your report will stretch horizontally, taking up all available space in the current region the report is placed in. Other options are available as well:

   ■ **Alternating Rows**   Use an alternating color pattern in your report.

   ■ **Row Highlighting**   Change the color of a row in a report when you mouse/hover over it.

   ■ **Report Border**   Change how your report looks. The Default option creates a report with both horizontal borders separating the rows, plus vertical lines separating the columns, for a spreadsheet look and feel. Horizontal Only removes any vertical lines and separates the rows with a black border, as shown in Figure 8-19 in the top image. In the middle image of the figure, the Report Border attribute is set to Vertical Only, which removes the borders separating the rows horizontally and replaces them with vertical lines separating the columns. The bottom option shows No Borders, which removes horizontal and vertical borders from the report. The last option, No Outer Borders (not shown), removes the borders around the outside of the report.

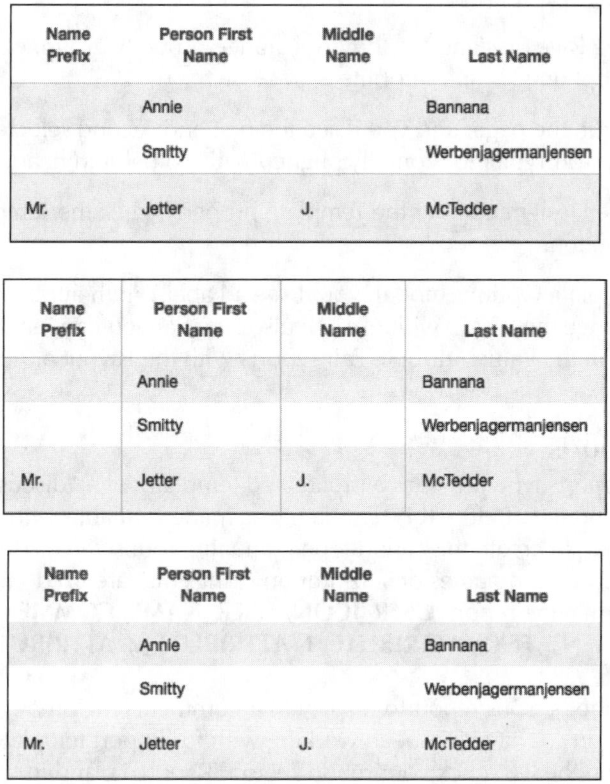

Name Prefix	Person First Name	Middle Name	Last Name
	Annie		Bannana
	Smitty		Werbenjagermanjensen
Mr.	Jetter	J.	McTedder

Name Prefix	Person First Name	Middle Name	Last Name
	Annie		Bannana
	Smitty		Werbenjagermanjensen
Mr.	Jetter	J.	McTedder

Name Prefix	Person First Name	Middle Name	Last Name
	Annie		Bannana
	Smitty		Werbenjagermanjensen
Mr.	Jetter	J.	McTedder

FIGURE 8-19.   *Different border layouts of a report template*

Value Attribute Pair Template

The Value Attribute Pair template includes two options: Row and Column. Let's start with Column:

1. In the Page Designer, click the Attributes node under your Report 1 region.

2. On the right in the Attributes tab, in the Appearance property group, for Template, select Value Attribute Pair – Column.

3. Save and run your page.

You'll see that your report is shifted, with the columns on the left side and the data on the right. Each row is represented as a block of columns and data. These reports are very useful when you need to see the column and row data paired up.

Now let's change to Value Attribute Pair – Row:

1. Back in the Page Designer, in the Appearance property group, change the Template option to Value Attribute Pair – Row.

2. Save and run the page, and you'll see the first and second selected columns (ID and Person Type) horizontally aligned with no column headers.

3. In the Page Designer, under the Template property, click the Template Options button.

4. In the Template Options modal, you'll see a Label Width attribute you can use to change the label's width. You'll also see that you can left or right align your data in the Value Attribute Pair reports with the Layout attribute.

Comments Reports

The Comments Reports type provides a precreated template for a "discussion and comments" look and feel. Before this template was made available with APEX 5, you would have had to create this report type manually from scratch. This template has a few required column names or substitution strings that are used to display the data as well as format the report: **USER_ICON**, **USER_NAME**, **COMMENT_DATE**, **ACTIONS**, **COMMENT_TEXT**, **ATTRIBUTE_1**, **ATTRIBUTE_2**, **ATTRIBUTE_3**, and **ATTRIBUTE_4**.

You can alter the persons report to display in a comments region by replacing the SQL in the report we have just been working with for Report templates. In the Rendering panel on the left, click your report region (Report 1), and in the Region tab, for SQL Query, add the following SQL:

```
Select
    person_first_name ||' '|| person_last_name user_name,
    upper(substr(person_first_name,0,1))||
    upper(substr(person_last_name,0,1)) user_icon,
    person_notes comment_text,
    person_birthday comment_date,
    ' '|| person_type attribute_1,
    ' ' attribute_2,
    ' ' attribute_3,
    ' ' attribute_4,
    ' ' actions
from persons_table
```

Once the SQL is replaced (the SQL here is renaming the table columns to be template column names), you need to change the Report Type to comments.

1. Back in the Rendering panel on the left, in your report region (Report 1) and below the columns is the Attributes node. Click the Attributes node.

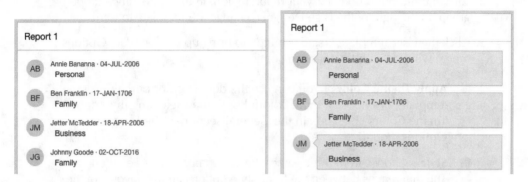

FIGURE 8-20.   *The Comments Report templates: the Basic style (left) and the Speech Bubbles style (right)*

2. Look on the right in the Attributes tab for the Appearance property group and the Template property. For this property, select Comments.

3. Click the Use Template Defaults button to bring up the Template Options modal window, which includes options for Comments and Comments Style. You can choose from the Basic style or Speech Bubbles style. The Basic style looks similar to a report, with the user icon on the left, and the Speech Bubbles style adds a text message–like bubble border around the comment. Both styles are shown in Figure 8-20.

4. Save and run the page to see the Comments Report template.

Cards Report

The Cards report is very useful for showing information in panels that have a title, icon or initials badge, and a few lines of text. To use the Cards Report template, you need to change the SQL query a bit so that the Cards Report template knows what rows to use and where to display them. You need to use a few substitution strings for your cards: **CARD_TITLE**, **CARD_INITIALS**, **CARD_TEXT**, and **CARD_SUBTEXT**.

1. In the Rendering panel, click your report region. On the right in the Region Attributes tab, find SQL Query and replace the SQL query with the following:

```
Select
    person_first_name ||' '|| person_last_name card_title,
    person_type card_text,
    upper(substr(person_first_name,0,1))||
    upper(substr(person_last_name,0,1)) card_initials,
    person_notes card_subtext
 from persons_table
```

2. Click the Attributes node for your report region. In the Appearance property group on the right of the Page Designer, change the Template to Cards.

3. Click the User Template Defaults button to bring up the Template Options modal window with the following options:

- **Apply Theme Colors**   You can use the default color of the Cards template, or choose a more colorful option by selecting the Apply Theme Colors checkbox in the General section in the Template Options modal.

- **Style**   Choose from three values: Basic, Compact, and Featured. The differences between the three style options are the layouts of the elements. The Basic style shows the card title on top with the initial badge/image to the right. The card text and subtext elements are below in the body of the card. The Compact style is similar to Basic, but the text size and initial badge/icon size are greatly reduced. The Featured style has the initial badge/icon on the top of the card, with the title under the initials badge/icon and the text and subtext elements separated below the card title with a horizontal border. Figure 8-21 shows examples of the three styles.

- **Icons**   Use these options to choose an initials badge, an icon, or neither. If you choose neither, the area is replaced with a colored horizontal line.

- **Layout**   Use these options to choose from a column layout, a float layout that has multiple rows that span the entire region based on text amount, or a layout that spans each card horizontally with an equal width.

FIGURE 8-21.   *The Cards Report styles*

Next, choose how your text and subtext elements behave with the Body Text attribute. You can determine how many lines of text are shown by choosing two lines, three lines, or four lines; let the region decide with the auto option; or hide the text and subtext elements altogether with Hidden.

The last option, Animation, shows two options when you hover over the card. The Raise Card option gives the illusion of the card lifting off the page slightly. The Color Fill option fills the card with color in a burst pattern, starting in the center and working to the edges.

Buttons

Buttons have come a long way in APEX. Just recently APEX started using HTML5 buttons, and APEX 5 has taken it a step further. Using Template Options and buttons, you can craft buttons more in line with their intended use. Let's add a few buttons to the page we used for the report template:

1. In the Page Designer, Rendering panel, right-click the Report 1 region and choose Create Button. A button will be displayed in the main Canvas in the region and in the Rendering panel.

2. Click the button to select it and look on the left side at the Button Properties tab. In the Appearance property group, find the Button Template property.

Text Buttons

Let's create a text button with the Text Button template.

1. Just below the Button Template property is the Hot property, which lets you choose whether the button needs to draw more attention than a regular button. Set this attribute to Yes to change the color of the button to a blue solid color, as shown next. Blue is the default theme style; other theme styles may use different colors.

2. Back in the Page Designer, in the Button property panel on the right, click Use Template Defaults to bring up the Template Options modal for Text Buttons with several attributes:

   ■ **Size** Choose sizes of Tiny, Small, Default, or Large, as shown.

■ **Type**   Change the button's use on a page. In reality you are just changing the button's color, but the colors accent the corresponding type. Choose Normal, Danger, Primary, Success, or Warning.

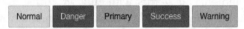

■ **Style**   Change how the button looks with either the default look, which is a color-filled button, or the Simple style, which is a white button with the corresponding type's border color. The last style is Remove UI Decoration, which renders the button as text only.

The Advanced template options deal mainly with button positioning and spacing.

Text and Icon Buttons

The Text + Icon Button template is similar in template options to the Text button, but you can use the Icon CSS Classes property to add an image within your button.

1. Change the Button Template to Text With Icon.

2. Click the Use Template Defaults button in Template Options.

3. You'll see a new attribute called Icon Position. Use this attribute to set the icon's position either to the left or right of the button text, as shown next:

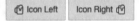

4. To set which icon to use for the button, use the pop-up LOV for the Icon CSS Classes property below the Template Options attribute in the Appearance property group.

Icon Buttons

The Icon Button template forgoes the button text for an icon only. The Template Options are the same as those for the Text Button template. Again, set the Icon you want to use with the pop-up LOV for the Icon CSS Classes property.

Forms

For ages, we have struggled with form layout in web applications—getting the labels or multiple-column forms aligned, and the list of troubles goes on and on. Lucky for us, the Universal Theme lends a helping hand with a few template options to help ease form alignment woes.

Let's create a new form in our application:

1. In the Page Designer, click the Create dropdown menu and select Page.

2. In the Create A Page modal, choose Form, and then Form On A Table.

3. On the Page Attributes step of the Create Form On Table wizard, enter the Page Name **My Form**.

4. Look at the Page Number. Select this Page Number for the Branch Here On Submit and the Cancel And Go To Page fields. Once done, the modal should look like Figure 8-22. Click Next.

5. For Navigation Menu, choose the Create A New Navigation Menu Entry radio button, and then click Next.

6. For the Source Step, Table / View Owner should default to your current schema.

7. Choose PERSONS_TABLE for the Table / View Name.

8. Keep all the columns selected in the Select Columns shuttle and click Next.

9. For Primary Key Type, select the Select Primary Key Column(s) radio button. The selection should default to PERSON_ID; if it doesn't, choose PERSON_ID.

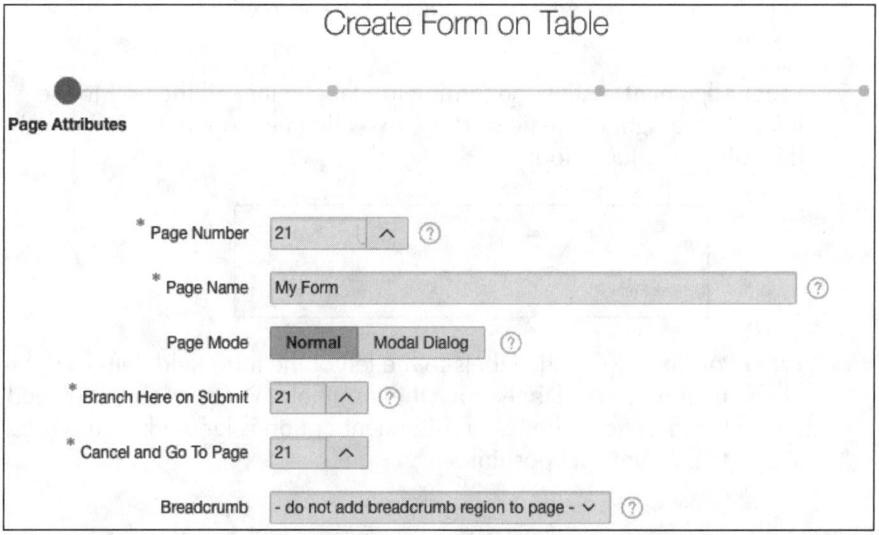

FIGURE 8-22. *Page Attributes when creating a Form Page*

10. We will use an existing trigger on the table, so leave the default values and click Create.

11. Run the page and you can see it's the standard form, with all the items in a vertical layout. Now let's go back to the Page Designer to apply some Template Options.

Form Modifiers

Let's start with form modifiers:

1. In the Rendering panel, click the My Form node.

2. On the right side in the Region Properties tab, find the Appearance property group. Start off by looking at the Template Options property. Click the Use Template Defaults button to open the Template Options modal.

3. In the Advanced section are several options (you may need to scroll the modal down to see all). Let's discuss a few:

   - **Item Size**   Change the size of the form fields and labels by choosing Default, Large, or Extra Large.

   - **Item Width**   Keep the width of the item to the set value in the Width attribute of the Item itself by selecting the Default option, or span all items across the region to use all available space with the Stretch Form Fields value.

   - **Label Alignment**   Align the form field's label either all the way to the left or to the right of the field. These two alignment options are shown in the following illustration:

   - **Label Position**   Keep the labels to the left of the form field (left- or right-aligned), or place the label above the form field. When a label is placed above the form field, the Label Alignment option is ignored. Figure 8-23 shows the above label position.

Multicolumn Layout

Tidy forms do not always span vertically down a page. Similar form fields are usually next to each other in a horizontal manner. A good example of this is our

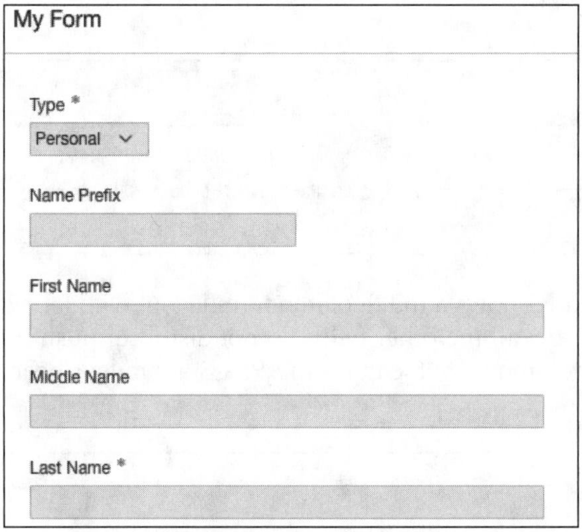

My Form

Type *

Personal ⌄

Name Prefix

First Name

Middle Name

Last Name *

FIGURE 8-23. *The above label position*

name fields. Placing the first, middle, and last name form fields on the same horizontal row helps with data entry and continuity. APEX 5 provides new methods to help with multicolumn layouts with the Universal Theme.

Creating multicolumn form layouts is easy:

1. In the Page Designer, Rendering panel, find your form (My Form) and then the items within that form just below the region in the Items node.

2. Find and click PERSON_MIDDLE_NAME and then shift-click PERSON_ LAST_NAME, and in the Page Item Properties tab on the right, find the Layout property group.

3. For the Start New Row property, click No. As you click No, you'll see in the Canvas that both items horizontally align with Person First Name.

4. Save and run your page. Existing items still line up vertically, and the new layout for the name fields has not altered other form fields or labels in the form.

You can even use the Template Options form modifiers discussed previously with a new multicolumn layout. Go ahead and experiment with the form layout. You can also drag-and-drop form items in the main Canvas in the Page Designer. Just drag an item all the way to the right of an existing item, and then drop the item when you see a new column appear and the item's shadow in that column, as shown here:

The next illustration shows a multicolumn form layout with labels above the form fields. Notice how all the other fields do not distort or push into new columns. The multicolumn layout features in APEX 5 are miles ahead of previous version features.

Layout Columns Mode   If you need some help aligning fields or elements, click the Show Layout Columns button on the Developer toolbar to bring the page into Layout Columns mode (Figure 8-24) to see all the columns and layouts of your page sections. Mouse over the sections to highlight the exact space each grid element is using.

Calendars

Calendar regions underwent some much needed changes in APEX 5. You might even say they were completely overhauled, because the final product looks and acts nothing like Calendars in previous APEX versions—and that's a good thing. Let's start by creating a new Calendar region page.

1. In the Page Designer, click the Create dropdown menu and select Page.

2. In the Create A Page modal, click Calendar.

3. In the next modal page, choose Calendar to launch the Create Page wizard.

4. Set the Page Name to My Calendar and then click Next.

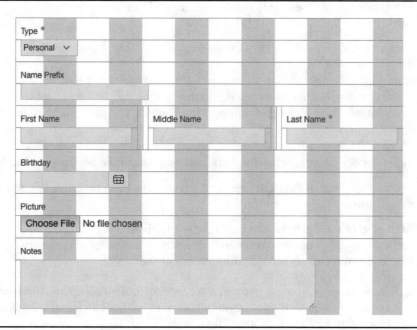

FIGURE 8-24.   *A form in Layout Columns mode*

5. On the Navigation Menu step, in the Navigation Preference section, select the Create A New Navigation Menu Entry radio button and click Next.

6. On the Source step, click the SQL Query radio button for Source Type.

7. Enter the following SQL statement for the Enter Region Source area:

```
select person_id,
person_first_name ||' '|| person_last_name person_name,
trunc(person_birthday) person_birthday
from persons_table
```

This SQL statement concatenates the first and last name into a single name and also selects the person's birthday—nothing fancy at all. (PERSON_ID is selected for something special later in the chapter.)

8. After you've entered the code, click Next.

9. The next step of the Calendar wizard asks you to choose the Display Column—what to show on the calendar. You also have the Date columns. Users can indicate multi-day events here if you include Start and End columns in your table. For this calendar, for the Display Column choose PERSON_NAME, and for Start Date Column choose PERSON_BIRTHDAY.

10. The Show Time property will show the date and time of the event on the calendar. Set this to Yes and click Create.

11. Back in the Page Designer, run the page.

Scroll through the months with the arrow buttons at the upper-left of the calendar. You can also reduce the view down to week or day, or see a list view of upcoming events. Edit the page and return to the Page Designer for some more new Calendar options.

1. In the Rendering panel, click the Attributes node under the My Calendar node.

2. On the right side of the Page Designer, in the Calendar Properties tab, you can customize the calendar further.

3. At the top of the Calendar attributes are the Display, Start Date, End Date, and Primary Key columns. You can change them here after you change any SQL code. You can set other attributes here as well:

   ■ **Show Time**   Choose Yes to see a set of some other properties: The Time Format property lets you toggle between a 12-hour clock and a 24-hour clock. The First Hour property defines at what hour your calendar starts in the week and day views.

   ■ **Calendar Views And Navigation**   Use these properties to control what views the end user sees and can switch between. If the Show Time property is set to No, this property will be named Additional Calendar Views and provided the options of List and Navigation. Month view is always displayed.

   ■ **Drag And Drop**   See the next step for information on this property.

   ■ **Create Link**   Use this to take the user to an event page with more details or to edit the event.

   ■ **Google Calendar ID, REST Webservice (JSON)**   Use these properties to link to external calendars—a Google Calendar or a calendar feed from a REST Web service.

4. Scroll back up the Property tab and enable Drag And Drop. With this feature enabled, you can drag events onto the calendar at new dates—the database will be updated in the process. Start by setting the Primary Key Column property to PERSON_ID. Without this setting, the Drag and Drop property will not be visible.

5. For the Drag And Drop property, just below the Calendar Views And Navigation property, change the value from No to Yes.

6. For the Drag And Drop PL/SQL Code, enter the following:

```
Begin
    update persons_table
        set person_birthday = to_date(:APEX$NEW_START_DATE, 'YYYYMMDDHH24MISS')
    where person_id = :APEX$PK_VALUE;
end;
```

This PL/SQL code updates the PERSON_BIRTHDAY column with the new date onto which you dropped the event. It uses the PERSON_ID to find the correct row in the database to update. You see in the PL/SQL some calendar substitution variables items, such as **:APEX$NEW_START_DATE** and **:APEX$PK_VALUE**. These are used for setting new dates and referencing the primary key when creating the PL/SQL for drag-and-drop. You'll see that another variable, **:APEX$NEW_END_DATE**, is also available to use.

7. Save and run your page.

8. Find a person's birthday on the calendar and drag and drop it to a new date, as shown next. The date is now updated on the calendar as well as in the database.

Theme Roller

Previous to APEX 5 and the Universal Theme, the colors of your applications were usually based around the theme you chose upon application creation. If you knew CSS well, you could change the color of components, but you had to keep that CSS code in page templates, files on the web server, or in the component template itself. This worked fine, but if you needed to make a change to that CSS, you would have to find the base code and change it there—and if the CSS was in multiple places, it got very messy. APEX 5 introduced the Theme Roller, a declarative tool that lets the developer change the color of all aspects of the application with a single click.

To start using the Theme Roller, run any page. On the Developer toolbar at the bottom of the page, click Theme Roller to launch the tool.

The toolbar across the top of the page includes buttons that are very similar in function to those in the Page Designer, Properties tab.

- **Show Common and Show All**   Use these two buttons to change how many application components you see in the tool; this works similarly to properties in the Page Designer.

- **Undo**   Make a change and hate it? Click the Undo button.

- **Redo**   Change your mind about hating that change? Click the Redo button.

- **Search bar**   Enter an element whose style you want to change and filter the results in the body of the tool.

- **Reset**   Restore the theme back to its default state

- **Help**   Bring up help on the Theme Roller.

Below the toolbar is the Style region, where you can change to a previously saved style or use one that APEX provides. The four default options are Vista, Vita, Vita – Red, and Vita – Slate.

You can also change the colors of components at the individual level. Click the Show All button on the Theme Roller toolbar, and then scroll down the center of the Theme Roller to see multiple component groups in collapsed regions:

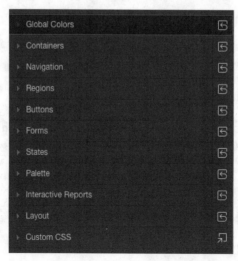

Expand the Buttons region. Here you can control the color of each of the button types. On the right of each button type, you'll see the following: a checkmark, a warning sign, or an X. Hover over these icons to see a Color Contrast Information report based on the Web Content Accessibility Guidelines (WCAG) 2.0, shown next, with a higher calculated contrast score indicating a color combination that is more accessible. This report is invaluable when you're working with applications that must conform to accessibility guidelines. This Web Content Accessibility will appear only for elements with two color boxes—thus the potential to have contrasting color.

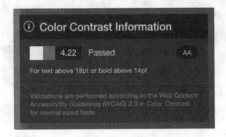

To the right of the contrast report are two color boxes. The first color box applies to the buttons text, and the second color box applies to the background color of the button. Click in a color box to open a color picker, shown next, where you can use a pointer to choose a color in the color region, enter HTML color code in the field at the bottom, or set the color via the RGB values along the right side. You can also move a slider to change the buttons border radius here.

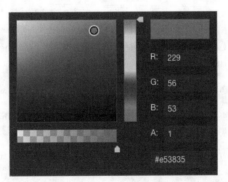

Other component groups may include one or two color boxes for other purposes. To see what a particular color box represents, hover your mouse over it. A tooltip will display which aspect of the component that particular box changes:

Need to revert a section back to its original color? Just to the right of a section is a reset button. Just as clicking the reset button on the Theme Roller toolbar resets the entire theme, clicking this button resets the particular section you are working in.

At the very bottom of the component areas is the Custom CSS section, where you can add custom CSS Classes to your theme to customize further every aspect of the UI:

Once you have chosen the color scheme you want for your application, save it. If you are altering an existing theme that is not read-only, you can also click the Save button on the bottom of the Theme Roller. If the theme is read-only, click the Save As button on the bottom, which will bring up the Save As dialog, where you can name and save your newly created theme. Once a Theme is saved, you can instantly apply it to your application with the Set As Current button on the lower left of the Theme Roller.

You can also set the theme as current in the Theme details page:

1. In the Shared Components page, click Themes, and then click the current theme in the theme report.

2. In the subtab navigation, click Styles.

3. In the Styles section of your current theme, click the name of the theme you just created.

4. Change the Current attribute to Yes and then click the Apply Changes button.

Note that there are a few other items on this page as well:

■ **Read Only**   This blocks all changes from being saved to this theme in the Theme Roller. You will still be able to use the Save As button to save the theme with a new name, but the Save button will not be present.

■ **Theme Roller JSON Configuration**   This section contains your theme in JSON notation. By copying and pasting this JSON notation, you can easily share themes via e-mail or in a blog post.

Live Template Options

Also new in APEX 5.1 is Live Template Options, which lets you change attributes of a template right from the running application. Here's how it works:

1. Run any page of your application.

2. On the Developer toolbar on the bottom of the page, click the Quick Edit option. You know from previous chapters that you can click an item to see its properties in the Page Designer, but now you can hover your mouse over a section and the Live Template Options icon, a little wrench, shows up in the upper-right corner of that section:

3. Click the Live Template Options icon to see a modal pop-up showing template options (Figure 8-25). You can change the particular item you selected. When you change an option and save, the template option is updated for that item and the change is immediately made in the UI. If the attribute is JavaScript–based, that change will be visible after a page refresh.

FIGURE 8-25. *The Live Template Options modal*

Summary

Crafting a powerful and good-looking UI previous to APEX 5 could be done, but it took someone who knew HTML and CSS to do the job. With APEX 5, this is no longer a requirement. As you have seen in this chapter, the Universal Theme makes altering templates, components, and regions on your page a snap. Template Options give end users the power to customize major pieces of the UI as well as the little things, to give application UIs a personal touch.

Have a corporate color scheme? Use the Theme Roller to change every aspect of your application to conform to the color scheme you want. Creating functional business apps that are ugly is a thing of the past: APEX 5 gives you the ability and power to create something beautiful.

CHAPTER
9

Dynamic Actions

When end users enter data into an online form or use their favorite web application (social or e-commerce), they expect certain events to happen. They expect that if they get a field wrong in a form or leave it blank, a message will pop up telling them so. They expect regions on a page to refresh automatically for them when their order is ready to pick up from the store. These client-side events help create a user experience that not only assists in guiding the user through forms, but also helps with the ease of use of our applications.

About Dynamic Actions

Dynamic Actions enable you to react to and create client-side events declaratively without needing to know JavaScript, page Document Object Models (DOMs), or Cascading Style Sheets (CSS). With that said, with a little knowledge of these technologies and how they fit into Dynamic Actions, you can go from novice to dangerous in no time at all.

Benefits of Dynamic Actions

Why use Dynamic Actions over hand-coding JavaScript in our pages? To start, when using Dynamic Actions, we are able to link browser events to pages, regions, and items that render on the page at runtime. We can reference these page items and events in our Dynamic Actions without having to traverse the web page's DOM or hand-write code that waits for a specific browser event. We also get the benefit of our Dynamic Actions living past upgrades of APEX. If the APEX development team decided to change how page items are named in version 6, for example, our Dynamic Actions would still continue to work, where hand-coded JavaScript would have to be rewritten to uptake any changes.

APEX puts these browser and JavaScript events into a human-readable context, making the terminology and naming more user friendly. For example, instead of a complex API name for showing and hiding a region, APEX names these events Show and Hide, putting the power of these events in the hands of everybody, no matter their skill level.

Getting Started

As previously mentioned, using Dynamic Actions does not require knowing JavaScript. You can create browser event–based actions on any APEX item without knowing or having to learn JavaScript. For example, with a Dynamic Action, you can show and hide page items based on a value a user entered.

We see these types of events every day in our web applications. When you enter a credit card number, for example, some web applications will auto-select the card type you are using after you enter the first four numbers of your card, and then highlight an icon of the type of card you are using. They can also expand the CVV/CVC field if you are using a card that uses four digits rather than three. Dynamic Actions can help enforce our business logic on the client side so that our users get instant feedback without the page having to contact the database server first.

We will create Dynamic Actions in this chapter to do exactly that: to help enforce some of our business logic we defined in Chapter 2. Just remember that an application must have the business logic enforced at the server level as well. Crafty or malicious users can bypass JavaScript client-side validations; the database must check for business logic on insert, update, and delete.

Bind Events

What types of events can we use with Dynamic Actions? APEX breaks them down into four categories:

■ **Browser**   Standard browser events such as Click and Scroll

■ **Framework**   Events triggered from within the Application Express framework such as closing an APEX dialog box or just before submitting a page for processing

■ **Component**   Custom events triggered from specific APEX application components or plug-in components containing custom events

■ **Custom**   Events triggered by your application, or components within your application, that were created by you

APEX further breaks down some of these events based on the user interface type being used (mobile or desktop). The next sections go over the events in detail so you can better grasp what browser and APEX framework events are available for you to use in your applications.

Browser Events

Choose from among these standard browser events:

■ **Change**   Fires when a value has been changed and focus is lost, such as choosing a value in a select list or filling out a text field and moving to the next.

■ **Click**   Fires when a user clicks a particular page element such as a button.

■ **Double Click**   Similar to the Click event but fires upon a double-click.

■ **Get Focus**   Fires when the element receives focus via a mouse click or tabbing into that particular element.

■ **Loose Focus**   Fires when a page element or component loses focus by the user clicking the mouse or tabbing out of the particular element.

■ **Key Down**   Fires when a key on the keyboard is depressed while the triggering element has focus.

■ **Key Press**   Fires when keyboard key is pressed—used in a textual element to capture the Key Press event.

■ **Key Release**   Similar to the Key Press event except the event fires upon key release.

■ **Mouse Button Press**   Fires when the user clicks a mouse button over the triggering element.

■ **Mouse Button Release**   Fires when the user releases a mouse button over the triggering element.

■ **Mouse Enter**   Fires when the mouse cursor enters the triggering component.

■ **Mouse Leave**   Fires when the mouse cursor leaves the triggering component.

■ **Mouse Move**   Fires when the mouse cursor moves within the triggering component.

■ **Page Load**   Fires when the page loads in the browser.

■ **Page Unload**   Fires when the user navigates away from the page, such as using the back/forward browser buttons, clicking a link, entering a new URL, or closing the browser.

■ **Resize**   Fires when the page is resized.

■ **Resource Load**   Fires when the browser finishes loading all content within a web page.

■ **Select**   Fires when a user selects some text in a text component in the page.

■ **Scroll**   Fires when a user scrolls the page. Good for loading content on demand as the user scrolls down a large vertical page. Component could be browser window, scrollable frames, or DOM elements with the CSS property **overflow** set to **scroll**.

APEX Framework Events

Choose from among these framework events:

- **Dialog Closed** Fires when a modal or dialog page is closed by the user; will not fire if the user cancels out of the modal dialog page.

- **After Refresh** Fires after the triggering page component has been refreshed. This event is valid only for page components that perform Partial Page Refresh and fire this event. The APEX components that support After Refresh are interactive reports, classic reports, charts, list view, and item types with cascading List of Values (LOV) support.

- **Before Page Submit** Fires before a page is submitted.

- **Before Refresh** Like the After Refresh event, fires before the triggering page component has been refreshed. This event is valid only for page components that perform Partial Page Refresh and fire this event. The APEX components that support Before Refresh are interactive reports, classic reports, charts, list view, and item types with cascading LOV support.

Component Events

Choose from among these component events:

- **Change Order [Shuttle]** Fires when you change the value of the right side of a shuttle using the following events: Move Top, Move Up, Move Down, or Move Bottom.

- **Date Selected [Calendar]** Fires when a user selects or clicks a date in the calendar.

- **Event Selected [Calendar]** Fires when a user clicks an event in the calendar.

- **View Changed [Calendar]** Fires when a user clicks the view change icon options such as month, day, week, and list.

- **Row Initialization [Interactive Grid]** Triggers or fires after the user clicks the Add Row button in an interactive editable grid.

- **Selection Change [Interactive Grid]** On interactive grids, triggers an event after one or multiple selections have been made—for example, having a chart or graph refresh after the selection of multiple rows in an interactive grid.

Custom Events

Select Custom and an additional field displays, enabling you to define a custom event. This is useful when the native or plug-in–provided events are insufficient.

Actions

Once you decide on when (which event) to fire your Dynamic Action, you have to decide what action to take. You can take the following actions once an event is fired.

Component Actions

Choose from among these component actions:

- **Clear**   Clears/empties the affected elements listed.

- **Collapse Tree**   Collapses the current node in an APEX tree region.

- **Expand Tree**   Expands the current node in an APEX tree region.

- **Disable**   Disables the affected elements listed. Disabling an element makes it read-only and not available for edit. Disabled elements also do not retain values when the page is submitted.

- **Enable**   Enables the affected element. Makes it available for edit in some cases.

- **Hide**   Hides the listed elements on the page.

- **Show**   Shows the listed elements on the page

- **Refresh**   Refreshes the listed elements. You can refresh content in interactive reports, classic reports, and all item types with cascading LOV support.

- **Set Focus**   Sets focus to the first listed affected element.

- **Set Value**   Sets the values of the listed affected elements.

Execute Actions

Choose from among these execute actions:

- **Execute JavaScript Code**   Enables the developer to define or call custom, page-specific JavaScript code to use within the Dynamic Action framework using the APEX JavaScript framework–specific attributes.

- **Execute PL/SQL Code**   Executes PL/SQL code on the database server.

Miscellaneous Actions

Choose a miscellaneous action:

- **Cancel Event**   Cancels out of the current event, stopping all following events in the Dynamic Action.

Navigation Actions

Choose from among these navigation actions:

- **Cancel Dialog**   Cancels a dialog page. Does not apply to inline dialogs.
- **Close Dialog**   Closes a dialog page. Does not apply to inline dialogs.
- **Submit Page**   Submits the page and enables the developer to set the request value.

Notification Actions

Choose from among these notification actions:

- **Alert**   Creates an alert dialog box with an OK button. Once a user clicks OK, the Dynamic Action continues to process any subsequent actions.
- **Confirm**   Creates a confirmation dialog box with OK and Cancel buttons. If the user clicks OK, the Dynamic Action continues to process any subsequent actions. If the user clicks Cancel, the current event is canceled.

Style Actions

Choose from among these style actions:

- **Add Class**   Adds CSS class(es) to the affected elements.
- **Remove Class**   Removes CSS class(es) from the affected elements.
- **Set Style**   Sets a style (CSS property) and the value of the style on one or more elements.

Anatomy of a Dynamic Action

Before we create a Dynamic Action, let's put all the parts in order and see how they relate to one another. We previously discussed events and actions. When creating a

Dynamic Action, we first start with an event and an element we want to place this event upon. Once we select that, we need to decide what action to take and what elements are affected by those actions taking place. Once we know the answers to these questions, we can start crafting our Dynamic Action. The next few sections will propose some situations in our Contacts in the Cloud application where a Dynamic Action could be used.

Creating a Dynamic Action

To start, let's create a simple Dynamic Action that will show or hide the Birthday field based on what type of contact we choose. If we choose a business contact type, we can hide the Birthday field. If we choose a family or personal contact, we will show the Birthday field.

Simple Show/Hide

1. In the **App Builder** for our Contacts in the Cloud application, navigate to the applications details page and find page 2. Click the page 2 icon (or if in list view, click Create/Edit Contacts) to launch the **Page Designer**.

2. On the left side, in the **Rendering Panel**, expand the **Items** node under the Create/Edit Contacts region node. Then right-click P2_PERSON_TYPE and select **Create Dynamic Action** to create a dynamic action upon that item:

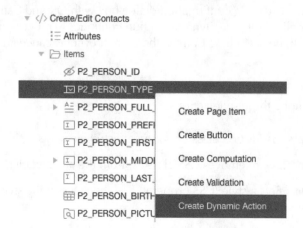

3. The new Dynamic Action is called NEW. Click the New Dynamic Action under P2_PERSON_TYPE if not already selected, and then look on the right of the Page Designer under the Dynamic Action property tab.

4. For the name of the Dynamic Action, enter **Show/Hide Birthday**. To do this, find the Name property under the Identification property group then click the Text field and enter the new text.

5. In the When property group, Event is the first property. You want to hide the field when the user changes the contact type, so set the Event to Change if it is not already set for you. The Selection Type and Item(s) properties should have defaulted to Items(s) and P2_PERSON_TYPE because you created this Dynamic Action on the item itself by right clicking and using the menu. (We will use this Selection Type property later in this chapter.)

6. In the **Client-Side Condition** property group, set the Type property to **Item = Value**. This will open up the Item and Value property fields under the Type property.

7. Keep the Item property set to P2_PERSON_TYPE and enter **Business** in the **Value** field. Here's what you have just done: if the contact Type is equal to Business, do something—which in this case is hide the Birthday field. If the contact Type is not equal to Business, do something else or don't do anything at all. Here's how the property group should look:

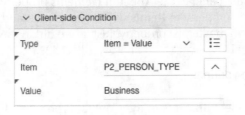

8. Back in the Rendering panel under the Dynamic Action you just created, expand the **True** folder node and then click **Show**. Look to the right side in the **Action** properties tab. For the Action property in the **Identification** property group, change the value to **Hide** using the select list.

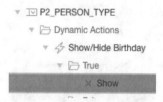

9. In the **Affected Elements** property group, you need to tell the Dynamic Action what elements, or in this case page items, to hide. Set the **Selection Type** property to **Item(s)** if not already selected, and then click the pop-up LOV in the **Item(s) Property**. In the pop-up LOV, select **P2_PERSON_BIRTHDAY**.

10. In the Rendering panel, right-click the **False** folder node under the Dynamic Action and select **Create FALSE Action**:

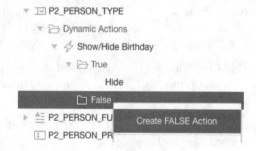

11. On the right of the Page Designer in the Action property panel, under Identification, set the **Action** property to **Show** if not already selected.

12. Scroll down the panel to the **Affected Elements** property group. Set the Selection Type property to **Item(s)** if not already set, and then click the pop-up LOV in the Item(s) property, just as we did in the True Action. In the pop-up LOV, select P2_PERSON_BIRTHDAY.

13. Save and run your page.

Now when you select Business in the Contact Type select list, you'll see that the Birthday field in the form disappears. When you select Family or Personal, it reappears. This simple hide/show dynamic action shows that you can quickly and easily create client-side business logic without knowing JavaScript.

Dynamic Actions Affecting Multiple Items

Dynamic Actions can also listen for an event that is tied to multiple items on a page. In the next Dynamic Action we build, we will have a client-side alert when a field is left blank. We can create one Dynamic Action for this and have it span across multiple items on our page. We are going to have a check on the First Name and Last Name fields to ensure that these fields are not empty.

Start by creating a Dynamic Action via the Dynamic Action panel, which contains all the Dynamic Actions on a page categorized by event type.

In the Page Designer, click the **Dynamic Actions** Panel (lightning bolt) on the left side, right next to the Rendering panel tab:

1. Right-click the Events folder and choose **Create Dynamic Action**. The newly created Dynamic Action is selected for you, so you can instantly use the Properties Panel on the right side. On the left side in the Dynamic Actions panel, each Dynamic Action on the page is categorized into the event associated with it. Because you have not defined the event for your new action, it is in the folder named **Not Specified**.

2. Now define your action. On the right side in the Property Panel, change the **Name** property in the **Identification** property group from New to **Highlight Null**.

3. In the **When** property group, change the **Event** to **Lose Focus**.

4. For the **Selection Type** property, because you want to set the event on your First and Last Name page items, set this property to **Item(s)**.

5. You need to add two page items here, and can do this either by entering a list of page items separated by a comma, or using the pop-up LOV to select the items. For the Item(s) property, enter (or select) **P2_PERSON_FIRST_NAME,P2_PERSON_LAST_NAME**.

6. In the **Client-side Condition** property group, set the Type property to JavaScript Expression.

7. In the JavaScript Expression text area, enter the following:

```
apex.da.testCondition( this.triggeringElement,'NULL')
```

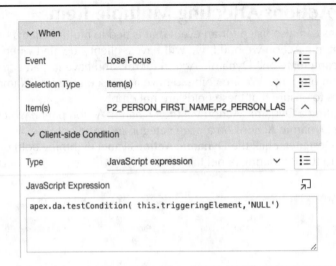

FIGURE 9-1. *Setting a Dynamic Action on multiple items in the Properties panel*

This simple line of code evaluates the triggering element, either First Name or Last Name, and determines whether the item is null. If it is null, the element fires or triggers the true action; if it's not null, the element fires or triggers the false action. Your When and Client-side Conditions property groups should look like Figure 9-1.

You have now set up an event that will fire when either the First Name or Last Name in a contacts form is null. Next you'll define what action to take when these conditions are met.

1. In the Dynamic Actions panel on the left, open the **True** folder under the Highlight Null dynamic action, and then click the **Show** node. This will change the Property Editor on the right to Action. In many modern forms in web applications, when leaving a required field null, that field will usually be highlighted in red, indicating an issue. You can add that same behavior here.

2. Under the **Identification** property group, change the Action property under the Identification property group to **Set Style**.

3. In the **Settings** property group, find the **Style Name** property and enter **border**. For the **Value** property, enter **1px solid red** as shown next:

∨ Settings	
Style Name	border
Value	1px solid red

4. In the **Affected Elements** property group, use the select list to set the value to **Triggering Element**. This value tells the Dynamic Action to watch for the null condition on the items you set in the previous section. The Triggering Elements, or in this case items, cascade down into the action without you having to set the values again here.

5. Scroll down to the **Execution Options** and set **Fire On Initialization** to **No**. Fire On Initialization enables us to have our actions fire as soon as a user loads a page. This is useful for setting up form or page elements before a user sees the final loaded page. If you leave this value set to Yes, the form will start with those two fields (First Name, Last Name) having red borders.

6. Now define a FALSE action—an action performed when the field is not null. On the left side, find the Dynamic Action we are working with, right-click the False folder node, and select **Create FALSE action**. This will change the Property panel on the right to Action and you can begin working with your FALSE action.

7. In the **Identification** property group, set the **Action** property to **Set Style**.

8. In the **Settings** property group, for the **Style Name**, enter **border**, as you did in step 3.

9. For the **Value** property, enter **1px solid #e0e0e0**.

10. In the next property group, **Affected Elements**, set the **Selection Type** to **Triggering Element**. This action will put the border of the text field back to its original color when it was previously in error from being null.

11. Save your work and run the page to try out the Dynamic Action.

Getting Away from Hard-Coding CSS

In step 9, you entered the value property **1px solid #e0e0e0** for ease of use and simplification. The concept is sound, but there is a potential issue going forward. If in the future the APEX development team decides to change the style of the universal theme input border (1px solid #e0e0e0), your border value will not match the other fields after the error is corrected. The more robust way is to define a style rule inline on the page: **.null-warning { border: 1px solid red; }**. Then use the add and remove class actions. Although this is a much more complex method and a bit beyond the scope of the book, continue

(continued)

reading to learn how to do this; otherwise, you can skip this sidebar. Still with us? OK, let's do this.

1. In the Page Designer, click the top level Page node at the top of the tree in the Rendering panel (on page 2, it's called Page 2: Create/Edit Contacts).

2. In the Property Editor on the right side, scroll down and find the CSS property group and the Inline property. Enter the following for Value:

   ```
   .null-warning { border: 1px solid red !important; }
   ```

3. Now you can edit your Dynamic Actions. With your True Action on the First Name and Last Name items, change the Action from Set Style to Add Class.

   In the Class property, enter **null-warning**.

4. In the False action, change the Action from Set Style to Remove Class.

   In the Class property, enter the following: **null-warning**.

5. Now Save and run the page. The Dynamic Action should perform just as it did before, but it has more longevity and survives Universal Template changes.

   You can also set this new property at the application level by adding this CSS in your theme details, so that you can use this across the application and not just on a single page.

Now in our running application, click the First Name field and then press the TAB key. The text field now has a red border, as shown next. Click the First Name field again, enter some text, and then press TAB; the border returns to normal.

First Name [   ]

Let's add one last TRUE action to this Dynamic Action:

1. The Rendering panel will probably not be selected and the Dynamic Actions panel will be showing. Click the Rendering panel tab in the upper right. Edit the page, and expand the **P2_PERSON_FIRST_NAME** in the **Page Items** in the Rendering panel on the left.

2. Expand the Dynamic Actions. Navigate to the **True** folder node, right-click the node, and select **Create TRUE Action**.

3. In the Property panel on the right, set the **Action** property in the Identification property group to **Alert**.

4. Set the **Text** property in the **Settings** property group to "Please Enter A Value".

5. In the **Execution Options** property group, make sure **Fire On Page Load** is set to **No**.

Now, to wrap this section up, we are going to prevent the user from submitting the page when those two page items are null.

1. On the left side in the Rendering panel, find the **Create** button in the Region Buttons folder node within the Create/Edit Contacts region (or find it in the page canvas). Click the button to bring up the **Button** property tab on the right side.

2. In the **Behavior** property group, change the **Action** property from **Submit Page** to **Defined By Dynamic Action**.

3. Back in the Rendering panel on the left side, right-click the Create button and select **Create Dynamic Action**.

4. On the right side of the Page Designer, in the Dynamic Actions properties tab, find the **Name** property in the **Identification** property group, and enter **"Dynamic Action Stop Submit"**.

5. In the **Client-side Condition** property group, set the **Type** property to **JavaScript Expression**. Now enter the following JavaScript code in that text area:

```
apex.item( "P2_PERSON_FIRST_NAME" ).isEmpty()
|| apex.item( "P2_PERSON_LAST_NAME" ).isEmpty()
```

This code uses some built-in JavaScript APIs provided by APEX. (Check the APEX documentation for a full list of JavaScript APIs.) As you can see from the code, you are using the **isEmpty** API to check whether those two page items are empty. APEX includes a complex set of JavaScript code in an easy-to-read function or API. The double pipe (||) is used in JavaScript as the OR operator. Putting this all together, the expression says: "If P2_PERSON_FIRST_NAME is empty or if P2_PERSON_LAST_NAME is empty, do something."

6. Now for that "something." Under your Dynamic Action in the Rendering panel, open the **True** folder. A Show action has been entered by default. Click the **Show** action and look at the Action property tab on the left side. Change the **Action** property in the **Identification** property group to **Alert**.

7. In the **Settings** property group, for the **Text** property, enter the following text:

```
Please Check Your Form Inputs.
```

8. Back on the left side, again find your Dynamic Action, right-click the False node, and choose **Create FALSE Action**.

9. Then, in the Action property tab on the left, change the **Action** property in the **Identification** property group to **Submit Page**.

10. In the **Settings** property group, set the property **Request / Button Name** to CREATE, in all capital letters.

Save and run your page. Now when you click the First Name field and TAB out, not only will you see a red border, but you'll get an alert message. In addition, when those fields are empty, regardless of the red border, you cannot submit the page by clicking the Create button. You will see the pop-up warning you just created:

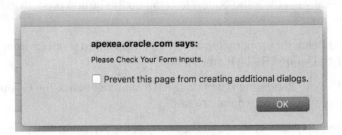

This section walked you through building up a Dynamic Action on various parts of a page, which is a new feature of Application Express 5.1 that can be accomplished with a single click. Look at any page item's properties, and in the **Validation** property group, you can see the **Value Required** property. In Application Express 5.1, this property is no longer just a server-side check, but it's a client-side one as well. Setting this property to **Yes** will make the item behave similarly to what we built. You now know both methods and understand how a Dynamic Action is built so that you can expand and create from this base.

Dynamic Actions Using PL/SQL

The next Dynamic Action we are going to create will perform an on-the-fly calculation. We'll calculate a person's age based on her birthday. Let's get started:

1. Edit page 2. In the Rendering panel, navigate to **Content Body**, and then right-click **Create/Edit Contacts** and select **Create Page Item**.

2. At the bottom of the page is a new item called P2_NEW. Drag-and-drop this item under P2_PERSON_BIRTHDAY, as shown next.

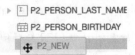

3. Now click P2_NEW to access the Property panel on the right.

4. In the **Identification** property group, change the **Name** property to **P2_PERSON_AGE** and the **Type** property to **Display Only**.

5. In the **Settings** property group, set **Save Session State** to **No**. This will ensure that you don't try and commit or save the value.

6. Scroll down the Property tab, for the **Source** property group, set the **Type** property to **Null**.

7. Now, on the left side in the Rendering panel, find and right-click the item P2_PERSON_BIRTHDAY and select **Create Dynamic Action**. A new Dynamic Action will be created (called NEW or NEW_X, with X being a number).

8. Click the newly created Dynamic Action and look at the Property panel on the right. In the **Identification** property group, change the **Name** property to **Calculate Age**.

9. In the **When** property group, ensure that the **Event** property is set to **Change**, and in the **Client-side Condition** property group, ensure that the **Type** is set to **Item Is Not Null**.

10. In the Rendering panel on the left, under your newly created Dynamic Action, expand the **True** folder if it is not already open.

11. Click the **Show** event and look at the **Action** property panel on the right. In the **Identification** property group, set the **Action** to **Execute PL/SQL Code**.

12. In the **Settings** property group, enter the following code for the **PL/SQL Code** property:

```
select trunc(months_between(sysdate, :P2_PERSON_BIRTHDAY)/12) || ' years old'
into :P2_PERSON_AGE from dual;
```

This code uses the **months_between** SQL function to calculate the date based on the item P2_PERSON_BIRTHDAY. This calculated value is then used to set the value of P2_PERSON_AGE page item.

Under the PL/SQL Code property are two properties, **Items To Submit** and **Items To Return**. The **Items To Submit** property takes the value of the item or items you entered in that field and submits them to the server, placing them into the APEX session state. When you select a birthday date in your form, that value is only in the HTML page. APEX or the database does not know about it until you either submit the page for processing or use the Items To Submit property of a Dynamic Action. Any items you place in this property can be used in your PL/SQL code.

The **Items To Return** property returns values that are set in APEX Session State and returns them to your page. In this example, the newly calculated value in item P2_PERSON_AGE is set only in the APEX session, and not on the page. Placing this item in the Items To Return property will ensure that the page item on the APEX page gets updated with this newly calculated value.

13. For the **Items To Submit** property, use the pop-up LOV to select P2_PERSON_BIRTHDAY or enter the text into the field.

14. For **Items To Return**, use the pop-up LOV to select P2_PERSON_AGE or enter that text into the field:

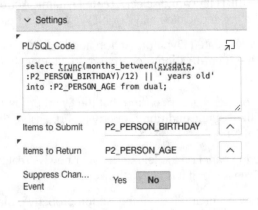

15. Scroll down in the Property Editor and in the **Execution Options** property group, set **Fire On Initialization** to Yes. This will have the Dynamic Action fire when you load the page, as well as fire when you look at an existing record calculating the age. Remember that this will fire on page load only if the P2_PERSON_BIRTHDAY item is not null.

16. You now need to add this page item to the show/hide event you created earlier in this chapter. It would look strange if we hid the birthday item and not the age item for business contacts. In the Page Designer, on the left side in the Rendering panel, expand the P2_PERSON_TYPE page item. This will expose the Dynamic Action you placed upon that item.

17. Expand the **True** folder node and click on **Hide**.

18. On the right side of the Page Designer, in the **Action** property editor, find the **Affected Elements** property group, and then the **Item(s)** property. Choose P2_PERSON_AGE from the pop-up LOV. Then click that item, and when returned to the Page Designer, the Item(s) property should read **P2_PERSON_BIRTHDAY,P2_PERSON_AGE**.

19. Now back on the left side, expand the **False** folder if isn't open and click the **Show** action node.

20. On the right in the **Action** property editor, as we did for the Hide action, find the **Item(s)** property under the **Affected Elements** property group. Choose P2_PERSON_AGE from the pop-up LOV to make the field look just like it does in the **Hide** action, with the following code: **P2_PERSON_ BIRTHDAY,P2_PERSON_AGE**.

Save and run your page. To see this Dynamic Action work, just click on the Date Picker in the Person Birthday Page item and select a date. Once that date is returned into the text field, you should see the **Person Age** item refresh with the calculated age, as shown next. You can test the hide and show action by changing the contact type.

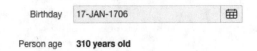

Advanced Dynamic Actions—Putting It All Together

Our next Dynamic Action will incorporate some UI, page, and report elements and is going to be a bit more advanced compared to the other Dynamic Actions we have created. It will give you an idea of how powerful and useful Dynamic Actions are. This section also incorporates some SQL code, but we will explain what that code is doing as we go.

We'll place a button on the Create/Edit Contacts page. When you click this button, a modal page opens, displaying a form. After you fill out this form and save it, the modal page will close and a new report on the Create/Edit Contacts page will refresh, showing the row you just entered.

Create the Modal Page

1. In the Page Designer, click the **Create** drop-down menu and select **Page**.

2. In the **Create A Page** modal, select **Form** by clicking it

3. Then, on the next step, select **Form On A Table**, again by clicking it.

4. On the first page of the **Create Form On Table** wizard, leave the **Page Number** at the default value, because APEX will auto-fill this with an available page number. For **Page Name**, enter **Enter Contact Information**. For **Page Mode**,

set the button to **Modal Dialog**. Once your page looks similar to the following (the page number may be different), click Next.

Create Form on Table

● ─────────────── ● ─────────────── ●

Page Attributes

* Page Number	17 ⌃ ⑦
* Page Name	Enter Contact Information ⑦
Page Mode	Normal **Modal Dialog** ⑦
Breadcrumb	- do not add breadcrumb region to page - ⌄ ⑦

5. For the Navigation Menu step, set the radio button to **Do Not Associate This Page With A Navigation Menu Entry** if it's not already selected. Then click **Next**.

6. For the **Source** step, select the schema you used when you created this workspace for Table / View Owner. For Table / View Name, select **CONTACTS_TABLE**.

7. For the **Select Columns** area, make sure all the columns are on the right side of the shuttle; if not, use the arrow button in the middle of the shuttle to move all the columns to the right. Then click Next.

8. Choosing a primary key is next. Click the radio button next to **Select Primary Key Column(s)** and make sure the Primary Key Column 1 select list is set to CONTACT_ID.

9. In the second step of the Primary Key section, select **Existing Trigger For Source Type** if it's not already selected and then click **Create**.

10. Back in the Page Designer for our modal form, in main canvas in the middle of the page is our Form region, and just below a Buttons region. A Modal or Dialog page type has a special display position called the **Dialog Footer**. This position contains your Button region and ensures that your dialog buttons are always affixed to the bottom of the dialog page.

11. On the main canvas, or in the Rendering panel on the left, click
PX_PERSON_ID (with *X* being the page number assigned to this page).

12. On the right, in the Property panel, change the **Type** in the **Identification**
property group to **Hidden**. Save the page.

NOTE
*If you try and run a model dialog page type, you
will get an error stating the following: "Changes
saved. Dialog pages cannot be run directly from
Page Designer. Review this page by running a page
that launches this dialog." In the following sections,
we are going to do exactly this create a button that
launches this dialog page.*

Create the Report
Next up is a new report on the bottom of our details page.

1. Change to page 2 in the Page Designer. (You can change pages at the top
center of the Page Designer.)

2. In the Rendering panel, right-click the Regions folder node and select
Create Region. This will add a new region to the bottom of your page,
called **New**.

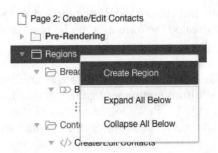

3. Find the New region and click it. In the right in the Region property tab,
in the **Identification** property group, change the **Title** property to **Contact
Information**.

4. Change the **Type** Property to **Classic Report**. Once this change is made, the **SQL Query** property in the **Source** property group will be in error. Click the pop-out editor button to use the code editor, or enter the following code in the text area:

```
select *
from contacts_table
where person_id = :P2_PERSON_ID
```

This code gets all the columns from your CONTACTS_TABLE, where the person_id matches the person_id you get from page 1. The person_id is passed to page 2 when you click an edit icon on your first page to edit a contact.

5. While still in the Region property editor, scroll down to the **Server-side Condition** property group and set the **Type** property to **Item Is NOT NULL**.

6. Set the **Item** property to P2_PERSON_ID, as shown next. This ensures that the report will not display if you are creating a new contact.

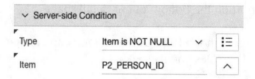

Create a Button

Now you have your form and your report, but you need a method of displaying the new form. Because you created the form as a modal page, you should display this modal with a button click.

1. From the Page Designer, in the middle Canvas grid layout, drag a **Text [Hot]** button from the **Buttons component gallery** on the bottom on the Grid Layout to right of the P2_PERSON_LAST_NAME item. You may have to drag it a bit farther right to see the drop location to the right of the item.

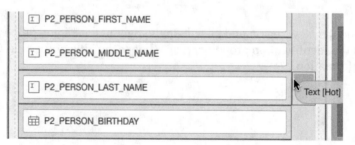

2. Click the **Text [Hot]** button, and in the Button property tab on the right, in the **Identification** property group, change the **Button Name** property to **ADD_CONTACT_INFO**.

3. Change the **Label** to Add Contact Info, if this is not already set for you.

4. Scroll down in the Property Editor to the **Behavior** property group. Change the **Action** property to **Redirect To Page In This Application**.

5. Click the **No Link Defined** button in the **Target** property.

6. In the **Link Builder – Target** modal dialog, the **Type** property should be set to **Page In This Application**.

7. In the Page property, click the List Of Values icon and find the Enter Contact Information page in the list and click on the page number:

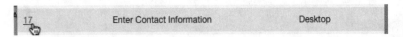

8. Back in the Link Builder, in the **Set Items** property group, click the list of values icon for the Name property and then choose the P*X*_PERSON_ID item from the list (*X* will be the page number that APEX assigned to the new page we created). So, for example, if your Enter Contact Information page was page 17, you would select P17_PERSON_ID.

9. Back in the Link Builder, click the list of values for the **Value Property** and choose **P2_PERSON_ID**.

10. When you return to the Link Builder, in the **Clear Session State** property group, set the **Clear Cache** property to the page number that APEX assigned to your Enter Contact Information modal page (the *X* in P*X*_PERSON_ID item). The Link Builder – Target model should look similar to Figure 9-2.

11. Click **OK** to return to the Page Designer.

12. Scroll down the Property Editor one last time and find the **Server-side Condition** property group. Set **Type** to **Item Is NOT NULL** and set the **Item** property to **P2_PERSON_ID**.

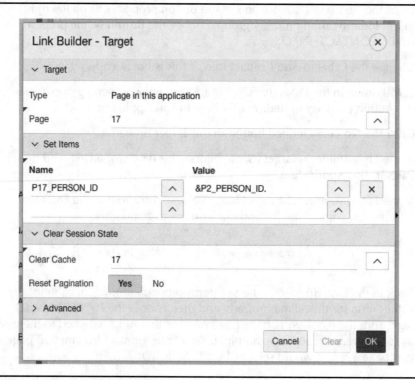

FIGURE 9-2. *The Finished Link Builder – Target Modal*

Create the Dynamic Action

1. In the Rendering panel on the left of the Page Designer, right-click the **Add Contact Info** button and select **Create Dynamic Action**:

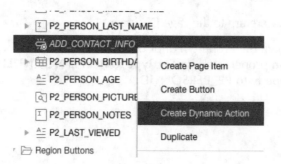

2. Click the New action if it's not already in focus

3. In the Dynamic Action property tab on the right, in the **Identification** property group, change the **Name** property to **Refresh Report**.

4. In the **When** property group, set the **Event** property to **Dialog Closed** if not already selected.

5. For the **Selection Type** property choose **Button**, and the **Button** property should be the button you just created and named ADD_CONTACT_INFO.

6. Back in the Rendering panel, click the action under the True node in your Dynamic Action. (You may have to open the Dynamic Action node to find the True node.)

7. In the Actions property editor on the right, change the **Action** property in the **Identification** property group to **Refresh** if not already set.

8. In the **Affected Elements** property group, change the **Selection Type** property to **Region**, and set the **Region** property to **Contact Information**. Save your page.

Test the New Form and Dynamic Action

Now let's test this new Dynamic Action and form:

1. On page 1 (run your application if not running), choose to edit any existing contact.

2. On page 2, click the new Add Contact Info button in the form to the right of the Person Last Name field. This should open your new form in a modal window.

3. For the Contact Type field, enter **Phone** and then enter a string of numbers in the Contact Number1 field (Figure 9-3).

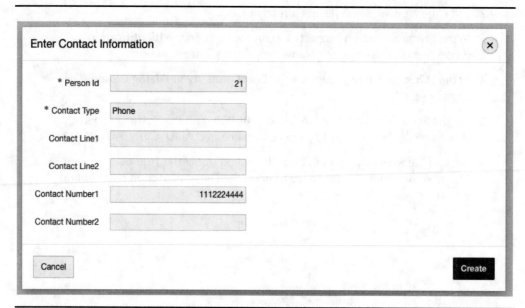

FIGURE 9-3. *Contact Information modal*

4. Now click the **Create** button, and you'll see the newly created row in the Contact Information report at the bottom of the page, shown next. The Dynamic Action was looking for the closing of your dialog window and refreshed that report for you, so you could see the newly created row without refreshing the entire page.

Contact Information

Contact id ↑≟	Person id	Contact type	Contact line1	Contact line2	Contact number1	Contact number2
1	21	Phone	-	-	1112224444	-

1 - 1

TIP
Want to take this a few steps farther? Start by putting a Dynamic Action on the Contact Information form that will show or hide fields based on the contact type (that is, create a static LOV for this page item). If a user chooses Email for the type, you can hide all the fields except Contact Line1. If Phone is chosen, hide all but Contact Number1. The possibilities are endless, but with the knowledge you've gained in this chapter, you should be well equipped to handle them.

Summary

Creating interactive user interfaces on your APEX components isn't difficult. In fact, it's quite easy with Dynamic Actions. With Dynamic Actions, control how forms guide the user, refresh reports to get the latest data, and even hide elements on the page that are not relevant to a particular user or data set. Remember, however, that you should not rely on Dynamic Actions for your business logic alone; instead, include this logic in two places: in the browser (via Dynamic Actions) and in the database (via PL/SQL).

CHAPTER
10

APEX Security

A fellow APEX developer and former APEX product manager (and my brother), Scott Spendolini, says in his security presentations, "Security is hard. If it's easy then you're doing it wrong." Implementing security always needs to walk that fine line of convenience and irritation. Application security needs to be crafted so that the user can use the application but security exists at all levels without getting in the user's way. Lucky for us, with APEX 5.1, setting up security is much easier than it was in the past.

When building application security, we all too often hear the phrase, "Well it has always been that way and nothing has happened," or "We can secure that part later; getting that cool button to work is more important." Security should never be an afterthought or something that happens to the other guys. It should be architected into the application from day one. As I was writing this chapter, I received yet another e-mail from a major retailer telling me my personal information was stolen. It's not a matter of *if* anymore; it's a matter of *when*.

This chapter will outline the security features of APEX. We will also cover how APEX helps to prevent or minimize some of the more dangerous web application attack methods. Access control, authentication, and authorization will be covered in depth as well.

Application Attack Points

Web applications have multiple attack points that hackers try to exploit. Lucky for us, APEX helps to prevent most of these attack vectors and gives us the ability through the database to prevent the others.

Following are the most common types of web application exploits:

- **Brute-force login attempts** In this type of attack, a malicious script will try multiple username/password combinations multiple times a second until it guesses the correct one. In a variation called a dictionary attack, the attacker uses a dictionary table of commonly used passwords as well as the dictionary itself to attempt to log in.

- **SQL injection** This attack attempts to take advantage of poorly constructed form elements, where the attacker can inject code such as **'** or **'1'='1**, which, when successful, will append that statement to a SQL query, resulting in a return of all available rows in the database table.

- **Cross-site scripting (XSS)** This attack takes advantage of unescaped text in pages. This could happen via a form input or a malicious URL. The attack is able to inject JavaScript code into the page that will run unbeknownst to the user. This code could steal authenticated cookies, watch users as they enter passwords, or hijack a browser session, all resulting in the theft of sensitive information.

■ **URL manipulation**   In this type of exploit, the attacker is able to change the URL to see information they might not be authorized to see. If a parameter such as **person_id=12** exists in the URL, the attacker can change that **person_id** number to see data belonging to people they should not be able to view.

■ **Unauthorized access**   Attackers like to test the limits of a web application's security, and searching for pages that are not part of the main application is a common abuse. Application developers might have left an administration page open to the public, or perhaps a metadata report or entry form is open. If unsecured, these pages can be found and exploited.

Instance-Level Security

Instance-level security is found in the internal or administrator application of APEX. You can get there via the internal Workspace or the /apex/apex_admin URL. If you are using a hosted version of APEX, chances are you don't have access these pages (that is, an account on apex.oracle.com). This section will go over the security options you can set at an instance level—for educational purposes (if you don't have access) or for practice.

Log into the internal Workspace/APEX admin application. On the right side under Instance Tasks, click Security. (Or, after clicking the Manage Instance icon [Figure 10-1] on the first page, click Security in the Instance Settings section on the following page.)

Manage Instance

FIGURE 10-1.   *The Manage Instance icon on the Instance Administration page*

Security Section

Security sessions are divided into multiple sections. The first section is Security (Figure 10-2).

- **Set Workspace Cookie** Sets a cookie in your browser that helps to prepopulate the sign-in page with the last Workspace you logged into as well as the user.

- **Disable Administrator Login** Prevents users from logging into the administrator application. This is a very useful option for production APEX environments.

- **Disable Workspace Login** Prevents users from getting to the App Builder. Again, in production environments, this will help with change management and for developers who like to test their code in production.

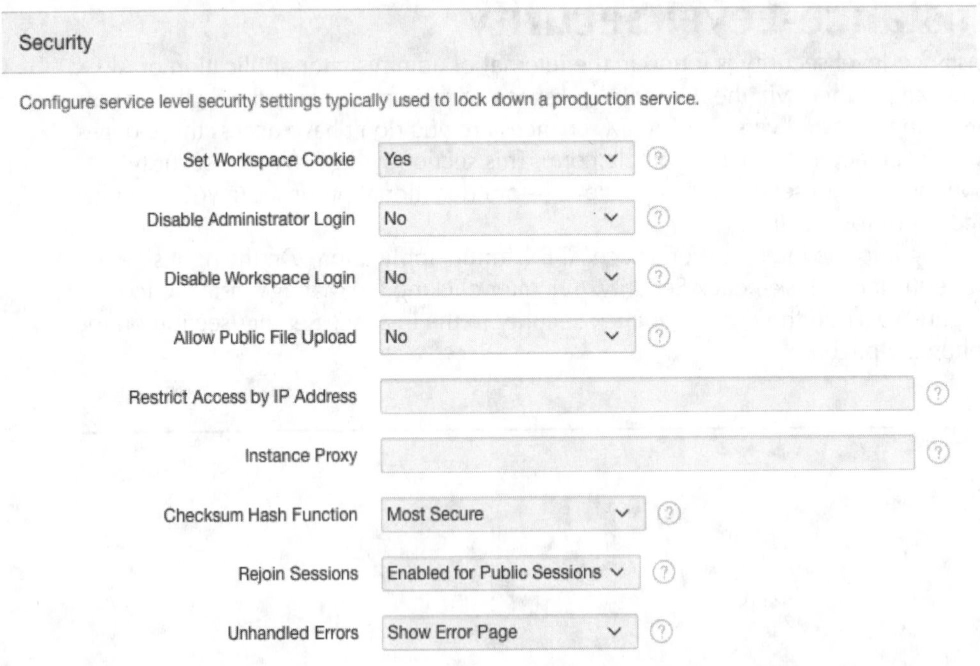

Security

Configure service level security settings typically used to lock down a production service.

Set Workspace Cookie	Yes
Disable Administrator Login	No
Disable Workspace Login	No
Allow Public File Upload	No
Restrict Access by IP Address	
Instance Proxy	
Checksum Hash Function	Most Secure
Rejoin Sessions	Enabled for Public Sessions
Unhandled Errors	Show Error Page

FIGURE 10-2. *Security settings*

- **Allow Public File Upload**   Enables or prevents public users who have not logged in from uploading files into file browse items on pages.

- **Restrict Access By IP Address**   Lets you set specific IPs or IP ranges to access your APEX instance. You can enter IP ranges in the format xxx.xxx.* or use specific IP addresses. Once set, only the IP/IP ranges you set here can access your APEX instance. This is very useful—just don't lock yourself out!

- **Instance Proxy**   Enables you to set all outbound traffic from an APEX instance to go through a proxy server.

- **Checksum Hash Function**   Enables you to select the algorithm to hash values. Setting it to Most Secure ensures that APEX always uses the most secure algorithm available. Pro tip: don't use MD5.

- **Rejoin Sessions**   Controls whether APEX should support application URLs that do not contain session IDs. This value can be overridden at the application level.

- **Unhandled Errors**   Enables you to select the behavior when APEX runs into an unhandled error. You can have APEX show the error in an error page or just return an HTTP 400. For development environments, show the error; in production, throw an HTTP 400.

HTTP Protocol Section

In this section (Figure 10-3), you can choose various options regarding using HTTPS. The Require HTTPS field has three options:

- **Always**   Enforces HTTPS for all applications, including the Application Express Development and Administration applications.

- **Application Specific**   Makes HTTPS dependent on the setting in your application.

- **For Development And Administration**   Allows authenticated pages within the APEX development and administration applications to require HTTPS.

Here are the other main options on the page:

- **Require Outbound HTTPS**   Makes all outbound traffic from your APEX instance require HTTPS.

- **HTTP Response Headers**   Enables you to add additional headers to your HTTP requests. More on this option and examples in the section "Application-Level Security."

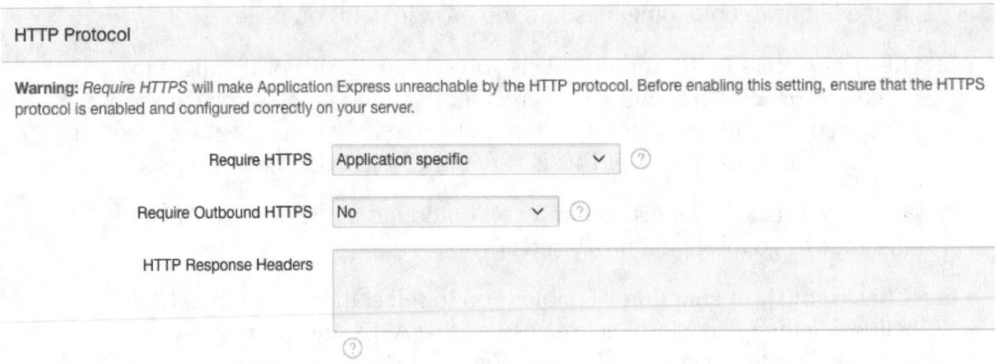

HTTP Protocol

Warning: *Require HTTPS* will make Application Express unreachable by the HTTP protocol. Before enabling this setting, ensure that the HTTPS protocol is enabled and configured correctly on your server.

Require HTTPS   `Application specific` ⌄ ⑦

Require Outbound HTTPS   `No` ⌄ ⑦

HTTP Response Headers

⑦

FIGURE 10-3. *HTTP Protocol settings*

Session Timeout Section

In the Session Timeout section, you can set the default values for the maximum time a user session lasts (Maximum Session Length In Seconds) as well as how long a session can stay idle (Maximum Session Idle Time In Seconds). These two values can be overridden at the application level. It is good security practice to have Maximum Session Idle Time In Seconds set to a low number. If a user steps away from her computer and does not lock her screen, a low number here will prevent someone from walking over and using her session for nefarious purposes.

Workspace Isolation Section

The Workspace Isolation section (Figure 10-4) includes the following settings:

- **Allow Hostnames**   Requires that the incoming HTTP request URL's hostname part must match one of the listed hostnames in the attribute. You can specify multiple hostnames in a comma-separated list.

- **Resource Consumer Group**   Lets you specify a Database Resource Manager profile to this instance. You can configure more specific values that override this one at Workspace level.

- **Maximum Concurrent Workspace Requests**   Sets the maximum number of concurrent page events that APEX supports for all applications. This can be overridden at the Workspace level.

- **Maximum Concurrent Session Requests**   Sets the maximum number of concurrent page events that APEX supports for each session for applications in this instance. This can be overridden at the Workspace level.

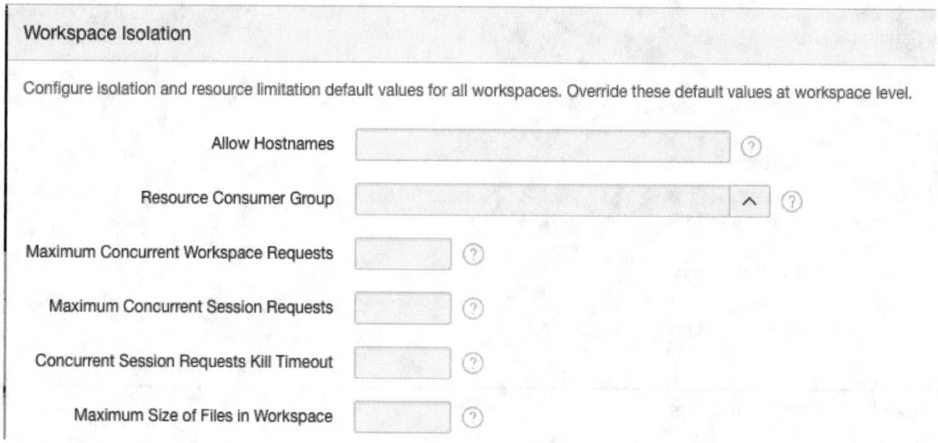

FIGURE 10-4. *Workspace Isolation settings*

- **Concurrent Session Requests Kill Timeout**   Specifies the number of seconds a database process has to be active before it can be killed. If you leave this blank, APEX will not kill any database sessions, but this may cause problems with the application server's database session pool.

- **Maximum Size Of Files In Workspace**   Lets you control the total size of uploads into APEX. Set this to prevent someone from uploading multiple very large files that might fill the database file space on the server. This can be overridden at the Workspace level.

Region and Web Service Excluded Domains Section

Use the Domain Must Not Contain attribute to prevent someone from calling a restricted domain in regions of type URL or accessed as a web service.

Authentication Control Section

The next three sections deal with how users log in, what happens then they fail at logging in, and development of authentication schemes.

General Settings Section

General Settings (Figure 10-5) is the first section in Authentication Control.

If you fail to log into APEX, you may have seen a countdown timer. This timer prevents you from logging in for a set number of seconds. If you fail again, the number doubles, and again, it triples. This prevents brute-force attacks in which

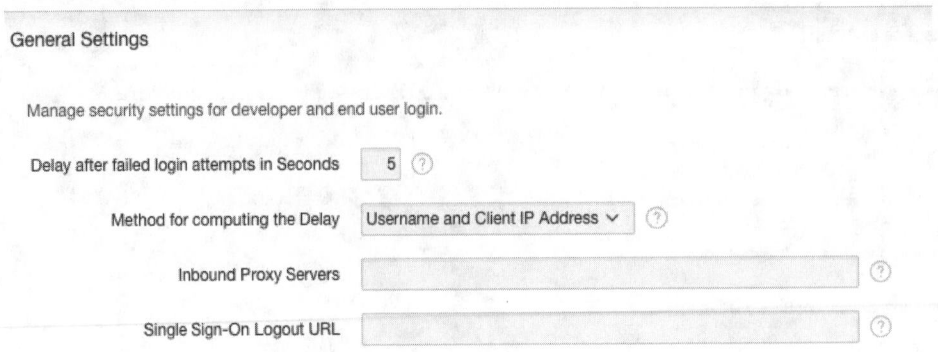

General Settings

Manage security settings for developer and end user login.

Delay after failed login attempts in Seconds   5 ⑦

Method for computing the Delay   Username and Client IP Address ∨   ⑦

Inbound Proxy Servers   [   ]   ⑦

Single Sign-On Logout URL   [   ]   ⑦

FIGURE 10-5. *General Settings*

an attacker runs a script against a login page. These scripts can run through many combinations a second.

- **Delay After Failed Login Attempts In Seconds** Sets the number of seconds a user must wait before logging in again. Attackers usually move on to another site when this is present, because the wait time can get very large after ten attempts when this is set to 5 seconds.

- **Method For Computing The Delay** Works hand-in-hand with Delay After Failed Login Attempts In Seconds. You can use combinations of username and IP address to recognize a failed attempt from the same client. Username And Client IP Address is a good setting in case an attacker is using a botnet with multiple IPs but the same username.

- **Inbound Proxy Servers** Gives APEX a list of known proxy servers for incoming traffic.

- **Single Sign-On Logout URL** Gives APEX URLs to pass the user if signing out when SSO is the authentication method.

Development Environment Settings Section

Next are the Development Environment settings (Figure 10-6).

- **Username Validation Expression** Lets you define a regular expression for how new usernames should be crafted. For example, using the regular expression,

```
^[[:alum:]._%-]+@[[:alnum:].-]+\.[[:alpha:]]{2,4}$
```

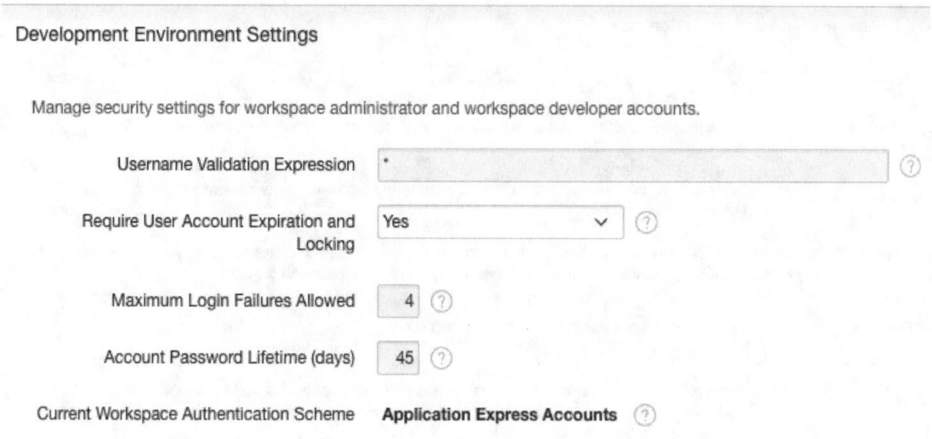

Development Environment Settings

Manage security settings for workspace administrator and workspace developer accounts.

Username Validation Expression	*
Require User Account Expiration and Locking	Yes
Maximum Login Failures Allowed	4
Account Password Lifetime (days)	45
Current Workspace Authentication Scheme	**Application Express Accounts**

FIGURE 10-6. *Development Environment Settings*

states that all accounts should be in the format of an e-mail address. Create your own expressions or use * to bypass this validation.

■ **Require User Account Expiration And Locking**   Lets you dictate whether all Workspaces in this instance of APEX follow the next two attributes in this section (Maximum Login Failures Allowed and Account Password Lifetime), or whether you want the individual Workspaces to decide these rules. Set this to No to relinquish control to each Workspace administrator. Both of the following settings ensure that users create new passwords and that if a hacker were to try to access an APEX Workspace, the account would lock after a specific number of tries. At that point, even with the correct password, you cannot log into a locked account.

■ **Maximum Login Failures Allowed**   Sets the number of unsuccessful user login attempts before the account is locked.

■ **Account Password Lifetime (Days)**   Sets the time interval in which a user is required to change his password.

■ **Current Workspace Authentication Scheme**   Displays what authentication scheme you have chosen as the method for logging into Workspaces and the administration application.

Development Environment Authentication Schemes Section
This section displays a list of authentication schemes in your repository (Figure 10-7).

Development Environment Authentication Schemes

	Name	Description	Status
✏	Application Express Accounts	This is the default authentication scheme. It authenticates users against the workspace user repository.	Current
✏	Database Accounts	This scheme utilizes database credentials. The user name and password of the database account is used to authenticate the user.	Not Current
✏	HTTP Header Variable	This scheme relies on a HTTP header variable to contain the username and on an external login method to log in. Application Express presents the available workspaces for the user.	Not Current
✏	LDAP Directory	This scheme checks credentials against an LDAP repository.	Not Current
✏	Oracle Application Server Single Sign-On	This scheme authenticates developers with Oracle Single Sign-On, using SSO's external login page. After authentication, Application Express presents the available workspaces for the user.	Not Current

FIGURE 10-7. *Development Environment Authentication Schemes*

You can change the method by which you authenticate for accessing Workspaces and the administration application. To change the scheme, click the edit icon (the pencil). Then, on the next page, click the Make Current Scheme button. Note that setting up a new authentication scheme incorrectly will lock you out of application Workspaces and administration app. If this happens, you can reset it back to Application Express Accounts by running the following SQL as sys in the database:

```
apex_instance_admin.set_parameter('APEX_BUILDER_AUTHENTICATION','APEX');
```

Password Policy Section

In this section (Figure 10-8), you can craft what type of password users need to use when setting or changing their passwords.

APEX gives you a host of options such as minimum password length, what letters and types of characters are required, and even the number of differences needed between the old and new passwords.

REST Administration Interface Section

Back on the main Instance Administration page, on the right, under Instance Tasks, is the REST Administration Interface. You can use this interface to create, delete, and issue tokens to OAuth clients. You can also view metrics about these clients.

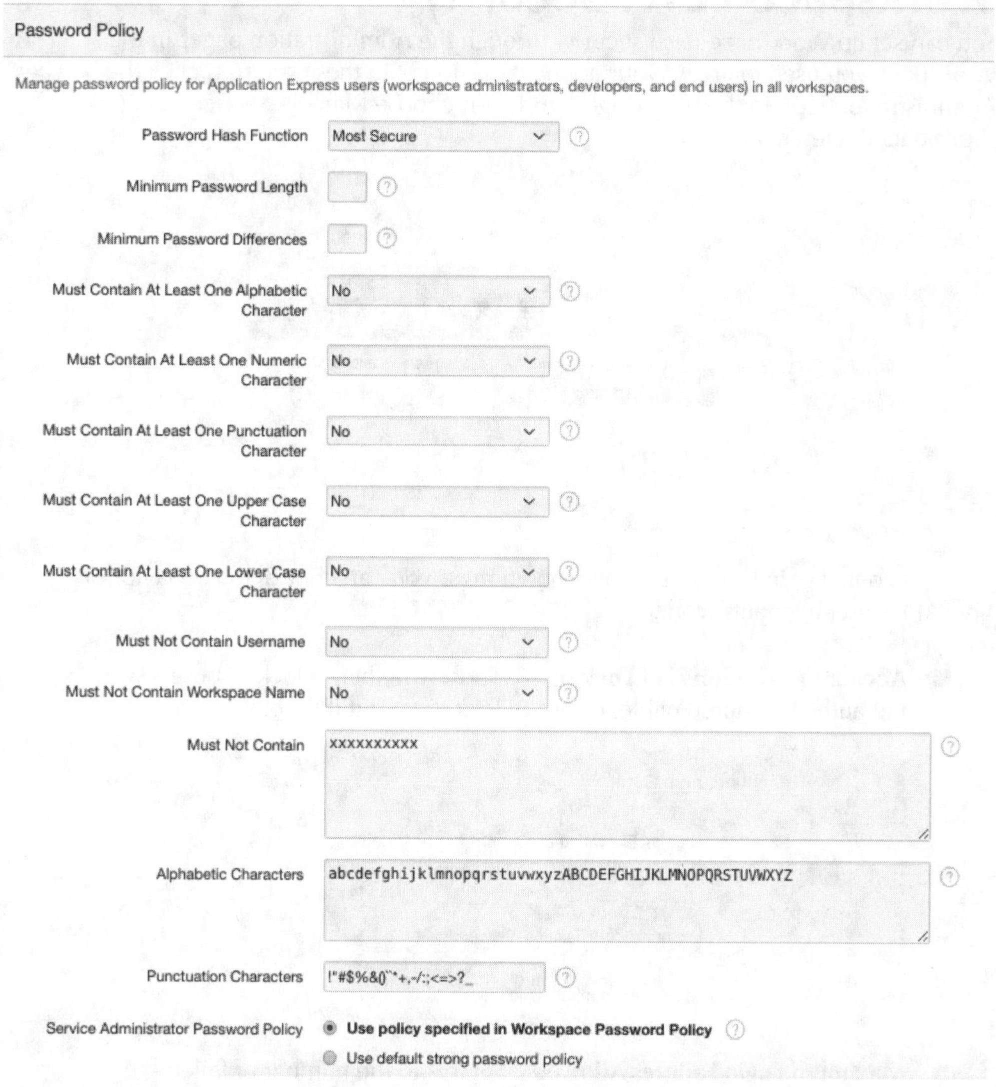

Password Policy

Manage password policy for Application Express users (workspace administrators, developers, and end users) in all workspaces.

Password Hash Function	Most Secure ⌄ ?
Minimum Password Length	?
Minimum Password Differences	?
Must Contain At Least One Alphabetic Character	No ⌄ ?
Must Contain At Least One Numeric Character	No ⌄ ?
Must Contain At Least One Punctuation Character	No ⌄ ?
Must Contain At Least One Upper Case Character	No ⌄ ?
Must Contain At Least One Lower Case Character	No ⌄ ?
Must Not Contain Username	No ⌄ ?
Must Not Contain Workspace Name	No ⌄ ?
Must Not Contain	XXXXXXXXXX ?
Alphabetic Characters	abcdefghijklmnopqrstuvwxyzABCDEFGHIJKLMNOPQRSTUVWXYZ ?
Punctuation Characters	!"#$%&()`'+,-/:;<=>?_ ?
Service Administrator Password Policy	● **Use policy specified in Workspace Password Policy** ?
	○ Use default strong password policy

FIGURE 10-8. *The Password Policy attributes*

Workspace-Level Security

You can set up Workspace level security through the Administration pages in the Workspace you used to create your application. To get to these settings, click the Administration icon in the upper right, and then choose Manage Service | Set Workspace Preferences:

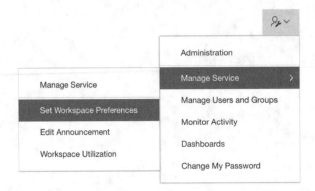

In Account Login Control section, shown next, you can control the behavior of how APEX user accounts work.

- ■ **Account Expiration And Locking** Choose whether to lock out users who fail authentication (Enable) or not to lock them out (Disable).

- ■ **Maximum Login Failures Allowed** Set this to the number of failed user login attempts before the account is locked. This attribute helps in preventing brute-force login attacks.

- ■ **End User Account Lifetime (Days)** Set this to determine how long an APEX user account's password can exist until it needs to be changed.

In the next three sections on this page—App Builder, SQL Workshop, and Team Development (Figure 10-9)—you can determine whether these sections are available to developers.

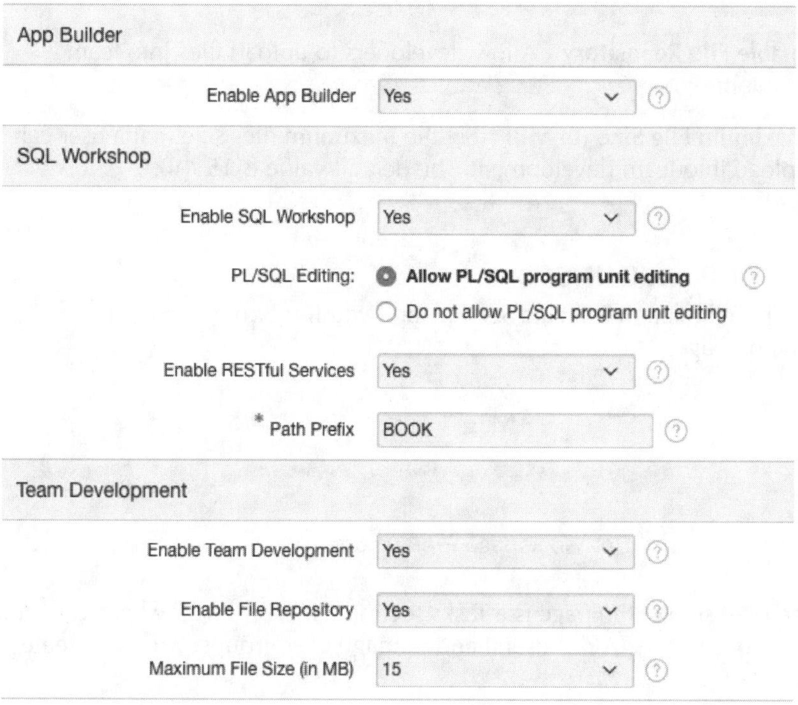

App Builder	
Enable App Builder	Yes

SQL Workshop	
Enable SQL Workshop	Yes
PL/SQL Editing:	● **Allow PL/SQL program unit editing**
	○ Do not allow PL/SQL program unit editing
Enable RESTful Services	Yes
* Path Prefix	BOOK

Team Development	
Enable Team Development	Yes
Enable File Repository	Yes
Maximum File Size (in MB)	15

FIGURE 10-9. *App Builder, SQL Workshop, and Team Development settings*

If you are not using a section or want to restrict the availability of that particular function, set the Enable option select list for each section to No.

Note the following attributes in the SQL Workshop section:

- **PL/SQL Editing** Allow or do not allow developer to edit and compile PL/SQL from the SQL Workshop.

- **Enable RESTful Services** Set whether or not to enable RESTful Services in the current Workspace.

- **Path Prefix** Used with RESTful services; specify the URI path prefix to be used in the current Workspace. The default path prefix value is the name of the Workspace. For example, if your Workspace is named "book," the URL to the RESTful services would be http://our_apex_instance_url/apex/book/our_rest_service.

Note the following attributes in the Team Development section:

- **Enable File Repository**   Allow developers to upload files into team development.

- **Maximum File Size (In MB)**   Set the maximum files size that a user can upload into team development. The default value is 15 MB.

Workspace Groups

Click the Up to the left of Manage Service, and you'll return to the main Administration page:

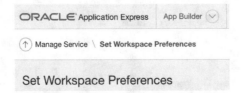

On the right side of the page is a Tasks section (Figure 10-10), where you can define workspace users (APEX users) and manage user groups. You can create

FIGURE 10-10.   *The Administration Tasks*

specialized user groups and assign users to one or more of them. These groups can then be used in conditional statements or authorization schemes.

To create a group, click Manage User Groups, and then click the Create User Group button at the upper right of the page. On the User Groups page, you can name the group, enter a description, and nest other groups within the group to create a hierarchical grouping, with the nested groups inheriting the privileges of the nested groups.

Managing Workspace Users

Back in the main Administration page (click the Up icon), you'll see the Manage Users And Groups icon (Figure 10-11).

Click the icon to open the Manage Users and Groups page, where you can create Workspace users and assign them different roles and functionality. Click an existing user to open the Edit User page (Figure 10-12), where you can enter the user's name, e-mail address, a description, a session date format (very useful for international users), and other user information.

Account Privileges Section

Click the Account Privileges tab to open the Account Privileges section (Figure 10-13), where you can set several options.

- **Default Schema**   This setting is useful for a Workspace tied to multiple schemas.

- **Accessible Schemas**   Enables you to restrict what schemas a user has access to in a multiple-schema Workspace. Provide the attribute within a comma-delimited list of schemas you want the user to be able to use. Leaving this field null will grant access to all schemas in this Workspace.

- **User Is A Workspace Administrator**   Choose Yes to grant the user unrestricted access to all the sections of the application, such as the SQL Workshop, Team Development, and the Administration pages. Choosing Yes also will lock out all the following attributes dealing with workspace access. Choose No to unlock the next set of attributes starting with User Is A Developer.

Manage Users and Groups

FIGURE 10-11.   *Manage Users And Groups icon*

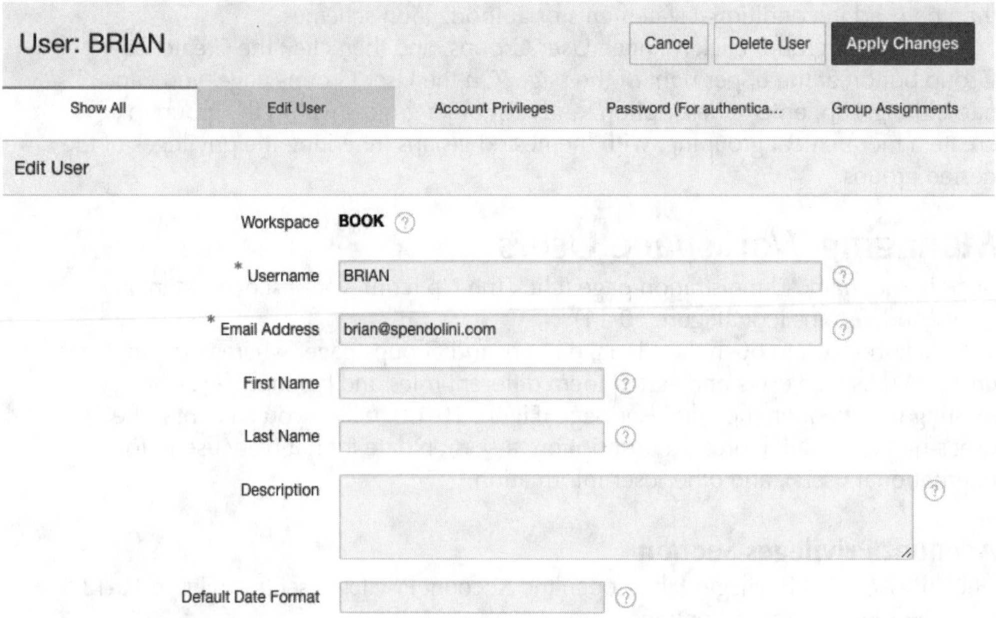

User: BRIAN			Cancel	Delete User	**Apply Changes**

Show All	Edit User	Account Privileges	Password (For authentica...	Group Assignments

Edit User

Workspace	**BOOK** ⑦
* Username	BRIAN ⑦
* Email Address	brian@spendolini.com ⑦
First Name	⑦
Last Name	⑦
Description	⑦
Default Date Format	⑦

FIGURE 10-12. *Edit User information*

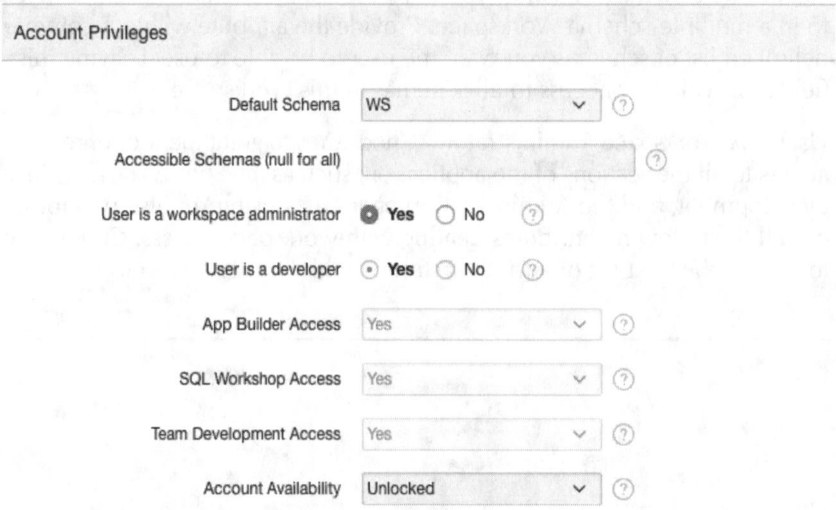

Account Privileges

Default Schema	WS ⑦
Accessible Schemas (null for all)	⑦
User is a workspace administrator	● Yes ○ No ⑦
User is a developer	◉ Yes ○ No ⑦
App Builder Access	Yes ⑦
SQL Workshop Access	Yes ⑦
Team Development Access	Yes ⑦
Account Availability	Unlocked ⑦

FIGURE 10-13. *The Account Privileges section*

- **User Is A Developer**   Choose Yes to give the user access to the main sections of your Workspace, the Builder, SQL Workshop, and Team Development. You can further restrict access with the individual select lists next to these workspace sections. Choose No to restrict the user to Team Development access only.

- **Account Availability**   Enables you to lock this user account out of APEX completely.

Password Section

In the Password section (Figure 10-14), you can change a user's password. You can also set the following attributes:

- **Require Change Of Password On First Use**   If you choose Yes, as soon as the user logs into APEX, she is prompted to change her password immediately before continuing. This attribute may not be shown for end user only accounts.

- **Developer/Administrator Password**   Shows the status (Valid or Invalid) of the User's password.

- **Expire Password**   Check this checkbox and the user will need to change her password upon the next login. There is also a read only field here. This attribute may not be shown for end user only accounts.

Password		
Password		Passwords are case sensitive ⑦
Confirm Password		⑦
Require Change of Password on First Use	Yes ⌄	⑦
Developer/Administrator Password	**Valid** ⑦	
Expire Password	☐ ⑦	

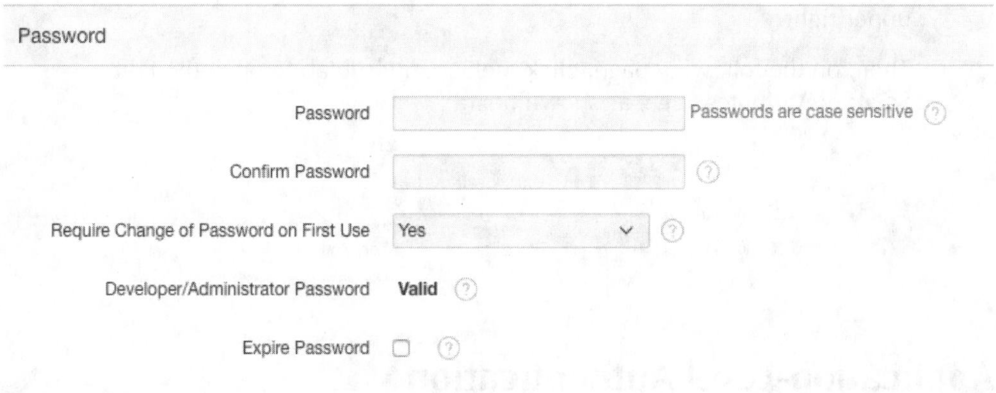

FIGURE 10-14.   *The Password section*

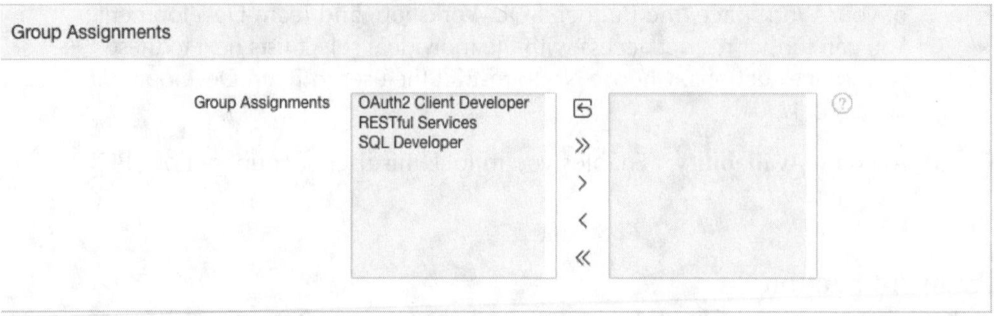

Group Assignments

| Group Assignments | OAuth2 Client Developer
RESTful Services
SQL Developer | |

FIGURE 10-15. *Group Assignments section*

Group Assignments Section

In the Group Assignments section (Figure 10-15), you can assign one or more groups to this user. The group functionality was discussed in the previous section.

Application-Level Security

In this section, we'll look at the APEX application-level security options.

1. Click the App Builder tab on the top of the page or App Build tile if on the home page, and then click your application name.

2. On the next page, click the Edit Applications Properties button in the upper right.

3. Then, on the following page, click the Security subtab to open the Edit Security Attributes page, as shown next:

Application-Level Authentication and Authorization Sections

The first section on the page is the Authentication section (Figure 10-16). The Public User attribute identifies the Oracle schema used to connect to the database through

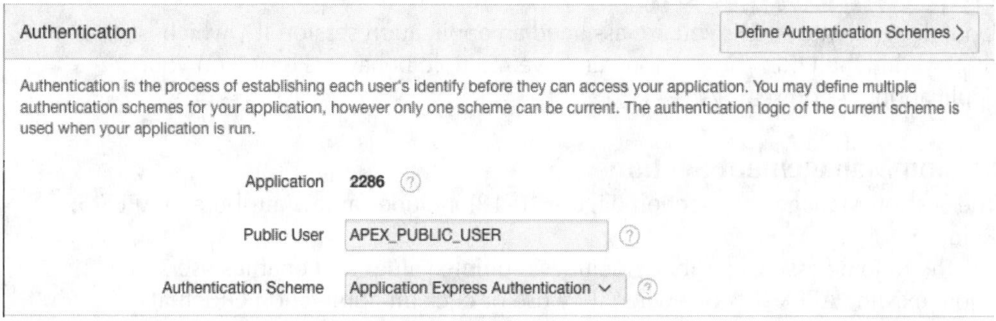

FIGURE 10-16. *Authentication settings*

your application server. The value that is most common is APEX_PUBLIC_USER. This user is the parsing schema user assigned by APEX. The user itself has very few privileges in the database and acts as a proxy user. When using the embedded PL/SQL gateway to access APEX, this user is the ANONYMOUS user.

The Authentication Scheme attribute controls what process will authenticate the user when he attempts to log in. Notice the Define Authentication Schemes button in this section; click it to open the Authentication Schemes page, where you can define new or edit existing authentication schemes.

In the Authorization section (Figure 10-17), you can set an application-wide authorization scheme.

An authorization scheme differs from an authentication scheme in that the former controls APEX elements and functionality at a lower, more granular level. You can opt to run this authorization scheme on public pages that you don't have to log into. This can help you set up a home page with a login link that is accessible to everyone— but once a user is logged in, you can control the content using the authorization scheme. Click the Define Authorization Schemes button to open the Authorization page, where you can define new or edit existing authorization schemes.

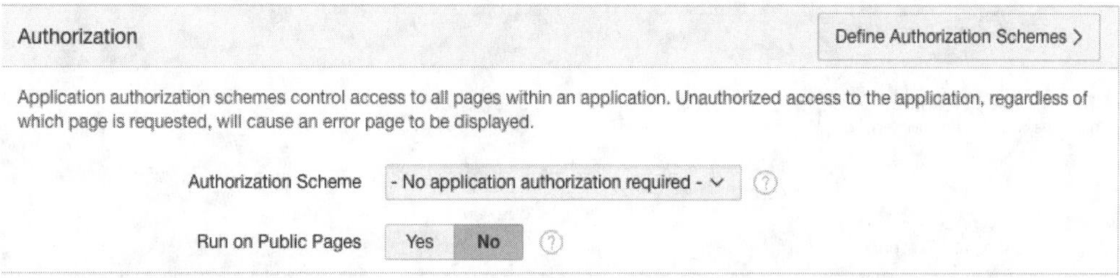

FIGURE 10-17. *Authorization settings*

Application Session

Upon logging into APEX, you are assigned an application session ID, which is displayed in the URL. This session can have multiple behaviors based on your application session settings.

Session Management Section

The Session Management section (Figure 10-18) includes a new attribute in APEX 5, Rejoin Sessions.

The Rejoin Sessions attribute includes multiple values and enables users to rejoin existing APEX sessions when they use or click an application URL that contains no session ID or an expired session ID. APEX does this by attempting to use the session cookie set in your browser. Here are the Rejoin Sessions settings:

- **Disabled**   If the URL does not have a session ID or contains an expired session ID, APEX will create a new session ID.

- **Enabled For Public Sessions**   If the URL goes to a public APEX page and does not contain a session ID or contains an expired session ID, APEX attempts to use the existing session cookie previously established.

- **Enabled For All Sessions**   If the URL does not contain a session ID or contains an expired session ID, APEX attempts to use the existing session cookie previously established.

Session Management

Rejoin Sessions	Disabled
Deep Linking	Disabled
Maximum Session Length in Seconds	

When Maximum Session Length is not set, the workspace level or instance level value will be used (currently, 28800 seconds).

Session Timeout URL	

Maximum Session Idle Time in Seconds	

When Maximum Session Idle Time is not set, the workspace level or instance level value will be used (currently, 3600 seconds).

Session Idle Timeout URL	

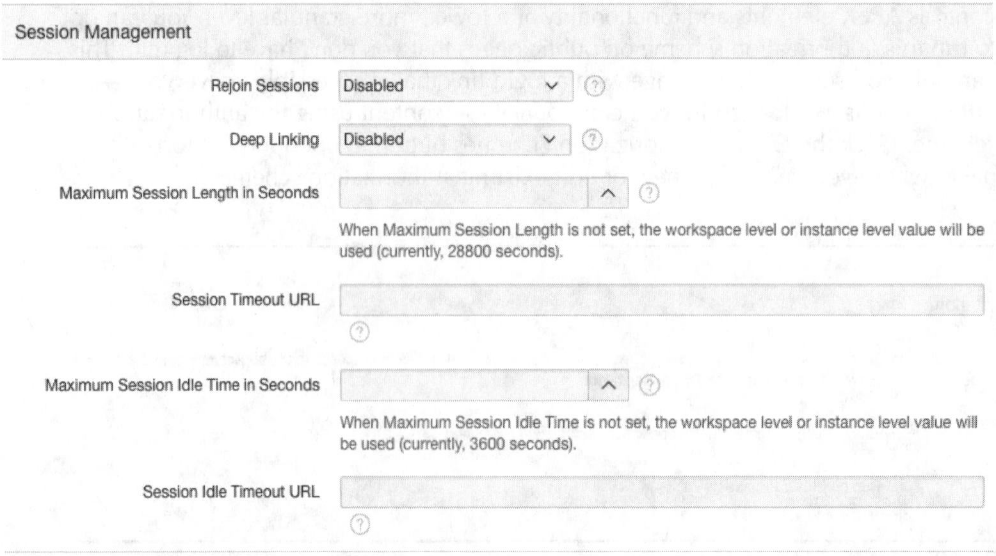

FIGURE 10-18.   *Session Management settings*

NOTE
To use Rejoin Sessions, the Embed In Frames attribute (discussed later in the section "Browser Security") must be set to Allow From Same Origin or to Deny for the application.

The Deep Linking attribute controls whether a user can go to an APEX URL that contains item values in the URL. For example, if Deep Linking is set to Enabled, a user can go to a product description page where the URL contains some product information such as an ID. This setting may be overridden at the Application page level. If a user attempted to access a page via a bookmark for which Deep Linking was set to Disabled, he would be redirected to the home page. Note that deep linking should be used with caution and tested thoroughly for correct functionality.

Use the Maximum Session Length In Seconds attribute to define how long an APEX session is valid for. Click the pop-up LOV next to this attribute to view multiple values, such as 1 Hour, 10 Minutes, and 1 Day. Click one of these values, and the returning value in the attribute is shown in seconds—so, for example, clicking 10 Minutes would result in an attribute setting of 600 seconds, and so on. Once this allotted time ends with an APEX session, the user is returned to the Authentication page to log in again.

The Session Timeout URL can be set to bring the user to the login/logout URL when the session ends, or to a custom page you indicate here.

Use the Maximum Session Idle Time In Seconds attribute to set how long a session can be idle before APEX invalidates the session and asks the user to log in again. This setting is particularly useful for applications with very sensitive data. For example, if an employee working with personal identifying data or financial data left her desk and forgot to lock her computer, after the idle time passed, anyone attempting to alter that data would be presented with a login page rather than having access to the data. Finally, as with the Session Timeout URL, you can set a Session Idle Timeout URL.

NOTE
When Maximum Session Length or Maximum Session Idle Time are not set, they inherit the instance-level settings. Messages are displayed under each attribute that state what instance level is being used and what that value is. For example, if Maximum Session Length In Seconds is not set, you would see a message similar to this: "When Maximum Session Length is not set, the workspace level or instance level value will be used (currently, 28800 seconds)."

Session State Protection Section

The Session State Protection section (Figure 10-19) can help you prevent URL tampering and manipulation.

- **Session State Protection** If set to Enabled, this attribute can help secure your URLs when accessing pages. It does this by using the Page Access Protection attributes and the Session State Protection attributes along with checksums to ensure the URL cannot be tampered with.

- **Allow URLs Created After** If the bookmarked link contains a checksum and Session State Protection is Enabled for the application, this attribute controls the date and time that those bookmarks will be valid.

- **Bookmark Hash Function** This attribute dictates the hash function that is used to create checksums for application-level and user-level checksums in "bookmarkable" URLs.

Browser Security Section

The Cache attribute in the Browser Security section (Figure 10-20) allows the application to cache pages so that when users click the Back button, for example, the page loads from the browser cache and not from the server.

This speeds up the page load times, but it could also be a potential security nightmare, because APEX may now be caching sensitive data on your local machine, which could be retrieved as easily as clicking through your browser history at a later time. This attribute should be evaluated on a per-application basis. APEX recommends that this attribute be set to Disabled and changed only after the security implications are thoroughly reviewed.

Session State Protection	Expire Bookmarks	Manage Session State Protection >

Enabling Session State Protection can prevent hackers from tampering with URLs within your application. URL tampering can adversely affect program logic, session state contents, and information privacy.

To enable Session State Protection for your application, select **Enabled** from the Session State Protection list. Enabling Session State Protection turns on session state protection controls defined at the page and item level. To configure Session State Protection, click **Manage Session State Protection**.

Session State Protection	Enabled
Allow URLs Created After	**(null)**
Bookmark Hash Function	**SHA-2, 512 bit (requires 12c)**

FIGURE 10-19. *Session State Protection settings*

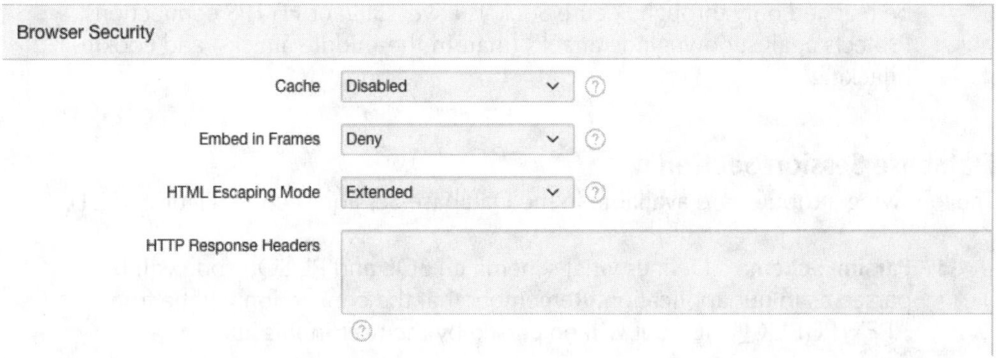

FIGURE 10-20. *Browser Security settings*

Using iFrames, you can embed an HTML documents within another. If used maliciously, iFrames can be susceptible to clickjacking attacks. The Embed In Frames attribute will Allow or Deny APEX pages to be embedded in iFrames. There three options for this attribute:

- **Deny**   Restricts this application from being displayed in iFrames completely.

- **Allow From Same Origin**   Pages in this application can be displayed in iFrames but only on the same server.

- **Allow**   Pages in this application can be used in iFrames.

The HTML Escaping Mode attribute setting will help prevent against XSS attacks by escaping special or control characters across the application. There are two options:

- **Basic**   Escapes &, ", <, and >

- **Extend**   Escapes &, ", <, >, ', /, and non-ASCII characters if the database character set is not AL32UTF8

The HTTP Response Headers attribute enables you to add HTTP headers to your HTTP response, which may help against specific hacks. Here are some of the more useful ones:

- **X-XSS-Protection**   Helps to prevent XSS attacks in Internet Explorer and Chrome browsers.

- **X-Content-Type-Options**   Enables the browser to opt out of *MIME-sniffing*—inspecting the content of a byte stream to attempt to determine the file format. This could trick a browser into executing malicious code.

■ **Strict-Transport-Security** Tells a browser that this site or application can be reached only through Secure Sockets Layer (SSL) or HTTPS connections. Protects against downgrade attacks (man-in-the-middle attacks) and cookie hijacking.

Database Session Section

The following attributes are available in the Database Session section (Figure 10-21)

■ **Parsing Schema** Defines what schema all SQL and PL/SQL code will be parsed as in our application. Remember that the connection will be from APEX_PUBLIC_USER but will be parsed by the user in this attribute.

■ **Initialization PL/SQL Code and Cleanup PL/SQL Code** Works hand-in-hand to set database context. Database context tells the database who is using the application. You set this context in the Initialization section and release it in the Clean-up section, ensuring that resources are freed up and no data is leaked if the session is reused later on.

■ **Runtime API Usage** Controls how an application can use the APEX_UTIL package within the application. The options are Modify This Application, Modify Other Applications, and Modify Workspace Repository. This attribute prevents an attacker from using injections to take over applications with wwv_flow_api calls.

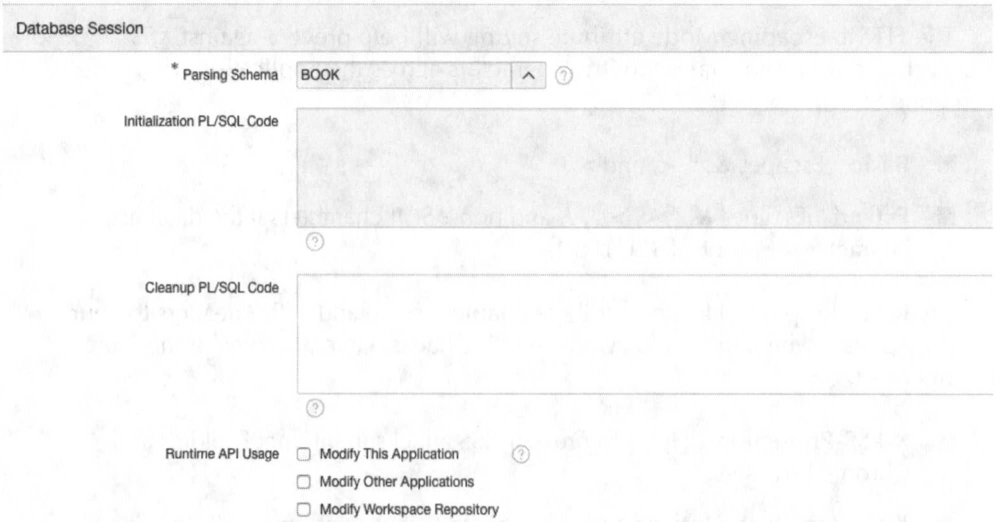

FIGURE 10-21. *Database Session settings*

Page-Level Security

Now let's look at some of the options available for page-level security. We can get there by editing a page in the Page Designer. Click the edit page 1 icon at the upper-right of the current Security page. Then, in the Page Designer, click the top-level page icon in the Rendering panel:

Security Properties

In the Property Editor – Page tab, scroll down to the Security section (Figure 10-22), or from the Go To Group dropdown menu, click Security. You'll see many of the same attributes you saw at the application level, but these are page-level attributes. Setting these attributes will override the application-level settings.

The first property is Authorization Scheme. Here we can set what group or privilege is needed to access this page. Next, we can define an Authentication method. We will be using both Authorization schemes and Authentication methods later in this chapter. Rejoin Sessions and Deep Linking will override the application level settings we discussed earlier in this chapter.

The Page Access Protection attribute has four options:

- ■ **Unrestricted**   This page can be linked to without needing a checksum for setting items.

- ■ **Arguments Must Have Checksum**   This page has to have a valid checksum for setting session items, clearing the page cache, or setting a request.

- ■ **No Arguments Supported**   You may link to this page, but no requests, cache clearing, or page items may be in the URL

- ■ **No URL Access**   This page can be reached only through an APEX page branch.

Setting the Form Auto Complete attribute to On will allow the browser to remember values for specific fields in a form. This is a huge time-saving for some forms, because all you need to do is double-click the field and you'll get a list of recently used values. This can also be a huge security risk, however, because you may be caching personal or sensitive data. This risk can be compounded when using a browser such as Chrome, because these auto-complete values are not only cached in the browser, but if signed into Chrome, they are cached on Google's servers.

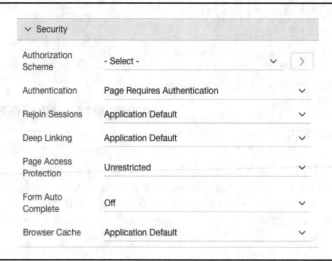

FIGURE 10-22. *Page-level Security attributes*

The Browser Cache property will allow the browser to cache pages. If a user were to click the browser back button, the page would be pulled from cache, not from the server. While this may seem like it would aid in the speed of the page being rendered, it is also a security risk. If the browser is able to cache sensitive data, anyone can access the browser history and potentially see that data. It is best left to Disabled. You can set the application default level so that all pages take on the value of that application level property.

Advanced Properties

In the Advanced property group, the Enable Duplicate Page Submissions property prevents a user from clicking the Submit button multiple times, thus resulting in multiple inserts; it also prevents the browser from submitting the data again if the Back/Reload button is clicked.

The Reload On Submit property is a new addition to APEX 5.1. This option shows errors in forms without reloading page on submit if the Only For Success option is chosen. It always reloads the page after a successful processing.

Server Cache Properties

In the Server Cache property group, the Caching property lets APEX cache HTML text on the server side to speed up page load. (This feature is unrelated to the Browser Cache attribute we discussed earlier.) There are four options for this property:

- **Disabled**   Content is not cached and computed for each request.

- **Enabled**   Content is cached and used by all users.

- **Cache By User**   Content is cached specifically for each user.

- **Cache By Session**   Content is cached specifically for each session.

When setting these properties, evaluate your security needs so that you are not caching sensitive data or page form items.

Region and Item-Level Security

Region- and item-level security share some properties—mainly the Authorization Scheme and Conditional properties.

Let's start by editing page 2 of our application in the Page Designer. On page 2, click the Create/Edit Contacts region in the Rendering panel. On the right side in the Region properties, find the Security property group, shown here. (Remember that you can find the Security section quickly by using the Go To Group icon.)

Regions Properties

For Regions, only Authorization Scheme is included in this section. But just above the Security sections, two groups away, is the Server-side Condition section. You can set conditions on almost every element in APEX. (Conditional statements will be discussed later in the chapter.) You can set the Server Cache attribute at a region level as well as a page level. This helps to control server caching at a more granular level if you have it turned off at the page level.

Items Properties

In the Rendering panel, scroll down and find the Items folder. Open the folder and click P2_PERSON_MIDDLE_NAME. On the right side, find the Security Properties group in the Properties panel. At the item level are many more Security settings:

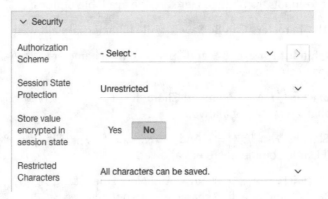

■ **Authorization Scheme**   This is the same property you saw with regions, but this setting can differ between the page, region, and item levels; the page level will always override the region level, and the region level overrides the item level.

■ **Session State Protection**   Once you set this at the application level, you can set it at the item level. You have five choices:

   ■ **Unrestricted**   The item may be set in the URL with no checksum.

   ■ **Checksum Required - Application Level**   The item may be set in the URL but it needs a checksum generated specific to the application and workspace.

   ■ **Checksum Required - User Level**   The item may be set in the URL but it needs a checksum generated specific to the user in the same application and workspace, but it may have a different session.

   ■ **Checksum Required - Session Level**   The item may be set in the URL but it needs a checksum generated for the specific session the user is currently in.

   ■ **Restricted - May Not Be Set From Browser**   This item cannot be set via a POST URL. Only internal server processes may change or set the items value.

■ **Store Value Encrypted In Session State**   Tells APEX to encrypt the value of this particular item in Session State so that it cannot be read by anyone with rights to read the APEX metadata tables. This is especially important when working with sensitive data.

■ **Restricted Characters**   Restricts certain characters from being passed back into the database. Restricted characters are very important because they can save you from an XSS attack by escaping a potentially dangerous input value. This attribute should be set as restrictive as possible when dealing with text inputs from users. Here are the available options:

   ■ **All Characters Can Be Saved**   All characters are allowed.

   ■ **Whitelist For a-Z, 0-9 and Space**   Only characters a–z, A–Z, 0–9, and space are allowed.

   ■ **Blacklist HTML Command Characters (<>")**   Reserved HTML characters are not allowed.

   ■ **Blacklist &<>"/;,*|=% And --**   &, <, >, ", /, ;, ",", *, |, =, %, and "--" (PL/SQL comment) are not allowed.

   ■ **Blacklist &<>"/;,*|=% or -- And New Line**   &, <, >, ", /, ;, ",", *, |, =, %, "--", and new line characters are not allowed.

Read Only Properties

Just above the Security property group for items is the Read Only property group. Here, you can set items on pages to be read-only based on a set condition. These conditions can range from "always be read-only" to "be read-only from 1 A.M. to 2 A.M. EST." The read-only options will not be available for hidden items. Read-only items are also not put into session when submitting a page.

Conditional Statements

Most components in APEX have a server-side condition property that controls when a component is rendered, or shown to a user, based on a conditional statement you set for the component. When setting a condition, the Value property will change based on the condition type. The Value property field is displayed after you chose a condition below the Type attribute, with two fields appearing for some conditions:

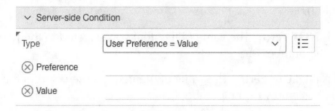

APEX comes with a multitude of conditions you can use to control access. Using these conditions on any component in APEX will help with access for a particular situation alongside authorization schemes:

- **Rows returned**   A SQL statement in a condition returns one or more rows.

- **No Rows returned**   A SQL statement in a condition returns no rows.

- **SQL Expression**   A SQL statement in a condition evaluates to TRUE.

- **PL/SQL Expression**   The PL/SQL expression returns TRUE.

- **PL/SQL Function Body**   The PL/SQL function body returns TRUE.

- **Request = Value**   The page REQUEST in the URL is equal to the value in the Value attribute.

- **Request != Value**   The page REQUEST in the URL is NOT equal to the value in the Value attribute.

- **Request is contained in Value**   The page REQUEST in the URL is equal to the Value attribute. You can include many values in the Value attribute, each separated by a single space.

- **Request is NOT contained in Value** The page REQUEST in the URL is NOT equal to the Value attribute. You can include many values in the value attribute, each separated by a single space.

- **Item = Value** The value of the item you selected in the Item attribute is equal to the text you entered in the Value attribute.

- **Item != Value** The value of the item you selected in the Item attribute is NOT equal to the text you entered in the Value attribute.

- **Item is NULL** The value of the item you selected in the Item attribute is empty.

- **Item is NOT NULL** The value of the item you selected in the Item attribute is not empty.

- **Item is zero** The value of the item you selected in the Item attribute is the number 0.

- **Item is NOT zero** The value of the item you selected in the Item attribute is not the number 0.

- **Item is NULL or zero** The value of the item you selected in the Item attribute is empty or the number 0.

- **Item is NOT NULL and NOT zero** The value of the item you selected in the Item attribute is not empty and not the number 0.

- **Item contains no spaces** The value of the item you selected in the Item attribute has no spaces.

- **Item is numeric** The value of the item you selected in the Item attribute is numeric.

- **Item is NOT numeric** The value of the item you selected in the Item attribute is not numeric.

- **Item is alphanumeric** The value of the item you selected in the Item attribute is alphanumeric; it contains only letters and numbers but not special characters.

- **Item is in colon-delimited list** The value of the item you selected in the Item attribute is contained within the colon-delimited list in the text you entered into the Value attribute.

- **Item is NOT in colon-delimited list** The value of the item you selected in the Item attribute is NOT contained within the colon-delimited list in the text you entered into the Value attribute.

- **User Preference = Value**   The value of the User Preference in the Preference attribute is equal to the text you entered into the Value attribute.

- **User Preference != Value**   The value of the User Preference in the Preference attribute is NOT equal to the text you entered into the Value attribute.

- **Current Page = Page**   The application's current page is equal to the value you entered into Page attribute.

- **Current Page != Page**   The application's current page is NOT equal to the value you entered into Page attribute.

- **Current Page is in comma-delimited list**   The application's current page is in the comma-separated list you entered into the Page attribute by typing it in or using the pop-up select list.

- **Current Page is NOT in comma-delimited list**   The application's current page is NOT in the comma-separated list you entered into the Page attribute by typing it in or using the pop-up select list.

- **Current Page is in Printer Friendly Mode**   The application's current page has been toggled to Printer Friendly Mode by a user.

- **Current page is NOT in Printer Friendly Mode**   The application's current page has NOT been toggled to Printer Friendly Mode by a user.

- **Page/Region is Read Only**   Either the page, parent region, or current region of this item's or subregion's Read Only condition evaluates to TRUE.

- **Page/Region is NOT Read Only**   Either the page, parent region, or current region of this item's or subregion's Read Only condition evaluates to FALSE or is not set.

- **User is Authenticated (not public)**   The current user has logged into the application via some form of authentication.

- **User is the Public User (user has not authenticated)**   The current user has NOT logged into the application via some form of authentication.

- **Inline Validation Errors displayed**   An inline validation error is displayed on the page after the user submits the page.

- **Inline Validation Errors NOT displayed**   An inline validation error is NOT displayed on the page after the user submits the page.

- **Current Language = Value**   The user is running the application using the language entered into the Value attribute.

- **Current Language != Value**   The user is running the application NOT using the language entered into the Value attribute.

- **Current Language is contained in Value**   The user is running the application using one of the languages entered into the Value attribute.

- **Current Language is NOT contained in Value**   The user is running the application NOT using one of the languages entered into the Value attribute.

- **Never**   The current component set to Never will not render on the page.

NOTE
Remember that conditions do not always have to deal with security issues but can also be tied to the business logic of your application, the layout of your page, or the nationality of the user accessing the application.

Authentication Schemes

On the Application's Shared Components page, we can create and use authentication schemes. From the App Builder main page, choose your application, then click the Shared Components Icon. Then click Authentication Schemes to see the report, shown next:

As you can see, only one authentication scheme is available at this time: Application Express Authentication - Current. This scheme uses your APEX developer username and password for authentication. Although this is good for development and the purposes of this book, it would not be appropriate in a production environment. Let's create a new authentication scheme.

1. In the upper-right corner of the report, click Create.

2. The Create Authentication Scheme wizard will step you through creating a new authentication scheme for the application. For the first step, Create Scheme, make sure Based On A Pre-configured Scheme From The Gallery is selected. Then click Next.

3. The value As A Copy Of An Existing Authentication Scheme lets you copy an existing scheme and alter it slightly without overwriting the original scheme.

4. On the next page of the wizard, you first name your new authentication scheme, but you can also choose from a list of prebuilt names. The list contains the following options:

- **Open Door Credentials** This scheme asks for a login name and uses that name as the app user in the application. No password is needed. This is a great method to use in development to test how different users see your application without the need for a password—just don't use it in production.

- **Application Express Accounts** This scheme uses the internal users we created when creating the workspace. These users will usually be developers but can be any user you want to use: developer, team development member, or end user.

- **Database Accounts** This authentication scheme uses database schema users.

- **LDAP Directory** This scheme lets you tie into an existing corporate LDAP directory such as Active Directory or Oracle Internet Directory.

- **No Authentication (Using DAD)** Uses the parsing schema that you set in the application for authentication.

- **Oracle Application Server Single Sign-On** Integrates into an existing Oracle SSO server. Note that you must have been registered as a partner application with the SSO server before using this method.

- **Custom** Create a custom login scheme. You tell APEX how to authenticate by setting the sentry, authentication, invalid session, and logout procedures.

- **HTTP Header Variable** This scheme lets you authenticate by using secure HTTP headers to identify the user. For example, you can have Oracle's Identity Federation authenticate and set the headers, and then use the headers to create an APEX session and get the username.

If you are using an Oracle Cloud Application Express instance such as the one in the Oracle Database Exadata Express Service, you will see another authentication scheme called Oracle Cloud Identity Management. This authentication scheme will enable you to create users using the Oracle Cloud Identity Management console, and enable them to log into your APEX accounts that are within the same cloud account or identity domain.

Use the application Authentication scheme type Application Express Accounts for now. As you can see, APEX has many built-in schemes that could work with your enterprise or existing authentication methods. Click Cancel to close this wizard.

Authorization Schemes

In addition to authentication schemes in shared components, you can set up authorization schemes. You can place these pass/fail checks on most components in APEX, from applications to items. For example, you can create an Administrator authorization scheme and place it on data setup pages in your application that a regular user does not need to access. You can also place it on items or reports in your application that you want to restrict to a particular level of user.

1. Click the Authorization Schemes link in shared components to open the Authorization Schemes report:

2. Click Create to start the wizard.

On the first page, for Create Authorization Scheme, select From Scratch. Then click Next.

The second page of the Create Authorization Scheme wizard is the details step. Here you define how your authorization scheme will work and where it will check for user authorization, as shown in Figure 10-23.

3. For the Name attribute, the more descriptive the better, because the name will help you determine its function later down the road.

4. For Scheme Type, the options are similar to those listed for conditions (in the "Conditional Statement" section). Two of these, however, are different: Is In Group and Is Not In Group. These conditions will use the groups at the Workspace level that you were introduced to earlier in this chapter. As with the item conditions, choosing an option here will expose the appropriate field(s) under your choice. For example, choosing a Scheme Type of PL/SQL Function Returning A Boolean will expose the PL/SQL Function Body text area.

5. The next attribute, Identify Error Message Displayed When Scheme Violated, is where you define a custom descriptive error message to display when the authorization scheme fails.

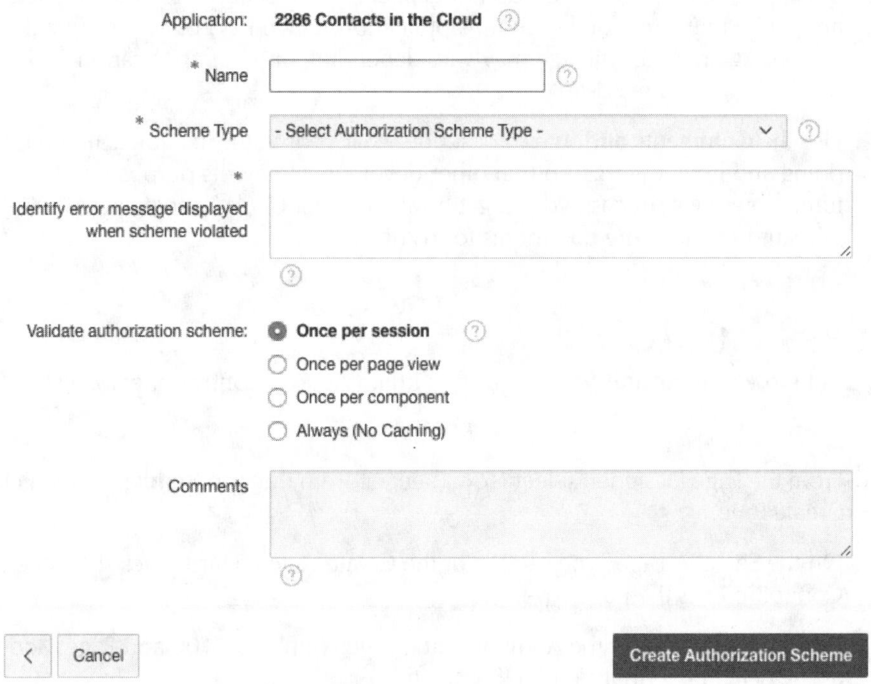

Application:	**2286 Contacts in the Cloud** ⑦
* Name	[ ] ⑦
* Scheme Type	- Select Authorization Scheme Type - ⌄ ⑦
* Identify error message displayed when scheme violated	[ ] ⑦
Validate authorization scheme:	◉ **Once per session** ⑦
	○ Once per page view
	○ Once per component
	○ Always (No Caching)
Comments	[ ] ⑦

| ‹ Cancel | | **Create Authorization Scheme** |

FIGURE 10-23. *The Create Authorization Scheme details step*

6. The Validate Authorization Scheme Selection tells APEX when and at which point to run this particular validation. Be aware that authorization schemes are always evaluated when a new session is created; these options let you fine-tune the execution point. The choices are as follows:

■ **Once per session (default)**   Evaluate this scheme upon session creation and memorize the result.

■ **Once per page view**   Evaluate this scheme on each page view or page submission. Also use the memorized result if APEX encounters this authorization scheme anywhere else in the page.

■ **Once per component**   Evaluate this scheme on each component that contains this scheme. Also use the memorized result if APEX encounters this authorization scheme anywhere else in the page.

■ **Always (No Caching)**   The authorization scheme will always be evaluated.

Using the default Once Per Session is the best option and reduces server activity for each page. If you do not expect a user's security to change often and while they are working in the application, Once Per Session is a great option. Again, your mileage may vary depending on your application and security/business needs.

7. Use the Comments attribute to describe what your authorization scheme is doing and how it works, so that other developers know its purpose (or for future reference, in case you forget how it works). Click Cancel and APEX will auto-create some comments for us next.

Access Control

APEX can help you jumpstart your security with an Access Control page. Let's create one:

1. From the Page Designer, select New Page; or, from the App Builder page, click Create Page.

2. On the Select A Page Type section of the Create Page wizard, click the Access Control icon as the page type.

3. In the next screen, set the Administration Page Number to 100 and Page Mode as the default (Normal). Then click Next

4. For the Navigation Menu step, Navigation Preference, choose Create A New Navigation Menu entry. Upon this selection, you will see two more attribute fields. For the New Navigation Menu entry field, enter **Security Administration**. For Parent Navigation Menu make sure – No parent selected – is chosen. Then click Next.

5. Check over the values on the Confirmation page and then click Create.

6. Back in the Page Designer, run the page. In the top section, Application Administration, set the Application Mode defining how the application will behave to Full Access To All, Access Control List Not Used:

Application Administration

Application Mode   ● **Full access to all, access control list not used.**   ⑦

          ○ Restricted access. Only users defined in the access control list are allowed.

          ○ Public read only. Edit and administrative privileges controlled by access control list.

          ○ Administrative access only.

          [Set Application Mode]

7. Next, in the Access Control List, you can assign users to specific privileges:

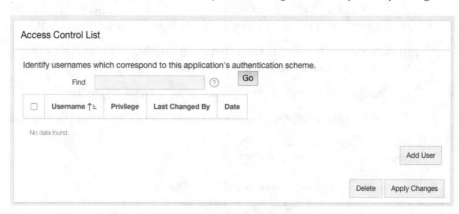

APEX has automatically created three groups for you: Administrator, Edit, and View. Behind the scenes, APEX has also created authorization schemes for you to use in your application. If you want to confirm the creation of these schemes, from the main App Builder page for your app, click Shared Components and then Authorization Schemes.

Let's do some quick setups so we can see this in action.

1. On the top of the page, the Application Administration section, click the radio button Restricted Access. Only Users Defined In The Access Control List Are Allowed. Then click Set Application Mode.

2. In the Access Control List, to add another row, click the Add User button.

3. Enter your user login name in the Username field, and then set the Privilege select list to Administrator.

4. Now add two fake users: Annie, with the Edit privilege, and Oliver, with the View privilege. When the table looks similar to the following, click the Apply Changes button.

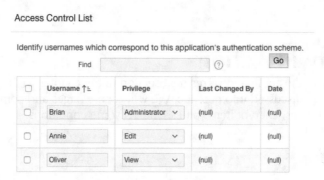

5. Now create an open door authentication scheme so you can use these users without actually creating them. Go to Shared Components, and then Authentication Schemes. Click the Create button to start the wizard.

6. In the Method step, or Create Scheme, choose Based On A Pre-Configured Scheme From The Gallery. Then click Next.

7. For the Scheme Name, enter **Open Door** or something similar.

8. From the drop-down select list, choose Open Door Credentials, as shown next:

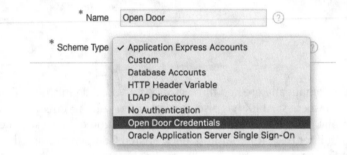

9. Click the Create Authentication Scheme button in the upper right.

10. On the next report page, you should see the created scheme, which is now the current one being used by either the check icon or the word "Current" after the name:

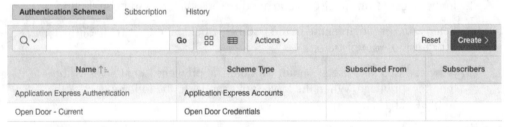

1 - 2

Security in Action

Now let's secure the application. This next section of the chapter will put many of the concepts we discussed into practice. We will secure pages and components, set checksums on items, encrypt item values, and set some conditions.

Authorization Schemes

We'll start by setting the application's authorization schemes.

1. Edit page 100 in the Page Designer via the Edit Page 100 link on the Developer toolbar.

2. In the Rendering panel on the left, click Page 100: Access Control Administration Page.

3. In the Property panel on the right, find the Security Property group and set the Authentication Scheme to Access Control – Administrator.

4. Save and run the page.

   Note that if you have not logged in for a while, you might see the new open door login page. Log in as the user you created with the Workspace and that you set as an administrator in the Access Control List tabular form. Then click the Login button.

Log In to Application 2286

Enter your credentials in this form to start a new session in this Application Express application.

* Username [　　　　　　　　　]

5. You should next see the Access Control Administration page. In the upper-right corner, click the Log Out link and you will be redirected to the open door login page.

6. For Username, enter **Annie**. Then click the Login button.

7. You should see your homepage. Find the Security Administration menu item on the left in the navigation menu bar and click it.

8. A new page states, "Access denied by Page security check." Because user Annie has only the edit privilege, access is denied from the page based on the authorization scheme you set. Click the browser back button or go back to your home page by clicking the OK button.

9. Back on the main page, you see that Annie can still see the Security Administration menu item on the right. Let's hide this menu item based on privilege so that the user can never find herself faced with an Access Denied page.

10. To hide the navigation menu item, you need to edit your application. Click the Edit Application button on the Developer toolbar (shown next). Then click the Shared Components icon.

11. In Shared Components, click Navigation Menu (in the Navigation section in the middle left of the page).

12. On the Navigation Menu report, click Desktop Navigation Menu and then click Security Administration.

13. Scroll down to or click the Authorization section and set Authorization Scheme to Access Control –Administrator, as shown next. Then click the Apply Changes button at the upper right.

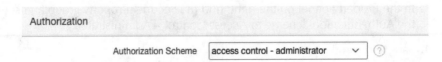

14. Reload the application main page, and Annie should no longer be able to see the Security Administration menu item.

Now let's secure the edit link and the new contacts button.

1. Edit page 1 via the link on the Developer toolbar 1.

2. On the left side, in the Rendering panel, My Contacts region, click the Attributes folder.

3. In the Attributes panel on the right, in the Link properties group, set the Authorization Scheme property to Access Control – Edit, as shown in Figure 10-24.

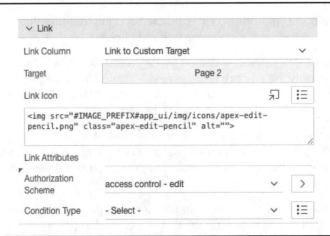

FIGURE 10-24. *Setting the Authorization Scheme on the Edit Link in an Interactive Report/Grid*

4. In the Grid Layout Canvas, My Contacts region, click the NEW_CONTACT button. This will change the Property Editor on the right to display the button properties.

5. In the Security Property group, set the Authorization Scheme property to Access Control – Edit. Save and run the page.

6. You should be logged in as Annie, so the Edit column and the Create button should be visible. Click the Log Out link at the upper right and log in as Oliver.

7. Upon logging in, you should no longer see the Create button or the Edit column in the report.

8. Log out and let's log back in as our main user. Next, we'll edit the page.

Session State Protection and Item Encryption

First, you need to do a bit of cleanup work. Remember how you set the page and menu authorization for the Security Administration page? You need to do the same for the edit/create contacts form.

1. In the Page Designer, switch to page 2.

2. In the Rendering panel on the left, ensure that Page 2: Create/Edit Contacts is highlighted

3. In the Page Properties tab, Security Properties group, change the Authorization Scheme to Access Control – Edit and save the page.

4. Back on the left side, change the Rendering panel to the Shared Components panel and expand the Navigation Menu folder. Right-click Desktop Navigation Menu and choose Edit:

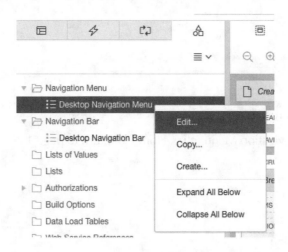

5. Click the New Contact entry, and in the Authorization section, set the Authorization Scheme to Access Control – Edit.

6. Click Apply Changes in the upper right.

You have now secured the pages and navigation menu item from users without the edit function. It is good practice to set up authorization schemes in your applications so that no page is without one.

Time to secure items.

1. In the Page Designer, edit Page 2.

2. The tab will probably be set to the Shared Components on the left. Click the Rendering panel tab, and then click the Page2: Create/Edit Contacts top-level node.

3. On the right, in the Security Properties group in the Page tab, set Page Access Protection property to Arguments Must Have Checksum if not already set.

4. Back in the Rendering panel on the left, under Page Items, click P2_PERSON_ID.

5. In the Properties - Page Item tab, in the Security properties group, set Session State Protection to Checksum Required – Session Level if not already set. Also set the Store Value Encrypted In Session State property to Yes:

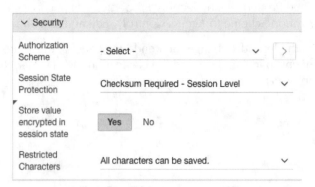

6. Save and run the page.

7. In the Navigation Menu, click Home to return to page 1.

8. Hover your mouse over the Edit links in the report to see the secured URL. You can see that APEX is appending a checksum similar to the following:

```
PERSON_ID:2&cs=3iKino6IgJW9oQfO7vW8_AV6ATGUHu4DsgrugtGO1Gy-
LmEQ7zNdXZhqnDHOys8QZ5UD4QWANDqafFaH6Lz6XB2
```

This secures the value of the item and prevents it from being set through the URL. This protection helps to prevent against URL tampering and SQL injection.

9. Click the Edit icon as though you were going to edit the contact, and look at the URL of the page. Let's try to change the contact ID via the URL. In the URL section of your browser (address bar), change the number after P2_PERSON_ID: to any number. (So for example, if my URL was :P2_PERSON_ID:22&cs=, I would change the "22" to another number, such as "31.") Keep the colons in the URL.

10. Submit the URL by pressing ENTER/RETURN on the keyboard.

11. You'll get a checksum error (Figure 10-25), preventing you from editing users via a URL change. Click OK to return to the Edit page.

12. On the Developer toolbar, click the Session link. You can also see that the Item Value for P2_PERSON_ID is encrypted in Session State as shown in Figure 10-26. It is encrypted not only here, but also in the database, preventing anyone with access to the APEX Session table from seeing this value and making this a good option when working with sensitive data.

The checksum computed on the request, clear cache, argument names, and argument values (RP,2P2_PERSON_ID31 [ZyOTNcE7d8rhw5w4MhcMjbtE1EvKyobz2oblsr1 did not match the checksum passed into the show procedure (iKino6IgJW9oQfO7vW8_AV6ATGUHu4DsgrugtG(Note: End users get a different error message.

Contact your application administrator.

FIGURE 10-25. *A checksum error*

Page Items

Application ↑≞	Page	Item Name	Display	Item Value	Status	Encrypted
2286	2	P2_PERSON_ID	Hidden	*****	Inserted	Yes
2286	2	P2_PERSON_BIRTHDAY	Date Picker	17-JAN-1706	Inserted	No
2286	2	P2_PERSON_FULL_NAME	Display Only	Ben Franklin	Inserted	No
2286	2	P2_LAST_VIEWED	Display Only	Oct 30 2016 15:57	Inserted	No
2286	2	P2_PERSON_AGE	Display Only	310 years old	Inserted	No

1 - 5

FIGURE 10-26. *The encrypted Item Value in Session State*

Conditions

As we have authorization schemes on just about every component in APEX, we also have conditions. Conditions don't always have to stem from security; they can also stem from data or page values. Although two conditions deal with whether a user is logged in or not, we have other conditional statements to deal with for a vast range of situations. For example, we can conditionally hide or show fields in a form if a particular language set by the user is not applicable to the data. We can conditionally render items or regions based on an application item value set upon login. We can create custom logic with PL/SQL that will determine what a user sees. And we can even render or run logic if our page submission results in error. Remember that not only can conditions be applied to items, but to PL/SQL processes, cache clearing, columns in reports, regions, or UI elements as well.

Application Context and Views

Back at the beginning of this chapter, we discussed application-level attributes you can set, with one being database context. Database, or application, context lets us store information about a user in a database session so we can refer back to these values at a later time without querying a table. Let's now use this in our application.

To be able to work on the following section, you must have the following GRANT and EXECUTE given to your database user:

```
GRANT CREATE ANY CONTEXT TO SCHEMA;
GRANT EXECUTE ON DBMS_SESSION TO SCHEMA;
```

The SCHEMA should be the database user you are using. In our case, it would be APEX5_BOOK_DEMO, which would make the preceding SQL look like the following:

```
GRANT CREATE ANY CONTEXT TO APEX5_BOOK_DEMO;
GRANT EXECUTE ON DBMS_SESSION TO APEX5_BOOK_DEMO;
```

First stop is the SQL Workshop. We need to create a package we can call to set our application context.

1. In SQL Workshop, click SQL Commands. Enter the following code and click Run. This code creates the specification of our context package.

```
create or replace package context_package as
  procedure set_app_context(p_app_user in varchar2);

  procedure clean_up_context;

end;
```

2. Next, create the body. Delete the specification code in the SQL Commands windows and replace it with the following:

```
create or replace package body context_package as
  procedure set_app_context(p_app_user in varchar2) as
  begin
    sys.dbms_session.set_context(
      namespace => 'my_application_context',
      attribute => 'app_user',
      value     => p_app_user
    );
  end;
  procedure clean_up_context as
  begin
    dbms_session.clear_context('my_application_context');

  end;
end;
```

3. Click Run.

This code will do a few things: First, **set_context** will create a context group or namespace called **my_application_context**. The namespace must be a unique name to this particular database schema. Then, it sets an attribute in the group called **app_user** with the value **p_app_user** that we pass into the procedure.

If in the future, you decide to reuse this package and add your own requirements to it, you can create additional contexts by using the following code outline:

```
sys.dbms_session.set_context(
  namespace => 'my_application_context',
  attribute => 'new_attribute',
  value     => attribute_value
);
```

The **namespace**, or context name, is the one you used in this app; the **attribute** is an attribute you create and name (for example, **user_role**); and the **value** is the value you want the attribute to have. This value can be passed in though the package or derived from a SQL statement run within the package.

Now let's create the context we can use:

1. In the SQL Commands window, delete all previous code and run the following:

```
CREATE CONTEXT my_application_context USING context_package;
```

2. Next, you'll alter a table in the database so that you can use this database context in your application. The following code adds a CREATED_BY column to our PERSONS table. Run the following in an empty SQL Worksheet:

```
ALTER TABLE PERSONS_TABLE
ADD (CREATED_BY VARCHAR2(100));
```

3. Now fill that column with your main user's name. Run the following in the SQL Worksheet:

```
UPDATE PERSONS_TABLE SET CREATED_BY = 'XXXX';
```

The **XXXX** is the main user you have been using. For example, if the user was Brian, the code would look like this:

```
UPDATE PERSONS_TABLE SET CREATED_BY = 'BRIAN';
```

4. The final SQL you need to run will create a VIEW that uses this context. Run the following SQL in the SQL Worksheet:

```
create or replace view PERSONS_VIEW as
select person_id, person_type, person_prefix,
       person_first_name, person_middle_name,
       person_last_name, person_birthday,
       person_picture, person_notes
  from persons_table
 where upper(created_by) =
   upper(sys_context('my_application_context','app_user'));
```

This code creates a database view for us and will show only data for which the **created_by** is the person logged into the application.

5. After running the preceding SQL, go back to the App Builder and find your contacts app. Click the app and then click the Edit Application Properties button at the upper right.

6. Click the Security Sub tab. At the bottom of the page, in the Database Session section, in the Initialization PL/SQL Code section, enter the following code:

```
context_package.set_app_context(:APP_USER);
```

This code will call your context creation package and pass it the value **:APP_USER**. The variable **:APP_USER** is a session level item APEX stores the username for a person who is logged in.

7. Now for the Cleanup PL/SQL Code section, enter the following code:

```
context_package.clean_up_context;
```

Your Database Session section should look similar to Figure 10-27.

8. The second set of code cleans up your context session. When it's done, click the Apply Changes button.

You can now reference the context in the database on a per-session basis. To try this out, let's go again to your My Contacts home page (Page 1).

1. Edit the page in Page Designer and click the My Contacts report region in the Rendering panel on the left.

FIGURE 10-27. *Setting database context*

2. In the Properties panel on the right, find the SQL Query property under the Source property group. Change the SQL in that region to the following:

```
SELECT
    "PERSONS_VIEW"."PERSON_ID" "PERSON_ID",
    "PERSONS_VIEW"."PERSON_TYPE" "PERSON_TYPE",
    "PERSONS_VIEW"."PERSON_PREFIX" "PERSON_PREFIX",
    "PERSONS_VIEW"."PERSON_FIRST_NAME" "PERSON_FIRST_NAME",
    "PERSONS_VIEW"."PERSON_MIDDLE_NAME" "PERSON_MIDDLE_NAME",
    "PERSONS_VIEW"."PERSON_LAST_NAME" "PERSON_LAST_NAME",
    "PERSONS_VIEW"."PERSON_BIRTHDAY" "PERSON_BIRTHDAY",
    "PERSONS_VIEW"."PERSON_NOTES" "PERSON_NOTES"
FROM
    "PERSONS_VIEW"
```

3. Save your changes and run the page. You should see all the contacts you have in the database because you ran the SQL to set the logged in user as the **created_by**.

4. Log out and log in as user Annie. You see the same page, but with no data. The Application Context is set upon login and the view uses it to fetch the data. Annie is not in the CREATED_BY column, so the viewer cannot see any data, as shown in Figure 10-28.

To complete this change over to a multitenant application, you need to fix a few things. On all pages that used PERSONS_TABLE, you need to change it to PERSONS_VIEW. Don't remember where we used it? APEX has you covered.

1. In the Page Designer, in the upper right, click or mouse over the magnifying glass icon to open application search.

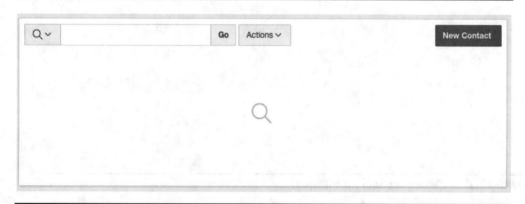

FIGURE 10-28. *Application Context prevents users from seeing other users' data*

2. Enter **PERSONS_TABLE** and press ENTER on your keyboard.

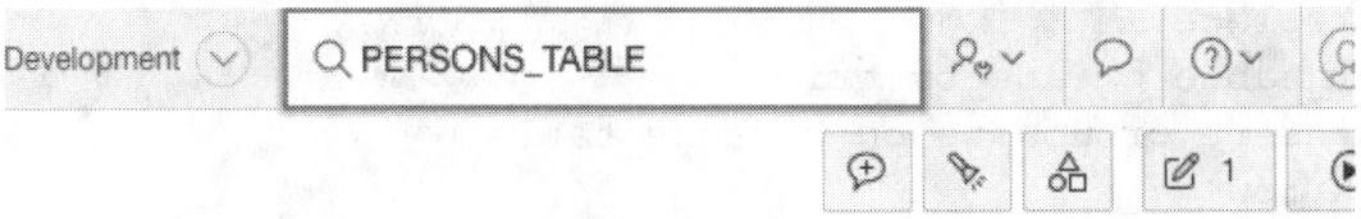

The next report (Figure 10-29) will show you all the places in the application where you used PERSONS_TABLE. Note that this search will also look into scripts you may have loaded into the application. Also remember that you do not need to replace occurrences of the PERSONS_TABLE in row processing. You will still be inserting into the base PERSONS_TABLE and not the secured view. With that said, you could use the new view on row fetches to prevent SQL injections.

The last change needs to be on the PERSONS_TABLE. You need to automatically enter the user's name into the CREATED_BY column. Easy enough—you can use a trigger for that:

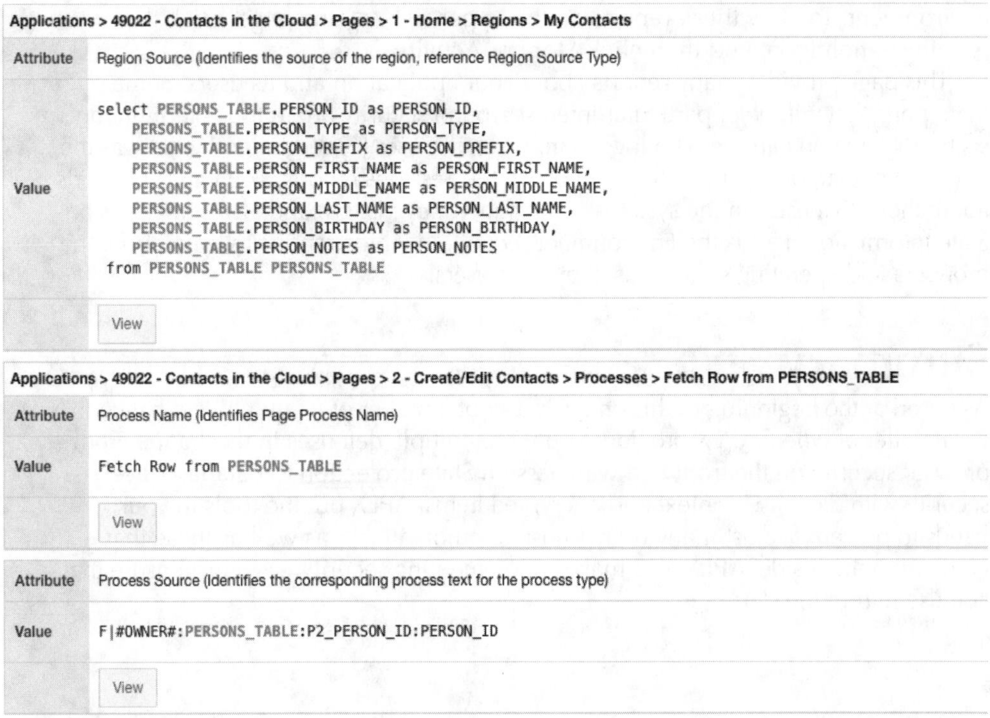

Applications > 49022 - Contacts in the Cloud > Pages > 1 - Home > Regions > My Contacts

Attribute	Region Source (Identifies the source of the region, reference Region Source Type)

Value	select PERSONS_TABLE.PERSON_ID as PERSON_ID,
	    PERSONS_TABLE.PERSON_TYPE as PERSON_TYPE,
	    PERSONS_TABLE.PERSON_PREFIX as PERSON_PREFIX,
	    PERSONS_TABLE.PERSON_FIRST_NAME as PERSON_FIRST_NAME,
	    PERSONS_TABLE.PERSON_MIDDLE_NAME as PERSON_MIDDLE_NAME,
	    PERSONS_TABLE.PERSON_LAST_NAME as PERSON_LAST_NAME,
	    PERSONS_TABLE.PERSON_BIRTHDAY as PERSON_BIRTHDAY,
	    PERSONS_TABLE.PERSON_NOTES as PERSON_NOTES
	  from PERSONS_TABLE PERSONS_TABLE

View

Applications > 49022 - Contacts in the Cloud > Pages > 2 - Create/Edit Contacts > Processes > Fetch Row from PERSONS_TABLE

Attribute	Process Name (Identifies Page Process Name)
Value	Fetch Row from PERSONS_TABLE

View

Attribute	Process Source (Identifies the corresponding process text for the process type)
Value	F|#OWNER#:PERSONS_TABLE:P2_PERSON_ID:PERSON_ID

View

FIGURE 10-29. *The results of an application search on PERSONS_TABLE*

In the SQL Workshop tab, run the following code in the SQL Commands page:

```
create or replace
trigger per_table_create_by_trig
    before insert or update on persons_table
    for each row
begin
    if :new.created_by is null then
        :new.created_by := upper(sys_context('my_application_
context','app_user'));
    end if;
end;
```

To test this, create a contact with another user. Then look at the table in the Object Browser in the SQL Workshop, and look in the new column for the user's name or log in as another user, to check to see if you can see that contact.

Security Reporting

APEX contains some prebuilt reporting for you to view about the security of your environment. To view these reports, at the upper right of any page, click the Administration icon, and then click Monitor Activity.

This page provides many reports about your application and its users. Some of the reports that will be of particular interest around security are in the Login Attempts section. Here you can see who logged in, when the user logged in, and what was the outcome of that login. Above that section, in the Sessions reports, you can see reports about the active users in the systems, what pages they visited, and also some Session State information. Last is the Environment section, in which reports tell you about the browsers and operating systems used by your users.

Summary

As stated at the beginning of this chapter, it's not a matter of *if* you will get hacked; it's a matter of *when*. APEX provides you with multiple defenses in this battle. From browser security on the front end with Session State protection to database-level security with database context and encrypted items, APEX put the tools in your hands to prevent against many of the most common attacks as well as those that come from the inside. APEX also makes implementing security easy; just ensure that you use it from the start.

CHAPTER
11

Packaging and Deployment

M oving a complete application from one environment to another is a challenge in itself, let alone moving individual application components. Moving an application from development, to user acceptance testing, to production, is not always an easy process. APEX gives you the ability to bundle all your components together quickly and move them from environment to environment, bringing along the database objects and application components seamlessly.

Packaging Overview

An APEX application can consist of many components: the application code, the database objects (tables, triggers, sequences, and so on), and even static files such as custom images or CSS files. When moving your applications to another environment, you have to consider whether you need to move these components as well.

When moving your application, you'll deal with the following three main deployment scenarios, in order of complexity:

- Copying your application in the same workspace

- Moving to a new workspace that uses the same schema

- Moving to a new workspace that uses a different schema

The complexity stems from which objects you need to move with your application. APEX enables you to create a packaged application—a bundle that contains not only the application, but the database objects and related application files needed for the application to run.

Packaged Applications

In many application development environments, the usual steps involved in moving or installing an application are

1. Run multiple SQL scripts to create the database objects.

2. Import all the needed libraries and archive files.

3. Install the application.

Packaged applications, however, contain the application itself as well as all the database objects needed, all of which can be installed into your APEX environment in one easy step.

Supporting Objects

The Supporting Objects utility combines all the database object scripts you would use into a single step that's performed during an application installation. To get to

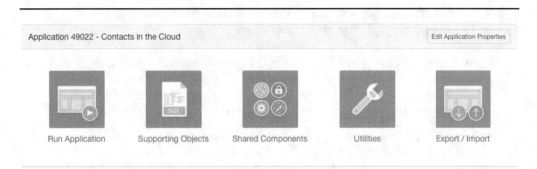

Application 49022 - Contacts in the Cloud   Edit Application Properties

Run Application   Supporting Objects   Shared Components   Utilities   Export / Import

FIGURE 11-1. *Click the Supporting Objects icon to launch the utility.*

the utility, go to your applications details page in the App Builder and click the
Supporting Objects icon on the upper icon row (Figure 11-1).

On the first page, in the Supporting Objects region (Figure 11-2) is a summary of
all the supporting objects this application contains (if any), how much space is
needed for this install, whether license text is used, and a check for system privileges
upon install. Supporting Objects are much more than DDL scripts.

The following sections will examine the subtabs within the Supporting
Objects pages:

Messages   **Prerequisites**   Substitutions   Build Options   Validations   Install   Upgrade   Deinstall   Export

Messages   In the Messages section, you can define custom (or keep the default)
messages for each step of the install process, as well as licensing, welcome,
upgrade, and deinstallation messages. If you do not have a specific component in

---

Supporting Objects

Use this utility to define the database object definitions, images, and seed data to be included in your application export.

Application:	**1420: Contacts in the Cloud** ⑦	Check for Objects:	**No** ⑦
Verify System Privileges:	**No** ⑦	Required Free KB:	**0** ⑦
Prompt for License:	**No** ⑦	Include in Export:	**Yes** ⑦

FIGURE 11-2. *The Supporting Objects region*

your supporting objects, this step will be skipped and the message will not be shown. You can define the following types of messages:

■ **Welcome** This message is shown after the application is installed and just before supporting objects are installed. Use this message to tell the user what is going to happen, what checks are done, or any important information you need to convey before the supporting objects are installed.

■ **License** Use this message to prompt the user to accept or decline a licensing agreement.

■ **Application Substitutions** This message is displayed above the application substitutions.

■ **Build Options** This message is displayed above the build option prompts step of the install.

■ **Validations** This message is displayed above the validations step of the supporting objects install. A good use of this message is to go over all the validations you have set up for your supporting objects just in case the install fails or the installer is missing a critical component.

■ **Confirmation** This message is shown just before the supporting objects are installed.

■ **Post Installation** This is two messages—a success message and a failure message. Use the failure message to help guide the user to a quick resolution. Include things to check in their environment and perhaps contact information.

The Upgrade Message section has four messages to set. Use these message areas to help describe to the installer what is happening on a particular step, what validations will take place and how to deal with them, as well as troubleshooting tips for issues that may arise.

■ **Upgrade Welcome Message** This message tells the user that supporting objects have been discovered that can be upgraded and prepares them for the upgrade process.

■ **Upgrade Confirmation Message** Similar to the install confirmation message, this message is shown just before the install occurs.

■ **Upgrade Success/Failure Message** These messages will be shown after the upgrade takes place. Use the failure message to suggest resolutions or provide contact information.

- **Deinstallation** Here we have two messages—a Deinstall Message and a Post-Deinstall Message. Use the Deinstall Message to prepare the user for the deinstall and the Post-Deinstall Message when the deinstall is completed. You may want to remind the user that any data in the table that is to be dropped will be lost, so back up the data if necessary.

Prerequisites On the Prerequisites page, you can define how much space you think your application will need. When installing your application, the parsing schema's default tablespace is checked to see if the space is available or not.

In the Required System Privileges section, you can select which database system privileges are needed to install your application.

In the Objects That Will Be Installed section, select the objects whose existence will be validated before you install your application. If any of these objects exist when the prerequisite check occurs, the installation will stop and present an error to the user, as shown in Figure 11-3.

To add an object, click the pop-up LOV icon to see a list of all the objects in your schema, with the objects type in parentheses. Select an item and you are returned to the main page. Click the Add button to add the item to the lower object area. To remove objects, select one or more objects in the lower area and click Remove.

Creating checks to ensure that all the required objects and tables do not already exist is a good practice to follow. This will prevent tables or other database objects

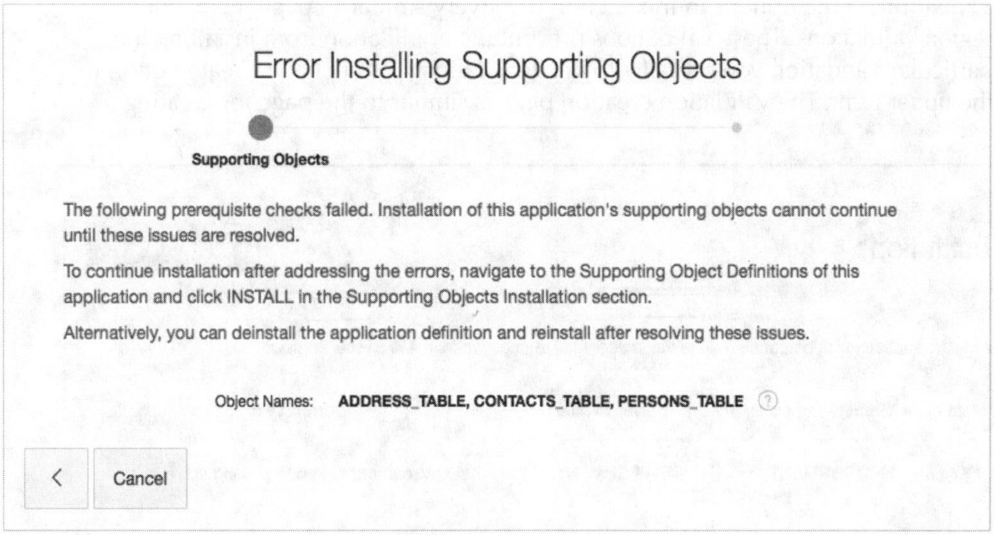

Error Installing Supporting Objects

Supporting Objects

The following prerequisite checks failed. Installation of this application's supporting objects cannot continue until these issues are resolved.

To continue installation after addressing the errors, navigate to the Supporting Object Definitions of this application and click INSTALL in the Supporting Objects Installation section.

Alternatively, you can deinstall the application definition and reinstall after resolving these issues.

Object Names: **ADDRESS_TABLE, CONTACTS_TABLE, PERSONS_TABLE**

< Cancel

FIGURE 11-3. *Failing a prerequisite check*

from being overwritten and critical data from being lost. It also prevents the users from facing ugly errors on application installation that may be cryptic or confusing.

Substitutions   In the Substitutions page (Figure 11-4), you can enable the user to change or keep application-level substitution strings. This page will be displayed to the user at install with a prompt text message you define, either to keep the existing value or change it. When installing the application, a step in the install wizard will present the user with this prompt if chosen and with the ability to change the substitution text or leave the default value. To ensure the user is prompted, be sure the Prompt? checkbox is checked.

Here's an example: Suppose you had a substitution string in your application with a server or environment name or an environment type (Development/User Acceptance Testing/Production). Upon install, you could change that name on this step (Figure 11-5). As a reminder, substitution strings can be created and maintained on the Edit Application Definition page on the Shared Components page, or by clicking the Edit Application Definition button on the main application details page. Once on the Edit Application Definition page, click the Substitutions subtab or scroll down to that section.

Build Options   The Build Options page displays all the build options you have defined for this application. By selecting the Prompt checkbox, you can have the installing user decide whether she wants to retain the build option's settings or leave the default setting. Build options are examined later in this chapter.

Validations   The options in this section work very similar to page, item, and region validations. These validations prevent the application from installing if a particular validation you set fails. To create a validation, click the Create button in the upper right. The validation creation page is similar to the page for creating a

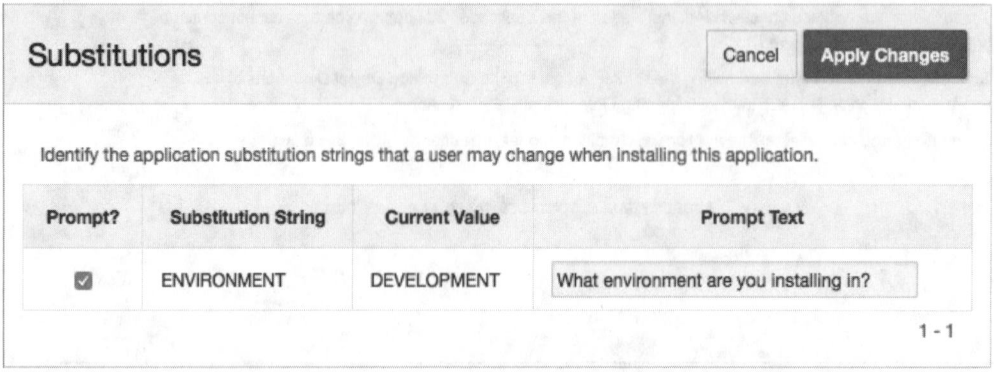

Prompt?	Substitution String	Current Value	Prompt Text
☑	ENVIRONMENT	DEVELOPMENT	What environment are you installing in?

1 - 1

FIGURE 11-4.   *The substitution strings supporting objects page*

FIGURE 11-5. *The substitution strings change prompt*

validation in our application, with a few changes. In the Validation Type dropdown list, you can see a few new values, validations dealing with CGI_ENV variables. The CGI_ENV variables, or Common Gateway Interface Environment variables, are a series of hidden values that the web server sends to every CGI program you run. The ones available to use in validations are DAD_NAME, HOST_NAME, and SERVER_NAME. A good example of using the CGI_ENV variables is to check the SERVER_NAME upon install to ensure this is being installed into the correct environment, preventing production apps from being overwritten by accident. When you're done looking around here, click the Cancel button.

Install   This is the meat of your supporting objects. Click the Install subtab to open the Installation Scripts page. Here you define what database objects to take when exporting your application.

1. Click the Create button in the upper right to launch the Create Script wizard.

2. The first step of the wizard asks you to choose your method for the script creation, as shown in Figure 11-6.

   ■ **Create From Scratch**   Click this option to be prompted to name the file. Then, on the last page of the wizard, you'll see a code canvas to create your SQL code, where you can copy and paste code from SQL Developer or another tool.

- **Create From File** Click this option to name the script and then upload the script with your code in it. Again, you can create a script in SQL Developer or in SQL Developer Data Modeler.

- **Create From Database Object** Click on this option to launch the Script Attributes step of the wizard. Enter a name in the Name field. Then enter a sequence number if you want to have scripts run in a sequence or specified order. Finally, the wizard asks for the database object types you want to use in your install scripts. Highlight the object types you want to move, and then click Next to move onto the third step of the wizard. (Quick note here: This object list is a multi-select list, so you can select one or many database object types in the list (CONTROL/COMMAND-click or SHIFT-click to add several objects). If you want to have one jumbo install script, select all the objects. If you want to separate out your scripts into a table script, a package script, and so on, select one object at a time per script—you can see how sequence numbering works.)

3. On the third step of the wizard, you'll see a shuttle, where you can move any object from the types you selected on the previous page, from the left

to the right. All objects on the right of the shuttle will be included in the created install script. Use the Filter text field to find the exact script(s) you are looking for. Type in the text field and press RETURN/ENTER to filter the results. If you selected only table object types in the previous step, you will see a checkbox, Include DDL Related To Tables. Check this checkbox if you want all the DLL associated with this table, such as triggers and indexes, to be present in the created script.

4. Once you have selected all the objects you want to use in your install script, click the Next button. The final page is the script itself, with all the code for the objects pregenerated for you. Look over the script and click the Create button to add it to your supporting objects.

Database objects may change over time, requiring you to upload new scripts or change the scripts by hand. If you choose the Create From Database Object option, you can use the Refresh Checked button to re-create the scripts, taking up any database object changes automatically. Click the checkbox on a script's row, and then click the Refresh Checked button:

On the Installation Scripts page, you can run a few tasks to help check the health and order of your support objects:

- **Install Supporting Objects**   Runs you through actually installing the objects in your database to check for errors.

- **Upgrade Supporting Objects**   Runs you through your upgrade scripts, just as Deinstall Application guides you through your deinstallation scripts.

- **Edit Application**   Brings you back to your applications details page

- **View And Download Single Script**   Concatenates all your scripts into a single file you can edit or download.

■ **Resequence Scripts** Resequences the installation scripts, changing the numbers into multiples of 10, as shown next:

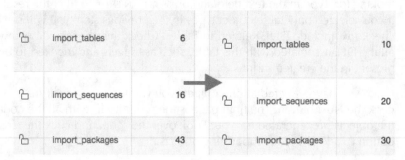

Upgrade The options on the Upgrade page are similar to those for creating install scripts, with a new region on the first page, Query To Detect Existing Supporting Objects. The query should determine whether the supporting objects already exist and need to be upgraded. If the query returns a row, the upgrade scripts will be run. When creating the upgrade script, you have two options: Create From Scratch and Create From File.

Deinstall On the Deinstall page, you can create a deinstall script that will be run when a user selects to remove the application from his workspace. This script will drop all the database objects you defined in its creation. When creating the deinstall script, you can choose from Create From Scratch and Create From File.

Export On the Export page, you can define whether the supporting objects will be exported by default when exporting your application. You have three choices here:

■ **No** Does not include the supporting object definitions in the export.

■ **Yes** Includes supporting object definitions in the application export.

■ **Yes And Install On Import Automatically** Includes the supporting object definitions in the export as well as a call to install them. (Note that this option is valid only for command line installs and will install or upgrade your supporting objects automatically.)

Supporting Objects Tasks
Back on the Supporting Objects main or summary page are a few tasks you can perform directly.

■ **View Install Summary** This task shows a list of all the scripts you have with your application's supporting objects.

- **Export Application**   This task is a shortcut to the export page. This page can be also found on the application details main page, Export / Import icon.

- **Install Supporting Objects, Upgrade Supporting Objects, and Deinstall Supporting Objects**   These tasks enable you to run your scripts in your environment for testing and error checking. (Note that some of these tasks will be present only when a particular supporting object is present. For example, you will not see the Deinstall Supporting Objects task unless there is a deinstall script.)

- **Remove All Supporting Objects**   This task removes all scripts, messages, and options associated with your application.

Application Exports

The application export is the basis for moving your application to another environment, workspace, or archive. As stated in the beginning of this chapter, the three common deployment scenarios are

- Copying your application in the same workspace

- Moving to a new workspace that uses the same schema

- Moving to a new workspace that uses a different schema

Copy Your Application in the Same Workspace

If you are copying the application in the same workspace and using the same schema, your job is quite simple—in fact, APEX can do this for you.

To copy an application, in the App Builder, follow these steps:

1. On the applications details page (use the breadcrumbs in the upper-left to navigate there), under Tasks, click Copy This Application to launch the Copy Application Modal wizard. This two-page wizard first asks you to select a New Application ID and a New Application Name. Changing the name is not required, but you do have to change the application ID.

2. The last option is Copy Supporting Object Definitions. If you want to retain all of your supporting objects' install/upgrade/deinstall scripts, choose Yes. (Note that setting this to Yes and copying the application will not run the install scripts. You are copying the application and supporting object definitions, configuration options, and scripts, not installing them.)

3. Click Next to open a summary page. Review the values and click Copy Application. APEX will copy your application and display the Application Details page for the new app, as indicated by the new application number on the upper left.

Move to a New Workspace that Uses the Same or a Different Schema

Export / Import

Moving our application to a new workspace that uses the same or different schema is a similar process, with only a slight difference—the supporting objects.

First, export the application. On the main applications detail page, click the icon for Export / Import to start the wizard.

The wizard asks if you want to import or export: click the Export icon. The next page defines how you export this application and offers some options you can choose upon export. In the first section of the Export Application page, click the dropdown select list to see all the other applications in the workspace. The wizard should default to the application you chose to export.

In the Export Application section, the first three attributes are informational: your Selected Application name, how many pages are in the application (Page Count) and the database schema Owner.

For the File Format attribute, choose DOS, UNIX, or Database. Choose DOS and the lines in the file will be terminated by carriage returns and line feeds. Choose UNIX and the lines in the file are terminated by line feeds. Choose Database to save the export to the APEX Export Repository rather than downloading it immediately. You can download it at a later time from the Export Repository if needed.

For Owner Override, you can define a different database schema owner upon export.

Build Status Override lets you lock down your application with two settings:

- **Run And Build Application**   Select this option to, upon install, have the application available to use and continue to develop. You will see the Edit and Run icon on the application developer page.

- **Run Application Only**   This option will export the application in runtime only mode. When installing, you will not be able to edit this application unless an administrator changes the status to Run And Build Application.

Options for the Debugging attribute are On or Off. Setting this to Off in a production environment will prevent users from seeing application logic and debug information. This should be kept to On in development environments.

The As Of attribute enables you to export the application as it looked in the past. This attribute specifies the number of minutes in the past APEX should go. This utility uses the dbms_flashback package and has a default flashback time of 3 hours (defined by the **undo_retention** database parameter).

Last in the section is File Character Set, which is informational and usually the character set of the database. You can see all these options in Figure 11-7.

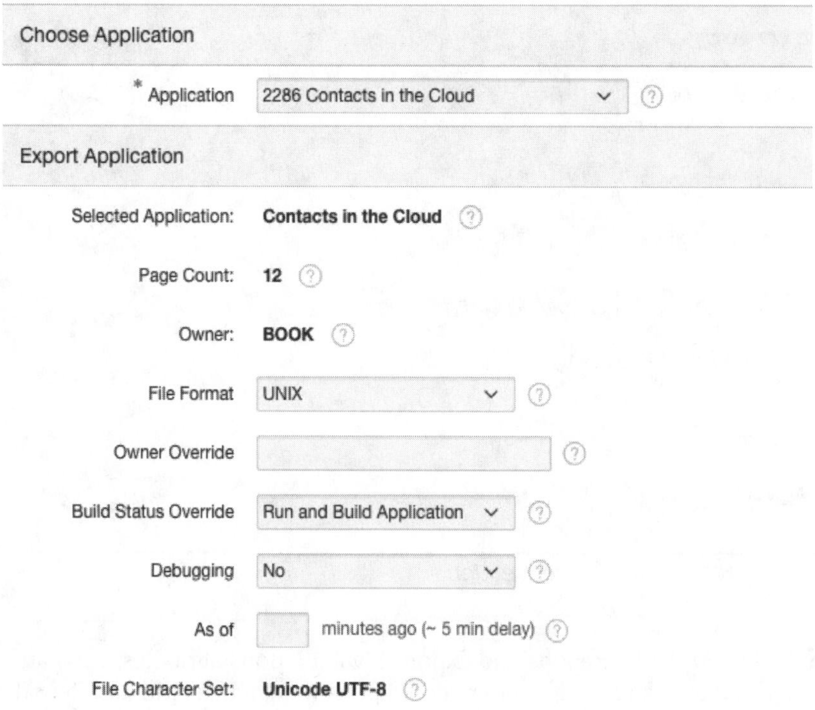

Choose Application

* Application   [2286 Contacts in the Cloud   ⌄] (?)

Export Application

Selected Application: **Contacts in the Cloud** (?)

Page Count: **12** (?)

Owner: **BOOK** (?)

File Format   [UNIX   ⌄] (?)

Owner Override   [   ] (?)

Build Status Override   [Run and Build Application ⌄] (?)

Debugging   [No   ⌄] (?)

As of   [   ] minutes ago (~ 5 min delay) (?)

File Character Set: **Unicode UTF-8** (?)

FIGURE 11-7.   *The Export Application section*

The next section on this page is Export Preferences (Figure 11-8). For Export Supporting Object Definitions, the three values are Yes, No, and Yes And Install On Import Automatically.

- **No**   Does not include the supporting object definitions in the export. This is best for when moving within the same workspace, especially if your Supporting Object scripts have prerequisite checks.

- **Yes**   Includes supporting object definitions in the application export. When installing from a command line (SQLPlus) this does not automatically load supporting objects.

- **Yes And Install On Import Automatically**   Includes supporting object definitions and a call to install supporting objects in the application export. This option is best used for command line installs because when run, it automatically installs or upgrades the supporting objects.

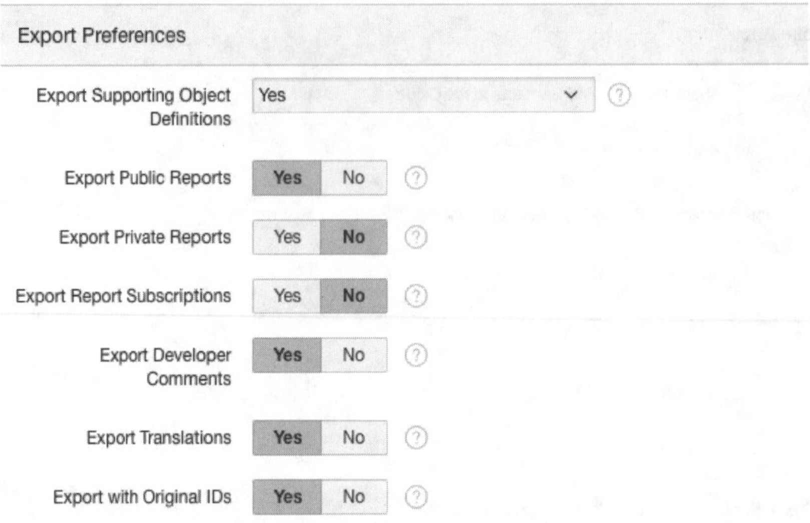

FIGURE 11-8. *The Export Preferences section*

With the Export Public Reports and Export Private Reports attributes, you can export all user-created and developer-created reports (Interactive Grid and Reports), preserving the user's work in customizing a report to their exact specifications. You can also export a user's Report Subscriptions, retaining the frequency the user receive the report via e-mail.

For the Export Developer Comments attribute, depending on where the developers are entering comments, you can choose to include or exclude these comments on export.

The Export Translations attribute will preserve all translation mappings and all text from the Translation Repository if set to Yes.

The last attribute, Export With Original IDs, will preserve the component IDs so that a developer can spot changes in two export files without the component IDs showing as file changes when comparing files in, say, a text editor.

When you are satisfied with your choices on this page, click the Export button at the upper right. If you chose DOS or UNIX as the File Format, you should see a browser-download dialog asking where you would like to save the file (or if your browser is set to automatically download to the downloads folder, check there). The filename format of an APEX export is f#APP_NUMBER#.sql, so, for example, if I exported application 123, the file would be named f123.sql. Of note on this page, next to the Export button is the Reset button. Clicking the Reset button will change all the attributes on this page to their default values.

Application Import/Export Strategies

When exporting or importing your application, APEX gives you some options to restrict what is exported and to gain full control on how you import our applications.

Exporting Components

There are times when you might want to export a single application component or a group of application components without exporting your entire application. Here's how to do this:

1. Navigate to the Shared Components page for your application.

2. On the right side, under Tasks, click Export Application Components to open the Component Export wizard.

3. Select one or many individual components of your application to export to file (Figure 11-9).

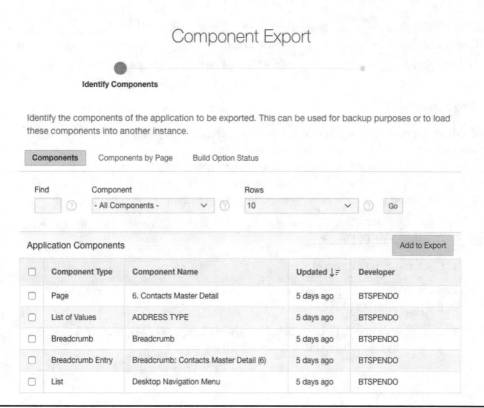

FIGURE 11-9. *Component Export page*

At the top of the report section are three subtabs to help you find your components for a report:

- **Components**   Filter by name or type.

- **Components By Page**   Find a component on a particular page.

- **Build Option Status**   See all the components with build options attached to them.

You can export the following component types on an individual level:

Application Computation	Application Item	Application Process
Authentication Scheme	Authorization Scheme	Breadcrumb
Breadcrumb Entry	Breadcrumb Template	Build Option
Button Template	Calendar Template	Data Loading
Label Template	List	List Template
List of Values	Navigation Bar Entry	Page
Page Template	Parent Tab	Plug-in
Popup List of Values Template	Region Template	Report Layout
Report Query	Report Template	Shortcut
Tab	Text Message	Tree
Web Service		

Just about every piece of your application can be exported and reused in another application, workspace, or environment.

Once you find the components you want to export,

1. Select the checkbox next to the component's/components' name.

2. Click Add To Export. This creates a report on the bottom of the page called Components To Export.

3. Click the Next button.

4. As with an application export, you can choose a File Format and a point in the past with As Of.

5. Once the options are set, click the Export Components button to download a file in the format f#APP_ID#_components.sql.

Exporting and importing components are helpful when your application is in multiple environments and you need to update or move a small portion, such as a page or list of values.

NOTE
Component exports cannot be installed into applications with different IDs.

Build Options

On the application details main page, click the Shared Components icon. On the next page, you'll see Build Options listed in the Security section. Build options act similarly to conditions on application components, enabling or disabling functionality. Build options also have a trick up their sleeves: you can use them to restrict components from being included in your exports—perfect for that experimental functionality that's just not ready for prime time.

Let's create a build option.

1. Click Build Options:

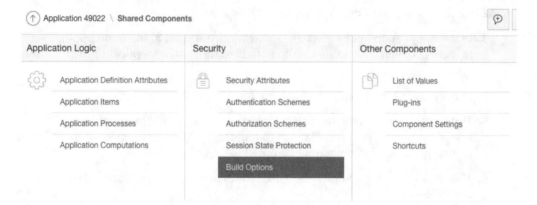

On the Build Option page (Figure 11-10), you'll see that a report has been created that includes all existing build options in your application (which would be a blank report if you have no build options defined). You'll also see two subreport tabs: the Utilization subreport shows where build options are being used, and the History subreport shows recent changes made to your build options.

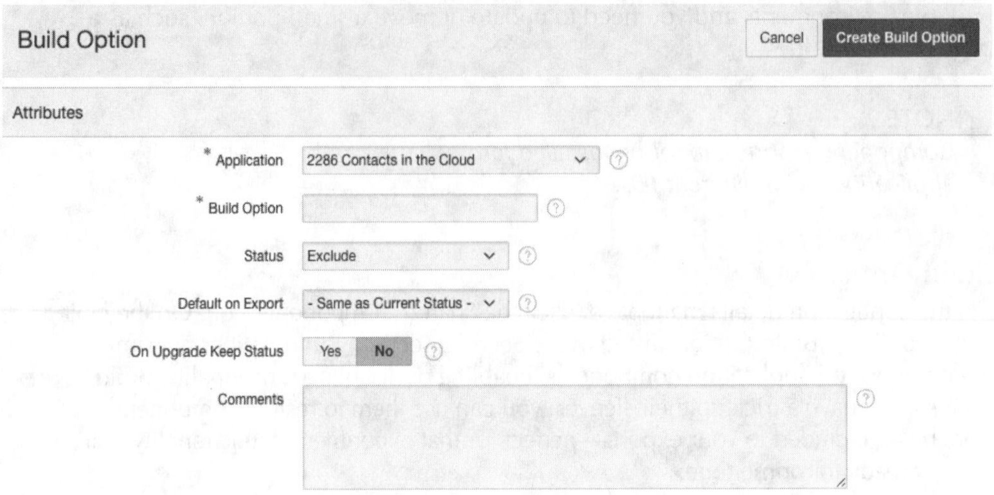

FIGURE 11-10. *Build Option page*

2. Click Create Build Option at the upper right.

3. In the Application field, select the application you want to the build option to associate with. This value should default to the current application you are working with.

4. In the Build Option field, enter a name for the Build Option.

5. The Status field has options: Select Include to indicate that this component or feature is used, or select Exclude to indicate that this component or feature is not used in your application.

6. The Default On Export attribute is used for exporting the application. There are three options:

   ■ **Include** This component or functionality will be included with the application export.

   ■ **Exclude** This component or functionality will not be included with the application export.

   ■ **Same As Current Status** This option defaults to the value in the Status attribute.

7. Use the On Upgrade Keep Status toggle switch to keep the build status or overwrite it when upgrading the application. Click Yes to keep the current application status if the application supports build option configuration via the APEX_UTIL APIs to enable or disable the build option, and where you want to respect those settings upon an application upgrade.

8. In the Comments field, add comments to describe this build option.

You can see how build options can be useful in hiding components or functionalities that are still under development without exposing them or exporting them to your final application.

Importing an Application or Component

To import an application or component, start from the main page of the App Builder. Click the App Builder tab on the top of the page.

1. Click the Import icon, shown here, to open the Import wizard.

Import

2. On the first page of the Import wizard (Figure 11-11), click the Import File button and choose an application file to import from your local computer. (For the next few steps, use an export from any application. We will not actually import the application, but needed it to progress through the wizard steps.)

3. For File or Export type, choose the first option: Database Application, Page Or Component Export.

4. For File Character Set, choose the character set encoding of the file to be imported. Then click Next.

5. The import file will be uploaded into the export repository, and you'll see the next step of the Import wizard: File Import Confirmation. Here you will be notified if the file uploaded successfully and given the option to perform some tasks. At the bottom of this page is an expandable Tasks region (Figure 11-12).

Import

Select the file you wish to import to the export repository. Once imported, you can install your file.

If the imported file is a packaged application export, the installation wizard will allow you to run the packaged installation scripts after installing the application definition.

* Import file   [Choose File] No file chosen   ⑦

* File Type: ● **Database Application, Page or Component Export** ⑦
     ○ Websheet Application Export
     ○ Plug-in
     ○ Theme Export
     ○ User Interface Defaults
     ○ Team Development Feedback
     ○ CSS Export [Deprecated]
     ○ Image Export [Deprecated]
     ○ File Export [Deprecated]

File Character Set   [Unicode UTF-8   ⌄] ⑦

FIGURE 11-11. *Import wizard*

Import

File Import Confirmation

The export file has been imported successfully.

If you wish to install now, click the **Next** button. You can also install this file at a later time by navigating to the Export Repository.

⌄ **Tasks**

Manage Export Repository   ›

Preview File   ›

FIGURE 11-12. *Import file tasks*

6. Click Manage Export Repository to leave the wizard and move to the Export Repository, where you can manage your application and component exports. Click Preview File to open a window where you can view the contents of your application or component export.

7. Click the Next button at the bottom of the page to go to the next step.

8. The last step of our application import is an Install Summary, as well as a chance to change the Parsing Schema, the Build Status, and the Application ID number:

   ■ Change the Parsing Schema to move the application to another schema in the database as well as set the new owner of the application.

   ■ Use the Build Status to restrict editing of this application. Set it to Run Application Only to prevent the developer toolbar from showing when you run the application as a developer or to prevent editing the application with the Page Designer. Set it to Run And Build Application allows you to edit the application as a developer. Install As Application has three options: Auto Assign New Application ID (let APEX decide the application ID), Reuse Application ID From Export File (retain the original ID), and Change Application ID (a text field to enter an application ID yourself).

   Whether you change the application ID or use an existing one, upon install, APEX will double-check to ensure that an application with that ID does not already exist in this workspace. If an existing application does have this ID, you will be prompted to change it before you can continue the installation.

9. Click the Install Application button at the bottom on the page.

10. If your application has supporting objects, the Install Application wizard will start with an option, Install Supporting Objects. You can also see on this page the size of the application you set on the supporting objects pages previously in this chapter. Choose Yes to Install Supporting Objects and click the Next button.

11. If any Substitutions were defined on the supporting objects page, the Application Substitutions step of the wizard enables you to change the values. After you have changed any values, click the Next button.

12. On the Confirmation page of the wizard, you can view the scripts to be run for supporting the object install. Open the Tasks dropdown and click Preview Installation Script.

13. In the preview script summary, you can scroll through the script names, the required database roles, and the code itself. Part of the preview is shown next. Click the Install button to start the process.

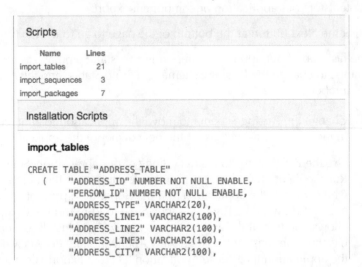

```
Scripts

        Name        Lines
import_tables        21
import_sequences      3
import_packages       7

Installation Scripts

import_tables

CREATE TABLE "ADDRESS_TABLE"
   (    "ADDRESS_ID" NUMBER NOT NULL ENABLE,
        "PERSON_ID" NUMBER NOT NULL ENABLE,
        "ADDRESS_TYPE" VARCHAR2(20),
        "ADDRESS_LINE1" VARCHAR2(100),
        "ADDRESS_LINE2" VARCHAR2(100),
        "ADDRESS_LINE3" VARCHAR2(100),
        "ADDRESS_CITY" VARCHAR2(100),
```

14. If your install fails, the following page will state, "Installation of database objects and seed data has failed" in an alert region. You can see what happened when the script ran by clicking the Install Summary button. The Install Summary page will break down your scripts and errors and show you the errors encountered at each step of your supporting object scripts:

```
ORA-02275: such a referential constraint already exists in the table
```

```
import_sequences

CREATE SEQUENCE  "PERSONS_SEQ"  MINVALUE 1 MAXVALUE 9999999999999999999999999999

ORA-00955: name is already used by an existing object
```

On the right side of the Install Summary page are some tasks. Of importance to this step of the install is the Edit Installation Scripts task. Here you can directly link to the supporting objects install scripts page, where you can modify your install scripts and rerun them.

15. If your supporting objects installed successfully, you will see the message, "Your application's supporting objects have been installed." Click the Install Summary button to see how the scripts ran, or just run or edit your application.

Install Application

Your application's supporting objects have been installed.

Other Import File Types

Several other import file types are available:

- **Websheet Application Export** Import websheet applications, which are exported and imported in the same manner as database applications.
- **Plug-in** Import plug-ins created by you or from third parties.
- **Theme Export** Export and share themes. Can also be used to import themes created by third parties.
- **User Interface Defaults** Keep your user interface defaults in sync by exporting and importing them into all your environments.
- **Team Development Feedback** Export and import all the feedback collected in team development between environments.

Summary

In our application development life cycles, we have to move code constantly, fix bugs, and create and replace database objects. APEX makes this process easy and straightforward by providing multiple point-and-click tools. The import/export utilities for moving applications across environments provide users with the ability to control exactly what is being packaged in the application. Supporting objects has us covered on the database side to ensure a smooth application install, with the ability to create install, upgrade, and deinstall scripts; prerequisite checks; and validations. We can also define messages to guide and provide help to users if issues occur during the import process. All these components create an environment that sets up users for successful and easy application migrations.

Index

B

Join the Largest Tech Community in the World

 Download the latest software, tools, and developer templates

 Get exclusive access to hands-on trainings and workshops

 Grow your professional network through the Oracle ACE Program

 Publish your technical articles – and get paid to share your expertise

Join the Oracle Technology Network
Membership is free. Visit community.oracle.com

@OracleOTN   facebook.com/OracleTechnologyNetwork

Climb the Career Ladder

Think about it—97 percent of the Fortune 500 companies run Oracle solutions. Why wouldn't you choose Oracle certification to secure your future? With certification through Oracle, your resume gets noticed, your chances of landing your dream job improve, you become more marketable, and you earn more money. It's simple. Oracle certification helps you get hired and get paid for your skills.

93% Hiring managers who say IT certifications are beneficial and provide value to the company[1]

7% Salary growth for Oracle Certified professionals[5]

70% Believe that Oracle certification improved their earning power[2]

90% Say that Oracle certification gives them credibility when looking for a new job[2]

68% Think that certification has made them more in demand[3]

6x Increased LinkedIn profile views for people with certifications, boosting their visibility and career opportunities[4]

Take the next step
http://education.oracle.com/certification/press

[1] "Value of IT Certifications," CompTIA, October 14, 2014, [2] Oracle Certification Survey, [3] "Certification: It's a Journey Not a Destination," Certification Magazine 2015 Salary Edition, [4] "The Future Value of Certifications: Insights from LinkedIn's Data Trove," ATP 2015 Innovations in Testing, [5] Certification Magazine 2015 Annual Salary Survey

ORACLE®

Push a Button
Move Your Java Apps to the Oracle Cloud

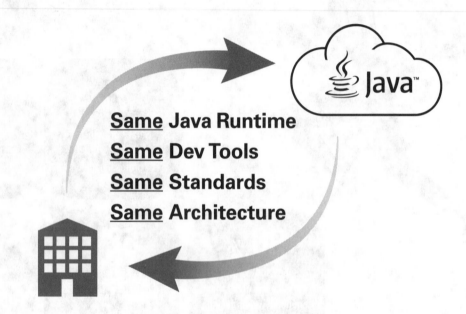

Same Java Runtime
Same Dev Tools
Same Standards
Same Architecture

...or Back to Your Data Center

cloud.oracle.com/java

Reach More than 640,000 Oracle Customers with Oracle Publishing Group

Connect with the Audience that Matters Most to Your Business

Oracle Magazine
The Largest IT Publication in the World
Circulation: 325,000
Audience: IT Managers, DBAs, Programmers, and Developers

Profit
Business Insight for Enterprise-Class Business Leaders to Help Them Build a Better Business Using Oracle Technology
Circulation: 90,000
Audience: Top Executives and Line of Business Managers

Java Magazine
The Essential Source on Java Technology, the Java Programming Language, and Java-Based Applications
Circulation: 225,00 and Growing Steady
Audience: Corporate and Independent Java Developers, Programmers, and Architects

For more information or to sign up for a FREE subscription: Scan the QR code to visit Oracle Publishing online.

Beta Test Oracle Software

Get a first look at our newest products—and help
perfect them. You must meet the following criteria:

- ✔ Licensed Oracle customer or
  Oracle PartnerNetwork member

- ✔ Oracle software expert

- ✔ Early adopter of Oracle products

Please apply at: pdpm.oracle.com/BPO/userprofile

If your interests match upcoming activities, we'll contact you. Profiles are kept on file for 12 months.